Growing Gaps

Growing Gaps

Educational Inequality around the World

EDITED BY

Paul Attewell

Katherine S. Newman

OXFORD
UNIVERSITY PRESS
2010

OXFORD
UNIVERSITY PRESS

Oxford University Press, Inc., publishes works that further
Oxford University's objective of excellence
in research, scholarship, and education.

Oxford   New York
Auckland   Cape Town   Dar es Salaam   Hong Kong   Karachi
Kuala Lumpur   Madrid   Melbourne   Mexico City   Nairobi
New Delhi   Shanghai   Taipei   Toronto

With offices in
Argentina   Austria   Brazil   Chile   Czech Republic   France   Greece
Guatemala   Hungary   Italy   Japan   Poland   Portugal   Singapore
South Korea   Switzerland   Thailand   Turkey   Ukraine   Vietnam

Published by Oxford University Press, Inc.
198 Madison Avenue, New York, New York 10016

www.oup.com

Oxford is a registered trademark of Oxford University Press

Library of Congress Cataloging-in-Publication Data
Growing gaps: educational inequality around the world /
edited by Paul Attewell, Katherine S. Newman.
    p. cm.
Includes bibliographical references and index.
ISBN 978–0–19–973218–0; 978–0–19–973219–7 (pbk.)
1. Critical pedagogy.   2. Comparative education—Philosophy.
3. Educational equalization—Cross-cultural studies.
4. Education and globalization.
I. Attewell, Paul.   II. Newman, Katherine S., 1953–
LC196.G78 2010
306.43'2—dc22   2009044157

9 8 7 6 5 4 3 2 1

Printed in the United States of America
on acid-free paper

Preface

This volume grew out of an annual conference sponsored by Princeton University's Global Network on Inequality, a group of twenty-five research institutions around the world that are actively engaged in research on the causes, consequences, and remedies for inequality. Now spanning universities and research institutes in Latin America (Brazil and Chile), Africa (South Africa), Asia (China, Korea, India, Japan), the Middle East (Israel), and Europe (Ireland, England, Spain, Italy, France, Finland, Denmark, Germany, and Poland), the network has been in existence since 2004 and continues to grow to incorporate new countries and new fields of study.

Inequality is growing rapidly both in postindustrial societies and in the high growth economies of the developing world. The symptoms can be measured in Gini coefficients and gated communities, in unequal access to institutions of social mobility and the emergence of stark health disparities, in the flows of international migration and the local patterns of segregation. The consequences are visible in unequal patterns of educational attainment, lopsided engagement in elections, and earlier mortality for some groups rather than others. Indeed, few problems of interest to sociologists, political scientists, labor economists, and social psychologists are unrelated to the broad patterns of inequality sweeping the modern world.

Access to education is a critical piece of this puzzle. Whether education is regarded as a proxy (or crucible) of skill and therefore the engine of human capital development, or a set of credentials that permit status groups to close ranks and claim advantage in a competitive market, it is clear that individual life chances and national wealth depends centrally on educational outcomes. Whether economic growth leads to an opening of opportunity (as has been the case in the social democracies) or a ferocious competition for the small number of slots available in public institutions (as is true in the developed countries with weaker welfare states) is a key question for scholars interested in the intersection between inequality and education. The staggering growth of private higher education has developed in response to the inadequate supply of opportunity, but poses serious problems of debt for families who must fund this human capital accumulation on their own.

A comparative approach is essential for understanding the worldwide race for educational advantage in the context of widening inequality. This volume aims to contribute to the debate with careful national case studies that do more than describe systems of education; it weaves the case studies into a larger framework of stratification, one of the key foci for the Global Network on Inequality.

The contributors to this volume are indebted to the Princeton Institute for International and Regional Studies, which supports the Global Network and funded this research, and to Jill Fraser, whose editorial eye helped to transform the original papers into their present form. Nancy Turco was an essential ingredient in the production of the manuscript, as was our editor at Oxford, James Cook.

Katherine S. Newman
Director of the Global Network on Inequality

Contents

Contributors

Paul Attewell is a professor of sociology teaching in the doctoral programs in sociology and in urban education at the Graduate Center of the City University of New York. His most recent book, coauthored with David Lavin, was *Passing the Torch: Does Higher Education for the Disadvantaged Pay Off Across the Generations?*, which won the 2009 Grawemeyer Award in Education and the American Education Research Association's Outstanding Book Award for 2009.

Louis Chauvel is Professor of Sociology and director of the PhD program of sociology at Sciences Po Paris, and member of Institut Universitaire de France.

Li Chunling is Professor of Sociology at the Institute of Sociology, Chinese Academy of Social Sciences, Beijing, China.

Cristián Cox is head of the Centre for Research on Educational Policy and Practice at the Catholic University of Chile.

Jaap Dronkers is honorary professor of international comparison of education performance and social inequality at the Maastricht University, the Netherlands.

Fenella Fleischmann is a PhD researcher at the European Research Centre on Migration and Ethnic Relations (Ercomer) at Utrecht University and at the Centre for Social and Cultural Psychology (CSCP) at Leuven University.

Yaakov Gilboa is a senior lecturer of economics at Sapir Academic College and one of the founding members of the Department of Applied Economics.

Antonio S. A. Guimarães is Professor Titular at the University of São Paulo, Brazil.

Angel L. Harris is an assistant professor of sociology and African American studies at Princeton University.

Moshe Justman is Professor of Economics and Dean of Humanities and Social Sciences at Ben Gurion University in Israel.

Malcolm Keswell is Associate Professor of Economics at Stellenbosch University and Honorary Research Associate of the Southern Africa Labour and Development Research Unit at the University of Cape Town, in South Africa.

Byoung-Hoon Lee is a professor in the Department of Sociology at Chung-Ang University, South Korea.

Katherine S. Newman is the founder of the Global Network on Inequality and the James B. Knapp Dean of the Krieger School of Arts and Sciences at Johns Hopkins University. Until the fall of 2010, she was the Malcolm Forbes Class of 1941 Professor of Sociology and Public Affairs and the Director of the Institute for International and Regional Studies at Princeton University. Her most recent books include *Taxing the Poor* (forthcoming) and *Who Cares? Public Ambivalence and Government Activism from the New Deal to the Second Gilded Age* (2010).

Pawel Polawski is an assistant professor and codirector for evening studies at the Institute of Sociology, Warsaw University, and Secretary of the Polish Academy of Science Committee on Sociology.

Karen Robson is an assistant professor of sociology at York University in England.

Kwang-Yeong Shin is a professor in the Department of Sociology at Chung-Ang University, South Korea.

Yi-Lee Wong is a sociologist working as an assistant professor at University of Macau, China.

Growing Gaps

1

Education and Inequality in a Global Context

Paul Attewell

All around the world, young people are attending school for more years, and record proportions are continuing into higher education (Schofer and Meyer 2005). In the affluent countries of the Organization for Economic Cooperation and Development (OECD), the proportion of youth enrolling in university-level education increased by 20 percentage points in the decade between 1995 and 2006 (OECD 2008:13). The growth rate was even faster within middle-income nations:[1] their college enrollments increased by 77 percent over eight years (UNESCO 2005:43, 180).

This expansion is part of a long-term trend that began with mandatory primary education in developed countries in the late nineteenth century. As the twentieth century unfolded, increasing proportions of youth in most OECD nations attended school beyond the compulsory minimum. From the 1960s onward, it was the turn of post-secondary education: in many countries, universities were founded and new kinds of tertiary institutions came into being to accommodate a burgeoning demand for higher education.

So far, the growth in demand for more years of education seems to have no limit. Increasingly, a baccalaureate degree no longer suffices; enrollment in master's, professional, and higher degree programs is booming. Each new generation exceeds its parents in terms of average years of schooling completed.[2]

This portrait of educational expansion may seem grounded in the Western European and North American historical experience; however, trends over time in the economically less developed parts of the world are not so dissimilar. Less-developed countries typically started their educational expansion at a later date. Many are still challenged by high rates of illiteracy, and markedly smaller proportions of their populations complete secondary or tertiary education. Nevertheless, developing nations have made immense efforts to catch up, as Cristián Cox's chapter 2, on Latin America, attests. Pushed on one side by burgeoning popular demand for access and on the other by the belief among elites that education drives a nation's economic growth, governments on many parts of the political spectrum have prioritized public investment in education (Bashir 2007).

State investment in education dwarfs private investment in all countries,[3] and public subsidies drive educational demand to much higher levels than would occur in a purely market-based system. Growing demand places increasing fiscal pressures on governments, and they look for ways to limit expenditures, which, *ceteris paribus*, tend to exacerbate inequalities in access. Nevertheless, education has consumed an increasing portion of GNP in most countries.[4]

Even in the wealthiest nations, popular demand for more education—especially at the tertiary level—potentially exceeds supply, causing institutions to ration or limit access. This imbalance is exacerbated by differences in institutional prestige: applicants clamor to get into the most esteemed universities.[5] The most common strategy for rationing access has been through competitive entrance examinations. The contest for access to higher education ramifies through the other levels of an educational system: certain secondary schools develop a reputation for providing superior chances for admission to high-status universities, so they in turn become highly sought after. A cascade of unequal prestige and competition ensues, and differentiation and inequalities among schools emerge and solidify.

Where there is limited or competitive access to public institutions, families with means can turn to private educational providers. Global economic growth in recent years has swelled the number of families that can afford to purchase private educational services. (Yi-Lee Wong's chapter 8 illustrates this phenomenon in the case of Hong Kong.) As a result, private primary and secondary schools, after-school academies, and tutoring and test-preparation services, along with private colleges and universities, are mushrooming worldwide, offering educational opportunity to paying customers. A diverse range of private institutions serves, in a very unequal way, a spectrum of income levels.

Public and private educational institutions are frequently intertwined in symbiotic fashion. In nations like Brazil, the most prestigious universities are public, as chapter 3 in this volume by Antonio S. A. Guimarães indicates. However, affluent Brazilian families often send their children to private elementary and secondary schools, believing that these will better prepare them for admission to the highly selective public universities. In other countries, including the United States, there is a contrasting pattern, whereby many affluent families send their children to public primary and secondary schools, but where top high-school graduates enter a fierce competition to gain admission to the most prestigious colleges and universities, most of which are private.[6] In both situations, economically advantaged families act strategically, seeking superior educational opportunities for their children by moving between private and public educational institutions. In so doing, they widen the gaps in educational attainment between children from affluent and poorer families (Haveman and Wilson 2007).

At the same time, public institutions lose legitimacy if they are viewed as closed to those from lower social strata. In several societies, "affirmative action" policies have come into play to improve access to sought-after public universities for disadvantaged groups. The Guimarães chapter in this volume show how these efforts play out in one case, but there are many others, including, for example, India, with its nationwide system of "reservations" for low-caste applicants to the public universities (Newman and Deshpande in press).

Increasingly, the thirst for educational access has spilled over national borders: worldwide, nearly 3 million students travel overseas to enroll in higher education. Currently, the largest recipients of overseas students are the United States (20%) and the United Kingdom (11%), followed by Germany, France, and Australia (OECD 2008:353–354). The largest numbers of foreign undergraduates come from Asia, but there are also large flows within the European Union (EU) and among OECD countries. Efforts to harmonize divergent national education systems within the EU—the Bologna Process—testify to the growing importance of these flows across political boundaries.

Multiple forces drive the burgeoning student demand for a university education overseas (Altbach and Knight 2006; IOM 2008:111–113). One common motivation is to gain a prestigious credential and attain fluency in English—stepping stones to a better job in one's home country. Some undergraduates pursue an education overseas because they did not succeed in the intense competition for access to a prestigious university in their native country; here, overseas study functions as a safety valve where domestic educational opportunities are restricted. In other cases, overseas study provides a route for immigration or employment in the host country. For yet other students, an overseas education or a semester or two of study abroad is partly an adventure and/or a way of cultivating a more cosmopolitan outlook. Driven by this varied mix of motivations, international enrollment in higher education has accelerated quite rapidly over the last two decades (OECD 2008:353).

This internationalization of higher education had its origins in colonialism and later in attempts by ex-colonial powers to maintain their spheres of influence by providing scholarships to foreign students. But that history is receding quickly; today, international education resembles a global business. The

Anglophone universities, which enroll most foreigners, typically charge higher tuition and fees to overseas students than to domestic students.[7] Tuition from foreign students provides a valuable new source of funds to universities where domestic government support is limited.[8] Some universities have become even more entrepreneurial; about one hundred have built satellite campuses in the sending countries, trading on their "brand names" to bring their services closer to the sources of demand (IOM 2008:114). Other universities have entered into collaborative arrangements whereby students remain in home-country institutions but take courses sponsored by or credentialed by Western universities. These are known as "cross-border programs" and they currently enroll at least 300,000 students (IOM 2008:113).

Relatively little is known to date about the impact of international education on global socioeconomic inequality. One the one hand, international education provides a potential route for students from poorer nations to gain access to educational institutions in relatively wealthy nations, and therefore might be viewed as redistributive. If these individuals return to their home countries and aid in the development of research and higher education institutions at home, then this would also act to lessen the knowledge and capacity gaps between nations. There is one instance of this "capacity-building approach" in China's current effort to recruit Western-trained Chinese academics to return to China and join in their efforts to build research capacity.

On the other hand, international education can act as a "brain drain," drawing talented and skilled individuals from the poorer countries to the economically more developed ones, and thereby exacerbating the education and skill gaps between nations. For example, according to the international Organization for Migration (IOM 2008:119), "27% of international students from within the EU were employed in the U.K. six months after obtaining their degrees," and between a fifth and a half of the immigrants in high-skill migration programs to countries like the United States, Canada, and Australia have previously been foreign students in those nations (Suter and Jandl 2006).

Moreover, to the extent that students who study abroad tend to come from economically and socially more privileged families in their home societies, their access to Australasian, European, and North American universities may act to consolidate class differences and socioeconomic divides in their home countries by providing greater educational opportunities to already-privileged social strata while less-privileged students at home compete for places in oversubscribed and less well funded institutions.

For scholars interested in education and inequality, the intellectual puzzle is first to understand why the demand for, and the earnings premium associated with, more years of education continue to be so strong in so many countries; and then to discover how the rapid educational growth of recent decades interacts with preexisting class and social inequalities or generates new forms of inequality. There is no consensus among scholars about the answers to these questions. Different conceptions of the role of education in the modern economy provide contrasting perspectives on the relationship between education and social inequality, so we begin with this theoretical or conceptual task.

"The core functions of higher education are the generation, dissemination, and preservation of systematic knowledge; we talk about research, teaching, and learning.... These are the essentials." Here, Teichler (2007:1) offers the conventional view of higher education, its manifest or intended function, as viewed from the perspective of academics and policymakers. When looked at from the undergraduate or consumer perspective, or from the bottom up, the purpose of higher education seems somewhat different. For many or perhaps most of its consumers, the main appeal of higher education is that it provides a stepping stone to a well-paying job. The latent function of a university education, as sociologists would term it, is to provide a credential with value in the labor market. If higher education is a global industry, then what it is selling to many undergraduates is the hope of social mobility. It is the prospect of "getting ahead in the world," of enjoying a comfortable standard of living, that powers the insatiable global demand for higher education.

But how and why is higher education so tightly linked to occupational and material success? This is where theories diverge.

THE HUMAN CAPITAL PERSPECTIVE

Economists Theodore Schultz, Gary Becker, and Jacob Mincer developed human capital theory as an explanation for the variations in earnings within a country and for differences in GNP growth across countries. Schultz's (1961) core argument was that human productive capabilities differ from individual to individual, and that "the quality of human effort can be greatly improved" by acquiring knowledge and skills through training, on-the-job experience, and formal education. Employers are willing to pay higher wages to employees with greater human capital because these workers are more productive and bring more skill to their work. Earnings can, therefore, be viewed as a monetary return on one's human capital investment.

This theory provides a parsimonious and powerful explanation for the observed relationship between education and earnings, arguing for a straightforward causal link between education and/or experience and productivity as it is reflected in earnings. It also explicitly addresses inequality: the absence of human capital translates into low wages; accordingly, among those in the social strata with less education or work experience, we find lower incomes (Schultz 1961; Thurow 1965:85). Beyond this, parents who invest less time and energy in raising their children, or in guiding their offsprings' educational progress, curtail their children's human capital and future earning power, causing the reproduction of inequality across generations (Mulligan 1997). Countries that underinvest in education also limit their nation's future growth.

Earnings inequality and social inequality are generated by differences in education and skill, but human capital theory does not envision a zero-sum competition between social groups over access to these background characteristics. The more accomplished social group or stratum does not gain economically from another's educational disadvantage. Becker (1971) theorized about discrimination; his conclusion was that employers with a "taste for discrimination" against a group of potential employees would be driven out of business by nondiscriminatory competitors, and that racist employees would have to take positions with lower wages if they wanted to work in racially segregated workplaces. Unfortunately, Becker's view that discrimination is anachronistic, and that it cannot persist in a modern competitive capitalist economy, is quite at variance with current empirical evidence, which suggests that racial, ethnic, and gender discrimination remain widespread and intractable features of labor markets in modern market economies (Pager and Shepherd 2008; Centeno and Newman 2010).

Nevertheless, the human capital perspective suggests that everyone can gain from an expansion of educational and training opportunities. Nor does the theory presuppose any necessary limit on the accumulation of human capital via increased education. The more educated a nation's population becomes, the higher the average productivity will be and the greater that nation's GNP growth is likely to be.

A sharp increase in income inequality occurred in the United States (and several other nations) from the late 1970s on, during an era of educational expansion. These "facts on the ground" posed a challenge to human capital theory. The explosion of income inequality reflected a marked shift in the earnings return to different amounts of education. That is, workers who did not complete their high school education experienced a sharp drop in their earnings power relative to other groups. High school graduates also fell behind. Conversely, four-year college graduates pulled away from the less educated, and the earnings of those with masters, professional, and higher degrees diverged even faster from those with less education. Does this imply that having a more educated populace necessarily creates a more economically unequal society?

This "fan pattern" of increasing earnings inequality over time was anomalous from a human capital perspective; typically, when the supply of college-educated labor is increasing rapidly, one would expect a drop in the earnings premium for a college degree because increased supply relative to demand drives down price. Empirically, the reverse happened: the earnings premium for higher education grew even while higher education enrollments were expanding. This led economists to develop a theory of "skill-biased technological change," or the notion that technological change—particularly the spread of information and computer-based technologies—required a more highly educated workforce. In this view, rapid technological change generated greater demand for educated labor and drove up the incomes of highly educated workers relative to those of less educated employees (Griliches 1969; see Berman, Bound, and Machin 1998 for international evidence).

The idea that technological change is "skill biased," and therefore requires more educated employees over time, has been widely accepted by social scientists; however, some criticize the next step in the argument: the explanation for rising income inequality in the United States and elsewhere. Card and DiNardo (2002) have pointed out that the spread of computer technologies did not coincide with the recent increases in income inequality. Gordon and Dew-Becker (2008) have documented a sharp increase in the share of income going to the very wealthiest individuals, a factor which has little to do with education or skills but a lot to do with their power within corporations and other institutions.

Most important, Goldin and Katz (2008) have modified the technological skill-bias argument by arguing for a "race between education and technology." Throughout the twentieth century, they note, technology has been changing in a manner that generates greater demand for higher-educated employees but at a constant rate: "the growth rate of the demand for more educated relative to less educated labor was fairly constant over the 1915 to 2005 period" (292). Consequently, there has *not* been a recent technology-induced surge of demand for educated labor, as some proponents of skill-biased technological change theory have suggested. Goldin and Katz argue instead that only in recent decades has the growth of educated labor in the United States not been able to keep up with technologically driven increases in demand for higher education. In the United States in the early 1970s, "Secondary-school graduation rates reached a plateau; college graduation rates slid backwards; education by cohort reached a standstill" (324). Since the 1980s, educational attainment has improved slightly in the United States. There has been "sluggish" growth in the college-educated labor force, mainly owing to more women entering college, but not enough growth to prevent a rising college wage premium. However, educational growth is still falling behind demand.

In sum, according to this theory, technological change requires greater numbers of increasingly educated employees, a trend that has held for a century or more; but educational growth has recently fallen behind in the race, causing income premiums for higher education to grow and generating greater income inequality in recent decades.

Projected onto a global stage, the imagery of a "race between education and technology" implies that, in some times and places, education may fall behind technology, causing the relative incomes of educated employees to rise. But it leaves open the possibility that, at other times and places, the reverse might happen: educational production might exceed the demands of technological change, creating gluts of educated labor, higher unemployment among highly educated youth, and/or drops in the wage premium paid to university-educated labor. Two chapters in this volume—one by Louis Chauvel (chapter 10) and the other by Pawel Polawski (chapter 11)—provide evidence for the second negative scenario in several countries (see also UNESCO 2005:19.) Chapter 9, by Karen Robson, looks at youth across several European countries who have fallen behind in this educational race and who face employment difficulties as a result.

A different topic within human capital theory that remains problematic concerns *how* education creates useful skills. Many researchers in this tradition focus on the importance of cognitive skills of the kind that are measured by IQ tests or the Armed Forces Qualification Test (AFQT), and they view these capacities as central to human capital. These kinds of cognitive skills are typically viewed as acquired primarily through family socialization and from schooling, rather than primarily genetically determined (Bowles, Gintis, and Groves 2005; Flynn 2007). There is evidence that the earnings return for cognitive skills has increased in recent decades; an implication is that modern workplaces make greater cognitive demands on employees than in earlier years (Murnane, Levy, and Willett 1995).

Other scholars stress that "soft skills" are very important forms of human capital; interpersonal skills and behavioral qualities, such as promptness, being neat and organized, diligence, perseverance, teamwork, and initiative are important for workplace productivity. These skills are learned through family upbringing and as a by-product of schooling (Heckman, Stixrud, and Urzula 2006; Farkas 1996).

It is easy to understand why the basic literacy, numeracy, and good work habits obtained during elementary and secondary education might dramatically affect individuals' productivity in the workplace. However, the greatest earnings payoffs from human capital currently come from higher education, implying that the greatest increases in productivity and the most valuable knowledge and skills should be those obtained at the university level. But what are these skills? Many undergraduates obtain college degrees in majors that are far removed from the work world; the substantive knowledge they have learned since high school would seem to have limited occupational application. Surveys of employers and recent graduates attempt to discern what important skills university-trained employees bring into their workplaces, but these tend to emphasize quite abstract capacities such as critical thinking, teamwork, and so on that are not drawn in any straightforward way from a university-level curriculum (Teichler 2007).

I would argue that the human capital perspective has provided a convincing argument for why elementary and secondary education provide crucial work-related cognitive and behavioral skills that should be rewarded by higher earnings; however, a much less complete or compelling case has been made to explain why *university-level* education provides skills that have become increasingly important for workplace productivity in the current period. On this last issue, a different theoretical approach provides a credible alternative explanation.

EDUCATION AS A SIGNAL

A very different perspective on the link between education and earnings derives from a tradition in economics that stresses the asymmetry and uncertainty of knowledge and information in transactions. In work that led to a Nobel Prize in Economics, Michael Spence (1974) considered situations in which one side of a market has better information (or private information) than the other side. For example, a job seeker knows much more about his or her own work skills and abilities than does the employer who is making the hiring decision. When hiring, the employer is, therefore, working with limited information about the quality of an applicant.

Spence showed that in these kinds of situations, both applicant and employer benefit if the former "signals" his or her worth to the employer. The signal that Spence emphasizes is education: certain applicants will obtain degrees or credentials while others will not. Rational employers will choose to hire more educated or credentialed applicants rather than applicants who lack that education signal.

However, the value of this signal to employers is not that education itself results in higher productivity. On the contrary, Spence makes the case that education may have no productivity-enhancing properties whatsoever, but nevertheless it functions as a useful signal. What matters in Spence's model is that obtaining an education exacts a cost on all applicants; that is, it must not be easy for individuals to obtain the signal. In addition, the theory requires that employees who have the traits that the employer wants to select (i.e., are more productive, or more conscientious, or more ambitious workers) will find it easier, or less costly, or at any rate are more willing to obtain the credential compared to less productive applicants. Ackerlof (1976) provided a similar argument in his notion of "the rat race" among those competing for employment opportunities.

The "self-sorting" aspects of education enable signaling to work: those who succeed in the difficult struggle to complete an education thereby signal that they will more likely turn out to be good employees; those who fail in the educational rat race signal that they lack self-discipline, or ambition, or sustained effort, and are therefore avoided by employers. From a signaling perspective, the substantive content of education does not matter, and the hours and years in the classroom need not impart useful workplace skills. What matters is that education is a race, and that it is simple to pick the winners and losers of that race by comparing their credentials.

The signaling model of education carries quite different implications from those of human capital theory. Signaling is premised on *unequal access* to education and/or on unequal opportunities to graduate with a credential. Education is valuable only as a signal for job seekers and for employers so long as many people are unable or unwilling to obtain it. Signaling implies that existing social inequality (in this case, in access to education) plays a very important functional role for capitalist employers.

Although its proponents have not made this argument, signaling theory can also easily explain the long-term increase in educational attainment that is under way worldwide. When most of a population does not complete high school, then a high school diploma has value as a signal to employers; but once high school graduation becomes widespread, the value of this credential as a signal should decline, creating a premium on extending one's education to college. More recently, as bachelor's degrees proliferate, more young people find it valuable to attain a master's or higher degree. Educational growth, or "credential inflation," would be predicted from this perspective.

The logic of signaling theory allows that other individual characteristics besides education might also be used by employers in hiring decisions. Arrow (1973) argued that, when faced with incomplete knowledge of an individual's capacities, it was economically rational for employers to use an applicant's race as a basis for hiring. He termed this process "statistical discrimination" rather than racism. That is, if, in a statistical or probabilistic sense, an employer has reason to believe that minority workers on average have been less productive than white employees, then, according to Arrow, the employer is rational in treating all members of the same race as having less productivity and in discriminating against minorities in hiring.

Contrary to Becker's view that discrimination in hiring is economically irrational and inimical to competitive capitalism, signaling theory implies that discrimination (whether on the basis of race, education, or other visible criterion) is rational because it correctly imputes—on average—characteristics that employers cannot easily measure but that they depend on to enhance the bottom line. Accordingly, discrimination is likely to persist.

We can speculate further that as certain forms of discrimination—racism, caste or class discrimination, sexism—have become less socially acceptable around the world, educational discrimination becomes ever more important. It is socially legitimate for employers to discriminate in hiring if this is based on education credentials; and according to signaling theory, employers depend on simple signals in order to make hiring decisions that involve preferences for individuals with certain traits over others.

Looked at from a global perspective, signaling theory predicts a never-ending race for more education as each individual seeks to distinguish him or herself from others, a process that spreads across borders when educational credentials become linked to immigration policies. Unlike human capital theory, signaling theory does not view this race for education as socially productive. It may, indeed, be a drain both on individuals and on governments—an educational equivalent of the arms race.

STATUS GROUP COMPETITION AND EDUCATIONAL CREDENTIALISM

Max Weber (1968) developed a sociological perspective on social stratification that emphasized the importance of status groups within capitalist societies. "Status groups" are communities of people who enjoy different amounts of social honor. They may encompass racial, ethnic, occupational, or religious groups, but they can also encompass larger social groups, such as the college-educated. Status groups share a certain style of life and maintain their solidarity through shared tastes and social activities and rituals, on the one hand, and through social closure, on the other, reducing their intercourse with social inferiors. In Weber's framework, status groups are not considered anachronistic holdovers from pre-industrial times; they are important elements in modern stratification systems (Chan and Goldthorpe 2007). New status groups are constantly emerging (Weber 1968:309).

One important element of Weber's theory is his assertion that members of status groups seek to monopolize valued economic opportunities (Weber 1968; Tilly 1998). Collins (1971, 1979, 1988) argued that certain occupational status groups persuaded American legislatures in the nineteenth and twentieth centuries that various jobs ought to be reserved for persons with college degrees; laws were passed that licensed many occupations and required educational credentials for those applying for those licenses. This process limited competition for entry into credentialed jobs. Nowadays, credentialed jobs in America include relatively low-level occupations, from child daycare workers to real estate salespeople to haircutters—for which some U.S. states require college coursework—and where the rationale for requiring government-sanctioned licenses or degrees is that consumers need to be protected from unscrupulous or inept practitioners. Credentialed occupations also include the highly paid "professions" of law and medicine, where the government delegates licensing authority to professional associations that require degrees and institute their own exams for those who wish to practice the profession.

A process of social emulation has spread credentialism far beyond occupations formally licensed by government. Many managerial, administrative, and professional jobs in the private sector have come to expect BA and/or higher degrees from all applicants. Both colonialism and multinational companies have carried Western cultural assumptions and practices concerning the importance of educational credentials for hiring into nations around the world, spreading credentialism worldwide.

Once an occupation has become credentialed, large sectors of society are excluded from entry simply by their lack of formal qualification. But additional dynamics come into play, whereby persons from privileged social strata who hire applicants for these jobs tend to favor those of their own class or status group when selecting among applicants. At one level, this involves unconscious social psychological processes that bias a person's judgment such that in-group individuals are perceived as more competent and/or more trustworthy, while out-group individuals are perceived as less able and less dependable (Fiske 1998). At another level, social networks prove important for finding and securing jobs in the United States and other countries, both at the professional end of the labor market (Granovetter 1974) and at the blue-collar end (Royster 2003). Social networks often run along status-group lines; and when a job opening occurs, individuals sponsor credentialed people from their own networks who are "like us" (Elliott 2001; Smith 2003). Institution prestige adds to this process; it is not simply having a degree or credential, but whether one has received a qualification from a college whose prestige matches that of current employees.

Under educational credentialism, certain jobs come to resemble sinecures or social monopolies; their high earnings reflect the privileged kinds of people who typically occupy them, both their social origins and their educational career paths, rather than the nature of skills required for the job. Credentialed occupations may portray themselves as exceptionally skillful and requiring years of training, but studies of those occupations suggest that most of their skills are learned on the job rather than during college, and that the long years of training function primarily to protect already-established practitioners from new competition (Collins 1979). In sum, according to Collins (1988:180), "the educational credentialing process has become a prime basis for stratification" in modern societies.

Credentialism widens earnings inequalities between jobs, and individuals respond by seeking more education, preferably from the most prestigious institution possible, in order to qualify themselves for top-quality jobs. The whole education system turns into a contest or race, in which different social classes and status groups compete for the best credentials from the best institutions. Part of this competition involves cultural capital: prestigious schools draw upon forms of knowledge and linguistic skills that children from privileged families obtain at home, but that poorer families lack; consequently, children from upper-class families tend to outperform classmates from less affluent or less educated families (Bourdieu and Passeron 1977). Gilboa and Justman's chapter 6 in this volume examines the importance of family cultural resources for student success in Israel.

Part of the competition for education is a matter of affordability: can a student and her or his family pay for superior schools and ancillary services from elementary to high school? Beyond this, can a young person afford to stay out of the paid labor market and instead devote years to obtaining a baccalaureate or higher degree, which are both the direct costs and the opportunity costs of higher education? There is also a geographical aspect to this competition: superior schools that provide the best chances for entry to the next higher level are often located in affluent neighborhoods. Conversely, children living in rural areas and in poor urban areas often attend inferior schools (Kozol 1991).

Educational competition generates a differentiation among and within schools that prepare children for widely differing roles in adult society by sorting them into groups with ostensibly different abilities—groups that are subsequently educated in divergent ways (Bowles and Gintis 1976; Oakes 1985). This process of sorting students is characterized by a *hidden curriculum*: beyond the academic subject matter learned in class, children are acquiring attitudes and behaviors in school that prepare them for one adult socioeconomic destination rather than another. Schools also tend to be internally differentiated with respect to the formal curriculum, with lower socioeconomic status (SES) pupils concentrated in the lower curricular tracks and more affluent students concentrated in the more advanced subjects and classes that lead to higher education (Gamoran 1986; Lucas 1999; Oakes 1985.)

To summarize, the sociological, neo-Weberian perspective views education as a competition between status groups, in which each family is trying to obtain an education for their children that best prepares them for obtaining a well-paying job. It is a very unequal competition, a highly unfair race.

Privileged families provide their children with linguistic and other skills that give them an advantage in the competition within schools. Moreover, their money allows them better access to superior quality schooling, which turns into better access to higher education, more years of educational attainment, more valuable credentials, and ultimately better paying jobs. Students from less affluent or less occupationally privileged families struggle to participate in this educational competition, but they generally receive an inferior education. Their chances of crossing the finishing line and receiving the best credentials from the most desirable institutions are greatly diminished.

MAXIMALLY MAINTAINED INEQUALITY

Maximally maintained inequality (MMI) is a sociological explanation for educational inequality that concerns educational systems worldwide (Hout 2004, 2006; Raftery and Hout 1993; Shavit, Arum, and Gamoran 2007; Shavit and Blossfeld 1993). Unlike the emphasis on collective actors (classes, status groups) characteristic of credentialism, MMI begins with the perspective of individual rational actors—parents, families, and teachers—in advancing their interests to the greatest extent possible. In most countries, the theory argues, access to certain levels of education is limited by the availability of spaces, such that only a fraction of young people can enroll. The level at which a bottleneck occurs will vary across countries and over time: in some nations, access to primary education is highly unequal; in many others, access to secondary education is the problematic transition; and more recently, access to college or university is the choke point.

As Hout (2004) explains, "Educational stratification works like a queue. The initial phases of educational expansion—first of some schooling, then of secondary schooling, and, for the last 50 years, post-secondary schooling—benefit the privileged families at the front of the queue. Then the benefits pass down the hierarchy" (12). MMI perceives the skill and educational advantages of children from the more privileged strata to be so powerful that very few students of lower status groups are able to make the transition into a given level of education until almost *all* of the children of more elite classes have already been accommodated at that educational level. Only after the demand for access from elite children is fully accommodated for a particular level of education—Raftery and Hout's (1993) term for this is "saturated"—do children of nonelite classes begin to enter that level in substantial numbers. Their ability to enter in large numbers is dependent on further expansion at that level: more schools or college places must open up. Thus, reductions in class-based inequality in educational access always follow the expansion of an educational level or sector. Nonelite students are never able to displace elite students; they gain access only when additional openings are generated and only after the more advantaged social stratum has accessed the most valued level of education.

This process creates a social sorting, whereby children of elite families consistently receive more years of education than children of less affluent families; consequently, there is at the national level a persistent correlation over time between the social class of parents and the offspring's educational attainment, even though average educational levels are increasing over time. That is why this perspective is labeled "maximally maintained inequality."

MMI theory has stimulated a large body of comparative scholarship, and the predicted "exclusion, saturation, expansion with inclusion" pattern has been documented for many developed and less developed nations. The theory explains why, in most cross-country studies to date, educational expansion over time has not reduced the educational inequality associated with parental social class (Shavit and Blossfeld 1993; Shavit et al. 2007).

Lucas (2001) disputed whether the MMI pattern fully applied to the United States, arguing that the effect of family class background was reduced well before saturation was attained. He offered a modified theory that he termed "efficiently maximized inequality." The latter suggests that inequality begins to drop before saturation has been achieved (when about 80% of the elite group completes that level of education); moreover, expansion of educational opportunity beyond the elite is often accompanied by institutional differentiation or tracking.

Put bluntly, as nonelite students begin to be accepted into higher levels of education, they tend to be diverted into different and inferior tracks from the elite. Thus, the expansion of higher education in many countries has been accompanied by the creation of new kinds of postsecondary institutions, which are less well funded and offer different curricula from the older, more prestigious institutions. Lower SES students tend to be disproportionately diverted into these lower status options. Thus, several scholars have added differentiation and diversion to the earlier ideas about access, to create a modified picture of educational inequality (Shavit et al. 2007; Teichler 2007). The elaborated sequence becomes: exclusion, saturation, expanded access via institutional differentiation, inclusion primarily via diversion to lower status institutions, movement among the elite to yet higher levels of qualification.

There are some widely acknowledged exceptions to the predicted MMI pattern. In particular, socialist or communist societies have at times instituted powerful policies providing preferential access to higher education for children of lower socioeconomic strata and denying, or at least restricting, entry of children of the intelligentsia or other suspect affluent classes (Hanley and McKeever 1997). This would appear to turn MMI upside down.

In this volume, Li Chunling's chapter 7 shows how rapidly the socialist model of educational access reversed itself into a pattern consistent with the MMI model, as China entered the world economy.

REGIME THEORY

The realization that government policies may impact educational expansion and access, and socioeconomic inequality more generally, has led some scholars to try to link education to typologies of governments, drawing on a perspective called regime theory or welfare regime theory, first developed by political scientists. The Danish scholar Gøsta Esping-Andersen (1990) developed a classification of welfare states that distinguished between social-democratic welfare regimes (in the Nordic countries), liberal welfare regimes (like those in the United States), and conservative welfare regimes (such as in Germany). Walther (2006) has modified this typology to distinguish among four types: universalistic (Nordic), employment-centered (Germany, France, Netherlands), liberal (U.S., U.K., Ireland), and subprotective welfare regime types (Italy, Spain, Portugal).

The central idea of regime theory is that each type of welfare regime tends to exhibit a particular orientation toward public policy. The liberal regimes favor free-market solutions to social needs; the social-democratic regimes emphasize government provision of services to all citizens irrespective of ability to pay; the employment-centered regimes emphasize the role of employers; and the subprotective type place primary responsibility on families to provide resources and support for all their members. Each social welfare regime type, it is also argued, takes a distinctive stance toward educational expansion, the incorporation of youth into the economy, mitigation of social inequality, and so on.

Esping-Anderson (1999) argued that the global trend toward education credentials is reinforcing class-based inequality. However, different national educational structures mediate this effect; in some nations, intensifying it and in others, mitigating the social reproduction of inequality through education. For example, some educational systems begin tracking—a differentiation of curricula between schools—at an earlier age than others; the earlier tracking is most common in conservative regime types. Conservative regimes also tend to have the highest enrollment in vocational education and to encourage more institutional differentiation in their educational systems (Estevez-Abe, Iversen, and Soskice, 2001; Hega and Hokenmaier 2002; Horn 2007).

Regime theory has become popular in part because of the recent availability of survey data sets that collect equivalent information on education from many countries and of compilations of national statistics by UNESCO, the United Nations, and the OECD. Scholars in this tradition can use these comparative statistics to contrast the alternative pathways that different welfare regimes take in dealing with education and other policy domains. Thus, instead of identifying a general global logic of educational expansion, scholars who employ welfare regime theory look for international contrasts in institutional structures in education, and in inequality outcomes, and then try to link those differences to distinct governmental regime types.

With these theoretical frameworks in mind, we now turn to a discussion of the individual chapters in this volume.

Chapter 2's Cristián Cox begins by providing an overview and analysis of changes in the educational systems of Latin American countries in the 1990–2006 period. Despite important differences in the political orientations of governments in this region, there has been a widespread push for educational expansion and for improvements in pedagogical quality. Educational reform has formed part of an economic development agenda across the region, an attempt to increase each nation's competitiveness in the global context, as well as to form part of a social agenda, integrating disadvantaged groups into the nation-state and improving civic engagement of the poorer parts of society. Cox suggests a terminology: *equity as inclusion* refers to access to education and equity in the number of years of schooling attained; while *equity as fairness* refers to equality of opportunity within educational institutions, in terms of degree and skill attainment, across social groups.

Cox initially analyzes development indicators that describe levels of inequality in both education and income in Latin American nations, and he notes that there is no simple relationship or correlation between the income inequality in a country and its level of educational inequality. This is a surprising but important finding, since some scholars assume that inequality in educational access is largely a reflection of a nation's general level of economic inequality. For Latin American countries, Cox discovers, that is not the case.

He does, however, identify two groups of countries that have contrasting agendas regarding educational expansion. One group of Latin American nations (mainly Andean countries plus some in Central America) are poorer and more agrarian, and less than one-half of their populations complete secondary school. For these countries, Cox argues, the focus has been on an *inclusion agenda*—on bringing large sections of the population into the school system for the first time. He next identifies a contrasting group of Latin American countries that are wealthier, have a small percentage of their population in rural areas, and have high secondary school completion rates. This latter group of countries, he argues, are facing a *fairness agenda*. Their concerns focus on class and income disparities in educational opportunity and performance within the educational system.

Educational investments have made big inroads into the inclusion agenda: a far larger proportion of children are going to school nowadays; they are attending for more years; boys and girls go to school in equivalent numbers; and rural—urban enrollment disparities have been greatly reduced.

Even so, Cox is pessimistic about the outcome. In Latin America, family background continues to exert a very strong influence on the quality of the schools that children attend, on students' scores on skills tests, and on their entry to and success with higher education. For example, on international educational tests such as PISA and TIMSS, test-score gaps between children from different family backgrounds are much larger within Latin American nations than within other OECD nations. Thus, the fairness agenda remains unfulfilled, even in Latin America's most affluent and urbanized nations.

Cox's approach stands in contrast to regime theory, as discussed earlier. His inclusion—fairness distinction is largely a reflection of national differences in GNP and urbanism. He does *not* find the political structure of individual nations in Latin America as determinative of educational expansion.

Antonio S. A. Guimarães (chapter 3) provides a case study of educational fairness or equity in Brazil, focusing on entrance into prestigious public universities, most particularly the elite University of São Paolo, known as USP. Brazil has long been proud of the high quality of its public universities, both federal and state institutions, Young people from many sectors of society—both the elite and the poor—aspire to enter them. However, admission is highly competitive and depends on a student's score on an entrance exam, the Vestibular. Children from socially and economically privileged families, who typically attend private high schools, tend to do well on this exam. Children from lower class backgrounds do less well and are therefore underrepresented at USP.

Guimarães assesses recent efforts to improve access to USP for less affluent students, especially those who are black. Recent policies have tried to improve access: one policy augments the Vestibular scores of public school applicants by 3 percent, as a form of affirmative action. Another provides federal grants to students from public high schools to enable them to attend university. Finally, USP has built a new campus in a poorer part of São Paolo and has expanded its number of university places.

Teasing apart the impacts of these various policy changes is the task that Guimarães sets himself. The longer term picture is not good when viewed from the perspective of equity, though. In 1980, the majority of students who took the USP entrance exam came from public high schools; over time this proportion has dropped. Guimarães says that this reflects a long-term deterioration in the academic quality of public high schools; their students are less likely to take the Vestibular, less likely to pass, and tend instead to apply to private or public universities whose entry standards are not so rigorous.

Despite this longer term trend, there are encouraging signs of recent progress at USP that are potentially attributable to policy shifts: in 2000, for example, 6 percent of those passing the Vestibular were black; by 2007, this had risen to 11.8 percent. The proportion of USP students from public high schools has also increased. In tying these recent gains to specific policies, Guimarães concludes that the extra points awarded to deserving students on the Vestibular are probably not the cause of progress for black students. More important has been the geographical expansion of USP into poorer parts of the city. This encouraged a spike in applications from local students, and thereby increased racial and class diversity in the university.

Guimarães concludes that although racial and class diversity has improved in recent years at USP, the affirmative-action policies aimed at improving equity in USP have not really reached those most in need of them. So far, the changes in access to USP are modest, leaving most disadvantaged students who aspire to college having to enter other, less-prestigious universities in São Paolo.

One theoretical implication of Guimarães's chapter is that the success or failure of policies aimed at reducing social inequality and increasing access and racial inclusion depends to a large extent on the details of implementation and on particular features of local context. The modest positive outcome of USP's attempts at racial inclusion via affirmative action is more a side effect of the location of USP's campus than of the planned intervention through adjustment of Vestibular scores.

Malcolm Keswell (chapter 4) also discusses changes in educational and racial inequality, but looks at another multiracial society: postapartheid South Africa. Under the old apartheid regime, educational opportunities for black South Africans were extremely limited and the best jobs were reserved for whites. This produced huge racial disparities in earnings: the average white earned over five times as much as the average black employee. Since 1994, the apartheid system has been dismantled, and considerable efforts have been made to open the nation's universities to students of all racial backgrounds and to ensure that employers hire nonwhite employees in professional and managerial positions.

Despite these changes, Keswell reports, the economic situation of the least-educated black South Africans remains dire. On average, since the end of apartheid, black wages have increased and white wages have decreased. Nevertheless, the proportion of the workforce that earns less than $2 per day has increased, from about 36 percent when apartheid ended to 52 percent today. Roughly half of South African society is underemployed and poor.

Using panel survey data, Keswell undertakes an econometric decomposition of wage data for full-time and casual workers. His goal is to separate out components of the racial wage gap that can be attributed to factors such as the amount of education, years of work experience, and quality of education, and contrast these differences in "factor endowments" from a "pure race effect" that is commonly understood as stemming from racial discrimination.

The picture that emerges from Keswell's analyses is complicated. In postapartheid South Africa, blacks continue to trail whites in terms of years of education completed: a four-year gap, on average. The effect of this education gap is to greatly lower the chances of employment for black South Africans compared to whites.

However, a second phenomenon has emerged concerning the wage returns for education of equivalently educated whites and blacks. In the early 1990s, education was rewarded similarly within each racial group, but there was a huge "pure race effect"—that is, racial discrimination in incomes occurred irrespective of educational level. In the latest period, the situation has reversed: the pure-race effect has decreased dramatically. Instead, a huge difference has surfaced in the returns for education of black and white South Africans. The former obtain a 7 percent earnings return per year of education, while whites gain a huge 43 percent return. This racial gap in returns for education occurs both among men and women workers, and it is not attributable to racial differences in educational equality, Keswell reports.

In sum, the South African story is not solely the longstanding one of racial inequalities in access to education but, rather, has recently become a matter of inequality in the ability of blacks and whites to translate their educational assets into reasonably paying jobs. As one form of racial inequality has shrunk in South Africa, another has taken its place.

Continuing this theme of the role of education in sustaining social inequality, Kwang-Yeong Shin and Byung-Hoon Lee (chapter 5) provide an analysis of social class and education in South Korea. The South Korean educational system is exceptional: the competition for admission into a prestigious college or university is probably the most intense in the world. Students and their parents begin strategizing many years before college, typically by seeking admission to academically superior elementary, middle, and high schools. Although the best schools are partly funded by the state, most are privately managed and charge tuition. In addition, over half of South Korean families enroll their children in expensive private after-school programs that prepare students for college entrance exams.

Korean students spend long hours studying inside and outside of school, knowing that their exam scores will determine which college they will be admitted to. At the end of the day, roughly 85 percent of high school students in South Korea go to college or university. However, the prestige of the university that a student attends matters a lot. Korean companies tend to recruit their employees from the most prestigious universities. Thus, in

South Korea, education is highly competitive, as a pathway to a good job and also as a major source of social status and self-esteem.

Shin and Lee's research examines the issue of access to the higher tracks within education, a situation that they characterize as a "silent class war." The first crossroads a Korean student encounters is whether to attend an academic or a vocational high school; the second is whether to attend a college or the more prestigious choice, a university. The authors find that a family's social class predicts a child's educational career, over and above the level of parental education. Holding parental education constant, children from middle-class families are more likely to attend academic high schools, and then attend universities rather than colleges, compared to children from capitalist, petty bourgeois, and working-class families. In this "silent class war" in South Korea, the middle class appears most successful in the competition for education.

Insofar as they document the disadvantages that children of manual workers experience in access to higher education, and they demonstrate the continuing importance of parental SES in predicting educational attainment, these findings are broadly consistent with prior research on South Korea in the MMI tradition (Park 2007; Arum et al. 2007:27). However, MMI theory would not predict Shin and Lee's finding that children of the South Korean middle class would outdo their counterparts from capitalist and petty bourgeois families in the competition for access to academic high schools and universities.

What explains the fact that middle-class students are more successful in the competition to enter higher education? Are material advantages—the ability to pay for better schools and after-school tutoring—what make the difference? Or is it the cultural knowledge and skills that a child gains from growing up with highly educated parents that matter most? These questions have been debated by researchers for decades, and there is no consensus in the literature. However, two Israeli contributors, Yaakov Gilboa and Moshe Justman (chapter 6), develop a creative approach to answering this puzzle.

The *kibbutz* is a distinctive Israeli institution: a rural commune or village whose members are committed to an egalitarian and collectivist ideology that leads them to minimize personal property and to invest equally in the education of all kibbutz children. After the first few months of life, babies are raised in the kibbutz's nursery, followed by kindergarten, followed by kibbutz-based schooling. A lot of the children's education and socialization, therefore, come from the community rather than from the nuclear family. On average, kibbutzim invest heavily in their schools, and their children attain more years of education than Israelis raised outside of this system.

The kibbutz provides a kind of natural experiment for understanding the effects of parental advantage on children's educational success because, within a given community, children have parents with different amounts of education, yet they receive similar schooling and other material investments in education. Gilboa and Justman have gained access to the national university entrance test scores of children who were raised on kibbutzim and those who were raised in the larger Israeli society, and they study the correlation between parental education and children's test scores for the two groups of children.

What they find is that the correlation between parental education and children's academic scores is significantly lower in the kibbutzim than outside. That is, the fact that these children have equal access to material resources for education makes parental education considerably less important for children's educational scores: the kibbutz correlation is about half of that for other Israelis.

This implies that, in Israeli society at large (outside the kibbutzim), some of the advantages gained by middle-class children are due to material inequality: the ability of affluent families, compared to less affluent families, to find better schools for their children and to invest in various kinds of educational enrichments for them. However, Gilboa and Justman's calculations indicate that only about one-third of the advantage that more educated parents pass on to their children is attributable to these material or financial advantages. The remaining two-thirds of that observed family advantage is presumably due to a mix of IQ, linguistic and conceptual skills, and cultural capital gained from parents.

Li Chunling (chapter 7) looks at another kind of natural experiment, examining the relationship between social class and university entrance in the People's Republic of China during a period of major economic change. Entrance examinations are the principal mechanism for selecting students for Chinese universities. However, prior to China's entry into the capitalist world economy, the Communist Party instituted policies that helped children of peasant and worker families attend institutions higher education (along with children of Communist Party members), while limiting the access to university education for students who came from families that had been landowners or capitalists in the pre-communist era. Li shows that, for many years, this policy greatly enhanced the educational prospects of previously disadvantaged classes. However, her analyses also show that, as China has liberalized its economy, the class balance of the university system has reversed dramatically. In the most recent period, educational access is much greater for the children of upper- and middle-class families, while students from peasant and working-class families are now disadvantaged in entering the universities, just as they were before the revolution.

Her study demonstrates the extent to which class differences in educational access and success are sensitive to public-policy choices and the nature of political regimes. Where there are large regional and school-level differences in educational quality, and where families differ in terms of their educational and cultural capital, a national policy that emphasizes exams for entry into higher education leads to large class-based inequalities that favor affluent families. However, where a government institutes compensatory or affirmative-action efforts for political reasons, as China once did, this pattern can be reversed, to the benefit of socially less privileged strata.

Yi-Lee Wong (chapter 8) provides additional insights into the class dynamics of educational access in today's China, through a qualitative study of "middle-class losers" in Hong Kong. Despite China's increasing affluence, the authorities have tried to limit the growth in public higher education. Nevertheless, university enrollment has grown from about 20 percent of the age group in the 1970s to about 60 percent in recent years. That still does not match the level of demand: in affluent areas, many students want to attend university but cannot gain admission. In Hong Kong, three universities have launched private subbaccalaureate community colleges to provide a "second chance" to students whose exam scores were too low to gain entry into the public university system. These booming new institutions are filled with students from affluent families who can afford to pay what, by Chinese standards, is very expensive tuition.

Yi-Lee Wong interviewed some of these "middle-class losers," and she found that they suffer considerable emotional and psychological distress. They have internalized an achievement ideology that views the exam system as fairly rewarding students who are smarter and harder working; and they are ashamed that they have failed within that exam system. Since many peers and relatives passed the exams and entered the public universities, these students feel publicly shamed within their social circle. Guilt piles on top of shame because they know their parents have made great efforts to provide a good educational environment and are now going into debt to send them to this expensive yet less prestigious kind of college. Culturally, they have failed their families as well as themselves. Thus, Yi-Lee Wong makes a strong case that scholars have neglected the emotional dimensions of class gaps in educational attainment. Not only do stratified educational systems create winners and losers, but the subjective reactions to higher education differ according to the class backgrounds of students at various levels.

Karen Robson (chapter 9) also looks at the "losers" in this educational race, through a comparative study of the least-educated young people in Europe. Roughly 10 percent of school leavers in Europe are "neither in education, nor employment, nor training"—NEETs, for short. This category of young people is of great concern to European scholars and policymakers since they seem to be socially excluded, making no progress through education or employment.

NEETs are disproportionately drawn from lower socioeconomic status families, where parental education and interest in children's education is low. Scholars have also debated, though not resolved, whether NEETs have unwillingly fallen into this situation or whether some NEETs actively choose to opt out of employment, training, and education.

Robson asks a different set of questions, Are NEETs stalled in the transition to adulthood? Or is this just a pause before they become reintegrated into the working world? Do different welfare regimes have different numbers of NEETs? Drawing on regime theory, she hypothesizes that the subprotective welfare regimes (countries such as Greece, Spain, and Italy) with the fewest safety nets will have the worst problems with long-term NEETs, and that the universalistic regimes found in the Nordic nations would provide resources to minimize NEET status and help these youths move into jobs. She anticipates that other regime types (the liberal welfare states of the U.K. and Ireland, and the employment-centered regimes that include France, Germany, and the Netherlands) would fall between these extremes.

European household survey data, covering seven nations, did not support the hypotheses drawn from regime theory: the results were mixed. The NEET phenomenon was *not* greatest in the subprotective welfare regimes of southern Europe, as was expected. On the contrary, the U.K. has about twice the proportion of NEETs (9.8%) of the next group of nations. Some employment-centered regimes (e.g., Germany) also have a higher NEET proportion than some subprotective regimes (e.g., Spain and Portugal). Moreover, the pattern of which country's NEETS stay in that status over time showed a weak relationship to regime type. The U.K., which has many NEETs, also shows the sharpest exit or recovery from the status over time. France and Germany, which are usually classified together in one regime type, had quite different patterns of NEET persistence. The data were more supportive of some other hypotheses from regime theory, however. Robson considers a number of potential reasons behind the complicated patterns she observes, including methodological and measurement issues, some of which may be addressable as more recent waves of panel data become available. Taken as a whole, however, her findings are not a success for regime theory.

Louis Chauvel (chapter 10) continues this focus on comparative research, also using welfare regime theory, but he adds a distinctive perspective by considering age cohorts within countries, and especially inequalities between age cohorts in the income returns on education. In many industrialized countries, the period from the end of the Second World War until the early 1970s was one of economic growth, leading to higher standards of living that were broadly shared. When that economic growth slowed down, as Chauvel demonstrates, very different dynamics came into play for different regime types and for different generations or age cohorts.

In countries such as Italy and France, employment protections and other social policies largely protected older employees from the worst consequences of the slowdown. Instead, the brunt of the slowdown, and of subsequent economic stresses such as deindustrialization and globalization, fell hard upon new young cohorts as they entered the labor market. These young cohorts found it difficult to find secure, well-paying jobs; even college-educated job entrants experienced a dramatic drop in the value of their educational credentials. So many college-educated young people were under- or unemployed that there appeared to be a crisis of "overeducation" in these countries. In sum, a large generational rift in standard of living and life chances opened up, in nations like Italy and France, between employees who were born before 1955 and those born later, leading to what Chauvel terms social "scarring effects"—high levels of youth unemployment, marginalization, and low youth self-esteem, even among the well-educated.

By contrast, in liberal welfare regimes like the United States, older generations of workers were not protected from economic pain; since the early 1970s, large numbers of them have been affected by layoffs, wage stagnation, and other economic stresses (Newman 2008). As a result, the economic pain was not concentrated on younger people entering the labor force. In contrast to countries like Italy and France, therefore, younger employees in America have not experienced sudden drops in employment prospects or in the value of their educational credentials. That is, the generational rift is minimal in the liberal welfare regimes. The effects of economic decline are seen, instead, in a marked increase in income inequality within each age cohort—there is polarization between economic winners and losers in liberal countries—but the impact is spread through the age pyramid.

In yet a third kind of regime, the Nordic social-democratic states, governments responded to economic hard times by greatly increasing their investment in youth, in education, and in skill creation—a strategy that seems to have minimized generational rifts, avoided overeducation, and limited youth unemployment and social marginalization.

Chauvel's concerns with overeducation and underemployment of French and Italian labor-market entrants are echoed by Pawel Polawski's research on Poland (chapter 11). Since its transition after 1990 from a socialist to a capitalist market economy, Poland has experienced considerable economic dislocation. Its overall labor-force participation rate is low because many of the older and least educated people are no longer employed, but depend on government support. Unemployment rates have fluctuated strongly; substantial numbers of Poles have also sought work abroad, principally in the U.K., in Ireland, and in Germany.

During this period, education has boomed. In part, this is because educated labor is now being paid significantly more than manual employment.

This was not the case under socialism, however. Polawski notes that Poles with tertiary education used to be paid less than the national average wage. Nowadays, the Polish wage structure looks much more like other Western nations, with increasing wages associated with more years of education. As higher education began to pay more, large numbers of Poles sought a college or university education. Student enrollments grew fivefold. Private tuition-charging colleges have opened, and even public institutions have developed tuition-charging extramural and evening courses.

Polawski is concerned that this rapid expansion is about to produce serious problems of overeducation or overqualification. He documents that so far, university graduates are earning more, and are less likely to be unemployed, than less educated workers, but he sees warning signs. The earnings of people with a college degree are much less than people with university or master's degrees, and at least one study finds that returns on bachelor's degrees have decreased. Polawski also notes that there is a skills mismatch in higher education: there are shortages of technical and skilled labor, yet most young Poles are studying the social sciences, business and law, and humanities and arts rather than technical subjects. The unemployment rate for tertiary graduates is rising. Access to higher education has boosted Polish expectations about highly paid jobs, but the pay in available jobs does not match young graduates' expectations. Polawski, therefore, concludes that expansion of higher education is only wise when a country's economic demand for educated labor is growing. Poland will harm itself if it produces a glut of graduates or if it provides a type of higher education that fails to prepare students for good jobs.

Fleishmann and Dronkers (chapter 12) examine the economic integration of first- and second-generation immigrants into thirteen countries in Europe, considering several possible determinants of successful integration, including the immigrant's own education and the education of the immigrant's parents. They also test whether welfare regime types of governments differ in their ability to integrate immigrants and whether immigrants' countries of origin, as well as their destination country, affect integration along such dimensions as employment and occupational status.

They find that, in general, both the immigrant's own educational attainment and the immigrant's parents' education do affect integration. That is, better-educated immigrants from more educated families are more successfully integrated. Various other factors also strongly affect the degree of integration, however. Country of origin matters: immigrants in the EU from Eastern Europe and Central Asia fare less well than immigrants from Western European countries, for example. The welfare regime in the receiving country also affects immigrant incorporation: immigrants in nations with social-democratic regimes have more success integrating than immigrants in the liberal regimes (like the U.K. and Ireland) and also more success than immigrants in the conservative welfare regimes of Spain and Italy. Other things held equal, Muslim immigrants were also less integrated economically than others and had lower returns to education than non-Muslims.

In sum, the educational background of immigrant families and the educational success of the second (European-born) generation are both important predictors of successful incorporation, but many other noneducational factors, including regime type, also determine the fates of immigrants.

Angel L. Harris (chapter 13) focuses on a different dimension of inequality in education: the gap between young men and young women in educational attainment. Harris points to a seeming paradox: in terms of earnings, women receive a lower payoff for education than do men. Nevertheless, in several countries, young women are more engaged in their education and are completing credentials at higher rates than are young men. From the perspective of rational choice theory, this is paradoxical: if young women benefit less than men from education, they ought to invest themselves less, not more, than men. Some scholars have attempted to explain this apparent paradox through the idea of a "Pollyanna hypothesis"—the notion that young women do not perceive themselves as economically underrewarded for their credentials and, being unaware, they continue eagerly to seek education.

Harris tests this Pollyanna notion using data on adolescent educational attainment in the U.S. state of Maryland, and he finds that it lacks empirical validity. The young women in his study are quite aware that, as women, they will face economic discrimination. (In fact, they perceive much more gender inequality than their male counterparts.) Notwithstanding this perception, young women invest themselves more in education than male adolescents: they spend more time on homework, are more likely to seek assistance with academic problems, and are more involved in school activities such as clubs.

The anomaly or paradox, therefore, remains. Young women do not enjoy the same labor-market benefits from education as young men do; they are quite aware of this inequity, nevertheless young women invest more in their education than do their male counterparts.

CONCLUSION

What general lessons should we draw from these international pieces of research? One lesson is that, although educational expansion is occurring nearly everywhere, educational growth is far from uniform in terms of its effects. In each nation, educational expansion has had a different impact on labor markets, on economic inequality, and on generational fortunes. In part, these differences reflect the vagaries of each nation's economic fortunes, but more important, the divergences in educational impacts reflect the different welfare regimes in each country and the details of how educational institutions have expanded in each country. Educational systems are embedded in their national political and economic contexts, and it is the interactions of these three realms that matters when assessing social impacts.

Nevertheless, we can observe certain commonalities or global trends. In all of the national studies, access to education—especially to higher education—has become the most important route for individual economic mobility for a large and growing part of the nation's population. This has led to increasing demands placed on states for greater educational access. Even in statist regimes such as China, ruling elites have accommodated this demand to some extent by expanding enrollments. Educational expansion, however, does not come cheap, and a pattern frequently recurs across countries in which governments allow private-sector institutions in higher education to supplement state-provisioned colleges and universities.

Private tuition-driven higher education is booming, and it is spilling over into primary and second education, and into ancillary educational activities such as test preparation and after-school study. Education has become an important industry, and this undoubtedly helps to satisfy the burgeoning demand for access. However, the private provision of education sold as a service to students and their families exacerbates preexisting class and income inequalities. Even where higher education is free, and where admission is strictly based on academic tests, research indicates that middle- and upper-class youth typically have a much better chance at access and graduation. When, in addition, access requires the ability to pay, these class-based differences are greatly magnified.

One adaptation that we see, albeit with variants in each country, is the emergence of differentiated educational institutions, whereby the affluent are more likely to attend elite colleges, while the lower classes mostly attend less prestigious institutions; or where affluent students attend full time or take higher degrees, while less affluent students attend part time or take shorter courses of study. Another common adaptation involves the international migration of students: more affluent families who confront difficulties in educational access in their home countries are increasingly sending their children abroad, especially to English-speaking countries. As higher education becomes a global industry, individuals with money can find educational opportunities for their offspring when they are confronted with local barriers.

Overall, the research presented here suggests that recent educational expansion maintains, and perhaps even amplifies, existing social inequalities even as it provides an important route upward for some individuals from the lower strata of society. Because education has become a competition among individuals and classes, it creates losers as well as winners. Several contributors to this volume alert us to the particular disadvantages suffered by young people who do not reach the higher levels of education when their age mates (or their nations) are becoming more and more credentialed. Economic opportunities for those who fail to complete an education, owing to either family circumstance or lack of talent or motivation, become increasingly constricted in an era of educational expansion. Education has become an important mechanism generating social exclusion, and this operates not only for youth from poorer families but also for middle-class losers in academic contests. The psychological and emotional toll of intense educational competition has barely begun to be studied.

Can the kind of educational expansion that we have seen for the last several decades continue? On this final important question, our contributors do not agree because the experiences of their nations differ. Some document that academic expansion can exceed the ability of national economies to absorb new graduates: what follows is overeducation, credential inflation, higher unemployment or underemployment among the well educated, and divergent economic fortunes for older and younger cohorts of people. In other countries, most notably the United States, scholars fear exactly the reverse, arguing that an observed slowdown in educational expansion is what endangers future economic growth. We leave the resolution of that matter to future research.

Notes

1. UNESCO's World Education Indicators Program reports statistics for 19 so-called middle income countries: Argentina, Brazil, Chile, China, Egypt, India, Indonesia, Jamaica, Jordan, Malaysia, Paraguay, Peru, the Philippines, the Russian Federation, Sri Lanka, Tunisia, Thailand, Uruguay, and Zimbabwe. The OECD countries in general are wealthier than the UNESCO sample and include Australia, Austria, Belgium, Canada, the Czech Republic, Denmark, Finland, France, Germany, Greece, Hungary, Iceland, Ireland, Italy, Japan, Korea, Luxembourg, Mexico, the Netherlands, New Zealand, Norway, Poland, Portugal, the Slovak Republic, Spain, Sweden, Switzerland, Turkey, the United Kingdom, and the United States.

2. Some scholars have argued that this expansion may be running out of steam in the most highly educated nations. For example, Carneiro and Heckman, in Heckman, Kreuger, and Friedman (2004), claimed that the current generation of Americans is the first ever to complete fewer years of education that their parents, although this is disputed. Government data suggest that enrollments in U.S. degree-granting institutions grew by 23% between 1996 and 2006, and are projected to increase somewhere between 9 and 16% between 2006 and 2017 (NCES 2008:8). These education growth rates exceed population growth and imply, *contra* Carneiro and Heckman, that larger proportions of Americans are entering college than

heretofore. What seems clear is that the rate of expansion of education has slowed markedly in the U.S. since the 1970s, and that America has lost its global leadership in college enrollment; several other nations now enroll a larger proportion of their youth in higher education than does the U.S. (Goldin and Katz 2008.)

3. On average in OECD countries, over 90% of total educational expenditures are paid for publicly, but private expenditures play a greater role at the higher tertiary level, from less than 5% in some Scandinavian countries, to 65% in the U.S., and to over 75% in Korea and Chile (OECD 2008:242).

4. The OECD nations now spend an average of 6.1% of their GNP on education as a whole, of which about one-third is spent on tertiary/higher education; the U.S. spends 7% of its GNP, of which 40% is devoted to higher education (OECD 2008: 226–227).

5. In many countries, there is an acknowledged prestige hierarchy among colleges and universities, sometimes based on historical precedence. These differences become crystallized if well-resourced institutions get richer through private endowments or via unequal government funding. Published rankings of universities tend to attract the academically most competitive applicants to the "best" colleges, and the most sought-after colleges in turn can be more selective in their student body and staff. In this way, inequalities in institutional "quality" become a self-fulfilling prophesy and are maintained or even intensified over time. A few countries resist this pattern and attempt to maintain equality across their higher education institutions; Germany and the Netherlands are examples. As Teichler (2007:257) notes, the growth of higher education in Europe led to the establishment of new kinds of tertiary institutions from the 1960s on (e.g., *instituts universitaires de technologie*, or IUT, in France; *Fachhochschule* in Germany and Austria; polytechnics in the U.K.. This further complicated prestige hierarchies.

6. While many middle-class American families send their children to well-regarded local public schools in affluent neighborhoods, some elite families have sent their children to private residential "prep schools" whose graduates are accepted in large numbers into Ivy League colleges. In recent decades, prep schools have found it increasingly difficult to gain access to the Ivies for their graduates (Powell 1996).

7. By contrast, public universities in France and Italy charge international students the same tuition and fees as their domestic students pay. The Scandinavian universities are exceptional since they charge neither foreign nor domestic students for tuition or fees (OECD 2008:356). Universities in EU member states typically charge students from other EU countries the same tuition as their own nationals.

8. A parallel process is under way in the United States, as state universities wrestle with the desire to attract higher fees from out-of-state students, while citizens in the state seek to monopolize positions in public higher education for their own offspring. These conflicts have become more pronounced as state-level budget support for higher education has dwindled to historic lows, thus increasing the value of "hard currency" obtained from out-of-state students.

2

Educational Inequality in Latin America

Patterns, Policies, and Issues

Cristián Cox

Latin America exhibits one of the highest levels of income inequality in the world, and by international standards, it has middling levels of educational inequality. The historic roots of both inequalities are deep, and the contemporary economic, social, and political institutions and forces that sustain them are durable and powerful. Yet improved participation by the disadvantaged in quality education is nowadays considered critical, not only on ethical grounds for citizenship and social integration but also in terms of lost potential for economic competitiveness (ECLAC-UNESCO 1992; World Bank 2005). This double-edged justification for reforms that aim to build more equitable educational institutions and processes has, in the last decade and a half, transformed the political economy of educational change in the region. Across the different countries' political spectra, education is seen as holding a strategic key for change and growth; and as a direct result, the 1990–2006 period has witnessed the greatest activism in education in the history of the region. Most governments have considerably increased their expenditures in the sector; carried forward institutional and curricular reforms; and developed programs that give disadvantaged territories or groups priority, with improvements in quality and equity as driving goals and criteria. The policies impact not only coverage, which was the main focus of state actions in education throughout the twentieth century, but also institutional and curricular arrangements.

In the context of an inheritance of marked inequalities and of policies aimed at reducing them, we address the following questions: First, how do the different countries of the region compare in terms of income and educational inequalities, and what is the pattern of relationships between these two dimensions. Second, which are the key policy continuities across countries in the examined period, and how do they relate to the issue of inequality? Are there any tradeoffs among policies so as to close the gap between quantity and quality of education among socioeconomic groups? Third, which dimensions of inequality, if any, can be said to have been affected by policies of the 1990–2006 period, and to what extent?

Equity is about justice and fairness in the distribution of resources and opportunities—criteria ultimately based on moral considerations, with roots that go back to religion and classical philosophy. As with any crucial normative concept, its meaning varies with groups and history, by country, and even by academic discipline. For a policy framework, we take equity criteria to be the orienting principles in public action that strive to achieve equality of opportunity—that ensure any predetermined circumstances (gender, race, place of birth, family origins) and social group a person is born into do not determine his or her opportunities and outcomes, nor are those opportunities and outcomes determined by groups in the economic, social, and political domains (World Bank 2005).

Three levels of equity frame the contemporary debates and policymaking in education: (1) equity in access to education, or unhindered opportunity regarding participation in formal education; (2) equity within education, or equality of opportunity in the educational process; and (3) equity as equality of opportunity with reference to results or achieved capacities (Reimers 2000; García-Huidobro and Eduardo 2005). There is an evident hierarchy in this triad, with equity of results being the most demanding and presupposing the presence of the other two levels. Here, we use these categories to describe and analyze policies and the evolution of patterns of inequalities in Latin American education, distinguishing: (1) *equity as inclusion*, when referring to the first level of equality of opportunity in education—that is, access to and participation in education in terms of grades completed; and (2) *equity as fairness*, when referring to equality of opportunity regarding the processes and results of education (OECD 2007b).

The first section of this chapter sketches the general picture of educational inequality in the region, compares income inequality, and distinguishes the different development agendas for the quite different levels of development that exist among the countries of the region. The second section describes the main components of educational reform in the Latin American region for the period 1990–2006, and discusses their impact on the historical patterns of inequality in the social distribution of education. The third section examines available data about years of education and grade completion by countries and social categories, by way of assessing the expansion of access to education by different generations and different socioeconomic categories. The fourth section describes learning outcomes in six Latin American countries and analyses their association with socioeconomic and institutional factors, as well as comparing them with selected OECD countries. This permits an assessment of the region's educational structures in terms of equity of their results. A final section returns to policy issues.

LEVELS OF INCOME, EDUCATION, AND INEQUALITIES
IN LATIN AMERICA

For all its historical and cultural continuities, Latin American countries diverge markedly in terms of their levels of economic and educational development and in terms of their degrees of inequality.

Table 2.1 presents the per capita income and the mean years of schooling for the eighteen countries of the region. The range of income is US $2399 (measured as per capita income in year 2001 PPP dollars) for Bolivia to US $12,174 for Argentina; and the range of mean years of schooling is 5.55 years for Honduras to 10.33 years for Argentina.

Table 2.2 shows the income Gini coefficient and the education Gini coefficient for the countries of the region. It can be noted that there appears to be no direct consistency between the two, except that in all cases except Nicaragua, the education Gini is always below that of the income Gini.

Table 2.1 Per capita income and mean years of schooling Latin American countries.

	GDP per capita, PPP (constant 2000 international $)	Mean Years of Schooling 1999–2001
Argentina	12174	10.33
Chile	9115	10.27
Mexico	9046	7.78
Uruguay	8782	9.41
Costa Rica	8621	7.90
Brazil	7301	8.38
Dominican Republic	6411	7.47
Colombia	6244	7.19
Panama	6164	9.52
Venezuela, RB	5685	8.29
Peru	4723	8.76
El Salvador	4594	6.56
Paraguay	4553	7.26
Guatemala	3974	4.58
Ecuador	3373	8.12
Nicaragua	3278	5.57
Honduras	2506	5.55
Bolivia	2399	7.63

Source: World Bank 2006, 2005, Table A4.

Table 2.2 Income and education inequality measures in Latin America.

	Income			Education		Share due to	
	Year	Gini index	90/10 percentile ratio	Year	Gini index	Location	Gender
Argentina-U	2001	0.51	13.71	2001	0.22	—	0.00
Bolivia	2002	0.58	29.65	1998	0.38	0.16	0.2
Brazil	2001	0.59	16.25	2001	0.39	0.01	0.00
Chile	2000	0.51	10.72	2000	0.23	0.08	
Colombia	1999	0.54	15.00	2000	0.36	0.13	0.00
Costa Rica	2000	0.46	9.65	2000	0.30	—	0.00
Dominican Rep	1997	0.47	9.17	2002	0.38	0.04	0.00
Ecuador	1998	0.54	16.09	1988–9	0.33	0.12	0.00
El Salvador	2002	0.50	15.88	2000	0.45	0.13	0.00
Guatemala	2000	0.58	16.81	1998–9	0.54	0.07	0.01
Honduras	1999	0.52	11.72	2001	0.45	0.11	0.00
Mexico	2002	0.49	11.87	1999	0.34	0.09	—
Nicaragua	2001	0.40	6.52	2001	0.49	0.13	0.00
Panama	2000	0.55	18.65	2000	0.27	0.11	0.00
Paraguay	2001	0.55	18.26	2000	0.35	0.12	—
Peru	2000	0.48	14.6	2000	0.30	0.14	0.01
Uruguay-U	2000	0.43	7.73	2000	0.24		0.00
Venezuela	2000	0.42	7.94	2000	0.30	0.01	0.00

Source: World Bank 2005, Tables A2 and A4.

These are two different dynamics, of course, where education appears as more malleable and ahead of the labor markets and ahead of society generally. For the World Bank, this disconnect "between the convergence in education and the divergence in incomes is that education is not translating into human capital and that the rise in per capita schooling explains only a small part of growth in output per worker" (World Bank 2005:68). More directly connected to our focus here, table 2.2 (columns 6 and 7) also shows that gender is less relevant in the region in terms of inequity (measured by years of education). In fact, gender parity was attained in Latin America in the 1980s. Today, because of boys' higher grade repetition and lower secondary-level survival rates, girls have become the majority at the secondary and tertiary education levels (EFA-UNESCO 2006). Location, instead, contributes a greater share to inequality, which is higher in the Andean countries (Bolivia, Peru, and Ecuador) and some of the Central American ones (Nicaragua, El Salvador) than in the remaining Latin American countries. This is a relevant factor when considering decentralization policies.

The educational agendas of such different societies clearly diverge in terms of levels of development and inequalities, while facing similar secular challenges of globalization in the information age. That is, many countries confront an *inclusion agenda*, with per capita incomes of less than US $4,000 PPP, with a third or more of their population living in rural areas, and with half or more of their youngsters not completing secondary education. Others, meanwhile, have per capita incomes around the US $ 10,000 PPP mark, have only about 15 percent of their population living in rural areas, and have high secondary-education completion rates, and so are challenged by the social segmentation of educational institutions and results, thus confronting a *fairness agenda*.

Race, Ethnicity, and Rural Residence as Factors in Educational Inequality

There is limited information about the impact of race and ethnicity on educational inequality. However, the data indicate that black people in Brazil, as with indigenous groups and those living in rural locations elsewhere in Latin America, consistently have fewer educational opportunities than the rest of the population (Reimers 2000; IIPE-OEI 2006).When the school attendance of white and *mestizo*/black/indigenous households in Brazil is compared, the data show that both groups participate in primary school, but there are significant differences, by up to two or three years, in grade completion. Mixed, black, and indigenous children all have a greater probability of facing difficulties in school (IIPE-OEI 2006:120).

Rural location carries greater weight in Central American countries. In Honduras, Guatemala, Nicaragua, and El Salvador, more than 40 percent of their populations live in rural areas, compared to approximately 10 percent of populations in Argentina, Chile, and Uruguay. However, in both situations and using whatever indicator, we find that urban schools show advantages over rural schools in terms of both access and results. Both Bolivia and the Central American countries have exclusion rates of school-age children in rural areas that are double those of their urban areas, ranging from 7.8 percent for Bolivia to 18.2 percent for Guatemala (IIPE-OEI 2006: table A4).

EDUCATIONAL POLICIES OF THE 1990S AND THE EQUITY CRITERIA

Around the turn of the millennium, we saw unprecedented public and private changes in education, as politicians and policymakers defined education as the key lever for economic and democratic development. In spite of decisive differences between countries, there is a uniformity to this period's policies that is embedded in both secular and political factors. First, state actions in education during this period were deeply influenced by structural-adjustment models and economic liberalization, on the one hand, and cultural pressures brought about by globalization and the arrival of the information age, on the other. These developments produced the longest period in Latin America's history with elected democratic governments in all the countries of the region. Thus, while the concept of equity was not part of the vocabulary of most military governments of the 1980s, let alone their policies, the transition to democratic regimes led to the opposite: an explicit emphasis on education as a standard for producing equality of opportunity.

Second, this period was characterized by the growing influence of multilateral development agencies like the World Bank, the Inter-American Development Bank, and UNESCO; their influence on government education policies and programs was reinforced by the spread of international tests like PISA and TIMSS. Their aggregate impact has arguably had an isomorphic effect on educational systems, which, independent of national specificities and agendas, needed to react to common worldwide pressures (Benavot et al. 1991; Schriewer 2004). In this environment, the educational policies of the period 1990–2006 are characterized by the following common components: (1) expansion and rationalization of expenditures; (2) administrative decentralization; (3) programs that focus on specific population groups; (4) curriculum reform; and (5) evaluation of results, information, and accountability (Gajardo 1999; Kaufman and Nelson 2005; PREAL 2006; Carnoy 2007; Grindle 2004). Their links with equity issues and their impact is the focus of this section.

The Evolution and Allocation of Expenditures

The level and evolution of educational expenditure are simultaneously a portrait of government priorities and the framework that conditions the sector's expansion and redistribution. In Latin America, this recent period shows both the high priority given to education and rising expenditures. That is, on average in the region public educational expenditure increased from 2.7 percent in 1990 as a percentage of the gross domestic product (GDP) to 4.3 percent in 2002–2003; it is estimated that when private expenditures are added, the proportion of money now spent on education in Latin America was around 10 percent of GDP (PREAL 2006; Vegas and Petrow 2007).

Expenditure per student increased at this time in the majority of Latin American countries, together with the processes of standardization and rationalization that accompany the modern management of decentralization. Thus, for example, Chile allocated resources on the basis of an identical subsidy per student across the country, to which were added other pro-equity features. Brazil changed its allocation mechanism to be on the basis of an annual per student contribution, which leveled the dramatic differences that existed between the states and between municipalities, thereby altering historic patterns of inequality. In Argentina, too, there was, though ineffective, a dynamic attempt to alter inequities among provinces (Carnoy et al. 2004). And Colombia specified ways by which its decentralized units could spend centrally transferred funds (Filgueira, Bogliaccini, and Molina 2006).

Put simply, the greater expenditures and more equal and improved allocations between administrative units and territories point to both an expansion of educational opportunities and an improvement in their distribution. Both objectives are reflected in the marked increase in coverage and, as will be seen, in a reduction in educational inequalities, measured by the educational years completed by different income groups.

In terms of allocations between levels of their education systems, large differences remain between the countries. Chile drastically reduced the differences in per student expenditures among primary, secondary, and tertiary education. Mexico experienced steady growth at all levels, thereby continuing its unequal education patterns, while Brazil maintained a bias toward tertiary education, which received seven times more funding per student than did secondary education (de Ferranti et al. 2004).

Decentralization

Recent educational policy has been framed by the process of decentralization itself, based on substantial institutional change, and this decentralization has been an influential component of educational reform. Countries have dealt differently with this transfer of power and responsibility. For example, Chile, Argentina, and Brazil made the transfer to subnational governments; Colombia and Bolivia shifted to combined subnational and national jurisdictions; Nicaragua and El Salvador make direct transfers to schools (Di Gropello 2004). However, from the point of view of equity and social cohesion, decentralization has had a broad but contradictory significance. Specifically, it has given rise to a profound change in the functioning of the state, and thus of the function of education. The historic models of identity and social cohesion based on a common public education are changing, as central and vertical control shifts (with great variety among countries) to another model, yet in its infancy, with diversity, horizontal interactions, and local control making up its leitmotiv (Iaies and Delich 2007).

For Latin America, educational decentralization signals a historic change. For nineteenth-century elites, public education was a fundamental instrument in the creation of the nation and its development, the inculcation of national and moral ideas, a basic pillar for its unity. The idea of a common formative experience, universal and identical for all, that dissolves differences in the mix of public school, that is organized by the centralized provision of education and its supporting mechanisms of nationally defined institutions, norms, curriculum, and teacher training, was based on common principles. The term *normal*—meaning to conform to a type or standard or norm—is at the center of the organizing principle of public education: the norm of buildings, school desks, and educational materials; normal schools for teacher education; the normative curriculum; the normative bureaucracy and its national role of regimenting educational services, with its legal and bureaucratic logic of equality before the law.

At the beginning of the 1990s, the Economic Commission for Latin America (ECLAC),[1] and UNESCO made a critical diagnosis of Latin America's national systems of education, training, technology, and scientific research. Their recommendations were tantamount to a new educational policy paradigm for the region. The judgment was that, while from the end of the Second World War to the 1980s there had been substantial, but socially segmented, gains in educational access, those gains had resulted in poor-quality education that was unconnected to social needs (ECLAC-UNESCO 1992). At its core was criticism of the institutions, of the management and bureaucracy of the school systems, and of their growing lack of connection with the new needs of socioeconomic development. Specifically, this diagnosis called attention to the administration of educational systems that "became so bureaucratic that they closed in upon themselves and answered to no one" and that encouraged a "radical separation between human resources training and development needs" (ECLAC-UNESCO 1992:73).

What emerged from this analysis was a recommendation for decentralization and autonomy of schools from the center (ministries of education). It proposed changing policies from those promoting homogeneity to those supporting diversity. And it suggested a complete shift from the norms of steady and uniform *top-down* policy responses to *bottom-up* initiatives, with incentives and institutions encouraging greater system flexibility and with an ability to respond rapidly to changing needs.[2]

The new strategy had competitiveness and citizenship (the latter with an explicit reference to equity and social cohesion) as its key objectives, through the decentralization of the management of educational systems and a more open policy. This strategy received fundamental support via loans from the World Bank and the Inter-American Bank for projects to improve quality and equity. The rationale reflected the economic reasoning that educational decentralization leads to (1) improvements in the management of technical and social efficiency; (2) greater information flow to improve decision making by ensuring that principal actors are close to the issues; and (3) improved accountability between the government and the governed, or client and agent, thereby neutralizing the capture of educational systems by vested interests (Winkler and Gershberg 2000; World Bank 2004; Di Gropello 2004; De Ferranti et al. 2004; Grindle 2004).

However, the promoters of decentralization did not consider equity as a goal. In fact, the effects of decentralization are ambivalent in terms of equity. On the one hand, the processes can erode the unifying and equalizing power of centralized systems while, on the other hand, it can create a landscape that favors basic inequalities. Decentralization can bring greater efficiency, participation, and accountability; and this may enhance mechanisms for voicing needs and greater power for the disadvantaged, with potential implications for greater educational coverage, retention, and content relevance. However, these positive effects have to be weighed against highly unequal social contexts and institutions, where the state has a dwindling capacity to provide a level playing field and the local communities differ substantially in terms of their capacities for controlling and supporting education.

A recent assessment of decentralization in the region concluded:

> Single-country evidence shows that the impacts of decentralization may vary depending on which actors or institutions have control over which types of

decisions.... Community and school-based management has proven promising in many of these areas, but like other decentralization policies, these policies can increase educational inequality between communities of differing income levels and management capacities. (Vegas and Petrow 2007: 151–152)

The tradeoffs between gains in efficiencies and accountability and increased basis for inequality, especially in societies marked by strong differences in state capacities at different levels and in different local contexts, were not made visible and were not, on the whole, considered as part of the political deliberation and decisions about decentralization. Research and discussions on decentralization focused instead on the assessment of gains in efficiency, the transfer of powers, and accountability issues. The questions of how, and to what extent, decentralization processes have negatively affected people, by weakening the central capacities to level the field or close the gaps in educational access and participation by different groups, remain unanswered.

Targeting Strategies and Compensatory Programs

The policies that give precedence to special demographic subgroups or other special categories of people are highly important and characterize this reform period. These programs were the direct heirs of priority action and targeting inaugurated in Europe and North America during the 1960s and 1970s (Zones Educatives Prioritaires, in France; Educational Priority Areas, in Britain; and similar programs in the U.S.), and they began to be practiced in Latin America a quarter of a century later, coinciding with the end of military governments. These policies presupposed a turnaround in the states' operating framework: from a legal-logic centered on principles of equality before the law to a socio-cultural one that aims to differentiate between groups in terms of priority actions and positive discrimination criteria.[3] The new paradigm was based on pro-equity socio-cultural criteria that saw students of unequal socioeconomic, ethnic, or other origins as requiring a differentiated education in order to obtain average learning outcomes. For the first time, programs were established for subgroups of the population with criteria that included preferential actions.

There is both richness and variety in the types and forms of priority action programs for education during the nineties and post-2000 years (Reimers 2000; Vegas and Petrow 2007). In general, all aim to reduce the gap between the most favored and the lowest income groups or those excluded from educational opportunities. The differences are in the strategies (Vegas and Petrow 2007; García-Huidobro and Eduardo 2005), which include:

- Financial equalization among groups, jurisdictions, institutional categories (e.g., expansion and rationalization of public expenditures in education with equity criteria between states and municipalities, as in Brazil, and between the provinces, as in Argentina).
- Greater access to education in poor rural and urban areas, from the construction of schools and hiring of more teachers to the use of television in secondary education (Telesecundaria, in Mexico) or, in general, the expansion of school coverage in rural areas (e.g., the EDUCO program in El Salvador).
- Radical expansion of the provision of learning resources to lowest-income schools similar to those commonly available to affluent schools, such as textbooks, school libraries, and ICT (e.g., Pare, Mexico's program to overcome educational backwardness; Colombia's Escuela Nueva program to enhance the quality of rural schools; Argentina's Plan Social; Chile's P900 program to improve the quality of the schools with lowest levels of student achievement).
- A set of educational mechanisms to decrease the cost of education for poorer families and provide incentives for them and/or the school systems to attract students and maintain enrollment of the most at-risk groups, in terms of repetition and dropping out (e.g., the conditional cash transfer programs Bolsa Escola/Bolsa Família in Brazil and Progresa/Oportunidades in Mexico, both on a huge scale affecting 30 to 40 percent of primary education enrollment, the latter in the case of Brazil; Nicaragua's conditional cash transfers to families; Chile's Subvención de Reforzamiento Educativo, involving allocation of per student differentiated subsidies, or vouchers, to its rural enrollments and its most at-risk students from both urban and rural areas).

State efforts to address inequalities, as we shall see, had a distinct impact on the lowest-income and marginalized groups, in terms of both access to and permanence in primary and secondary schools. Regarding "quantity of education," or completed grades by the different socioeconomic groups, these efforts have had a positive impact on those in the first quintile, the children of families with parents who did not complete primary education, and the rural poor. Whatever form of identifying exclusion is chosen to be studied, we find that these are the groups that show the greatest advances in access to and participation in education during this period in terms of the first level of inequality, defined as being included (or not) in an educational sequence comparable to that experienced by the more favored groups.

Curriculum Reforms and Inequalities

As with the First World, Latin America's curricular reform of the nineties attempted to respond to the burgeoning of information technologies, globalization, and changes in the knowledge bases of school disciplines, together with offering new competencies required by a democratic citizenship and the economic competitiveness required in this new context (Braslavsky 2001). While there are differences between the countries, the curriculum challenges have been strongly influenced by the proposals of the international agencies in the field of education, such as UNESCO and the OECD. In general, they emphasized skills as much as knowledge as main objectives: reflexive abilities, critical and creative thought, collaborative work habits and capacity to resolve problems; and development of learner-centered paradigms for teaching and apprenticeship (Ferrer 2004). The new curricular prescriptions raised the level of traditional competencies and added new competencies, such as the focus on problem resolution, ICT literacy, and the ability to work with others. This substantially increased the formative ambition and complexity of the schooling experience, particularly at the secondary level. Table 2.3 systematizes some of the shifts toward greater abstraction and complexity, exemplified by the new curriculum for Chilean secondary education.

Table 2.3 Curriculum refom: moves to increased abstraction and complexity in secondary education; Chile.

Competencies	Contents	*FROM*	*TO (and/or)*
-Know what	Language	Sentence analysis	Discourse analysis
	Mathematics	Fixed and closed algorithms for	Mathematical reasoning in
-Know how		calculation	resolution of applied problems
-Know why	History and Social Sciences	Events	Contexts and trends
-Assess	Biology	Organisms and environment	Microbiology
-Judge	Art	Artistic Expression	Artistic expression, knowledge, perception and critical interpretation

Source: Based on Chile's new curriculum for secondary education; Ministerio de Educación 2005.

Most of the curriculum reforms have not dealt with the specific learning challenges faced by children and young people in poor environments, who are confronted by the need to learn new contents and competencies. It is an unanswered question as to whether the new curriculum increases learning achievements for different groups and whether the greater complexity of the knowledge and competencies is being communicated successfully by the schools. The curriculum reforms, while undoubtedly prescribing new material that encourages capacity building for personal growth and a better functioning society, weigh most heavily on teachers. They have to find ways to create learning opportunities for poorer groups with less cultural capital. The greater variance observed in the learning results of Argentina and Chile between 2000 and 2006, for example (see table 2.6 later), may reflect the changes in the curriculum, with the "new literacies" and higher learning goals having perhaps created a terrain for increased social differentiation in learning results.

Assessment and the Potential of Increased Accountability

During the nineties, the majority of countries in the region began to evaluate their learning results through standardized testing, and some of them participated in the unprecedented wave of international assessments of education (TIMSS, PISA, and others). The publication of these results has become an issue in most Latin American countries, principally because they are comparative scores rather than broken down by socioeconomic segments, which would have very different results. While teachers resent these comparative results because of their accountability implications, the tests have untapped potential to create voice and pro-equity (as fairness) demands as the public becomes better informed and exerts pressure for better educational performance by all groups (Ferrer 2006; Vegas and Petrow 2007). We shall come back to this point in the closing section.

PROGRESS IN EQUITY OF EDUCATION AS INCLUSION

The social distribution of education in the region has been unequivocally positive; the substantial expansion of education has significantly reduced educational inequality as exclusion. In terms of access to and length of school attendance, there has been progress particularly for the disadvantaged groups. The key measure here is the growing years of schooling achieved and the derived "completion of levels of education," an evolution described in figures 2.1 and 2.2.

Figure 2.1 provides a comparative view of completed education for six generations in three groups of countries, categorized by the pattern of expansion in primary and secondary education The generations on the horizontal axis and their participation in completion of studies mirror the inclusion capacities of the schooling systems of the different countries, from the decade of the 1940s ("65 plus" generation) to the mid-nineties ("19 to 24" generation). The countries that expanded their education first (and have the greatest coverage today)—Argentina, Chile, and Uruguay—have practically universalized primary education (over 90 percent student-completion rates), a goal that they reached in the seventies ("35 to 44" generation); whereas this continues to be a distant goal for the other countries, which at the end of the 1990s reached between 60 (Group 2) and 65 percent (Group 3) of the

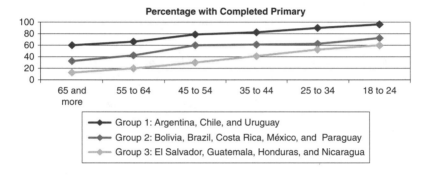

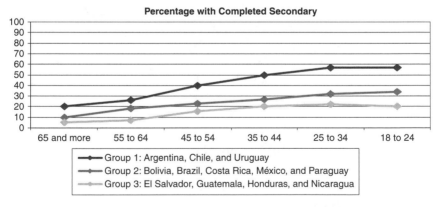

Figure 2.1. Latin America: Completion of primary and secondary education by age group.

Note: Data are for 18 countries in Latin America. Primary education is for young people ages 15–19, secondary education is for ages 20–24, 2005.

Source: IIPE-OEI, 2006. *Informe sobre Tendencias Sociales y Educativas en América Latina*. SITEAL, figs. 2.5 and 2.2.

relevant cohort completing their primary education. With regard to secondary education, the first group of countries show that almost 20 percent of
today's grandparents, 40 percent of their children, and just below 60 percent
of their grandchildren between 18 and 24 years have finished secondary
school. Only in the nineties did the remaining countries of the region reach
that 20 percent of cohorts completing the secondary level. Irrespective of the
different starting and finishing points, we see that the patterns of growth are
similar across the region for a fifty-year period of remarkable economic,
social, and political change. French historian Fernand Braudel's (2002: 18)
"brief, quick and nervous oscillations" that distinguish the history of political events from social history seem appropriate here: the consistent intergenerational march of education proceeds at a slower but steadier rate than
does political history.

The *longue durée* upward movement of inclusion is shown in more detail
(and with particular reference to the last decade and a half) in figure 2.2,
which compares completion of primary and secondary level schooling for
eighteen countries in the region, at two moments in time—1990 and
2005—according to five levels of household's "educational environment"
(measured by parents' education).

There are the expected differences, with the children of less educated
parents showing smaller proportions completing primary or secondary education. At the same time, for both primary and secondary education, the
figure shows an increase in the total number of students during the last
decade and a half; but while the changes are minimal in primary education,
as its universalization was nearly complete in 1990, the numbers are more
substantial at the secondary level. In primary education, the increase is most
significant for the poorest group, with a 21.4 percentage jump in the 1990–
2005 period (the same figure varying between 0.7 and 3.7% for the other
groups). This implies a reduction in the access gap compared to other categories—a change linked to active pro-equity programs across the region,
with both targeted programs in education and poverty-reduction programs
in other sectors (housing, health, adult education) contributing to this
effect.

At the secondary level, there is an upward and substantial movement for
all groups, as the comparison between the 1990 and 2005 curves clearly
shows. The two categories with the largest increases are those with parents
that have "primary incomplete" and "secondary incomplete" educational
records, with a leap in the proportion that complete studies that is equivalent to increases of 102 and 58.7 percent, respectively. The other three
groups also show increases, in ascending order, from parents with "secondary complete and above" to "higher education complete' (13.8, 19.3, and
20.6%, respectively).

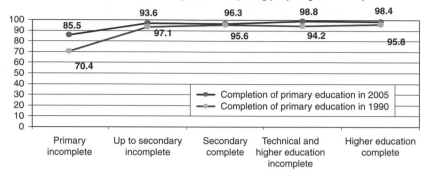

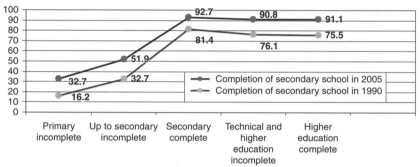

Figure 2.2. Completion of primary and secondary education by educational level of parents, for 18 countries, 1990–2005.

Note: Average number of years of schooling is for head of household and spouse. Data are based on special tabulations of household surveys in the different countries. The comparative data exclude Guatemala and consider 8 main cities of Bolivia and only the urban areas of Argentina, Ecuador, Paraguay, and Uruguay.

Source: ECLAC-UNESCO, 2007. *Panorama Social 2007*, gráfico 3.7.

The greater access to and completion of secondary schooling for those with the least cultural capital accelerated faster during the 1990s than for other groups that followed an upward trend. As with primary education, we interpret this as a result of targeting strategies and compensatory programs that were characteristic of the policies of the period. Further, the general increase in secondary education completion rates is an upward movement in the structure of opportunities. It corresponds to Pierre Bourdieu's concept of competition struggles, where "all groups concerned run in the same direction, toward the same objectives" and where "the competing groups are separated by differences which are essentially located in the order of time," with each group's past represented by the group below and its future in the group immediately above (Bourdieu 2003:163). This structure shows a closing gap between the less advantaged groups—in terms of cultural and economic capital—and the rest of the distribution, attributable, as said, to the policies of the period.

One can conclude that a fundamental result of educational policy of the last decade and an half has been the increase in coverage and school retention, so that the level of educational inequality (by years of education completed) between the present and previous generations has decreased significantly. The Gini coefficients for education inequality in the present generation (see table 2.2, above) represent an improvement of over twenty percentage points compared to its parents' generation, according to Latinobarómetro survey evidence of 2005 (Crouch, Gove, and Gustafsson 2007).

NO PROGRESS IN FAIRNESS: INEQUALITIES IN LEARNING AND THE WEIGHT OF SOCIOECONOMIC AND INSTITUTIONAL FACTORS

The participation of Latin American countries in international learning tests such as TIMSS and PISA since the latter half of the 1990s has produced information that, for the first time, allows more rigorous comparative analysis of educational systems and the social distribution of their learning outcomes (Vegas and Petrow 2007). Equity can be examined with the most demanding of criteria—results in terms of people and their capacities—and judged not only in terms of inclusion but also fairness, or the extent to which learning outcomes (test scores) are achieved independent of socioeconomic, ethnic, location, and similar background factors.

Social Segmentation in Schools

School socialization does not depend only on the official curricula or state guidance concerning cultural transmission. It is commonplace to note that a "silent curriculum" also plays a decisive role, one that has formative consequences in the relations, practices, and rituals that constitute the social texture of school experience. In this regard, the social homogeneity or heterogeneity of institutions is crucial. Next, the evidence regarding Latin American schools' social homogeneity or heterogeneity is examined as a key dimension for equity and for the construction of the socio-cultural base for social cohesion.

Figure 2.3 offers a straightforward presentation of the level of social segmentation that characterizes schooling in Latin America, based on data from the 2000 version of the Program for International Student Assessment (PISA) for five countries in the region. The bars represent the ratios in

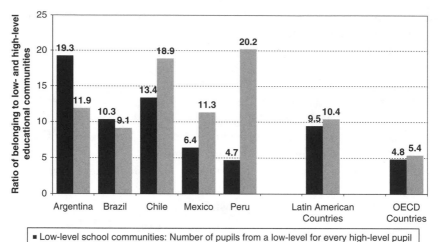

Figure 2.3. Latin America (5 countries) and OECD (7 countries): Composition of educational communities by socio-occupational level of parents, 2000.

Source: CEPAL, 2007. *Procesamientos especiales de la base de datos PISA 2000*, OECD (http://www.pisa.oecd.org).

socioeconomically low-level schools (in socioeconomic terms): the ratio between pupils from low socioeconomic levels and those from high levels;[4] and at high-income level schools, the ratio between pupils from the highest quartile in socioeconomic level and all low-level pupils. On average, the ratios in the school communities of Latin American countries are double the estimates of "social homogeneity" in the OECD countries—9.5 pupils of low socioeconomic status for every pupil of high socioeconomic status in poorer schools, whereas this figure is an average of 4.8 for OECD countries. There are also substantial differences among the five Latin American countries, with Peru, Argentina, and Chile having much higher levels of social segmentation in their lower secondary schools than Mexico and Brazil, although the rate of enrollment in these two countries is significantly lower, and therefore their intake is comparatively more selective and socially homogenous, than in the other countries.

Crouch et al. (2007) have constructed an "inclusion index" based on student responses, as part of PISA 2000 and 2003, to questions about whether the student feels excluded, if he or she makes friends with other students easily, if he or she feels part of the school, if the other students get on well with him or her, and if the student feels alone. They compared Latin American responses to OECD country responses. Latin American students—with the exception of Peru—declared themselves to be more "integrated" than students from OECD countries, perhaps replicating subjectively the social homogeneity of their schooling. Greater homogeneity is the foundation of bonding social capital (relations and trust within groups), but it has less weight in terms of bridging social capital, or relations and trust, between groups (Putnam 2000). This raises the question of how well socially segmented schools contribute to the construction of the cultural and dispositional bases of social cohesion (Cox 2008).

Table 2.4 sets out the scores for science, mathematics, and reading for the six Latin American PISA participants in 2006 (Argentina, Brazil, Colombia, Chile, Mexico, and Uruguay) as well as three OECD countries (Germany, Sweden, and the United Kingdom). The results have been ordered according to parents' educational level, comparing those with completed lower secondary education or less to those with completed tertiary education. The proportion of students in each category (columns 1 and 5) shows important variations between Latin America and Europe. For instance, there are 28.4 and 53.4 percent (Chile and Mexico) in the category showing parents with lower secondary education or less, while the proportions found in the three European countries vary between 5.3 percent (UK) and 15.1 percent (Germany).

What is important in this comparison between Latin American and European countries is that the differences in scores between the two categories of students are similar, albeit starting at quite different levels. The last column shows the score differences for reading competency (column 9) for children with parents having incomplete secondary education and those who have finished tertiary education; it is between 50 and 64 points in the Latin American countries (with Chile as an exception, with 93 points), but less than the average 73 points for OECD countries. If the data of figure 2.3 and table 2.4 are considered together, it is immediately apparent that Latin American schooling institutions do not differ markedly from the most advanced systems in terms of neutralizing the imprint of social class on learning results; but they do diverge clearly in terms of the social composition (homogeneity—heterogeneity) of their institutions. The following evidence on between- and within-school variance in learning outcomes permits us to study more this feature—of critical importance in terms of equity of education viewed as fairness.

Specifically, an examination of learning outcomes between and within schools, for the different countries and different regions, reveals the national and regional profiles of inequality in education. The *between-school* variance is strongly associated with students' socioeconomic background (family structure, parental occupation(s), number of books in the home, etc.) and institutional features of the school system. In some countries, like Chile, school choice is strongly related to socioeconomic variables, while in other

Table 2.4 Performance on the Science, Reading, and Mathematics PISA 2006 Test by level of education of parents[1]: Latin American and OECD countries.

Countries	Parents with completed lower secondary education or below: ISCED 0,1, or 2 [1]				Parents with completed tertiary education (ISCED 5 or 6)				Difference in scores between the two groups
	Percentage of students	PISA score in Science	PISA score in Reading	PISA score in Mathematics	Percentage of students	PISA score in Science	PISA score in Reading	PISA score in Mathematics	Pisa scores in Reading (Col 3–Col 7)
Argentina	34.2	353	338	344	45.5	422	402	408	64
Brazil	47.4	365	367	342	35.9	416	417	397	50
Chile	28.4	391	397	363	31.0	485	490	456	93
Colombia	42.3	368	361	346	42.7	410	411	394	50
Uruguay	34.4	392	373	385	54.3	452	438	451	59
Mexico	53.4	388	386	383	35.6	437	441	434	55
Average OECD	**15.0**	**446**	**443**	**448**	**46.6**	**525**	**516**	**522**	**73**
Sweden	7.6	456	463	462	69.4	515	519	514	56
U.K.	5.3	450	444	450	51.4	537	516	512	72
Germany	15.1	449	420	446	45.8	543	521	531	101

Source: OECD 2006. Science competencies for tomorrow's world. Volume 2: Table 2.4.7 a.

[1] Based on students self-report.

countries, such as Germany, the streaming of students by ability also strongly differentiates schools and segments the learning results socially. The *within-school* variance measures the differences associated with the distribution of capacities in any given group of students. In an education system, the greater the proportion of within-school variance in relation to the total variance obtained for a given student population's performance, the more equitable is the system. Thus, parents can send their children to any school, confident that both its social composition and the learning opportunities it provides will not differ much from those offered by any other school in the system.

Column 1 in table 2.5 shows that, with the exception of Mexico, the total variance in learning results is greater for the Latin American countries than for the OECD country average. Argentina and Uruguay exhibit the largest variance—50 percent more variance than the OECD average. The three European countries included in the table correspond to the three types of welfare regimes using Esping-Andersen's well-known categories: social-democratic (Sweden), with stronger pro-equity and socially cohesive institutions; liberal (U.K.), where markets and individual choice play a crucial role in the provision of welfare; and conservative-corporatist (Germany), in which the access to welfare is strongly segmented along status differences between groups (Esping-Andersen 1990). The differences between these countries in terms of between- and within-school variances, and their implications in terms of equity, provide an eloquent mirror by which to assess the situation in Latin American countries.

The between-schools variance (columns 2 and 6 in table 2.5) reveals the comparative social segmentation of the region's school systems. In the three southern-cone countries (Argentina, Chile, and Uruguay), the variance is over one and a half times that of the OECD average (38.4 percent). Colombia and Mexico are close to this OECD average, while Brazil is almost nine points higher. But Colombia and Mexico have smaller net enrollment coverage in secondary education (53 and 62%, respectively) compared to 80.8 percent for Argentina, 74.5 percent for Chile, and 71.7 percent for Uruguay (EFA-UNESCO 2006). The smaller total and between-schools variances of Colombia and Mexico result from the more selective character and the comparatively greater social and educational homogeneity of their intake.

The between-schools variances in relation to total variances is markedly lower in both Sweden (17.0%) and the U.K. (21.9%), while that of Germany, with its early tracking of students into different schools according to their ability, produces the highest variances of all the countries represented in table 2.2 (100.5%). The statistic "variance explained" (column 4) expresses the strength of the association between students'

Table 2.5 Between-school and within-school variance in student performance on the Reading scale in PISA 2006.[1]

| Countries | Total variance in student performance expressed as a percentage of the average variance in student performance across OECD countries | Total variance in student performance between schools[2] | Total variance in student performance within schools | Variance explained by the PISA index of economic, social and cultural status of students and schools | | Total variance between schools expressed as a percentage of the total variance within the country.[4] |
				Between-school variance explained[3]	Within-school variance explained	
Argentina	158.1	71.0	84.9	35.0	0.8	44.9
Brazil	107.9	47.0	55.3	23.6	0.3	43.5
Colombia	119.7	35.8	83.0	16.8	1.9	29.9
Chile	109.9	62.1	63.2	40.8	0.4	56.5
Mexico	94.2	33.9	48.8	15.9	0.2	36.0
Uruguay	151.4	62.4	87.8	31.4	1.3	41.2
OECD average	**100.0**	**38.4**	**63.4**	**21.5**	**2.7**	**—**
Sweden	96.4	17.0	81.0	7.9	4.0	17.7
U.K.	103.7	21.9	78.5	12.3	4.0	21.2
Germany	126.1	100.5	48.0	63.9	0.5	79.7

Source: OECD, 2006, Science Competencies for Tomorrow's World, Vol.2, Data, Table 2.4.1.d

[1] Variance expressed as a percentage of the average variance in students performance across OECD countries. The variance components were estimated for all students in participating countries with data on socioeconomic background and study programs.

[2] *Between-school variance*: average of the differences between the average score for each school and that for the country; *within-school variance*: average of differences between the individual score and the average score of the student's school. The sum of the between-and within-school variance components, as an estimate from a sample, does not necessarily add up to the total (Column 1).

[3] "Between-school variance explained," or what could be predicted about a school's average performance if the socioeconomic background of its intake were known; "within-school variance explained," or what could be predicted of a student's performance in a school if his/her socioeconomic background were known (measured by the PISA index of economic, social, and cultural status).

[4] This index expresses the relative size of the two variances by an intra-class correlation or a coefficient of the *variance between schools* divided by the sum of the *between-and within-school variance* (intra-class correlation, *rho*).

Table 2.6 Between-school and within-school variance in student performance on the Reading scale in PISA: Comparison between 2000 and 2006 for Argentina, Chile, and OECD countries.

Countries	Total variance in SP expressed as a percentage of the average variance in student performance across OECD countries		Total variance in student performance between schools		Total variance in student performance within schools		Variance explained by the PISA index of economic, social and cultural status of students and schools			
							Between-school variance explained		Within-school variance explained	
	Years		Years		Years		Years		Years	
	2000	2006	2000	2006	2000	2006	2000	2006	2000	2006
Argentina	129.4	158.1	67.9	71.0	61.3	84.9	43.9	35.0	0.6	0.8
Chile	91.1	109.9	56.2	62.1	44.6	63.2	34.7	40.8	0.9	0.4
OECD	100.0	100.0	34.3	38.4	67.4	63.4	21.6	21.5	4.2	2.7
Sweden	94.7	96.4	8.5	17.0	86.5	81.0	5.8	7.9	6.8	4.0
Germany	113.3	126.1	61.7	100.5	53.9	48.0	49.5	63.9	2.2	0.5

Source: OECD 2006, *Science Competencies for Tomorrow's World*, Vol.2, Data, Tables 4.1.d and 4.1.f. Table 2.6.

socioeconomic and cultural background factors and their performance—or what could be predicted about a school's average performance if the socioeconomic background of its enrollment were known.
In Chile, to take the extreme case among the Latin American countries,
that prediction would account for 40.8 percent of the cases, and in Mexico
and Colombia, it would account for around 16 percent of the cases. These
figures are well above those for Sweden and the U.K., and well below the
extreme for the German case.

How these relationships are evolving over time is a critical question for
policy assessment. Unfortunately, there are data only for Argentina and
Chile, as the only Latin American countries that participated in PISA 2000
and 2006. Table 2.6 examines total and between-school variance for these
years.

As the table shows, both the total variance in student performance and
the between-school variance have increased. It is an open question whether
this increase (column 1) is associated with changes in the curricula and its
implementation (its greater complexity probably contributing to the disper-
sion in results) or to changes in the social composition of the student body,
owing to the expansion of enrollment and increased inclusion of students
from poor groups (or a combination of both). The second column (2) shows
the increase in social segmentation between schools: relatively minor in
Argentina (67.9 to 71.0%), but significant in Chile (56.2 to 62.1%). In terms
of "variance explained" (column 4), the two countries differ in the direction
of the relationship: a drop in Argentina (43.9 to 35.0%) and an increase in
Chile (34.7 to 40.8%). It is interesting to note that OECD country averages
show an increase in the between-schools variance, with increments in the
cases of both Sweden and Germany. While there is no change in the strength
of association between socioeconomic background factors and student and
school performance for the OECD as a whole (column 4), Sweden shows
minor and Germany major changes in the indicator of social segmentation
of performance during this period.

The 2000–2006 comparisons for Argentina and Chile point in the opposite direction from equity, with larger differences in performance and
increased between-schools variances. That this is also the case for the two
European countries—with highly contrasting institutional arrangements—
questions the nature of the isomorphic processes at stake.

AGENDAS, PRIORITIES, AND THE PLACE OF EQUITY

In terms of the most basic equity criterion—access to education—the last
decade and a half in Latin America has been one of undoubted progress.

Half of the adult population has experienced upward educational mobility with respect to their parents. There has been a reduction in the gap between the poorest and the rest of the population in terms of years of education completed. Furthermore, in intergenerational terms, the inequality index of years of education of the present generation compared to that of their parents shows an important drop.

However, if inequality is considered in terms of learning outcomes, and not only attainment, the evidence shows schooling systems that, if compared with other regions, are socially segmented at much greater levels. Their learning results are ordered (as revealed by the PISA tests results) in forms strongly associated with socioeconomic inequalities. The great effect of these socioeconomic and ethnic inequalities on the education intake are not being attenuated by Latin American schools, as the analysis of the PISA tests of different years has revealed. Equity as fairness should be a crucial political aim, as improvements in social cohesion, economic competitiveness, and governance may be compromised by observed levels of inequality in the educational institutions and processes.

The marked differences in levels of development have produced different agendas. Many countries, as seen in figure 2.1, still confront the immense challenge of expanding their coverage in secondary education to include the whole cohort and to increase completion rates. The equity agenda in this case means breaking down the most damaging barrier of all—that of exclusion. For those countries with high completion rates, on the other hand, the crucial challenge is not inclusion but the socially segmented nature of their educational institutions.

Both agendas should give equity a higher priority; however, the political balance between quality and equity typically favors quality. Quality-oriented policies draw support from society as a whole, connecting to the future and linking national aspirations with a country's international position. In contrast, equity-oriented policies have to grapple with socioeconomic and other inequalities (or the weight of the past), and the divisive features of any social redistribution of goods, and so will typically garner less agreement and less political support. Pro-equity policies require even more political energy to confront the more entrenched obstacles than do quality-oriented agendas, which are widely recognized as more challenging than the expansion of access (Grindle 2004; Navarro 2006).

A central issue regarding equity in education is the relative absence of voices demanding more equity, as the disadvantaged are less likely to see their disadvantage in this domain and its value is often ignored in policymakers' calculations of costs and benefits.[5] As said, equity policies are more difficult to institute than are quality policies because the former challenge long-established societal patterns and structures, for both the elite and the poor. Change is likely also to antagonize participants with a voice. Furthermore, every step toward progress in quality will be differentially appropriated by the different socioeconomic groups.

For more than a century, educational opportunity in Latin America has been identified with the opening of schools and the provision of teaching posts. Access became paramount, subsuming what went on inside the institutions and how outcomes were distributed. In this respect, the potential of national and international assessments of learning results, and the accountability dynamics that they trigger, cannot be exaggerated. These measures might, in time, provide a basis for new and more powerful voices to be heard and new demands be met in education that transcends the pressures for inclusion and that requires state-policy answers in terms of fairness. These answers should certainly expand and sharpen compensatory programs, but perhaps more important, they can act against the social segmentation of public education institutions, which rather than reducing inequalities in society only mirrors them. This presupposes a national commitment to level the playing field of educational opportunity and to support social integration in schools—goals that tend to be subordinated to access and quality agendas.

Notes

1. An institution set up in the 1950s by the United Nations.

2. ECLAC-UNESCO (1992) is probably the most influential document on the thinking of governments responsible for some of the most important educational reforms in the region during the 1990s.

3. According to J. W. Kingdon, "people will see a problem quite differently if it is put in one category rather than another," and he exemplifies with the case of the transport of the handicapped and its classification as a civil rights or a transportation issue and the quite different policy frameworks which follow (Kingdon 2003:112). The case of the schools in need of "priority action" is similar. In the old legal framework, the problem did not exist or, rather, was invisible; in socio-cultural terms, the condition of categories of students or communities with regard to schooling and learning becomes an issue or policy problem.

4. "Low level" and "high level" refer here to the first and fourth income quartiles, respectively, in terms of the income of the parents, measured by the PISA 2000 questionnaires given to the students.

5. According to the World Bank (2006:3), "The point is that (the often implicit) cost-benefit calculus that policymakers use to assess the merits of various policies too often ignores the long-term, hard-to-measure but real benefits of greater equity."

3

Entrance into Prestigious Universities and the Performance of Groups That Have Been Discriminated Against on the Vestibular

Black Students in the University of São Paulo, 2001–2007

Antonio S. A. Guimarães

During the past few years, access to public higher education in Brazil has become the focus of significant political debate, as the aspirations of a large part of the Brazilian intelligentsia, who were raised with left-wing, universalist ideals, have clashed with those of young people from less-privileged social classes, who put their trust in affirmative actions of a particularist nature (Gomes 2001; Queiroz 2004; Feres 2005; Fry et al. 2007).[1] In the twenty-first century, the old struggle of the Brazilian black movement against color prejudice and racial discrimination has been transformed into a fight against racial inequality; and in the demand for university quotas for black people, it has found a legitimacy it never before had within Brazilian public life (Moura 1981; Mitchell 1985; Ferrara 1996; Pinto 1993; Guimarães 2003). Thus, the popularity of the demand for public university quotas, as measured by recent polling, was found to have greater support among respondents with lower levels of education.

The issues are widely known in Brazil, but I summarize them here. Brazilian public universities are free, and they hold a monopoly on educational excellence, as well as on scientific and artistic research in the country. Yet public elementary and high schools are run mainly by the municipalities and the states, and their performance is inadequate. For this reason, it is very difficult for a poor student, who is only able to attend public schools, to be successful in the Vestibular—the public universities' entrance examinations. It is, therefore, much easier—and now quite common—for pupils

Table 3.1 Approval of quotas in education and work, Brazil 2006.

Respondent's educational level	Quotas in education	Quotas in work
Elementary	71%	73%
High School	65%	67%
Higher Education	42%	45%
Total	65%	68%

Source: DataFolha 2006.

from private schools to attend public universities. As a result, public universities are, on the whole, populated by students with higher incomes and who are able to pay for their studies.

In this chapter, I describe the available historical data on the intake of black and public school students by the University of São Paulo (USP), the university with the greatest academic prestige in Brazil. My aim is to bring to light, by using the available data, the factors that have led to the increase in black students' gaining access to USP between 2000 and 2007, despite the absence of more incisive affirmative policies (such as the implementation of quotas). It is worth noting that I did not have access to a complete database, which would have facilitated a more refined statistical analysis.

From 2000 onward, USP started to react positively to the demands of the Brazilian black movement, making small changes to its selection system. These changes involved gathering information about the color of its students, as of 2001; exempting poor students from payment of the exam registration fee; increasing the number of spots by creating in 2005 a new campus; and finally, in 2007, establishing a policy of social inclusion that aims to increase the number of students from public high schools through a system of increasing exam marks by 3 percent.[2]

The analysis I develop in this chapter will serve as a preliminary introduction for future research, which will later analyze the academic and professional trajectories of those USP students who have benefited from the 3 percent bonus policy.

BLACK STUDENTS AND POOR STUDENTS AT USP

In 2000, only 6 percent of those approved in the Vestibular given by the Foundation for the University Entrance Examination (FUVEST), the foundation that produces and manages the vestibular examinations for USP, declared themselves *pretos* (black) or *pardos* (brown), which together fall within the definition of *black* used by Brazilian black movements.[3] In 2007, this number almost doubled, reaching 11.8 percent of those approved. Only 16.3 percent of the students approved in the Vestibular in 2000 had gone to public schools, whereas in 2007, that group constituted 20.5 percent. (Our baseline here is the number of students approved in the first round of the FUVEST Vestibular;[4] see table 3.2).

The University of São Paulo is the choice of almost 99 percent of approved students.[5] Despite its continuing practice of admitting a much smaller proportion of black students compared to white students (the latter were 79.5% in 2000 and 76.3% in 2007), USP seems to be slowly succeeding in its efforts to reduce racial inequality of access. This becomes even clearer when we consider the approval rates—that is, the ratio comparing those registered for the exam to those approved. This ratio provides a measure of black people's success, as shown in table 3.3.

Table 3.2 Annual intake by color and type of high school, USP 2000 to 2007.

Year	Blacks	Public Schools*	Whites
2000	6.0%	16.3%	79.5%
2001	7.0%	16.9%	78.4%
2002	7.7%	17.2%	79.6%
2003	8.5%	19.3%	80.0%
2004	9.7%	18.2%	78.9%
2005	11.5%	20.1%	76.7%
2006	11.1%	18.4%	76.5%
2007	11.8%	20.5%	76.8%

Source: FUVEST (Blacks = *pretos* +*pardos*)

(*) Municipal and state public schools.

Table 3.3 Approval rates by color and type of high school, USP 2000 to 2007.

Year	Total	Public Schools*	Blacks	Whites
2000	6.3%	3.4%	3.7%	5.0%
2001	6.6%	3.5%	3.8%	5.3%
2002	6.5%	3.4%	3.8%	5.3%
2003	6.1%	3.4%	3.6%	5.0%
2004	6.4%	3.4%	3.6%	5.1%
2005	7.2%	3.7%	3.9%	5.6%
2006	6.7%	3.0%	3.2%	5.2%
2007	8.1%	4.8%	4.8%	6.3%

Source: FUVEST

(*) Municipal and state public schools.

Which efforts have been made and which other factors are also at work to decrease the gap between white and black students entering USP? Among USP's efforts we can list three important measures: (1) the increase in the number of exam registration-fee exemptions for the Vestibular (see table 3.5); (2) the creation of ten new courses in 2005 on a new campus located in a poorer area of the city of São Paulo; and (3) the adoption in 2007 of a marking system that guarantees 3 extra points on the entry exams taken by students from public schools.

Among the external factors that have had a positive effect is a decline in the number of people registering for the FUVEST Vestibular in 2007, owing to an increase in non-USP university places in the Metropolitan Region of São Paulo. These offerings increased because of the inauguration of a new public university (UFABC),[6] as well as the opening of new campuses of another university, the Federal University of São Paulo (UNIFESP) in Grarulhos, Diadema, and São José dos Campos. Likewise, expansion of the University for All program (PROUNI), a federal package of government grants to poor students who are admitted to private universities, had an impact. This reduction in the number of applicants to the FUVEST Vestibular, however, also may have been at least partly due to the smaller number of students who finished high school in 2007.[7]

As we examine the factors that have favorably influenced greater access for black young people and students from public schools, we begin by looking at demand.

THE DEMAND FOR USP COURSES

The numbers of people who registered for the FUVEST Vestibular between 1980 and 2007 reveal something essential to our understanding of the current demand for affirmative action measures relating to the intake of black students at USP. In 1980, the majority of those registered to take the USP entrance exams still came from public schools; however, from 1987 onward, the percentage of students coming from private schools systematically grew higher than that of students coming from public schools. There is only one exception: 1995. (We note that there are no data available for the period between 1982 and 1986.) It is not only the case, therefore, that approval rates for those coming from private schools are higher, but that the demand for entrance spots has changed in favor of those from private schools. This suggests that many of the students coming from public schools have stopped trying to go to USP, which until very recently was the only public university in the Metropolitan Region of São Paulo. Increasingly, they either prefer to attend private universities, where it is easier for them to gain acceptance, or they give up their studies entirely.

Table 3.4 Number of registrations in the USP Vestibular, by type of high school.

Year	Public Schools (%)	Private Schools (%)
1980	48.2	39.8
1981	43.6	41.5
1987	38.2	47.3
1988	34.3	50.8
1989	31.6	53.8
1990	30.3	55.4
1991	31.8	51.9
1992	31.6	52.2
1993	28.9	56.4
1994	30.8	54
1995	39.7	39.3
1996	36.5	42.9
1997	29.5	58.7
1998	30.0	59.4
1999	29.6	60.2
2000	30.4	59.3
2001	32.8	57
2002	33.4	56.3
2003	34.8	55.3
2004	34.8	56
2005	38.7	53.1
2006	41.9	50.4
2007	34.9	57.9

Source: FUVEST

What has happened is familiar to Brazilians. With the exception of federal technical schools, the quality of teaching in the public schools has deteriorated over time, as the municipal and state high school network has expanded. The opposite occurred in the public universities, which grow more prestigious over time. The best public universities include federal universities that are located in almost all states of Brazil, plus some state university networks, especially the one in São Paulo.

Higher income families, therefore, prefer to send their children to private elementary and high schools, hoping that, in this way, they will pass the entrance exams for the public universities (whether federal or state), where teaching is not only excellent but also free. This strategy has resulted in the displacement of children from poorer families who, having gone to public schools, then attend private universities and colleges, which are less academically rigorous.[8]

EXAMINATION ENTRANCE-FEE EXEMPTION

The first USP measure that may have helped increase the intake of black people was to exempt students from families with incomes equal to, or below, 1,500 reais from having to pay the examination entrance fee. The entrance examination fee was a major obstacle for poor students who, when faced with the need to register also for other public and private universities' entrance exams,[9] ended up not registering at USP, which was considered to be the best university and, consequently, the one for which they would have less chance of success. This demand, first voiced by the Education and Citizenship for Afro-descendents and Those in Need (EDUCAFRO),[10] and the object of a hotly contested legal dispute, was finally accepted by FUVEST, which exempted 5,000 Vestibular candidates in 2001 and 55,396 in 2006 (with exemptions declining to 31,804 in 2007, owing to a decrease in demand).

Indeed, if we examine the records for registration and approval in the USP Vestibular between 2001 and 2007 (see table 3.5), it is clear that the relative number of registrations by black students (*pretos* and *pardos*) more than doubled between 2001 and 2006, an increase of 120 percent. Registrations abruptly declined in the last year, but still remained 58 percent higher than in 2001. The number of approved black students doubled during this period, rising by 102 percent. It is worth pointing out, however, that in absolute terms, the numbers are small. In 2001, for example, 668 black students (including 96 *pretos*) were approved; meanwhile, in 2007, this number reached 1,352 (including 203 *pretos*).

Between 2001 and 2006, the constant growth in the number of black students and those coming from public schools registered for the Vestibular can be related to the increased number of fee exemptions, although it is

Table 3.5 Annual registration in the Vestibular and the number of exemptions, USP 2001 to 2007.

	Registered	Approved	Black registered	Black approved	Exemptions	Public school approved
2001	144458	9527	17707	668	5000	1609
2002	146307	9531	19067	730	10500	1638
2003	161147	9910	23289	838	15799	1916
2004	157808	10127	27122	978	14680	1840
2005	154514	11094	32981	1274	39374	2226
2006	170474	11402	39000	1262	55396	2096
2007	142656	11502	28004	1352	31804	2360

Source: FUVEST

worth noting that the number of exemptions offered is always greater than the number accepted (shown in table 3.5).

The exemption from fees benefits public school students—that is, the poorest, as well as black students. For example, when making a statistical analysis using the Poisson model (see figure 3.1), there is correlation significant at the 95 percent level between the number of exemptions and the number of black people approved.

However, as figure 3.2 shows, the percentage of public school and black students approved does not change in accordance with the annual exemption percentage. The decline in the number of registrations for the entrance examination in 2007 in relation to 2006 (27,818) was very close to the number of exemptions given (23,592), and this produced a decline in the percentage of blacks and public school students registered. This was probably due to the fact that these students opted to take the entrance examinations of other public universities that had opened up during the year in the Metropolitan Region, while also being influenced by the number of places

$$f(Y) = \frac{\mu^Y e^{-\mu}}{Y!}$$

onde

$$\mu = \ln(X'\beta)$$

Figure 3.1. Poisson model for number of black students registered and proportion of exemptions.

Note: X is the explanatory variable, which in this case is the proportion of exemptions for those registered in the FUVEST Vestibular. Y is the response variable—that is, the number of black students registered in the FUVEST Vestibular.

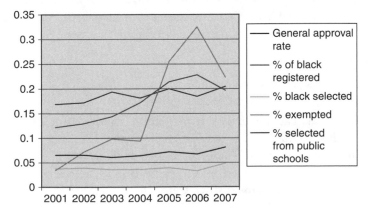

Figure 3.2. Annual Vestibular registration and number of exemptions, USP, 2001–2007.

Source: Foundation for the University Entrance Examination, University of São Paulo.

Table 3.6 Approval rates and percentages of registrations and exemptions.

Years	Total approval rate	% of blacks registered	Black approval rate	Exemptions registrations	%approved public school
2001	0.066	0,123	0.038	0.035	0.169
2002	0.065	0.130	0.038	0.072	0.172
2003	0.061	0.145	0.036	0.098	0.193
2004	0.064	0.172	0.036	0.093	0.182
2005	0.072	0.213	0.039	0.255	0.201
2006	0.067	0.229	0.032	0.325	0.184
2007	0.081	0.196	0.048	0.223	0.205

Source: FUVEST

being offered by PROUNI at private institutions. (We will return to this point further on.) In other words, if we look at the demand, the numbers of registrations and numbers of exemptions are very closely correlated.

However, in the case of Vestibular approval, things are slightly different. Approval rates for public school students are a growing, but irregular, trend, whereas approval rates for black students closely follow the general rate of approvals. This suggests that the growing numbers of black students enrolling at USP are more likely to be due to the growth of a higher income black population—one with greater access to good public or private schools—than to the new policies being implemented at USP.

It is worth noting, however, that the 30.7 percent increase in the number of black students approved in 2005, compared with 2004, is surprising. Certainly, the creation of ten new courses at USP's new campus in the Eastern Zone of São Paulo had a major impact. I now analyze the data from 2005—the year in which USP's Escola de Artes, Ciências e Humanidades, or EACH (School of Arts, Sciences and Humanities), was created.

SPACIAL DE-CONCENTRATION

In the city of São Paulo both wealth and educational opportunities are concentrated in a few districts, as defined by the census. This is a general feature of big cities, but in São Paulo, more than in other Brazilian cities, this phenomenon is distinguished by very little contact between poorer and richer areas within the same district. Generally speaking, the white population of the city of São Paulo is concentrated in the city's Centre and in the Western District, where the campus of the University of São Paulo is located, as well as, in much smaller numbers, in certain areas of the Eastern,

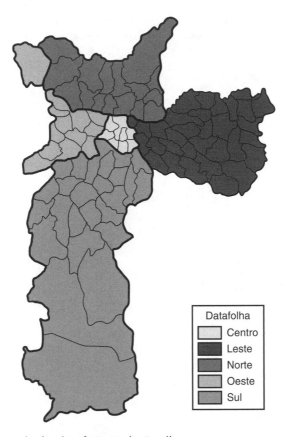

Figure 3.3. Zones in the city of São Paulo, Brazil.

Northern, and Southern Districts; meanwhile, the black population is concentrated in the South, East, and, partly, in the North of the city.

When some years ago the University of São Paulo decided to build an additional university campus and offer new higher education courses in the city's Eastern Zone (UPS-East), this initiative became central to its policy of greater social inclusion and democratization of access to public higher education. In 2005, rather than establishing on its West Campus (UPS-West) either quotas or goals for the inclusion of less-privileged sectors of the population (blacks, ethnic minorities, those who finished high school at a public institution, or members of low-income families), USP considered the possibility of obtaining similar results, over the long run, by geographically diversifying its learning opportunities and reaching the poorer areas. According to the Municipality of São Paulo data, there are 3.3 million people living in the Eastern Zone (33% of the city's total population and 17.76% of the population of the São Paulo Metropolitan Region).[11] They are under the administration of eleven

Table 3.7 Entrance examination approval rates by campus and color, USP 2005.

		COLOR GROUPS			
		WHITES	BLACKS	OTHERS*	TOTAL
USP	approved	7313 77,2%	1179 12,4%	983 10,4%	9475
RATES		(7.40%)	(3.67%)	(10.27%)	(6.74%)
	registered	98798	32166	9572	140536
USP-East	approved	694 69.1%	213 21.2%	98 9.8%	1005
RATES		(19.67%)	(10.27%)	(25.59%)	(16.79%)
	registered	3529	2075	383	5987
TOTAL	approved	8007 76.4%	1392 13.3%	1081 10.3%	10480
RATES		7.82%	4.07%	10.86%	7.15%
	registered	102327	34241	9955	146523

Source: FUVEST

* Ethnic Asians and native Indians.

submunicipalities. The average Human Development Index (HDI) for the Eastern zone is 0.478, compared with 0.52 for the entire the city of São Paulo and 0.850 for the state of São Paulo.[12]

In 2005, EACH offered 1,020 places for ten degree programs, distributed into three periods (morning, afternoon, and evenings), with classes of up to sixty pupils. The subjects were gerontology, environmental management, public policy management, leisure and tourism, teaching degree in natural sciences, marketing, obstetrics, IT, textiles, and fashion technology.

Has the aim of the University—to democratize opportunities in public higher education in São Paulo—been reached? Can a policy that focuses on poorer geographical areas be a substitute for a quota policy similar to the ones being implemented by some federal universities, which is what some sectors of the public would like to believe?

From data published by FUVEST concerning first-round approvals to the campuses of USP-West and USP-East (with breakdowns according to color, type of school, and level of income), the following can be shown:

- It is indeed the case that offering university places in poorer areas of São Paulo can achieve the objective of incorporating more students from among blacks, public school graduates, and poorer families. For example, the relative number of blacks approved at USP-East is 8.8 points higher than at USP-West—21.2 percent compared to 12.4 percent, respectively.
- The relative number of those approved from public high schools was 19.1 points higher at USP-East than at USP-West—46.7 percent compared to 27.6 percent, respectively.
- The relative number of students coming from poorer families was 11.8 points higher at USP-East than at USP-West—39.4 percent compared to 22.1 percent, respectively.

On its metropolitan campuses, USP as a whole has become blacker (13.3% of those approved in 2005 were black, compared to 12.4%, without including USP-East). USP has taken on a higher number of young people who were educated at public schools (29.5% in 2005) and coming from lower income families (23.7%, in the same year).

However, one must be careful when generalizing this model to other universities. First, USP's success may have been achieved not only because of its geographic expansion of university places but also because of two other factors associated specific to São Paulo. That is, USP-East offered courses with low social prestige (new courses), and the demand for them was, therefore, lower; also, the lack of good public transportation in the city of São Paulo restricts circulation between zones, limiting the competition for places to residents of areas close to its campuses.

Table 3.8 Entrance examination approval rates by campus and school of origin, USP 2005.

| | | TYPE OF HIGH SCHOOL | | | |
		Private	Public	Other	Total
USP	approved	6772 71.2%	2631 27.6%	113 1.2%	9516
RATES		(9.17%)	(4.11%)	(3.67%)	(6.75%)
	registered	73833	64018	3082	140933
USP-East	approved	517 51.1%	472 46.7%	22 2.2%	1011
RATES		(28.63%)	(11.81%)	(10.73%)	(16.83%)
	registered	1806	3996	205	6007
TOTAL	approved	7289 69.2%	3103 29.5%	135 1.3%	10527
RATES		(9.64%)	(4.56%)	(4.11%)	(7.16%)
	registered	75639	68014	3287	146940

Source: FUVEST

Table 3.9 Vestibular approval rates by campus and income, USP 2005.

		FAMILY INCOME BRACKET				
		Upto 1500	1500 to 7000	over 7000		total
USP	approved	2079	5721	1625		9425
RATES		(3.53%)	(8.64%)	(11.10%)		(6.74%)
	registered	58930	66221	14636		139787
		22.1%	60.7%		17.2%	
USP-East	approved	396	524	85		1005
RATES		(10.4%)	(26.9%)	(37.1%)		(16.8%)
	registered	3798	1948	229		5975
		39.4%	52.1%		8.5%	
TOTAL	approved	2475	6245	1710		10430
RATES		(3.9%)	(9.2%)	(11.5%)		(7.2%)
	registered	62728	68169	14865		145762
		23.7%	59.9%		16.4%	

Source: FUVEST

Table 3.10 Marginal increments in approval owing to income, schooling, and color, USP 2005.

	Up to 1500	1500 to 7000	Over 7000
Marginal return* of **Family income**	2,95544	3,113624	**3,343124**
	Private	**Public**	**Others**
Marginal return* of **Schooling**	**3.121091**	2.874073	2.927002
	Whites	**Blacks**	**Others**
Marginal return* of **Color**	2.656809	**2.800559**	2.491589

*Marginal Return = increase in the approval percentage in each category (USP-East/USP-West)

Second, from the data above, it can be seen that USP-East was far less difficult to enter (16.83 candidates were approved per 100 people registered, whereas at USP-West, this number was 6.75), so the marginal return on education and its economic capital (accumulated by having gone to a private school and being a member of a richer family) was greater than expected. I understand *marginal return* to mean an extra unit of capital, be it educational, economic, or social, that results in being approved in the entrance examinations. A measure that approximates this concept is that of the relative increase in the approval ratio between the two campuses of those students holding such capital. Thus, the data suggest that those who benefited most from this policy of expanded opportunities in the poorer areas were the students, regardless of their color, who attended private high schools and came from families with higher incomes.

This means that even non-racialized policies that focus on territory, not on racial or ethnic groups, and that adhere to models widely experienced in other countries, continue to be sensitive to the unequal distribution of capital in these areas—and it is possible that they may not be racially neutral. However, one cannot deny that the implementation of EACH (USP-East) favored the intake of more black students into USP. Comparing the years 2003–2004, which was before the implementation of the new campus, to the years 2005–2006, when EACH was opened without a bonus policy, we find that the increase from 10.28 to 12.74 percent, respectively, in the proportion of black students approved in the Vestibular did not happen by chance.

Finally, the main virtue of this model of social inclusion must be emphasized: It works by offering new places, contracting with new lecturers, and gaining new urban spaces for public higher education. By providing new investment in higher education, the government of the state of São Paulo

Table 3.11 Comparing the proportion of black incoming students in 2003/04 (without EACH) with 2005/06 (with EACH).

Year	Proportion
2003/04	0.1028
2005/06	0.1274
Estimated difference	0.0246
P-value	0
There was a significant difference.	

Source: NAEG

has included new social groups while avoiding the zero-sum game of dividing the already existing places among social groups or simply by overburdening the teaching staff.

But the fact that there has been a historical upward trend taking place since 2001, and also that only 28 percent of those entering USP-East in 2005 lived in the Eastern Zone (according to the data published by the Graduate Courses Administration Department) is an indication that it is not only geographic expansion that has helped increase the number of black students. It is worth asking whether the greater intake of black students into USP is not perhaps related more to the creation of courses with less prestige, and therefore less popularity with nonblack students? I now analyze this last point.

THE OFFER OF PLACES AND THE SOCIAL PRESTIGE OF COURSES

I found that the most practical method of classifying courses offered by USP according to social prestige was to group them by knowledge area; I relied upon a system using three classes demarcated by the value of the average approval marks, approximately half the standard deviation. In this way, I was able to retain the specificities of competition in each area, distinguishing nine different course types.

Table 3.12 shows the approval rates (the ratio between black and nonblack students for those approved and registered) for each of the nine types of courses offered in 2005. It is noticeable that nonblack students have approval rates that are, in general, double those of black students, except within low-prestige courses in the exact sciences, where the pattern of nonblack approval (17%) is only slightly higher than black approval. In other words, it is not true that in USP the greatest intake of black students has been in lower prestige humanity courses, as is sometimes implied. On the contrary, the approval of black students is best in the low-prestige exact

Table 3.12 Vestibular approval rates by color according to course type, USP 2005.

Area	Type	Blacks	Non-blacks	Total	Delta
Humanities	High	1.7%	4.3%	3.8%	150%
Biological Sciences	High	1.9%	4.1%	3.7%	120%
Biological Sciences	Medium	2.7%	7.8%	6.6%	189%
Humanities	Medium	3.0%	8.0%	6.8%	169%
Humanities	Low	5.0%	13.7%	10.9%	174%
Exact Sciences	High	5.4%	10.7%	9.7%	99%
Exact Sciences	Medium	7.8%	16.6%	13.5%	114%
Biological Sciences	Low	13.5%	21.9%	19.8%	63%
Exact Sciences	Low	40.9%	48.0%	44.9%	17%
Total		3.9%	8.0%	7.1%	107%

Source: FUVEST

sciences courses, while next best is the medium-prestige courses of the biological sciences. Even in the high-prestige exact-science courses, black students have a better approval rate than in low-prestige humanity courses.

Are these numbers specific to USP, owing to the fact that it has the most competitive Vestibular in the country? That may be so. It is the case that, despite the black approval rate's being usually half that of nonblacks, this group's performance in various types of courses is similar. This can be seen in table 3.12, which classifies the types of courses in decreasing order of difficulty for approval of black students. This order roughly follows that of nonblack students, without many discrepancies.

Indeed, it is very difficult to get into USP. The overall approval rate for 2005 was only 7.1 percent. Among the preparation factors that lead to high approval in the Vestibular, we find that black and nonblack students differ particularly in several respects. First, proportionally fewer black than nonblack students have attended private elementary and high schools and done preparatory exams. Second, relatively fewer black students attend daytime classes (see table 3.13); Third, the less effective preparation of black students reflects a less privileged social class, thus black and nonblack students differ in variables that reflect social class and origin, such as the father's or mother's level of education, family income, or the number of cars per family. These last markers, however, point to the fact that students getting into USP come from families with higher incomes compared to the families of students who go to other universities, such as the Federal University of Bahia (UFBA) and the University of Brasilia (UnB).[13] Even the majority of black students come from families that own at least one car.

In short, the entrance examination, and the performance of black and nonblack students in the competition for places in degree programs, shows

Table 3.13 Main factors affecting the success of black students in the Vestibular 2005.

Approval factors	Blacks	Non-blacks
Attending private elementary school	36.2	60.7
Doing preparatory exams	8.3	18.3
Attending private high school	46.3	71.9
Studying during the day	67.2	78.6
Father has a university education	28.3	47.2
Mother has a university education	27.7	45.8
Family income of 5 or more minimum salaries	16.5	32.7
Family has at least one car	68.7	87.4

Source: FUVEST

that, contrary to what happens at other public universities in Brazil, at USP the black students have not been systematically admitted into courses of lower prestige or into those less popular degree programs. The approval *pattern* for black and nonblack students is exactly the same, except that the former invariably have lower *rates* of approval than the latter. It is true that in general black students are found more often in lower prestige courses than are nonblacks (37% compared to 27%, respectively); however, black students take courses with low or high prestige in exactly the same proportion as do nonblacks, as shown in table 3.14.

I now examine why there has been a sharp fall in the number of registrations for the most recent Vestibular at USP (data for 2007). Apparently, the effect of this decline was positive: it decreased the candidate—places ratio while increasing the approval rates for black students and those coming from public schools.

Table 3.14 Distribution of students approved by color and courses, 2005.

Course Prestige	Blacks	Non-blacks	Blacks	Non-blacks
Low	443	2260	37%	27%
Medium	307	2180	26%	26%
High	433	4009	37%	47%
	1183	8449	100%	100%

Source: FUVEST

THE INCREASE IN PUBLIC OR SUBSIDIZED UNIVERSITY PLACES
IN THE CITY OF SÃO PAULO

Until 2005, USP, the most prestigious university in the country, was the only free and public university in the Metropolitan Region of São Paulo, providing around 10,000 places a year. Heavy competition limited the chances of poor and black students entering the university. Apart from USP, there was only the Escola Paulista de Medicina, now the Universidade Federal de São Paulo (UNIFESP), which in 2005 provided 273 places in five medical sciences degree programs. In 2006, however, UNIFESP opened a new campus in the Baixada Santista, providing a further five new courses and an extra 171 places; finally in 2007, three new campuses were opened, in Diadema, Guarulhos, and São Jose dos Campos, making available a further nine new degree programs and 545 places. Apart from these places, UNIFESP created 111 new places, distributed throughout its courses, reserved for black students only. The number of students registered for the UNIFESP Vestibular went in 2007 from 13,455 in 2005 to 22,799 for the general Vestibular and 2,491 for the "quotas" Vestibular. In total, demand for UNIFESP admission increased 115 percent in two years.[14]

Pari passu, in July 2006, the Universidade Federal do ABC (Federal University of ABC), based in São Bernardo, held its first entrance examinations. The UFABC began to offer 1,500 places annually; 750 of these were reserved for students coming from public schools.[15]

Without a doubt, the consolidation of the PROUNI—the University for All program offered by the Brazilian Ministry for Education, which offers poorer students grants for the payment of fees if they attend private universities—had the greatest impact on the increase in the numbers of places in São Paulo. To get an idea of the true impact of the PROUNI, consider that in 2006, the program assisted 8,724 students in the state of São Paulo, 6,581 on full grants (that is, full reimbursement of university fees); in 2007, PROUNI was granted to 34,199 students, with 20,326 on full grant. Thus, PROUNI grants increased 292 percent in São Paulo, nearly tripling in a single year. Enrollment at the PROUNI in São Paulo increased during the same period from 51,313 to 137,829—that is, by168 percent.[16]

This indicates that a decrease of 27,818 in the FUVEST Vestibular registration from 2006 to 2007, with a similar fall in the demand for exemptions, equates to a huge displacement from USP to other universities, public and private. In sum, this displacement reflects the additional offers of PROUNI's 25,475 study grants, 1,500 new public places offered by UFABC, and 666 new places created by UNIFESP. Out of a total of 27,641 new places, 25,697 (93%) were directed toward students who were poor, black, or graduates of public schools.

PRELIMINARY ASSESSMENT OF THE BONUS SYSTEM

As just shown, there was less demand from poor students and those coming from the public sector, at the same time as USP introduced its bonus a 3 percent on Vestibular marks, a program called INCLUSP. Did black students benefit from the bonus during the 2007 Vestibular? It is difficult to answer this question without having a complete database for the 2007 Vestibular. We can, however, statistically test whether the percentage distribution of those approved during the first round differs significantly from the 2006 distribution in terms of school origin, color, and student income. That is, we can ask the question preliminarily: Did the introduction of the 3 percent bonus added to the marks of students coming from public schools really benefit these pupils and alter the income and color distribution of the approved students, thus changing the intake composition in such a way that this variation was not by chance?

The Pró-Reitoria de Graduação (Graduation Affairs Administration) at USP reported the distribution in 2006 and 2007 by type of high school, as shown in table 3.15. The two- proportions test has a confidence interval of 95 percent, which indicates that the proportion of public school students has significantly increased after the use of INCLUSP.

With regard to color, however, the variation in proportion of black students approved in the last two years is not statistically significant, according to table 3.16. Finally, after testing for differences in the proportion of students with annual incomes lower than 3,000 reais in the years 2006 and

Table 3.15 Students called to register (1st round) by year and type of high school, USP.

Year	High School		Total
	Public		
2006	2343	24,22%	9675
2007	2645	26,30%	10058

Test and CI for Two Proportions: % of students from public high schools
Sample X N Sample p
2006   2343   9675   0,242171
2007   2645   10058   0,262975

Difference = p (2006) – p (2007)
Estimate for difference: –0,0208042
95% CI for difference: (–0,0329242; –0,00868424)
Test for difference = 0 (vs not = 0): Z = –3,36 P-Value = 0,001

Source: NAEG and FUVEST

Table 3.16 Black students called in the 1st round.

Year	Blacks		Total number of students called
2006	1186	12.26%	9675
2007	1278	12.71%	10058

Test and CI for Two Proportions: % of black students approved

Sample X N Sample p

2006   1186   9675   0,122584

2007   1278   10058   0,127063

Difference = p (2006) – p (2007)

Estimate for difference: –0,00447906

95% CI for difference: (–0,0137023; 0,00474421)

Test for difference = 0 (vs not = 0): Z = –0.95 P-Value = 0.341

Conclusion: There is no significant difference before or after the application of the 3% bonus.

Source: NAEG

Table 3.17 1st-round students with income lower than 3000 reais per month.

Year	Students with income lower than 3000 reais		Total number of students called
2006	4449	45.98%	9675
2007	4434	44.08%	10058

Test and CI for Two Proportions – % of students with an income lower than 3,000 reais

Sample X N Sample p

2006   4449   9675   0,459845

2007   4434   10058   0,440843

Difference = p (2006) – p (2007)

Estimate for difference: 0,0190019

95% CI for difference: (0,00511775; 0,0328860)

Test for difference = 0 (vs not = 0): Z = 2.68 P-Value = 0.007

Conclusion: The proportion of students with incomes lower than R$3,000 has significantly decreased after the application of the 3% bonus.

Source: NAEG and FUVEST

2007, they found that the proportion of low-income students approved at USP had significantly decreased.

Regardless, when the distribution of those approved was tested year by year, from 2001 to 2007, the constant increase in the intake of black students was statistically significant. That is, the introduction of the 3 percent bonus in 2007 has not significantly altered the proportion of black students approved in the USP Vestibular, but other factors are interacting since at least 2001 to produce a consistent increase in this population. The general trend, therefore, seems to be that black students coming to USP will have a profile similar to white students with regard to income, type of school they attended, preparation for the Vestibular, and so forth.

It is worth noting, however, that to explain the difference in the performance of students in the Vestibular, we find that color is more important than the type of high school attended.. In general, there is a greater difference between black and white students than between public and private school students. All this points to the fact that there is a racial factor—that is, some internalized effect of racism—that impairs the performance of young blacks beyond and above the simple lack of resources to study in private schools. As a result, the few black students who manage to get approved have a much closer performance profile to those in the white group.

Let us take, for example, the average approval mark for black students in the most prestigious courses in the biological sciences. In 2006, the difference between students from public and private schools was 0.19 points; the difference between white and black students in this regard was 0.08. This

Table 3.18 Differences in approval marks in the 2006 Vestibular between those going to private and public schools and between whites and blacks, according to the prestige of the courses.

Course Groups	Difference Private-Public	Difference Whites-Blacks
Biological sciences high	0.19	0.08
Biological Sciences medium	0.10	0.00
Biological Sciences low	0.33	0.22
Exact sciences high	0.11	0.06
Exact sciences medium	0.10	0.08
Exact sciences low	0.36	0.29
Humanities high	0.04	−0.07
Humanities medium	0.16	0.06
Humanities low	0.28	0.10

Source: NAEG

pattern repeats itself consistently within all the nine course groups (see table 3.18).

In short, all the measures taken by USP in the last few years to guarantee the inclusion of poorer students or those coming from public schools have given reasonably satisfactory results and have indirectly also benefited the intake of black students. However, these policies have not reached those who need them most: the students who are now looking toward other public universities and even more so to private institutions, with the help of the PROUNI grants. The socioeconomic profile and professional choices of black students approved at USP are very close to those of white students. Yet their lower performance in the Vestibular, in terms of their marks, indicates that socio-racial factors (effects produced by the idea of biological race to which their social interaction continues to be subjected) are not fully compensated for by their occasionally higher income or by the better schools that they might have attended.

Notes

This chapter was originally a report titled "OBSERVA—Assessing Affirmative Actions in Brazilian Higher Education," a project sponsored by the Ford Foundation and adapted to be presented to the Studies of Global Discrimination Conference at Princeton, May 18–20, 2007. I would like to express my gratitude to USP Pró-Reitoria de Graduação for providing data and assisting in the elaboration of some tables. The Vestibular is the universal examination used for university admissions in Brazil.

1. The bibliography concerning the debate about affirmative action in Brazil is already extensive; the easiest way to access this information is through a specialized Internet site, such as OBSERVA, www.ifcs.ufrj.br/~observa/ or GEMAA http://gemaa.iuperj.br/brasil/docs.html.

2. This policy is called INCLUSP, or the USP Inclusion Programme. For details, see the Pró-Reitoria de Graduação da USP site, www.naeg.prg.usp.br/siteprg/inclusp/inclusp_06–06.doc.

3. All the data concerning USP entrance exams cited in this chapter have been provided by the Foundation for the University Entrance Examination (FUVEST). The data about color have been taken from question 16 of the application form: "From the alternatives below, what color are you?" The alternatives offered were: white, preto (black), pardo (brown), amarelo (ethnic Asian), and indigenous. This question had a response rate of between 97.9 and 99 percent. In this chapter I use black as a combination of the preto and pardo categories.

4. Generally, FUVEST offers four rounds to judge candidacy for available places at USP, as some selected students prefer to enroll in more prestigious courses at other universities, where they have also taken entrance exams. The first round fills approximately 98 percent of available places at USP.

5. FUVEST also selects candidates for courses in the Military Police Academy and for medicine at Santa Casa da Misericórdia.

6. The ABC Federal University (UFABC) is located in São Bernardo, a city within the São Paulo Metropolitan Area. São Paulo Federal University (UNIFEST) is the old Escola Paulista de Medicina.

7. Although there are no annual data on the number of graduates from high school, we know from the INEP school census that the total number of students enrolled in high schools in the State of São Paulo fell by 8 percent between 2000 and 2005, from 2,079,141 to 1,913,848.

8. There are still a few private universities in Brazil, with excellent academic standards.

9. These other universities include UNESP, which has many campuses throughout the State of São Paulo, and UNICAMP, the other two universities under the State of São Paulo's administration.

10. The Education and Citizenship for Afro-descendents and Those in Need (EDUCAFRO) is a network of entrance-examination preparatory courses organized by the Franciscan Solidarity Service (SEFRAS), a nonprofit organization managed by Franciscan monks working in the metropolitan regions of Rio de Janeiro and São Paulo. EDUCAFRO's most important goal is ensuring the access of black people specifically, and more generally of poor people, to higher education, public or private.

11. See *portal.prefeitura.sp.gov.br/guia/urbanismo/zonaleste/0020.*

12. The Human Development Index (HDI) measures quality of life in terms of longevity, education, and income. Values are measured from 0 to 1.

13. For UFBA, see http://www.ifcs.ufrj.br/~observa/relatorios/Desempenho CotistasUFBA.pdf; for UnB see http://www.ifcs.ufrj.br/~observa/relatorios/Cursoe concurso_UnB.pdf.

14. Data available at www.unifesp.br/.

15. See data at http://www.ufabc.edu.br/index.php?p=menu/40Vestibular/50Es tatisticas.php.

16. All of the data are available at http://prouni-inscricao.mec.gov.br/prouni/.

4

Education and Racial Inequality in Post-Apartheid South Africa

Malcolm Keswell

One of the most far-reaching effects of apartheid was the role it played in generating extreme economic inequality between race groups in South Africa. Not only does South Africa have one of the highest levels of income inequality in the world, but also this inequality is strongly racial in nature. As figure 4.1 shows, the gap between white and black incomes just prior to the first democratic effections was substantial, with average real earnings of whites amounting to more than five times that of blacks. Equally influential was the social engineering via race and language that occurred in the sphere of public education, with the introduction of the Bantu Education Act of 1954, which sought to prescribe differential access to education based on race.

The decade since the end of apartheid, however, has brought about tremendous change in social and political life. South Africa is now heralded as a leading example of a modern liberal society, and many regard its constitutional guarantees as among the most ambitious statements of individual liberties enshrined in law. Yet these social and political freedoms have not led to tangible change in the economic realm. As figure 4.2 shows, compared to 1993, when about 36 percent of the workforce earned less than US $2 per day, the number of workers falling into this category now stands at 52 percent. Until recently, little could be said about such a process of change in South Africa, owing to the lack of both nationally representative data and a coherent framework within which to assess such a change. However, the recent accessibility of large-scale household datasets, capturing information on population groups previously excluded from national statistics, has led to a rapid expansion in studies devoted to understanding the changing structure of labor-market opportunities in the post-apartheid period. Examples are Kingdon and Knight (2003) on the changing structure of unemployment, Moll (1996) on the collapse of the returns to education for blacks, and most recently Hertz (2003) on measurement error in the returns to black education.

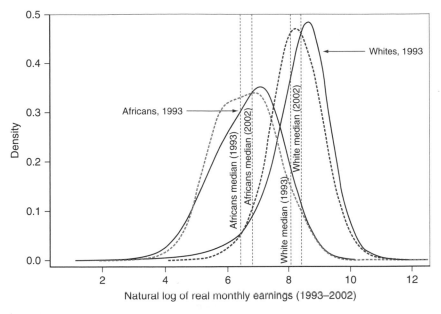

Figure 4.1. Racial distribution of earnings for full-time and casual workers, 1993 & 2000.

Note: Dotted lines represent 2002 income distribution. The income variable is measured in natural logs of monthly earnings in South African rand. All data are deflated by the average CPI for the months over which the survey work was conducted in the relevant years, with 2000 as the base year.

Source: Data for 1993 are from the World Bank's living standards measurement survey (also known as the PSLSD). Data for 2002 are from the Labour Force Survey (LFS).

This chapter adds to this new literature by examining changes in the causal structure of racial inequality in South Africa. An analytical framework is derived with testable hypotheses concerning equal opportunity. Using this framework and recent nationally representative panel data, it is demonstrated that while opportunities have been substantially equalized, as evidenced by an overall decline in the white-black wage differential, a new form of racial inequality has emerged, operating not directly on income, as in the heyday of job reservation, influx control, and school segregation, but indirectly, through inequality in the rewards for effort (as witnessed by sharply divergent patterns in the returns to education between the races). Differences in the returns to education now account for about 40 percent of the white-black wage differential, whereas a decade ago this effect was virtually zero. One consequence of this trend is an incentive structure likely to impede or possibly even reverse gains made in the equalization of schooling attainment.

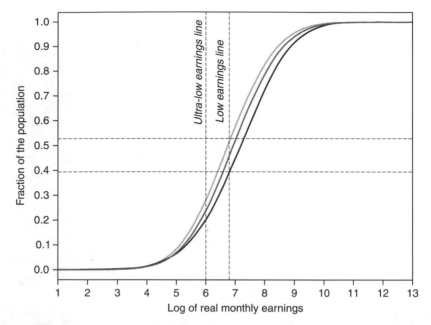

Figure 4.2. Evolving distribution of real earnings, 1993–2002.

Earnings are for full-time and casual workers for the years 1993, 2000, and 2002. The "low earnings line" refers to the wage required if a worker's family were to get to the household poverty line, given the average number of employed and unemployed workers in a household (see Chicello, Liebbrandt, and Fields 2001). The "ultra-low earnings" line is a per capita adult equivalent wage required to take a worker up to the the $1/day poverty line. The rand amounts used in calculating these reference lines are deflated to account for the new CPI benchmark of 2000.

Source: Predicted log monthly earnings.

The chapter is organized as follows. In the first section, I develop a framework for analyzing equality of opportunity in the attainment and reward of human capital. The next section presents the empirical approach, while the third section provides background information on the data used and a discussion of average sample characteristics. The key empirical estimates are presented in the fifth section, along with a discussion of the robustness of the estimates. The final section presents concluding remarks.

DEFINING EQUALITY OF OPPORTUNITY

Two views of equality of opportunity dominate public policy debates. Using the language of Roemer (2000), I refer to these as "nondiscrimination" and "leveling the playing field." The former is simply the meritocratic principle of the absence of one's ascriptive characteristics in determining one's success or failure to acquire some desirable outcome. In this world, such things as "blood, color and sex," to use the colorful words of Lester Frank Ward (1872), must be made irrelevant to success.

"Leveling the playing field" is a broader conception of both "what" to equalize and "how" to equalize, ranging from exceptionally broad-based compensation (such as equalization of resources in the Dworkinian sense, where resources are not limited to physical inputs that go into the production of the benefit, but extend also to include things that are beyond the control of any individual, such as "talent") to milder forms of compensation, such as proposed by Sen (1980).

Both views, however, embody a "before" and "after" notion of an intervention to equalize opportunity, the key idea being that once the intervention has taken place, competition should be allowed to play a role. Thus, more or less egalitarian views of equal opportunity can be reduced to differences about where to place the gate that marks "before" and "after"—a debate that often centers instead on what can reasonably be expected to be outside the scope of one's control and what individuals should be held accountable for.[1] Both the liberal view of equal opportunity (as embodied by the meritocratic principle of nondiscrimination) and modern theories of distributive justice recognize the importance of rendering the ascriptive aspects of one's personal characteristics to be inconsequential through the use of public policy or legislation. Thus, it seems uncontroversial that the absence of race as a determining factor in one's economic success or failure should feature prominently in a definition of a society in which opportunities are equal (see Arrow and Durlauf 2000; Benabou 2000; Bourguignon, Ferreira, and Menendez 2002; Bowles 1973; Roemer 1996; Dworkin 1981; and Sen 1980).

To derive a framework for analyzing equality of opportunity, I begin with the following canonical earnings function usually attributed to Mincer (1974):[2]

$$\ln y = \ln \alpha + \beta s \tag{1}$$

The constant term accounts for expected earnings in the absence of other factors, where the other factors in this model relate only to schooling. The schooling coefficient is the marginal private rate of return on education. Since earnings also are likely to be independently influenced by experience, Equation 1 is conventionally augmented with a measure of "potential experience" to account for the importance of on-the-job learning. But because this proxy is measured with considerable error in cases where grade repetition is high and spells of unemployment are long (both of which are true for South Africa), convention is not followed here.

Instead, age is used as opposed to the more standard proxy for "potential experience." We can then write:

$$\ln y = \ln \alpha + \beta s + \psi_1 Age + \psi_2 Age^2 + u \tag{2}$$

where u is an error term, which is assumed to be independent and identically distributed. Equations 1–2 can be derived from a solution to an optimization problem (i.e., a first-order condition that defines the optimal level of schooling that maximizes utility). However, I treat Equation 2 as a reduced form representation of an income-generating function. This is to account for the fact that, in the presence of credit constraints and other institutional impediments that restrict one's choice set (for example, the set of policies largely grouped under the heading of "Bantu Education"), the structure of choice will be inherently asymmetric across races. The standard microfoundation of the Mincerian Earnings function (see, for example, Willis 1986) will be of little value in this context, as it explicitly excludes the possibility that preferences for schooling might be endogenously determined (through constraints imposed by the institutions governing choices like these).[3]

Taking variances of the basic earnings equation gives a measure of the distribution of earnings as a linear function of the distribution of schooling. This is a proxy for earnings inequality attributable to schooling inequality. In a simple two-variable model, the coefficient of determination—that is, the R^2—measures the fraction of the variation in log earnings explained by education, adjusted for age. Likewise, in a more general model, such as Equation 2, the R^2 measure is a useful test of the fraction of earnings inequality explained by the particular combination of explanatory variables in question. However, when earnings are measured with error, unless the mean value of the error (transitory) component is zero, estimates of the intercept terms will be biased, and the R^2 measure is no longer a reliable estimate of so-called explained inequality. Yet as is well known, if the measurement error is "classical," then the estimated coefficients remain unbiased, even without correction. For this reason, and because of the likely effect of censoring, which I discuss below, I choose to focus not on the R^2 measure as an indication of the degree of inequality but on the coefficients themselves.

In the tradition of wage-differential decompositions by Oaxaca (1973), Blinder (1973), Newmark (1988), and Oaxaca and Ransom (1994), I seek to examine the contribution of personal versus nonpersonal characteristics in generating wage differences between groups. In the analysis to follow, I restrict my attention to the Mincerian representation of the earnings function, and therefore consider only the effects of education in generating racial wage differentials.[4]

Now, let there be two race groups—Whites and Africans—denoted by w and a, respectively.[5] Let $\bar{A}_j$ refer to the unweighted average age for of the two races in the j th year. By making use of the estimated coefficients from Equation 2 estimated separately for each group, the total expected earnings differential between Whites and Africans for the j th year can then be represented as: $\Delta_j = \bar{Y}_{wj} - \bar{Y}_{aj}$

$$= E(y_{wj} | \bar{s}_{wj}, \bar{A}_{wj}, \bar{A}^2_{wj}) - E(y_{aj} | \bar{s}_{aj}, \bar{A}_{aj}, \bar{A}^2_{aj})$$
$$= (\alpha_{wj} - \alpha_{aj}) + (\delta_{wj}\bar{A}_{wj} - \delta_{aj}\bar{A}_{aj}) + (\gamma_{wj}\bar{A}^2_{wj} - \gamma_{aj}\bar{A}^2_{aj}) \tag{3}$$
$$+ (\beta_{wj}\bar{s}_{wj} - \beta_{aj}\bar{s}_{aj})$$

This expression can then be decomposed into a "pure race" effect and a "schooling" effect, whereby the latter can be further decomposed into a "years" effect and a "returns" effect. In the Mincerian framework, the "pure race" effect is sometimes defined as the wage differential that would prevail in the absence of schooling; it could be measured as the difference in the intercepts of the two earnings functions, as in, for example, Lam (2001). However, this approach can potentially be confounding if either group has a nonzero minimum level of attainment. Since a "pure race" effect can, in principle, be calculated for any level of education, one solution is to restrict the benchmark to the lower bound of the common support of the two education distributions. I refer to this benchmark as $\bar{s}_{a1}$. Denoting Δ_j as the "pure race" effect (with the same age conditioning as in Equation 3), we can then write:

$$\Delta_j = \bar{Y}_{wj} - \bar{Y}_{aj}$$
$$= E(y_{wj} | \bar{s}_{a1}, \bar{A}_{wj}, \bar{A}^2_{wj}) - E(y_{aj} | \bar{s}_{a1}, \bar{A}_{aj}, \bar{A}^2_{aj})$$
$$= (\alpha_{wj} - \alpha_{aj}) + (\delta_{wj}\bar{A}_{wj} - \delta_{aj}\bar{A}_{aj}) + (\gamma_{wj}\bar{A}^2_{wj} - \gamma_{aj}\bar{A}^2_{aj}) \tag{4}$$
$$+ (\beta_{wj}\bar{s}_{a1} - \beta_{aj}\bar{s}_{a1})$$

Intuitively, this expression defines the wage differential that would result if Whites had the same average schooling attainment as Africans. If the estimation technique is linear in the parameters, Equation 4 is always contained in Equation 3. Thus the total wage differential given by Equation 3 can be expressed as the sum of the "pure race" effect given by Equation 4 and a residual term, Ω_j, so that:

$$\Omega_j = \Delta_j - \Delta_j$$
$$= \beta_{wj}\bar{s}_{wj} - \beta_{aj}\bar{s}_{aj} - (\beta_{wj}\bar{s}_{a1} - \beta_{aj}\bar{s}_{a1}) = \beta_{wj}(\bar{s}_{wj} - \bar{s}_{a1}) - \beta_{aj}(\bar{s}_{aj} - \bar{s}_{a1}) \tag{5}$$

How much of Ω_j can be attributed to differences in means as opposed to differences in rates of return differ between the two groups? Let the average return to schooling across groups be given as $\bar{\beta}_j = \dfrac{\beta_{wj} + \beta_{aj}}{2}$. Moreover, let the first term of Equation 5 equal ω_j and the second term equal, τ_j, so that:

$$\omega_j = \overline{\beta}_j(\overline{s}_{wj} - \overline{s}_{a1}) + (\beta_{wj} - \overline{\beta}_j)(\overline{s}_{wj} - \overline{s}_{a1})$$

$$= \overline{\beta}_j(\overline{s}_{wj} - \overline{s}_{a1}) + (\beta_{wj} - \beta_{aj})\left(\frac{\overline{s}_{wj} - \overline{s}_{a1}}{2}\right) \tag{6}$$

$$\tau_j = \overline{\beta}_j(\overline{s}_{aj} - \overline{s}_{a1}) + (\beta_{aj} - \overline{\beta}_j)(\overline{s}_{aj} - \overline{s}_{a1})$$

$$= \overline{\beta}_j(\overline{s}_{aj} - \overline{s}_{a1}) + (\beta_{aj} - \beta_{aj})\left(\frac{\overline{s}_{aj} - \overline{s}_{a1}}{2}\right) \tag{7}$$

Substituting Equations 6 and 7 into Equation 5 yields:

$$\Omega_j = \Delta_j - \Delta_j$$

$$= \underbrace{\overline{\beta}_j(\overline{s}_{wj} - \overline{s}_{aj})}_{years} + \underbrace{(\beta_{wj} - \beta_{aj})\left(\frac{\overline{s}_{wj} - 2\overline{s}_{a1} + \overline{s}_{aj}}{2}\right)}_{returns} \tag{8}$$

Given the above, we can now define precisely what is meant by equality of opportunity. As noted earlier, both the "nondiscrimination" and the "leveling the playing field" views of equal opportunity take as a given that a meritocratic society is one in which race should not be allowed to play a role. Both of these views also accept that in a meritocratic society, effort should be rewarded. Taking these two requirements as guiding principles, the following set of conditions can be specified:

Hypothesis 1. Whites and Africans should have the same expected incomes, contingent on a given level of schooling.

Hypothesis 2. Investment in education should reap a positive rate of return.

Hypothesis 3. There should be no income differential generated by race (that is, there should be no "pure race" effect).

Hypothesis 4. There should be no income differential generated by differences in mean schooling (that is, there should be no "years" effect).

Hypothesis 5. There should be no income differential generated by differences in rates of return (that is, there should be no "returns" effect).

In the above setup, the reffection of conditions 3–5 are necessary and sufficient (in the context of the Mincerian framework) for the reffection of Hypothesis 1. Thus, taken together the "race," "years," and "returns" effects can be thought of as constituting the causal structure of the racial wage differential. Condition 4 might be seen as potentially controversial in a deracialized schooling system. However, to the extent that present differences in attainment reffect past discrimination, a leveling of the playing field between the races requires special attention be paid to equalizing schooling attainment. In this respect, income differentials that arise because of limited progress on this front are no less a form of unequal opportunity than that which is introduced by more direct forms of discrimination.

ESTIMATION

A key challenge to estimating standard earnings functions based on household surveys is finding an appropriate method for dealing with zero earners. This problem is especially acute in the case of South Africa, since the rate of unemployment is known to be catastrophically high. Because of this, most now recognize the importance of including the zero earners. However, there is little consensus in the econometric literature on precisely how to deal with the zeros once included. While the Tobit estimator has become something of a workhorse in dealing with this problem, as Greene (2003) and others discuss, Deaton (1997) is among those that advocate Ordinary Least Squares (OLS) simply on the basis that zero earnings represent valid observations. As is well known, the argument for the latter position is especially convincing in the presence of heteroskedastic disturbances (see Johnston and Dinardo 1997). Indeed, Monte Carlo experiments frequently show poor performance of the Tobit estimator relative to OLS under such conditions (Breen 1996). For this reason, the analysis that follows reports both OLS and Tobit estimates. Given chronic unemployment in South Africa, it is arguably instructive to consider the joint process of employment and earnings determination. The Tobit estimator is useful for this purpose, as it lends itself to a useful decomposition of each of these effects. To see how this works, consider the following latent condensed form representation of the Mincer model:

$$y^* = x'\beta + u \text{ where } y = 0 \quad \text{If} \quad y^* \leq 0 \text{ and } y = y^* \quad \text{If} \quad y^* > 0 \quad (9)$$

The slope vector of the resulting conditional mean function for left censored data is:

$$\frac{\partial E(y|x)}{\partial x} = \beta \times Prob(y > 0 | \quad (10)$$

An intuitively appealing decomposition of this marginal effect, first proposed by McDonald and Moffitt (1980), allows an assessment of the relative earnings and employment effects of a given explanatory variable. The decomposition, obtained by applying the product rule when differentiating the conditional mean function for left censored data (assuming normality of the errors), is as follows:

$$\frac{\partial E(y|\mathbf{x})}{\partial \mathbf{x}} = pr(y > 0 \,|\, \mathbf{x})\frac{\partial E(y|y > 0, \mathbf{x})}{\partial \mathbf{x}} + E(y \,|\, \mathbf{x})\frac{\partial pr(y > 0)}{\partial \mathbf{x}}$$

$$= \underbrace{pr(y > 0 \,|\, \mathbf{x}) \times \beta\left(1 - \sigma\frac{\phi(z)}{\Phi(z)} - \frac{\phi(z)^2}{\Phi(z)^2}\right)}_{earnings} + \underbrace{E(y \,|\, \mathbf{x}) \times \phi(z)\frac{\beta}{\sigma}}_{employment} \qquad (11)$$

where $\phi(z)$ and $\Phi(z)$ refer to the probability density and cumulative distributions functions, respectively, of z, the normalized explanatory variable. The term labeled "earnings" is a useful way of approximating the rate of return on education when the Tobit estimator is used.

DATA AND BACKGROUND

Two racially representative data sets covering the decade since 1993 are used in the analysis to follow. The data for 1993 are drawn from the Project for Statistics on Living Standards and Development (PSLSD), the first racially representative national survey of living standards to be conducted in South Africa. Undertaken at a time of great political and economic turmoil, this survey captured, for the first time, the conditions under which the majority of South Africans lived during apartheid. It therefore offers a unique set of information with which to assess changes that have taken place since the advent of democracy. The body of data generated by this study is also unique because it was the first study of its kind to capture outcomes for all population groups, in all parts of the country, on a wide range of issues; and so it is frequently used as a basis for comparing reforms undertaken since 1994.[6] Examples of its use include Case and Deaton (1998) on the economic consequences of the deradicalization of social pensions; Carter and May (2001) on poverty dynamics; and Kingdon and Knight (2003) on unemployment.

The second and third sources of data are drawn from the Labour Force Surveys (LFS) of 2001/2002. The LFS is a bi-annual rotating household panel survey, which began in February 2000; it is designed specifically to track labor-market outcomes, making it ideal for the topic at hand. Table 4.1 shows the mean sample characteristics for each of these surveys, stratified according to race.

All estimates are for individuals and not for households. Earnings are measured as gross monthly pay, including overtime and bonuses. Income earners are restricted for several reasons to full-time and casual workers between the ages of 15 and 65. First, while full-time and casual employment are similarly defined across the surveys, "self-employment" is poorly defined in both the PSLSD and the LFS, thus rendering any meaningful comparisons of this group impossible.

Table 4.1 Mean sample characteristics.

Variable	African 1993	African 2002	White 1993	White 2002
Age	32.82	34.35	34.67	37.86
	(11.34)	(11.50)	(11.60)	(12.81)
Schooling (years)	6.78	8.18	11.19	12.00
	(3.89)	(3.82)	(3.31)	(1.94)
Natural Log of Monthly wage (full-time and casual)	2.86	3.02	7.15	6.26
	(3.20)	(3.44)	(2.49)	(3.74)
Females (percent)	0.48	0.52	0.47	0.47
	(0.50)	(0.49)	(0.50)	(0.49)
n	6929	31384	953	1939

Note: Standard deviations are in parentheses. Data for 1993 are from the PSLSD. Data for 2002 are from the LFS. Years of schooling are derived from categorical data on educational attainment. Monthly earnings are for individuals of working age (15–65) with full-time and/or casual employment and includes zero earners classified according to the "broad" definition (i.e., including unemployed individuals not searching for work). See Kingdon and Knight (2000), Nattrass (2000), Wittenberg (2003), and Dinkelman and Pirouz (2002) for more on why the standard ILO definition is considered inappropriate in the context of South Africa.

Moreover, even in the absence of these problems, including these categories would compound the opposing effects of seasonality (where the measurement error is systematic and therefore predictable) and inter-temporal income fluctuations owing to the transitory nature of many types of self-employment in the informal sector.

Years of education are derived from categorical data on level of education attainment. Table 4.1 indicates that, although mean educational attainment rose over the intervening years for both races, Africans still average about four years less schooling attainment than Whites. The distribution of education also shows some interesting asymmetries between the two races, with Whites exhibiting a much smaller standard deviation in years of schooling attainment than Africans.

EMPIRICAL ESTIMATES

Rates of Return to Education

Table 4.2 summarizes OLS and Tobit estimates of the coefficient on the schooling variable. Those estimates labeled "Ordinary Least Squares" and

Table 4.2 Mincerian returns to education.

Model	White 1993	White 2002	White M.Error	African 1993	African 2002	African M.Error
Ordinary Least Squares (OLS)	0.11	0.43	0.33	0.11	0.07	0.05
	(4.6)	(10.3)	(4.95)	(10.9)	(14.1)	(4.99)
Tobit Index	0.11	0.56	0.33	0.17	0.10	0.05
	(4.4)	(9.8)	(4.95)	(7.9)	(8.9)	(4.99)
Tobit Marginal Effects	0.11	0.49	0.33	0.09	0.05	0.04
Earnings Effect: $Pr(y>0\|\mathbf{x})\times\dfrac{\partial E(y\|y>0,\mathbf{x})}{\partial s}$	0.11	0.34	0.32	0.03	0.02	0.02
Employment Effect: $E(y\|\mathbf{x})\times\dfrac{\partial pr(y>0)}{\partial s}$	0.00	0.15	0.01	0.05	0.03	0.02
n	953	1939	531	6929	31384	14966

Note: Estimates of the coefficient on the schooling variable β from a simple mincer equation. Absolute values of t-ratios shown in parentheses. The dependant variable is the natural log of monthly earnings. OLS and Tobit estimates are presented for comparison. The full set of regression estimates are contained in table 4.3. The Tobit marginal effects are then decomposed into "earnings" and "employment" effects according to the method proposed by McDonald and Moffit (1980). Those estimates pertaining to earnings can be interpreted as a rate of return applicable only to employed individuals, conditioned on their probability of employment.

Table 4.3 Returns to education: detailed regression results.

Variable	Whites 1993		Whites 2000		Whites 2002		Africans 1993		Africans 2000		Africans 2002	
	Panel A											
	Ordinary Least Squares Estimates											
Constant	−0.307	(0.43)	−3.167	(5.35)	−4.520	(5.79)	−3.774	(11.88)	−5.755	(34.56)	−5.625	(34.64)
Age	0.335	(8.88)	0.240	(9.35)	0.259	(7.59)	0.272	(15.37)	0.368	(42.89)	0.354	(42.48)
Age^2	−0.004	(8.08)	−0.002	(7.88)	−0.003	(6.36)	−0.002	(10.64)	−0.003	(29.45)	−0.003	(29.31)
Education	0.105	(4.57)	0.418	(13.6)	0.430	(10.3)	0.107	(10.91)	0.106	(21.01)	0.072	(14.14)
R^2	0.11		0.14		0.10		0.10		0.16		0.15	
	Panel B											
	Tobit Index Estimates											
Constant	−0.813	(1.03)	−4.663	(6.73)	−8.422	(7.84)	−13.893	(18.88)	−16.469	(48.24)	−20.063	(49.88)
Age	0.353	(8.49)	0.272	(9.15)	0.340	(7.33)	0.605	(15.45)	0.743	(44.28)	0.864	(44.37)
Age^2	−0.004	(7.72)	−0.003	(7.71)	−0.003	(6.16)	−0.006	(11.22)	−0.007	(32.53)	−0.008	(33.32)
Education	0.113	(4.45)	0.467	(13.15)	0.557	(9.79)	0.166	(7.86)	0.150	(16.10)	0.098	(8.90)
σ	2.581	(40.03)	3.143	(58.29)	4.631	(49.26)	5.824	(68.54)	5.428	(158.09)	6.149	(144.15)
R^2_{ANOVA} [†]	0.120		0.171		0.099		0.032		0.034		0.078	
Likelihood Ratio[‡]	100.950		426.600		256.670		710.740		673.320		6471.150	
	Panel C											
	Decomposed Tobit Marginal Effects (Earnings and Employment)*											
Constant	−0.811	(1.03)	−4.608	(6.74)	−7.482	(7.90)	−7.163	(19.74)	−10.108	(50.57)	−10.005	(53.30)
Earnings	−0.790	(1.03)	−4.278	(6.76)	−5.191	(7.94)	−2.664	(19.61)	−4.358	(50.06)	−3.628	(52.31)
Employment	−0.021	(1.00)	−0.330	(5.60)	−2.291	(7.42)	−4.498	(19.47)	−5.750	(49.19)	−6.376	(52.43)
Age	0.352	(8.49)	0.269	(9.15)	0.302	(7.34)	0.312	(15.59)	0.456	(44.95)	0.431	(45.42)

(continued)

Table 4.3 Continued.

Variable	Whites 1993		Whites 2000		Whites 2002		Africans 1993		Africans 2000		Africans 2002	
Earnings	0.343	(8.49)	0.250	(9.15)	0.209	(7.29)	0.116	(15.31)	0.197	(43.63)	0.156	(43.93)
Employment	0.009	(4.54)	0.019	(7.13)	0.092	(7.12)	0.196	(15.60)	0.259	(44.70)	0.275	(45.40)
Age^2	−0.004	(7.73)	−0.003	(7.72)	−0.003	(6.17)	−0.003	(11.28)	−0.004	(32.82)	−0.004	(33.81)
Earnings	−0.004	(7.72)	−0.003	(7.71)	−0.002	(6.13)	−0.001	(11.17)	−0.002	(32.33)	−0.001	(33.22)
Employment	0.000	(4.41)	0.000	(6.38)	−0.001	(6.04)	−0.002	(11.28)	−0.002	(32.70)	−0.003	(33.78)
Education	0.113	(4.45)	0.462	(13.15)	0.495	(9.81)	0.085	(7.86)	0.092	(16.09)	0.049	(8.90)
Earnings	0.110	(4.45)	0.429	(13.12)	0.343	(9.68)	0.032	(7.80)	0.040	(15.99)	0.018	(8.87)
Employment	0.003	(3.42)	0.033	(8.61)	0.152	(9.32)	0.054	(7.87)	0.052	(16.11)	0.031	(8.90)
n	953		2171		1939		6929		30697		31384	

Note: The dependant variable is the natural log of monthly earnings in South African rand. All explanatory variables are measured in years. Absolute values of t-ratios are in parentheses.

† The Annova R-squared is a goodness of fit measure that roughly mimics its OLS counterpart, converging on this measure as the censoring probability goes to zero. It is computed by taking the variance of the predicted mean divided by the variance of the dependant variable—see Veall and Zimmerman (1992) and Greene (2003).

‡ The more common goodness of fit measure—the Likelihood ratio—is also reported. It tests the joint hypothesis that all the slope coefficients equal zero and follows a Chi-squared distribution with k degrees of freedom. In all cases reported above, the null hypothesis is rejected at the 1% level.

* Panel C of the table shows a decomposition of the marginal effects into two additive components: the independent effects of each explanatory variable on both earnings and employment. The decomposition, first suggested by McDonald and Moffit (1980), is achieved by applying the product rule when differentiating the conditional mean function. See Equation 11 for more details.

"Earnings Effect" are to be interpreted as private rates of return to education. (The full set of regression results are reported in table 4.3.)

The results are quite striking. At the end of apartheid, the rate of return on education stood at approximately 11 percent for both races. Although marginally lower than what is typically reported for other parts of Sub-Saharan Africa, during roughly the same time period (Psacharopoulos 1994, for example, reports a cross-country average Mincerian return for the nation of 13.7%), this estimate is extremely close to what is generally reported for South Africa at the end of the apartheid period: see Erichsen and Wakeford (2001), Kingdon and Knight (1999), and Hertz (2003). A decade later, however, the return to education for Whites stood at a dramatic 43 percent, although that of Africans declined to about 7 percent. These estimates stand in stark contrast to the most recent estimates for the Sub-Saharan Africa region of 12 percent, as reported by Psacharopoulos and Patrinos (2002).

Figure 4.3 is a graphic representation of the estimated return functions for the 18- to 25-year-old cohort. The picture shows that, at the end of apartheid,

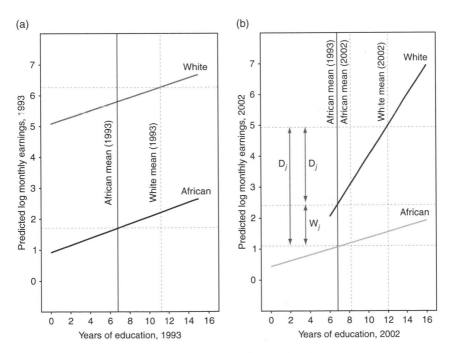

Figure 4.3. Education and racial inequality, 1993 & 2002.

Panel (a) shows predicted earnings of both races in 1993 and 2002. The figures are derived from OLS predicted values based on the estimates reported in tables 2 and 3, for the 18–25-year cohort only. The vertical reference lines indicate the mean level of attainment for each race group.

both races had virtually identical return functions, whereas a decade later the slopes of the two functions had diverged dramatically.

Robustness

One potential explanation for the unusually high returns to education for Whites concerns a measurement error relating to schooling. By exploiting the panel structure of the LFS, an inter-temporal schooling correlation of 0.74 was found. By the classical-errors-in-variables (CEV) assumption, this would lead to attenuation bias in the estimated rate of return, thus posing no problems for the conclusion of divergence in the return structures facing the two races. However, there is no obvious reason one should expect the CEV assumption to hold. Because data on schooling are usually recoded from a categorical structure to one that is discrete, owing to coding errors, the variance of observed schooling in years could, in principle, be larger than the variance of its unobserved component, thus violating a necessary condition for measurement error to be considered classical. Indeed, Hertz (2003) shows that the rate of return to black education drops to 5 to 6 percent after controlling for mean-reverting measurement error in reported schooling. By averaging reported schooling over successive waves of the LFS, one is able to approximate the true rate of return, assuming a nonclassical measurement error structure. This method of controlling for measurement error did result in a reduction in the rate of return (to levels roughly on a par with what Hertz found to be the case for Africans). However, the reduction for Whites was much smaller, with the decline not exceeding 10 percent.[7]

Controlling, however, in a similar fashion for measurement error in incomes (for those who reported incomes in both waves of the survey) generally increased, rather than decreased, the rate of return. Averaging both income and schooling (columns 4 and 7 of table 4.2) resulted in marginal reductions in the rate of return. But even in this instance, most estimates exceeded 30 percent.

Censoring also does not account for the result. Table 4.2 reports the Tobit index coefficient and corresponding marginal effect of the schooling variable. (See table 4.3, panels B and C, for the full set of regression results.) As is clear from these results, the marginal effect of education was approximately 11 percent for Whites and 9 percent for Africans at the end of apartheid, with a similar pattern ten years later, when censoring is not accounted for, as is evidenced by the OLS results. Since the Tobit marginal effect captures the combined effect of both earnings and employment, decomposing this coefficient is instructive for the purpose of evaluating the fraction of the total effect of education that can then be interpreted as a rate of return. This is accomplished by applying Equation 11 to the Tobit marginal effects, the results of which are summarized in table 4.2, and shown in more detail in panel C of table 4.3.

Given the large racial differences in employment, it is no surprise that most of the marginal effect of education for Whites is attributable to changes in earnings, conditional on their being employed; whereas, for Africans, most of the effect of education operates through marginal changes in the probability of being employed, given average wages. These two effects, separately labeled "Earnings Effect" and "Employment Effect" in table 4.2, sum to the overall Tobit marginal effect. The rate of return to education for Whites estimated in this fashion (i.e., the part of the marginal effect labeled "Earnings Effect" in table 4.2) follows a similar pattern as that depicted by the OLS estimates. Although this method gives an estimate of the White rate of return that is somewhat lower than the OLS estimate, even after conditioning on the probability of employment, the result is still in excess of 34 percent. Moreover, controlling both for measurement error (as described above) and censoring simultaneously, did not change this finding.[8]

Differences in the age composition between the African and White populations could also introduce confounding effects. Recall that table 4.1 shows slight differences in average age between the two races. Controlling for these effects (results not shown) did little to change the magnitude of the difference in rates of return. Running separate regressions by age cohort revealed that, while the youngest cohort of White workers (those aged 25 to 35) exhibited exceptionally high rates of return (in excess of 0.6), all other cohorts that were considered exhibited rates of return in excess of 0.30. By contrast, Africans exhibited extremely low rates of return, generally ranging between 6 and 13 percent.

Finally, the results appear not to be driven by assumptions about functional form. Figure 4.4 shows semi-parametric estimates of the return functions. The top panel shows a semi-parametric representation of the earnings-education relation at the end of apartheid, with the corresponding relation roughly a decade later. For each race group, two sets of curves are shown: the solid curves are for the simple Mincer equation (i.e., Equation 2); meanwhile, the underlying regression in the case of the dotted curves includes other regressors that can reasonably be assumed to be exogenous, such as gender, age-education interactions, and within-household fixed effects. Examining figure 4.4 tells a remarkably consistent story to that of figure 4.3 (albeit one that is somewhat more nuanced at the top end of the education distribution). We see the same sharp gradient emerging for Whites in the post-apartheid period, and a declining gradient for Africans, for all but those with tertiary educational qualifications. The emerging convexity of the African return structure, evident in 1993 and previously

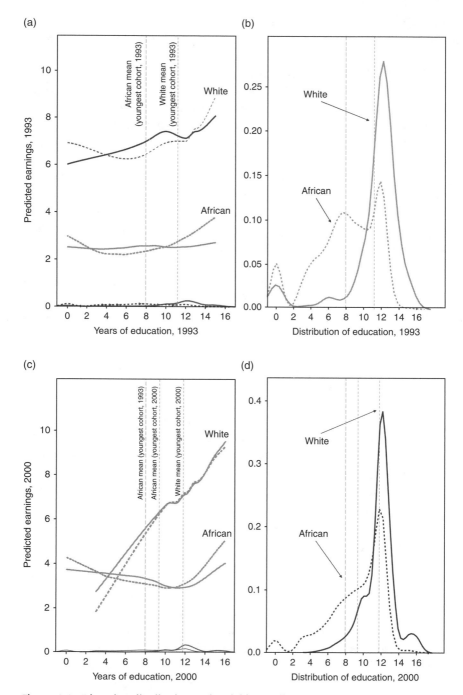

Figure 4.4. Education distribution and racial inequality, 1993 & 2002.

Panels (a) and (c) show nonparametric estimates of the return to education. Panels (b) and (d) show evolution of the distribution of education. Vertical reference lines indicate the mean level of attainment for all 18–25-year-olds. Solid curves in panels (b) and documented by Moll (1996) and others, seems to have become even more pronounced over the decade that followed.

Collectively, these tests suggest that the sharp increase in the gradient of the White return function, witnessed over the last decade, is robust to potential confounds that could be introduced through measurement error, age-cohort effects, functional form, and model misspecification.

The Effect of Omitted School Quality

Reconsider Equation 1 again, but now assume that school quality q is not observed. Under this scenario, q is captured as part of the error term, so that:

$$y = \ln \alpha + \beta s + \gamma q + \upsilon \tag{12}$$

Now, if q is correlated with s, then the composite error term $u = \gamma q + \upsilon$, will also be correlated with s. This will tend to bias the estimated return on schooling, the extent of which is given by:

$$p \lim \hat{\beta} = \beta + \gamma \delta_s = \beta + \gamma \left(\frac{Cov(s,q)}{Var(s)} \right) \tag{13}$$

The probability limit of the education returns function given in Equation 13 shows that if $\gamma > 0$ & $Cov(s, q) > 0$, then $\hat{\beta}$ is upwardly biased. The same result holds if $\gamma < 0$ & $Cov(s, q) < 0$. A standard solution to this problem is to find a valid proxy for q. However, since q itself is generally measured with error, we employ the multiple indicator method to control for this source of bias, as our data contain more than one measure of school quality. The source from which we derive our measures of school quality is the 1996 School Register of Needs. This is an administrative database maintained by the South African National Department of Education, and it contains a broad range of questions relating to school inputs. Our primary measure of school quality is the average pupil-teacher ratio of the magisterial district in which an individual resides:

$$q_1 = N^{-1} \sum_i^N \left(\frac{pupils}{teachers} \right) \tag{14}$$

Figure 4.4. (continued) (d) are nonparametric estimates of the Mincer equation. Dotted curves include other regressors that can reasonably be treated as exogenous, such as gender, location, age-education interactions, a remoteness indicator, and household fixed effects. Other regressors, such as union membership and occupation, are excluded on the grounds that they are endogenous (i.e., determined in part by schooling). The fitted values are for 13,627 working-age individuals in regular and casual wage employment.

Table 4.4 The effect of school quality on the return structure.

Model	White OLS	White 2SLS	African OLS	African 2SLS
Schooling	0.449	0.422	0.071	0.067
	(8.71)	(6.88)	(6.21)	(4.48)
q	0.019	−0.053	−0.052	−0.195
	(0.59)	(0.51)	(4.37)	(3.35)
n	1905	1256	29065	24678

Note: Absolute values of t-ratios shown in parentheses and are based on standard errors that are robust to district-level clustering; 95% confidence intervals for βw and βa do not overlap in both OLS and 2SLS specifications.

where N refers to the number of schools in a magisterial district and j indexes the district.

We then instrument this variable with residential district averages of the number of support staff employed by a school and the number of sheltered areas contained in the school. Our logic is that both of these variables have direct influences on the pupil-teacher ratio, but should not influence earnings once the pupil-teacher ratio has been controlled for. Table 4.4 summarizes estimates of the return to schooling, accounting for school quality in this manner. The key observation here is that school quality does not appear to have a marked impact on the racial differences in the return structure observed previously.

Testing for Equality of Opportunity

Given these dramatic changes in the manner in which education is rewarded in the labor market, what can be said about equality of opportunity? Applying the method outlined in Equations 3–8, table 4.5 presents a summary breakdown of the changing structure of the total wage differential for the period 1993–2002. (See table 4.6 for a more detailed breakdown.)

At first glance, it appears that the decade since the end of apartheid has brought about absolute gains in this respect. However, even though there has been an overall reduction in the total wage differential between Whites and Africans (evaluated at mean education of each group, holding age constant as shown in table 4.6), the structure of the differential has changed. Table 4.5 indicates that in 1993, almost 90 percent of the White—African wage differential could be said to be driven by "pure race" effects, with the remainder accounted for by differences in mean schooling attainment between the races.

Table 4.5 Decomposed White-African wage differential.

Differential	Pure Race	Years Effect	Returns Effect
	Δ_j	μ_j	ρ_j
1993	0.89	0.11	0.00
2000	0.34	0.34	0.32
2002	0.24	0.36	0.40

Note: The table shows the % breakdown of the total wage differential between Whites and Africans, evaluated at mean educational attainment of each race group, for each time period, holding age constant at the mean of the two means (rounded to the nearest whole number). The "pure race" effect is calculated according to Equation 4. The "years" effect and "returns" effect are calculated according to Equation 8. The three effects sum to the total differential, given by Equation 3.

Table 4.6 Detailed White-African wage differential decomposition.

Component	1993	%	2000	%	2002	%
White Mean Earnings $(E(y_{wj} \mid \overline{s}_{wj}, \overline{A}_j, \overline{A}_j^2))$	7.648		7.526		6.722	
African Mean Earnings $(E(y_{aj} \mid \overline{s}_{aj}, \overline{A}_j, \overline{A}_j^2))$	3.309		4.298		3.764	
Total Differential (Δ_j)	4.338		3.228		2.958	
Pure Race Effect (Δ_j)	3.873	(0.89)	1.087	(0.34)	0.711	(0.24)
Schooling Effect $(\Omega_j = \Delta_j - \Delta_j)$	0.465		2.142		2.247	
Years Effect (μ_j)	0.469	(0.11)	1.113	(0.34)	1.066	(0.36)
3mm]0mm0mmReturns Effect (ρ_j)	−0.004	(0.00)	1.028	(0.32)	1.181	(0.40)

The results a decade later, however, show a dramatically different causal structure, with more than three-quarters of the total differential accounted for by factors relating to schooling. More precisely, by 2002, only 24 percent of the overall wage differential operated through race directly, whereas about 36 percent of the 1993 wage differential was explained by differences in average educational attainment. The most striking finding, however, is the large increase in the fraction of the total differential accounted for by changes in the return functions. As table 4.5 shows, the so-called "returns" effect now explains about 40 percent of the total wage differential. Calculations based on the estimated Tobit coefficients, adjusted for measurement error on schooling and earnings from the LFS September 2001 and February 2002 waves (columns 4 and 7 of table 4.2), showed that the contribution of the total wage differential explained by differences in the rate of return to education was 32 percent. Restricting the analysis to the "earnings" effect reduces this estimate to about 30 percent.

Table 4.7 Hypothesis tests concerning equality of opportunity.

Hypothesis	1993	2000	2002	Progress
Hypothesis 1: $\Delta_j = 0$	No	No	No	Yes
Hypothesis 2: $\beta_{kj} > 0$	Yes	Yes	Yes	Yes
Hypothesis 3: $\Delta_j = 0$	No	No	No	Yes
Hypothesis 4: $\mu_j = 0$	No	No	No	No
Hypothesis 5: $\rho_j = 0$	No	No	No	No

Finally, the same general pattern holds across both genders, though there are large differences in magnitude. In 1993, "pure race" effects accounted for virtually the entire wage differential between White females and African females. By 2002, however, the race effect is small (about 10%) and negative. The entire wage differential is driven through differences related to schooling, with differences in the rate of return now accounting for 58 percent of the overall wage differential.[9] The same general pattern holds for the White-male—African-male wage differential (the returns effect increases from 7% in 1993 to 31% in 2002), though "pure race" effects remain high, at 42%).

Given these changes, what can one say about equal opportunity? Table 4.7 summarizes the main findings concerning each of the five dimensions of equal opportunity outlined earlier. As noted, although gains have been made in the form of moderate reductions in the overall wage differential (including the between-race—within-gender comparison just discussed), on most counts equal opportunity does not exist in present-day South Africa, and progress toward leveling the playing field has been slow.

CONCLUSION

While equality in the acquisition of education has seen modest improvements, the translation of educational opportunities into labor-market gains has diverged for Africans and Whites over the last decade. Unlike the case during apartheid, the direct effect of race on earnings is no longer as strong a factor in generating wage differentials between individuals. Rather, race now plays a strong role in determining how educational attainment comes to be *valued* in the labor market. The potential economic consequences of such a dramatic divergence in opportunities available to Whites and Africans are likely to be far-reaching.

One implication is that if standard models of human capital accumulation, such as of Mincer (1974), Becker (1975), and more recently Card (2001), are accurate in their description of the preferences, beliefs, and constraints governing individuals' decisions to acquire more education, then racial divergence in the return functions (on the order of magnitude suggested by the evidence presented here) might lead to an incentive structure facing blacks that is at odds with the further acquisition of schooling. This may impede or possibly even reverse gains made over the past decade in the equalization of schooling attainment, and could have the potential to further entrench racial inequalities as the old forms of (taste-based) labor-market discrimination that characterized the height of apartheid become displaced by statistical discrimination on the basis of schooling.

Notes

This chapter was written as a paper while I was a visiting scholar at the Santa Fe Institute and is a contribution to the Institute's Persistent Inequalities research initiative. I especially thank Sam Bowles for his encouragement and advice. I also thank Michael Ash, Abigail Barr, Justine Burns, James Heintz, Tom Hertz, Leonce Ndikumana, Chris Udry, and Libby Wood, participants of the bi-weekly researchers meeting of the Santa Fe Institute, for their comments and suggestions on earlier drafts, as well as participants of the 2005 meetings of the SFI Social Dynmics Working Group. Comments can be sent to keswell@sun.ac.za.

1. See Roemer (1996) for a survey of the differences in approach taken by Arneson (1989), Dworkin (1981), and Cohen (1989), particularly on the issue of defining "individual responsibility."

2. Note that individual subscripts, though applicable, have been suppressed to reduce notational clutter.

3. See Card (2001) for one recent attempt at resolving this problem.

4. It can be shown that altering the above earnings function to control for other variables that can reasonably be treated as exogenous (such as gender, age-education interactions, and within-household fixed effects) does not alter the main findings. However, for ease of exposition, I maintain a standard Mincer specification throughout.

5. During apartheid, there were four racial classifications for the South African population: White, African, Asian, and Coloured. This classification system was the basis for segregating the population in terms of residential areas, schools, and basic economic and political rights. When the term "black" is used in this and other work on South Africa, it is generally meant to refer to the African, Asian, and Coloured populations collectively. In what follows, I confine my analysis to differences between the African and White populations. If a statement applies to all nonwhite populations, the term "black" will be used. More precisely, "African" refers to individuals who are native to Africa (excluding the Asian and so-called Coloured populations), whereas "White" refers to individuals of European descent, a group comprising individuals primarily of British, Dutch, French, Portuguese, and German origin.

6. All previous surveys (including population censuses prior to 1991) excluded all homeland areas and the so-called TBVC states of Transkei (now part of the Eastern Cape Province), Bophutatswana (now part of the North West Province), Venda (on the Zimbabwe border now part of the Northern Province), and Ciskei (now part of

the Eastern Cape). This effectively meant that, prior to 1994, the overwhelming majority of the African population was never included in any of the sampling frames used by government statistical agencies.

7. In this section, not all results discussed in the text are reported fully (as is the case with the present result) owing to space considerations. Where this occurs, I clearly indicate as much. However, this mostly occurs where either the result is not central to the argument or it can be excluded because it reappears in a different regression specification without loss of generality.

8. These results are not reported here, but can be made available on request.

9. The relevant regression results (stratified by gender) that pertain to this decomposition are omitted from the paper for purposes of brevity, but these can be made available on request.

5

Social Class and Educational Inequality in South Korea

Kwang-Yeong Shin
Byoung-Hoon Lee

The educational system is a key institution for guaranteeing the openness of a society in our contemporary time. Equal opportunity to compete for success is a core principle of liberal capitalism, and the educational system provides an institutional backbone for a marketbased democracy. Meritocracy has become the dominant ideology in the achieving society as a contrasted to the ascribed society. Thus, educational opportunity has continuously grown with the expansion of higher education, while social barriers to education have been lowered.

However, the ideology of equal opportunity and meritocracy has always contrasted with the reality of educational inequality. For example, children's educational achievement has been affected by the economic resources associated with the class position of their parents (Bowles and Gintis 1976, 2002; Willis 1977). Parents' class-based cultural factors exert significant effects on their children's educational achievement even in those advanced industrial countries where public education systems are well established (Berstein 1971; Bourdieu 1984). Thus, persistent class inequalities in education haven't been eradicated by the expansion of public education itself, or even by an increase in the public expenditure for public education.

Though there are cross-national differences in the strength of the relationship between social class and educational achievement, researchers agree that school mediates the relationship between social class and educational achievement (Breen and Jonsson 2005; Goldthorpe 1997; Shavit and Blossfeld 1993). For instance, there is still strong belief that education can be a vehicle for equal opportunity and for a more open society. It is true that expansion of public education and higher education attempts to foster equality of opportunity and eventually a just society. Furthermore, it is also true that the meritocracy that underlines educational competition allows lower class members to aspire to upward social mobility. Since there is little alternative for the lower classes to move up the socioeconomic hierarchy, education plays a role not only as an ideology that makes people perceive the openness of a society but also as a channel for that social mobility, though the probability for upward mobility is low. Thus, education helps relieve the inherent social tensions in an unequal society by providing some possibility of success for talented students of the lower classes.

South Korea is an interesting case of this relationship between social class and educational inequality, since it has experienced an intensified silent class war as opportunities for higher education have expanded. In the 1990s, there was extensive development of tertiary education.. At the same time, the role of the marketplace in education, especially private after-school education, grew enough to outstrip the offerings of public education. Owing to the fierce competition for university entrance via examination, private after-school education has become very important. Nowadays, Korean parents and students regard private after-school education as more effective than public education in preparing for the highly competitive university entrance examinations.

Analyzing panel data for students who graduated high schools, we investigated how the social class of the parents affects children's educational achievement. Is it valid to argue that parents' social class does influence children's transition to higher education in Korea's current market-dominated educational system? This is the topic of this chapter.

THE KOREAN EDUCATIONAL SYSTEM IN COMPARATIVE PERSPECTIVE

For the last four decades, education in South Korea has been a focal point of social and political debate. Educational competition has become so intense that families spend a large proportion of their income to educate their children for university entrance exams. Because of its link to social mobility, higher education is strongly desired across all social classes. In 1994, 92.9 percent of Korean parents wanted their children to get a university education, a very high percentage compared with parents in other countries (KEDI 1994: 22).[1] The proportion of young students who expected to go to university was 95 percent in South Korea, which was the highest among OECD countries in 2003 (OECD 2007a). Figure 5.1 presents the percentage of young people who in 2003 expected to complete Level 5A or Level 6, the first or second stage of tertiary education, respectively, as defined by the International Standard Classification of Education (ISCED). Korea shows the highest percentage with 95 percent, whereas Germany the lowest percentage with some 21 percent.

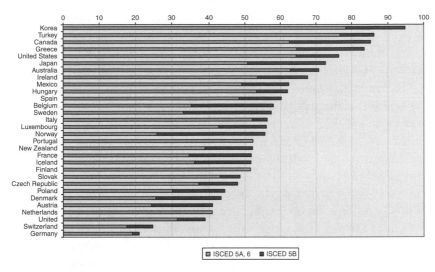

Figure 5.1. Percentage of students expecting to complete different levels of education, 2003.

Source: OECD, 2007[a]. *Education at a Glance 2007*. Paris: OECD, chart A.4-1.

Koreans have very high educational aspirations for two reasons. One is the economic reason that there has been no other way to guarantee financial security except by gaining a secure job through education. The country's recent history bears this out. The Korean economy was ravaged by the Korean War, which dominated the three years from 1950 to 1953. Most people suffered extreme poverty during that time, but a small number of highly educated people were able to maintain relatively secure lives with regular wages or salaries.

Public employees were the group mostly favored with employment during the 1950s and the 1960s. Employment in big companies offered an alternative form of secure employment, especially when the South Korean economy began to grow in the 1970s. In sum, educational credentials have played a key role in Korean people's getting and keeping secure jobs.

Another reason for this strong emphasis on educational attainment is that an educational credential has become linked to social status. The old status system based on a social hierarchy associated with Confucianism was abolished during the colonial period and the Korean War. A new form of social status, associated with a modern educational system, emerged as its replacement. Educational credentials thus became cultural capital, affecting marriage as well as employment. Indeed, as reported in Smiths, Ultee, and Lammers (1998), the level of educational assortative marriage in Korea was the highest among sixty-five countries studied. Even independent of economic status, in Korea assortative marriage based on education grows ever stronger (Park and Smits 2005).

Educational inequality has become institutionalized in Korea's educational system. High schools are divided into two types. The first is the general high school, where most students are expected to go on to university. The sole goal of the general high school, in fact, is to educate students to get good scores on the university entrance examination, which is given by the Ministry of Education once a year. The other type of high school is the vocational, where students are educated to fulfill specific jobs. These vocational schools were set up by the state to supply skilled workers to the industrial sector during the period of state-driven industrialization. Senior students in these schools serve an internship for a particular job.

Prior to the 1990s, the high expectations of both parents and students for educational achievement was not fully met, owing to parents' severely limited economic resources available for their children's education. As economic growth has continued, the proportion of students who go on to obtain higher education has increased. Strong economic growth, in fact, has generated two related changes in attitudes toward education. First, students are more likely to attend general high schools instead of vocational schools. The vocational schools are the less favored, and the gap between general and vocational schools is getting even larger. Thus, the proportion of middle-school students who attend vocational school has continued to diminish since the mid-1990s (see figure 5.2).

Second, increasing numbers of high school graduates want to go on to university. Figure 5.3 reports that the educational transition from middle school to high school (M → H) reached almost 100 percent in the early 1990s. The transition from high school to university (H →U) also began to soar during the same period. Currently, the proportion of high school students who go on to university is almost 85 percent, which is the highest in the world.

There are two reasons for South Korea's exceptionally high level of enrollment in tertiary education. First, a decreased fertility rate has affected the absolute number of children who wanted to go on to tertiary education. If we assume that expectations for higher education remain constant, then the decrease in the number of high school students has lessened the competition for entry into universities. Since Korea's fertility rate in the 1970s was very high, the government encouraged birth control for decades. Consequently, the fertility rate began to drop, from 2.8 percent in 1980 to 1.08 percent, the world's lowest, in 2005 (NSO 2006). This steadily decreasing fertility rate reduced the size of the student population, causing a shortage of new students for some local universities by the 2000s.

Second, for political purposes, educational organizations were expanded in 1980 and again in 1996. To begin, in July 1980, the military regime carried

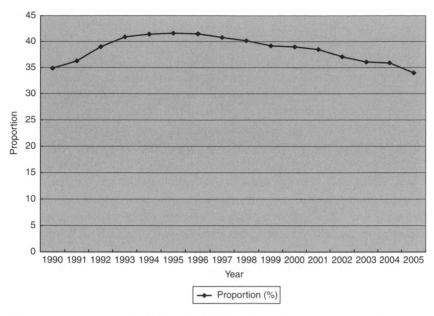

Figure 5.2. Percentage of middle-school children in South Korea who attend vocational high school.

Source: Ministry of Education and Human Resource Development, annual volumes of *Statistical Yearbook of Education*.

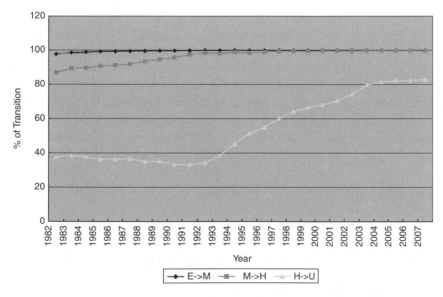

Figure 5.3. Upward trend in students transitioning to higher education, 1982–2007.

Note: M = middle school; H = high school; E = elementary school; U = university.

Source: Ministry of Education and Human Resource Development, annual volumes of *Statistical Yearbook of Education*.

out several educational reforms that increased the number of university places by 50 percent. Then, in 1982, the authoritarian regime expanded enrollment of new entrants to the universities by 30 percent and by 15 percent in the two-year colleges. The military government wanted support from parents whose children had suffered earlier in the severe competition for university entrance. This enrollment expansion was a drastic measure that the universities could not resist while under the military regime.

Then another expansion of higher education took place when the Kim Young Sam government announced a loosening of the regulations governing educational institutions, emphasizing autonomy in education. The government introduced a new rule: anyone could establish a new university without approval of the state agency if some basic criteria were satisfied. As we can see in table 5.1, the number of universities shapely increased from 131 in 1995 to 150 in 1997. Accordingly, the number of university students grew by 180,726 for the same period.

So while the number of high school students diminished with the declining fertility rate in the 1980s, the number of universities and university students increased in the 1990s and 2000s. As some universities began experiencing serious problems in recruiting new students in local cities, in the early 2000s, the Ministry of Education encouraged restructuring, such as limiting the number of new students majoring in unpopular disciplines and urging mergers and acquisitions among the universities by providing financial incentives.

While the Korean educational system has displayed remarkable changes over the last three decades, one constant has been the funding by parents of their children's education. Because the private school system so dominates, and there is such a highly developed system of private after-school education, Korea's public expenditures on education are the lowest among the OECD countries (see figure 5.4). The system of higher education is predominantly private. Though most high schools are financially supported by the state, they are managed by private organizations. The Ministry of Education controls the public high schools, based on the state's financial subsidy. The school fees at public schools are much lower than at private schools.

Korea's university system is even more predominantly private than are the high schools. Only 25 of the 175 universities are public, and have less than 20 percent of the university enrollment. Two-year colleges are also mostly private. The average number of students entering the universities (319,882 in 2007), is much larger than the number entering two-year colleges (283,069 in 2007).

Students can apply to three universities. A university's reputation, rather than a specific department or major, tends to be the most important factor

Table 5.1 Number of higher education and student enrollment.

Year	Total	University	University Students	Two-year College	Two-year College Students	Industrial College	Industrial College Student
1990	1,490,809	107	1,040,166	117	323,825	6	—
1991	1,540,961	115	1,052,140	118	359,049	8	—
1992	1,982,510	121	1,070,169	126	404,996	8	—
1993	2,099,735	127	1,092,464	128	456,227	12	—
1994	2,196,940	131	1,132,437	135	506,806	14	—
1995	2,343,894	131	1,187,735	145	569,820	17	—
1996	2,541,659	134	1,266,876	152	642,697	18	—
1997	2,792,410	150	1,368,461	155	724,741	19	—
1998	2,950,826	156	1,477,715	158	801,681	18	146,563
1999	3,154,245	158	1,587,667	161	859,547	19	158,444
2000	3,363,549	161	1,665,398	158	913,273	19	170,622
2001	3,500,560	162	1,729,638	158	952,649	19	180,068
2002	3,577,447	163	1,771,738	159	963,129	19	187,240
2003	3,558,111	169	1,808,539	158	925,963	19	191,656
2004	3,555,115	171	1,836,649	158	897,589	18	189,231
2005	3,548,728	173	1,859,639	158	853,089	18	188,753

Source: Ministry of Education and Human Resource Department 2006.

Note: Number of students in teacher's colleges and open university are included in the total number of students in tertiary education.

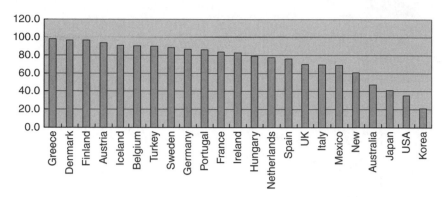

Figure 5.4. Public expediture on tertiary education as a percent of total expenditure, 2004.

Note: Figures for Denmark, Iceland, and Japan include some additional levels of education.

Source: OECD, 2007[a]. *Education at a Glance 2007*. Paris: OECD, 214.

for students and parents because hiring companies generally pay more attention to the job applicant's university than to any undergraduate major. Thus, the universities are ranked in a hierarchal order that corresponds to the entrance test scores of their students. From the individual's perspective, getting a high score on the national scholastic test is the best way to guarantee entrance to a good university, to a good job, and hence to a successful career.

That is why parents spend lots of money to educate their children, enrolling them in after-school programs by the time they start elementary school. Educational competition becomes a marathon race from pre-school to high school. At the beginning of this race, almost all parents expect their children to be excellent students. However, over time some of them realize that their children cannot compete with other children, owing to a lack of economic resources or the child's intellectual capacity. Thus, the proportion of students who participate in private after-school education begins to diminish, from 88.8 percent at elementary school, through 74.6 percent at middle school, to 55 percent at high school (KNSO, 2008:3).

Private after-school education is very costly, a severe burden for parents to bear. Moreover, the private educational market itself is highly stratified, ranging from very cheap group study to expensive private tutoring. On average, parents of high school students who participate in private after-school education spend almost US $3,000 per year, while 9.3 percent spend more than US $6,000 a year. Fittingly, the majority of students in private after-school programs study mathematics and English, which are the key subjects tested on the national scholastic achievement test (KNSO 2008:4–5).

In summary, there are three distinctive features of the Korean education from a comparative perspective. First, there is fierce competition for university entrance which has resulted in the emergence of private after-school education. According to a survey of these private schools conducted in 2007 by the Korea National Statistical Office, 55 percent of high school students participate in private after-school education, and students with higher scores on exams tend more to participate in these programs.

Second, Korea has the world's highest percentage of high school students going on to university. This reflects both parents' and students' high expectations for tertiary education and the declining number of high school students.. Owing to Korea's low fertility rate, the ratio of students who want to go to university to the number accepted has been decreasing since the early 1990s.

Third, Korea has a very high proportion of its students enrolled in the private school system, which requires extensive private expenditure for education. This implies that a family's economic resources likely affect a child's educational achievement.

DATA AND RESULTS

To explore the effects of social class on educational achievement, the Korean Education and Employment Panel (hereafter KEEP), survey conducted by the Korea Research Institute for Vocational Training & Education (KRIVET), is used in the following analysis. KEEP is a panel survey that investigates youths' educational experiences, educational progress, transition from school to the labor market, and career development. It comprises 2,000 middle school senior students, 2,000 high school senior students, and 2,000 vocational and technical high school senior students. Information about family and school environment that affects students' education is also surveyed in the KEEP.

The first wave of the KEEP survey was conducted in 2004. Owing to the attrition of the interviewees, the final sample used in the following analysis—the sample size of 3,327 cases—is much smaller than the first-wave sample, with 3,880 cases. The sample consists of those who went to a two-year college or to a university (1,391 general high school graduates and 1,085 vocational high school graduates) and those who stopped at high school (1,022). In addition, 151 incomplete cases were excluded from the final analysis. The first wave of the KEEP contains information about households and school administrators including teachers and principals.

Social Class

To explore the effects of parents' social class on children's education, we use the simplified class classification suggested by Wright (1985, 1997). In this study, four categories of social class are used: capitalists, petty bourgeoisie, the middle class, and the working class. Those who participate in the labor force are divided into two categories: the owning class and the nonowning class. The owning class is further divided into two social classes: the capitalist class, which owns the means of production and hires other people, and the petty bourgeoisie, which owns the means of production without hiring others. In our analyses, those who employ more than five persons are classified into the capitalist class. Those who employ fewer than five persons are classified as petty bourgeoisie. The nonowning class is further divided into two classes: the middle class of individuals who control other employees (having authority within organizations) or possess scarce knowledge or technical skills (skill assets), and the working class of individuals who have neither educational credentials nor technical skills (Wright 1985:8691; 1997:15–21). Those who have managerial and supervisory jobs or professional jobs are classified as the middle class. The working class is a residual category in the sense that it includes people who do not have means of production, authority, or skill assets.

Education

Children's educational attainment is measured at two transition points. The first is the transition from middle school to high school. Compulsory education ends at middle school, after nine years of education. Thereafter, students either go to a general high school or to a vocational high school. Because of large wage differentials by level of education, advancement to a vocational school is the less favored choice for both parents and students. Parents' social class significantly influences the transition from middle school to high school.

The second educational transition is from high school to post high school, which is either advancement to university, or advancement to a two-year college; or entrance into the labor market. The choice after one's high school education is influenced by a student's educational performance in high school.

The father's education is measured by four levels of educational attainment: those who completed middle school or below, those who completed high school, those who completed a two-year college, and those who completed university or above. Those who had started but had not completed a given stage of education were classified as having the next lower level of

education. Classification of a father's educational attainment is not a difficult issue in our analysis, because all fathers belong to the same generation
and experienced the same educational system.

In order to examine the relationship between social class and educational
attainment, we use an educational attainment model that is similar to the
status attainment model suggested by Blau and Duncan (1967). Figure 5.5
presents a path model of the process of educational attainment based on
parental class (C) and respondent's education (E). In the parental generation, the parents' education affected the parent's class position, the children's transition from middle school to high school (H), and the children's
transition from high school to university (U). The parents' class position
affects the children's educational attainment in two ways. First, a parent's
social class affects the transition from middle school to high school, from
the compulsory public education to the educational system based on individual choice. The choice between general high school and vocational high
school is made by parents; more students from poor families tend to go to
vocational high school. Second, a parent's social class influences the transition from high school to post high school. High school graduates make a
choice among three possibilities: stop studying and finding a job, advance to
a two-year college, or advance to a university.

Table 5.2 Characteristics of major variables of the data.

Variable		
Father's Education	Middle School and below	888(27.6%)
	High School	1,473(44.3%)
	Two-Year College	658(19.8%)
	University	308(9.3%)
Father's Social Class	Capitalist	481(17.3%)
	Petty Bourgeoisie	953(33.7%)
	Middle Class	364(12.9%)
	Working Class	1,031(36.4%)
Respondent's Gender	Male	1,822(54.8%)
	Female	1,505(45.2%)
High School Type	General High School	1,675(50.3%)
	Vocational High School	1,652(49.7%)
Transition after High School	University	1,555(46.7%)
	Two-Year College	806(24.2%)
	Employment or Not Studying	971(29.2%)
Total		3,327(100.0%)

Parental generation filial generation

Parent's education (E)

↓ ↘ ↘

↓ Transition to high school (H) → transition to university (U)

↓ ↗   ↗

Parent's class position (C)

Figure 5.5. Model for testing class effect on education.

Descriptive Analysis

Table 5.3 shows clear differences in children's educational attainment according to the father's social class. The odds of going to general high school instead of vocational high school is highest in the middle class, with 3.789 and lowest in the working class, with .826 (see panel A in table 5.3). The ratio of odds of the capitalist class to odds of the middle class is .454, revealing that the middle class is less than half as likely to go to general high school instead of vocational high school than the capitalist class. The working class is much less likely to go to general high school than the middle class; the odds ratio there is .217. Overall, the gender difference in the association between father's social class and child's advancement to high school is negligible.

The transition from high school to tertiary education reveals a more complex relationship between social class and educational achievement. First, as we see in panel B in table 5.3, middle-class children are much more likely to go on to tertiary education than those of other classes. They are also more likely to go to university and less likely to attend two-year college, compared to children of other classes (see panels C, D, and E in table 5.3). For example, .509 in panel E in table 5.3 indicates that children of the middle class are almost twice as likely to go to university, instead of to a two-year college, than those of the capitalist class. The advantage of the middle class over other classes maintains in the transition from high school to the post high school education.

Second, there is a significant gender difference in the association between fathers' social class and children's advancement from high school to tertiary education. Overall, female students are less likely to go to university or two-year college instead of nonadvancement than are male students for all social classes except the middle class. Panel B in table 5.3 shows the gender difference of the odds; for males, they are 1.346 for the capitalist class, .951 for the petty bourgeoisie, 1.548 for the middle class, and 1.028 for the working class. For females, they are .991, .841, 2.000, and .655, respectively. This is a noticeable pattern for panels C, D, and E as well.

Table 5.3 Odds and odds ratio of transition.

A	General High School vs. Vocational High School		
Class	Total	Male	Female
Odds			
Capitalists	1.646	1.660	1.624
Petty Bourgeoisie	.929	.951	.905
Middle Class	3.789	3.652	3.000
Working Class	.826	.850	.816
Odds Ratio			
Capitalists: Middle Class	.434	.454	.541
Petty Bourgeoisie: Middle Class	.245	.260	.301
Working Class: Middle Class	.217	.233	.272

B	University + College vs. High School Only		
Class	Total	Male	Female
Odds			
Capitalists	1.167	1.346	.991
Petty Bourgeoisie	.898	.951	.841
Middle Class	1.717	1.548	2.000
Working Class	.750	1.028	.655
Odds Ratio			
Capitalists: Middle Class	.680	.870	.496
Petty Bourgeoisie: Middle Class	.523	.614	.420
Working Class: Middle Class	.438	.664	.327

C	College vs. High School Only			
Class	Total	Male	Female	Odds
Odds				
Capitalists	1.075	1.115	1.036	
Petty Bourgeoisie	.916	1.267	.637	
Middle Class	.634	.527	.852	
Working Class	.900	1.013	.790	
Odds Ratio				
Capitalists: Middle Class	1.695	2.115	1.217	
Petty Bourgeoisie: Middle Class	1.445	2.403	.748	
Working Class: Middle Class	1.419	1.921	.927	

(*continued*)

Table 5.3 Continued

D	University vs. High School Only		
Class	Total	Male	Female
Odds			
Capitalists	2.406	2.846	2.018
Petty Bourgeoisie	1.721	2.155	1.377
Middle Class	2.805	2.364	3.704
Working Class	1.426	1.686	1.172
Odds Ratio			
Capitalists: Middle Class	.858	1.204	.545
Petty Bourgeoisie: Middle Class	.614	.912	.372
Working Class: Middle Class	.508	.713	.316

E	University vs. College		
Class	Total	Male	Female
Odds			
Capitalists	2.252	2.552	1.947
Petty Bourgeoisie	1.879	2.161	1.701
Middle Class	4.423	3.333	4.348
Working Class	1.584	1.665	1.484
Odds Ratio			
Capitalists: Middle Class	.509	.766	.448
Petty Bourgeoisie: Middle Class	.425	.510	.497
Working Class: Middle Class	.358	.500	.341

However, class differences, measured by the difference between the middle class and the other classes, are more salient for women than for men. When a father is middle class, female students' transition to tertiary education is more likely to happen than for male students. It means that regarding the transition from high school to tertiary education, the association between gender and class is not uniform and the middle class is an exception, in that the advantage of the middle class is greater for female students than for male students.

Log-linear Models

To explore further the relationship between social class and educational inequality, we use log-linear models for contingency tables (Christensen

1990:99166; Clogg and Shihadeh 1994; Power and Xie 2000:129146). Loglinear models are appropriate to investigate the association between fathers' social class and children's educational achievement, examining multi-way interaction terms affecting educational attainment.

Table 5.4 shows goodness of fit statistics of log-linear models for male students only. We divide the sample by gender because five- way interaction terms cause some difficulty to interpret if we include five categorical variables. Assuming gender dynamics in the association between social class and educational attainment, we initially divide the sample into a male student sample and a female student sample. Model 1 in table 5.4 is the baseline model with four categorical variables, assuming that father's education (E), father's social class (C), respondent's high school type (H), and respondent's transition to university (U) are all independent. Testing models is done by comparing hierarchically nested models.

First, comparing model 3 with model 2, we find that the association between father's social class and respondent's high school type (CH) is significant with the difference of G^2 of 73.62 with 3 degrees of freedom.[2] The association between father's education and respondent's high school type (EH) is also significant with a difference of G^2 of 161.01 with 2 degrees of freedom. Model 7 added the interaction of father's education and respondent's advancement to university (EU), showing a significant improvement of the model. However, the interaction term of father's social class and respondent's advancement to university (CU) is not significant, implying

Table 5.4 Goodness of fit statistics of log-linear models (for male).

Model	G^2	df	BIC
(1) (E, C, H, U)	893.25	63	430.41
(2) (EC, H, U)	523.2	57	104.44
(3) (EC, CH, U)	450.58	54	143.86
(4) (EC, EH, U)	362.19	55	−41.88
(5) (EC, CH, EH, U)	345.6	52	−36.43
(6) (EC, CH, EH, HU)	108.61	50	−258.72
(7) (EC, CH, EH, HU, EU)	97.22	46	−240.73
(8) (EC, CH, EH, HU, CU)	99.34	44	−223.91
(9) (EC, CH, EH, HU, EU, EHU)	62.52	42	−246.04
(10) (EC, CH, EH, HU, EU, CU)	90.71	40	−203.16
(11) (EC, CH, EH, HU, EU, CU, EHU)	56.75	36	−258.73
(12) (EC, CH, EH, HU, EU, CU, ECH)	85.81	34	−163.98
(13) (EC, CH, EH, HU, EU, CU, CHU)	54.77	34	−244.02
(14) (EC, CH, EH, HU, EU, CU, ECU)	70.29	28	−135.42
(15) (EC, CH, EH, HU, EU, CU, EHU, CHU)	31.94	30	−188.46

that there is no difference in transition to the tertiary education across social classes when we control for other interactions. When we compare model 10 with model 7, we also found that the interaction term of father's social class and respondent's advancement to university (CU) is not significant.

However, when we introduce a three-way interaction term among father's social class, respondent's high school type, and respondent's university (CHU), it shows a significant improvement in fit. Comparing model 13 with model 10, we find that the association between high school types and advancement to university varies across social classes. Comparing model 6 with model 7, we also found that another three-way interaction term, EHU, also shows significant improvement in model fitting with the difference of G^2 of 34.70 with 4 degrees of freedom. This is also true when we test other models such as model 12 and model 15.

To select parsimonious models, we include BIC test statistics. The model with the lowest value of BIC is better than others. Model 11 shows the lowest value of BIC with -258.73. Model 6 also shows almost the same value of BIC with -258.72. Model 6 assumes that there is neither an interaction between father's education and respondent's advancement to university nor an interaction between father's social class and respondent's advancement to university. However, model 11 assumes that both interaction between father's education and respondent's advancement to university and an interaction between father's social class and respondent's advancement to

Table 5.5 Goodness of fit statistics of log-linear models (for female).

Model	G^2	df	BIC
(1) (E, C, H, U)	743.55	63	293.2
(2) (EC, H, U)	481.68	57	74.22
(3) (EC, CH, U)	411.84	54	25.83
(4) (EC, EH, U)	326.17	55	−66.99
(5) (EC, CH, EH, U)	310.16	52	−61.55
(6) (EC, CH, EH, HU)	107.35	50	−172.94
(7) (EC, CH, EH, HU, EU)	88.97	46	−239.85
(8) (EC, CH, EH, HU, CU)	92.24	44	−222.29
(9) (EC, CH, EH, HU, EU, EHU)	54.19	42	−246.04
(10) (EC, CH, EH, HU, EU, CU)	76.23	40	−209.7
(11) (EC, CH, EH, HU, EU, CU, EHU)	40.24	36	−257.1
(12) (EC, CH, EH, HU, EU, CU, ECH)	73.01	34	−170.03
(13) (EC, CH, EH, HU, EU, CU, CHU)	53.88	34	−189.16
(14) (EC, CH, EH, HU, EU, CU, ECU)	64.05	28	−136.11
(15) (EC, CH, EH, HU, EU, CU, EHU, CHU)	-	-	-

Note: Model (14) is not estimable owing to some sampling zero cells.

university are significant. In addition, one three-way interaction term (EHU) is included.

Table 5.5 presents the results of log-linear models for female students. The difference between male students and female students is that both father's education and father's social class significantly affect respondent's advancement to university, as well as respondent's high school type. Compared with model 6, both model 7 and model 8 significantly reduce goodness of fit statistics. Model 11 and model 13 also show that three-way interaction terms improve goodness of fit. However, the best model based on BIC statistics for female students is model 11, with six two-way interaction terms and only one three-way interaction term.

Can we conclude that the association between father's social class and respondent's education differs across father's social class? Yes, we confirm that for both male students and female students. Next, is the direct effect of father's social class and father's education on respondent's advancement to university significant? This is true for female students, but not for male students. Considering two-way interactions between parent's social class and respondent's advancement to the tertiary education (CU), it is reasonable to choose model model 6 over model 11 as the better fitting model. However, when we only apply the Bayesian Information Criteria (BIC) value, we cannot prefer model 6 to model 11. However, when we consider an insignificant interaction, CU, in model 11, it might be safer for us to prefer model 6 to model 11.

Choosing models among fifteen models for each subset of data, we conclude that there is a gender difference in the association of father's social class and respondent's educational attainment. For male students, parents'

(a) Male students

Parental generation filial generation
 Parent's education (E)
 ↓   ↘
 ↓ Transition to high school (H) → Transition to university (U)
 ↓   ↗
 Parents' class position (C)

(b) Female students

Parental generation filial generation
 Parent's education (E)
 ↓   ↘ ↘
 ↓ Transition to high school (H) → Transition to university (U)
 ↓   ↗   ↗
 Parents' class position (C)

Figure 5.6. Model for testing class effect on education, by gender.

social class affects children's educational attainment in the mid-stage of educational attainment in the transition from the middle school to high school. In contrast, for female students, fathers' social class affects the whole trajectory of educational attainment. Figure 5.6 shows simplified path diagrams for male students and female students, describing effects of parent's social class on children's educational attainment.

CONCLUSION

In this chapter, we apply log-linear models to investigate the effects of fathers' social class on children's educational attainment in the transition from middle school to university in South Korea. Analyzing panel data that contain information about the process of educational status attainment, we found that with respect to educational attainment, the middle class is the most privileged class among four social classes: the capitalist class, the petty bourgeoisie, the middle class, and the working class. Among social classes, the middle class in South Korea shows the highest odds of going to a general high school instead of a vocational high school. The ratio of children of the middle class who go to general high school rather than to vocational school is even larger than that for the capitalist class, let alone the petty bourgeoisie and the working class.

However, the odds of going to university instead of not going to university or to a two-year college decrease for all social classes, implying that fathers' class effect on children's transition after high school is weaker than that during the transition from middle school to high school. Children of the middle class are more likely to advance to university than those of other classes. Class differentials, measured by the odds ratio, reveal that there is a clear association between fathers' social class and children's education attainment. The difference between the middle class and other classes is the most salient.

Gender differentials are noticeable in the association between fathers' social class and children's educational attainment. The class difference between male students and female students is not so big in the transition from middle school to high school. But it is big in the transition from high school to post high school. The gender difference is greatest in the transition from high school to college. In the case of the transition from high school to college, class differentials are more severe for male students than for female students.

Log-linear models reveal an interesting gender difference in the process of educational attainment. The effects of fathers' social class are strong in the early stage and not significant in the later stage of educational attainment for male students. In contrast, for female students, the effects of fathers' social class on educational attainment persists throughout the process of educational attainment. Because female students are less likely to go on to tertiary education, the effects of social class are more salient for female students than for male students.

Within a costly educational system, the middle class takes a greater advantage of educational attainment compared to other classes in South Korea. Remarkable class differentials in educational attainment indicate that unequal opportunity is an institutional principle of the South Korean educational system. However, because the KEEP survey does not include students studying overseas, class differences may be underestimated.[3]

Notes

1. It was 73.7 percent among the Japanese parents who wanted their children to complete university education in 1994 (Office of the Prime Minister 1994: 133).

2. In the following test statistics, we use the level of significance with .05.

3. The number of students studying overseas has been increasing for the last ten years. In 2007, more than 35,000 students from elementary school to high school went to foreign countries to study, mainly English-speaking countries. They are mostly children of wealthy professionals, such as doctors or lawyers and businessmen.

6

Equal Opportunity in Higher Education in Israel

Lessons from the Kibbutz

Yaakov Gilboa
Moshe Justman

There is broad consensus that children from all social classes deserve equal opportunity in education, but there is little agreement on what is meant by "equal opportunity" in practice and how it should be implemented. Roemer (1998), among others, has suggested defining the phrase as "origin-independence": the extent to which educational outcomes are statistically independent of irrelevant factors. Roemer's analysis, like ours here, focuses on the influence of parents' socioeconomic status on educational outcomes, but other applications are also clearly possible.

Full origin-independence, interpreted in this context as the complete statistical independence of educational outcomes from parents' socioeconomic status, is in all likelihood prohibitively expensive, if it can be achieved at all. Betts and Roemer (2005) maintain that it would require a hugely disproportionate investment of differential resources in the children of less-advantaged parents. While some find this a desirable goal, it is not a practical standard by which to measure actual policies in a world in which even equal investment of education resources in the children of less-advantaged families is a rarely achieved goal.[1]

In this chapter we offer a more modest standard, drawn from the experience of Israeli *kibbutzim*, rural communal villages ideologically committed to a collectivist ethos where the material resources invested in each child are independent of parental income or education or of the number of siblings. The degree of equal opportunity in education that kibbutzim achieve in practice provides a useful bound on the degree of equal opportunity that can be achieved in the general population through public policies; clearly, such policies cannot be expected to achieve more than the kibbutz, whose members are committed to an egalitarian way of life.

We apply this approach here to assessing equal opportunity in access to higher education in Israel. Access to higher education in Israel is not distributed equally among socioeconomic classes. Though tuition is relatively low, access is regulated by academic requirements that exhibit a strong positive correlation with parental socioeconomic background. We estimate the degree to which college-entrance test scores are statistically linked to parents' education (which we use as a proxy for socioeconomic status) in the general population, and we compare this to the strength of this link in the kibbutz population. We find, as expected, greater dependence in the general population. However, the size of the effect in the kibbutz population is larger than the difference between the kibbutz and the general population. This highlights the importance of parents' influence on their children's educational achievements through nonmonetary factors "that money can't buy," as earlier studies using diverse methodologies have shown.[2]

The rest of this chapter is organized as follows: the next section provides a conceptual framework for measuring equal opportunity in education; we then describe the problem of equal opportunity in access to higher education in Israel; a fourth section provides some background on the organization of the kibbutz and its education system; we then present the data and the findings of our statistical analysis, and draw our conclusions.

EQUAL OPPORTUNITY IN EDUCATION

There is generally strong support for the principle of equal opportunity in education, but there is considerable disagreement over how it should be measured and, consequently, implemented in practice. Different approaches can be classified according to whether they focus on resources or on achievements; and on whether they interpret the goal of equal opportunity as reducing disparities between individuals or ensuring that as large a fraction of the population achieves some minimal, "adequate" level.

Thus, the education finance reforms that followed two decisions of the California Supreme Court in *Serrano v. Priest* (1971, 1976) interpreted the government's obligations in providing public education as requiring a limit on *disparities* in the distribution of education *resources* between school districts. In contrast, the current federal initiative No Child Left Behind aims at ensuring that by 2014 all children achieve an *adequate* level of *achievement*. Yet a third approach, that which informed the plaintiff's case in *Williams v. State of California*, sought to hold the state to a standard of *adequacy* of *resources*.

A fourth approach to implementing equal opportunity, which we adopt here, follows Roemer (1998) in focusing on origin-independence in the

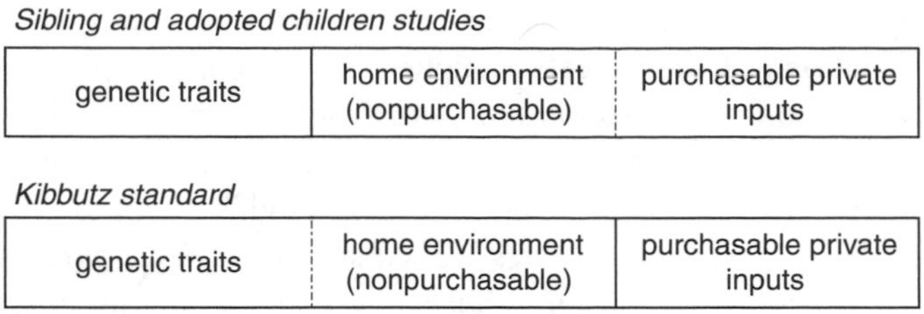

Sibling and adopted children studies

genetic traits	home environment (nonpurchasable)	purchasable private inputs

Kibbutz standard

genetic traits	home environment (nonpurchasable)	purchasable private inputs

Figure 6.1. Two decompositions of the parental effect.

distribution of *achievement* (or outcomes) as a measure of equal opportunity in education, specifically measuring the degree to which students' educational outcomes are statistically independent of their parents' social circumstances. The use of origin-independence to gauge social mobility is well established in economics and sociology. Among its most common applications in the literature is in measuring intergenerational social mobility, typically by calculating summary statistics drawn from transition matrices (Erikson and Goldthorpe 1992; Shorrocks 1978; Checchi 1997, among many others) or by regressing the logarithm of individual income on the logarithm of parental income (Solon 2002, among many others).

In the latter method, which we apply here, the size of the estimated coefficient of parental socioeconomic status serves as a measure of (im)mobility.[3] Specifically, individual scores of young adults on college admissions tests are regressed on their parents' formal education, which we take as a proxy for their socioeconomic status (cf. Betts and Roemer 2005; Checchi, Ichino, and Rustichini 1999).[4] A smaller estimated effect of parental education on test scores is an indication of greater equality of educational opportunity.

This raises the normative question: what is a reasonable standard to which specific measured levels of origin independence might be held? Theoretically, complete equal opportunity should result in full origin-independence. Applying it to education would seem to imply that educational achievement should be statistically independent of the socioeconomic status of the home. But this is not a practical standard, for several reasons.

First, while this approach requires that outcomes should be independent of socioeconomic background, it accepts that they should reflect differences in effort that children invest in their studies (Roemer 1998). However, it is conceptually difficult to separate circumstances from effort, as circumstances often shape effort, a point vividly illustrated by Jencks (1988).[5] Second, Betts and Roemer's (2005) calculations indicate that the differential investment of resources required to compensate children from disadvantaged socioeconomic circumstances to an extent that would render outcomes statistically independent of background is prohibitively expensive, clearly much beyond what society is willing to pay (see note 1). Third, full compensation in education may undermine global equality of opportunity if similar compensating investments are not made in other areas to offset other inherited differences—better health; a more attractive appearance; athletic, artistic or musical skill; and so on (Calsamiglia 2004).

A different standard that has been the subject of considerable interest aims at separating the effects of nature and nurture. This is generally achieved through sibling studies that analyze, for example, differences in achievement between identical twins separated at birth, or between adopted and biological children raised in the same family, in order to separate the impact of genetic factors from the impact of the home and school environment.[6]

While this is a less demanding standard than full equal opportunity, it is more demanding than the kibbutz standard, as can be inferred from figure 6.2: where sibling studies separate the genetic effect from the effect of the home and school environment, the kibbutz standard draws a different distinction, essentially separating the effect of genetic and nonmaterial resources from the effect of material resources.[7] As the kibbutz standard is clearly an upper bound on what public policy can be expected to deliver in the general population, a more demanding standard based on sibling studies is less relevant.

This does not imply that the degree of origin-independence achieved in the kibbutz is a tight bound on what public policy can be expected to achieve in the general population. The kibbutz is committed to an egalitarian ethos beyond that which is held in the general public; and in removing all differences in the circumstances of children's upbringing that derive from differences in their parents' *material* resources, it goes beyond the instruments available to general public policy. But it would appear to be a tighter, and hence more useful, bound than other available standards for what

	Ensuring adequacy	Limiting disparities
Resource-based criteria	Ensuring adequacy of resources: *Williams v State of California*	Limiting disparities in resources: *Serrano v Priest*
Outcome-based criteria	Ensuring adequacy of resources: *No Child Left Behind*	Ensuring origin-independence of outcomes (Roemer 1998)

Figure 6.2. Different approaches to implementing equal opportunity.

education policy can achieve in providing socially disadvantaged children equal opportunity in education.

ACCESS TO HIGHER EDUCATION IN ISRAEL

Strong demand for academic education has led to rapid expansion of Israel's higher education system in the last two decades. Since 1989, the number of academic institutions in Israel increased eightfold, and the number of students in academic institutions almost tripled: from 76,056 students in 1989 to 214,005 students in 2006 (excluding students of the Open University).[8] While the number of universities has remained constant (eight institutions including the Open University and the Weizmann Institute, which awards only advanced degrees), many new colleges have been established to meet the increased demand for education.

This general rise in the number of students in higher education is not distributed equally among socioeconomic classes, largely because entry is regulated by academic entry requirements. (Annual tuition, while not negligible, is low—about IS 8,700, equal to US $2000–2,500 at recent exchange rates.) Admission to higher education institutions in Israel typically requires a certificate of matriculation, obtained through national examinations usually taken at the end of high school, and some minimal score on a weighted average of individual matriculation grades and a psychometric test score.[9] Figure 6.3 presents the share of twelfth-grade graduates who took the matriculation exams, the share that obtained a certificate of matriculation, and the share that obtained a certificate good enough to allow admission to a university, each tabulated by the socioeconomic status of the examinee's locality of residence (1–2 is the lowest, 9–10 the highest). It highlights the importance of socioeconomic status for educational attainment. While in the highest status group 95.8 percent of students chose to take matriculation exams, in the lowest status group only 24 percent chose to take it them; and while 74 percent of higher status examinees met the universities' requirements, only 35 percent of low-status examinees met these requirements. Dahan, Mironichev, Dvir, and Shye's (2003) multivariate analysis of student achievement on matriculation exams also finds significant positive effects of parents' income and education on matriculation.[10]

Figure 6.4 illustrates the relation between socioeconomic status and access to higher education in Israel: in the highest status cluster, over 70 percent of high school graduates continue their education, about half in a university; in the lowest status cluster, only 37 percent continue their education, and less than a quarter of these attend a university.[11] Shavit et al,'s (2003) analysis of the expansion of the higher education system in Israel

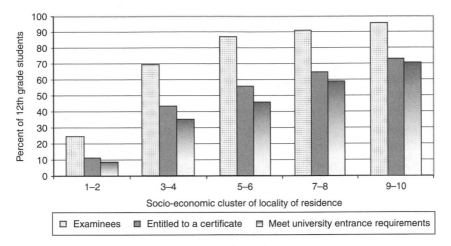

Figure 6.3. Matriculation achievements of 12th-grade students, by socioeconomic status of locality of residence.

Source: Central Bureau of Statistics, 2007. *Statistical Abstract of Israel*, table 6.st08-24.

over the last twenty years found that it did not improve access to higher education for families from lower socioeconomic strata. The universities increased their student numbers at a rate similar to the increase in the population with little change in the socioeconomic composition of their student bodies, while the new academic colleges, established with the specific purpose of improving access to higher education, mostly drew middle- and upper-class low-achieving students, who did not have the academic qualifications for admission to a university.

That participation in higher education is positively associated with socioeconomic class is, of course, not unique to Israel. Blanden, Greg, and Machin (2005) show that in the United States, of persons born at the end of the 1970s, only 9 percent of those born to parents from the lowest quintile of income obtained a college degree by the age of twenty-three, as opposed to 46 percent of those born to parents from the highest income quintile. In earlier work, Blanden and Machin (2004) found similar disparities in participation rates in the United Kingdom. Similarly, Conley (2001) finds that the transition from high school to college depends on parents' wealth, and Hansen (1997) finds that it depends on parents' income and their socioeconomic status. Finally, Schnitzer et al. (1996) show that in 1994, 40.1 percent of higher education students in former West Germany came from families in the upper quartile of parents' income and only 17.6 percent came from families in the lowest income quartile.

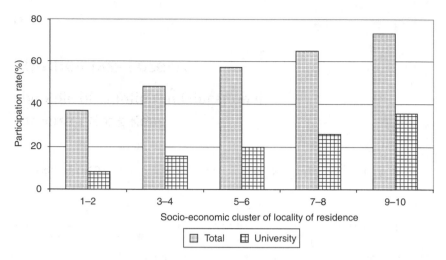

Figure 6.4. Continuation of studies within eight years of high school graduation, by socioeconomic status of locality of residence, 1997–98.

Source: Central Bureau of Statistics, 2007. *Statistical Abstract of Israel*, table 6.st08-40.

THE KIBBUTZ

The Israeli *kibbutz* (plural: *kibbutzim*) is a small, rural, voluntary community based on a socialist ideology, whose members maintain a communal way of life: all the property belongs to the kibbutz and the kibbutz provides for all its members' needs—food, housing, health, education—on an equal basis. The first kibbutz was founded in 1910 by young Russian immigrants near the Sea of Galilee, then at the frontier of Jewish settlement in Palestine. Since then the kibbutz movement flourished and many new kibbutzim were established all over Israel. At the time the state of Israel was established, about 6 percent of the Jewish population lived in kibbutzim, but this share has constantly declined, and in 2004 just over 2 percent of Israel's Jewish population lived on its 266 kibbutzim.

Initially, kibbutzim depended mainly on agriculture for their livelihood, but in the 1960s and 1970s the kibbutzim underwent a process of industrialization. Today, after the economic crisis the kibbutzim experienced in the 1980s, the kibbutz economy is even more diversified, as table 6.1 shows. Kibbutz members work either in kibbutz enterprises (in industry, agriculture, tourism, and community services) or outside the kibbutz, in which case all their income goes to the kibbutz. In addition, the kibbutzim employ outside workers.

From its inception and until the last twenty or thirty years, the kibbutzim were an important part of the Israeli elite. During the British Mandate in

Table 6.1 Revenue shares in the kibbutz of different economic sector, 1998–2003.

	1998	1999	2000	2001	2002	2003
Agriculture	22.2	21.5	21.0	20.2	19.3	18.7
Services	8.6	8.4	8.0	6.8	6.5	5.7
Work outside kibbutz	5.8	6.2	6.2	6.2	6.5	6.2
Industry's revenues	63.3	63.9	64.6	66.7	67.6	69.3
Total revenues	100.0	100.0	100.0	100.0	100.0	100.0

Source: Pavin 2006, Table 6.F2.

Palestine, and following the foundation of the state of Israel in 1948, much of the defense of Jewish settlement in Palestine and then Israel relied on the kibbutzim, and many kibbutz members were high-ranking officers in its defense forces. The kibbutzim also played an important role in absorbing the hundreds of thousands of refugees who came to Israel, as survivors of the Holocaust and as Jewish refugees from Arab countries. Kibbutz members were prominently involved in Israeli politics. In the 1960s, when the kibbutzim made up about 4 percent of the country's population, they accounted for 15 percent of the Israeli Knesset (parliament). The nation's first prime minister, David Ben-Gurion, was a proud kibbutz member, as were many other leading figures in government, the civil service and the cultural arena (including the noted author Amos Oz).

Since the mid-1980s, the kibbutzim have found themselves in the throes of an economic, ideological, and social crisis. Many members have left their kibbutzim, including many young sons and daughters of kibbutz members, whom their parents had hoped would follow in their footsteps (see figure 6.5). And many kibbutzim have undergone profound structural changes, departing from their socialist ideology of equality in various degrees to adopt a more market-oriented form of internal organization. Yet politically the kibbutzim retain a form of direct democracy. Major decisions in the kibbutz are determined by majority vote in the members' general meeting, usually held once a week, with minor decisions made by committees elected by the general meeting.

Our data pertain to kibbutz children born in the 1960s and the early 1970s who spent most of their formative years while the kibbutz's original ideology remained largely intact. A brief description of how these children were raised is useful for understanding the extent in which education in the kibbutz is egalitarian.[12] After birth, babies remain with their mothers at

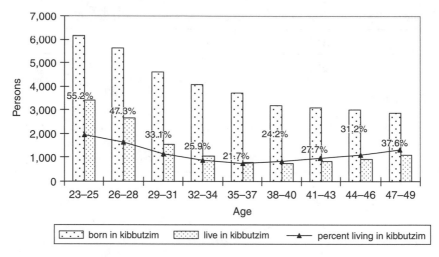

Figure 6.5. Population of kibbutzim, resident vs. as birthplace.

home for a few months. When mothers return to work, children are placed first in a nursery and then in a kindergarten during work hours, under the supervision of professional kindergarten teachers. Parents see their children for a few hours each day, in the late afternoon, after they return from work. As cooking and washing in the kibbutz is communal, this is a time that is largely free of chores, in which parents are able to give their children their full attention.

The kibbutz education system is part of the national education system, so the curriculum in these schools is similar to that taught in other schools in Israel. Kibbutz children, like all children in Israel, begin school in the year they turn six. Kibbutzim generally operate their elementary and high schools as regional schools in which children from nearby kibbutzim study together. Schools are nationally funded but kibbutzim, like other local authorities, can supplement national funding from their own resources. Typically, the kibbutzim invest more money in educating their children than do families with the same income in the cities, and on average, the kibbutz population has more years of schooling than the Jewish population in general.[13] As table 6.2 shows, 47 percent of the kibbutz population aged fifteen and over have some postsecondary education, compared to 39 percent in the Jewish population at large; and only 11 percent of the kibbutz population have ten years of schooling or less, compared to 24 percent in the Jewish population at large.

Kibbutz children who want to continue their education at a university or college must take the required nationwide matriculation exams and

Table 6.2 Years of schooling, aged 15+, 1998.

Years of Schooling	Kibbutz Population	General (Jewish) Population
0–8	4%	13%
9–10	7%	11%
11–12	42%	37%
13–15	30%	22%
16+	17%	17%

Source: CBS Statistical 5.

psychometric test (requirements vary by program and institution). As the large majority of kibbutz children expect to leave the kibbutz at some point, they have a similar incentive to take the psychometric test as does the general population (Avrahami 1997). Decisions on education, including decisions on university studies, are made by the kibbutz's education committee subject to the approval of the general committee. In the past this was a major hurdle to attending university, but in the last twenty years, with the changes in the kibbutz and in Israeli society, approval has become routine.

Many studies have compared the education system of the kibbutzim to Israel's general education system. Aviezer and Rosental (1997) have shown that at very young ages (about two years), kibbutz kindergartens are better than kindergartens in the cities in every respect: the staff is more educated, the ratio of children to staff is lower, and achievements are higher. Dar (1994) compared the educational attainments of kibbutz and city children at age thirteen and found that the average score in the kibbutz was over a third of a standard deviation higher than the average score in the city and its variance was smaller. Dar also found that the gap between the average scores was much smaller—about a tenth of a standard deviation—when the comparison was limited to children of families with high socioeconomic status (based on parents' education and father's occupation), indicating that differences in economic resources may explain at least part of the gap in average scores.

EMPIRICAL ESTIMATION

In this section, we regress psychometric test scores on age, gender, parents' education, and parents' ethnic identity, first for kibbutz children and then for the population at large. We then use the kibbutz estimates to decompose the parental effect in the general population into two parts: the core effect, which even the kibbutz's egalitarian education policies cannot remove; and the residual parental effect in the general population.

Data

Our data include the psychometric scores of all examinees educated as children in kibbutzim during the years 1992–1996 (6,164 examinees) and a representative sample of examinees from cities and other localities in that period (12,099 examinees). We restrict the sample to native-born Jews under the age of thirty-one, to reduce the extraneous bias introduced by differences in the time a person was exposed to the Israeli education system. This leaves 4,077 observations in the kibbutzim, of whom 54.8 percent are women and 7,487 observations in the general population, of whom 55.1 percent are women. The data we have on each observation include gender, the age of the examinee at the time the test was taken, and categorical information on the parents' education and country of origin. We use parents' education as a proxy for income in the general population and for the quality of the home environment in both the kibbutzim and the general population.

Table 6.3 presents summary statistics. The average psychometric test score in the general population is about 550 and its standard deviation is just under 100.[14] The average score in the kibbutzim is a quarter of a standard deviation higher than the average in the general population and the standard deviation is slightly smaller. Parents in the kibbutzim have on average just under a year more schooling than parents in the general population.

Table 6.3 Descriptive statistics.

		Test scores	Mother's years of schooling	Father's years of schooling	Age
Mean	Kibbutz	580	13.9	14.0	22.2
	General population	554	13.1	13.3	20.2
Standard deviation	Kibbutz	90	2.51	2.66	22.5
	General population	97	3.10	3.37	2.58

Kibbutzim: 4,077 observations, 54.8% women
General population: 7,487 observations, 55.1% women

Table 6.4 Spearman rank correlations between parents' education and test scores.

		Total Score	Verbal	Math	English
Kibbutzim	Mother's education	0.183	0.173	0.153	0.150
	Father's education	0.206	0.183	0.170	0.180
General population	Mother's education	0.366	0.330	0.292	0.367
	Father's education	0.359	0.304	0.297	0.373

Table 6.4 presents the Spearman rank correlation coefficients between test scores and parents' education. The correlations in the general population are about twice as large as those in the kibbutzim and the differences are statistically significant at the one-percent level. These differences indicate the importance of parents' socioeconomic status for educational attainment. In the kibbutz, investment in a child's education is independent of the contribution of his or her parents to the collective; in the city, parents invest according to their economic possibilities and rich parents can afford to invest more; hence the larger correlations in the general population. But the correlations in the kibbutzim are still significant, indicating that much of parental influence is exerted through factors that do not depend on material resources.

We ran a separate regression for each of the two samples: kibbutz-educated examinees and examinees from the general population, regressing test scores on gender, age, parents' schooling and parents' country of origin. Table 6.5 presents the results. Consider first the results for the kibbutz examinees. The base category for the education variables is "parent is a high-school graduate." Thus, for each of the other categories the coefficient listed in table 6.5 represents the difference, *ceritus paribus*, between the expected test scores of examinees with parents in that category and those of an examinee whose parents are high school graduates.

In the kibbutz and in the general population, the coefficients of both parents' postsecondary education, bachelor's degree and graduate studies, are positive, large, and highly significant, implying statistically significant origin-dependence both in the general population and in the kibbutz. However, the effects in the general population are larger. Thus, for example, in the kibbutz, the expected score of an examinee whose parents both have bachelor degrees is 40.8 points higher than the expected score of an examinee whose parents both are high school graduates. In the general

Table 6.5 OLS regression of total score on parents' education and place of birth.

	Kibbutz		General Population	
	Coefficient	Standard error	Coefficient	Standard error
Constant	505.58	71.634	368.62	46.111
Age	13.33	6.338	20.43	4.376
Age^2	−0.43	0.140	−0.53	0.103
Female	−54.85	2.841	−46.26	2.038
Father: less than 8 years	−38.29	24.394	−5.62	11.941
Father: 8 years of schooling	1.17	12.067	−1.375	5.04
Father: partial secondary	−2.70	5.420	−3.74	3.208
Father: post-secondary	24.64	4.973	22.02	3.769
Father: bachelor's degree	32.11	5.298	41.07	4.155
Father: graduate studies	45.01	6.205	48.32	4.618
Mother: less than 8 years	26.22	19.481	−55.85	11.635
Mother: 8 years of schooling	14.92	14.367	−13.70	5.403
Mother: partial secondary	−4.57	6.114	−7.24	3.304
Mother: post-secondary	23.48	4.746	23.09	3.812
Mother: bachelor's degree	26.77	5.322	37.12	4.347
Mother: graduate studies	44.53	6.512	59.57	5.022
Both parents have a degree	−18.06	5.946	−9.45	4.874
Father: North Africa, Asia	−19.56	5.112	−9.89	2.974
Father: W Europe, N America	−9.87	4.748	−6.34	4.064
Father: Eastern Europe	−17.62	4.872	−7.58	3.232
Father: Latin America	−18.01	6.843	4.94	8.994
Father: other foreign born	−34.22	11.060	−27.56	6.738
Mother: North Africa, Asia	−16.94	5.735	−5.42	3.088
Mother: W Europe, N America	2.97	4.430	−3.81	4.041
Mother: Eastern Europe	1.12	5.672	−6.81	3.383
Mother: Latin America	−1.54	6.795	2.92	9.084
Mother: other foreign born	−31.06	11.788	−17.74	7.062
R^2	0.158		0.231	
Number of observations	4077		7487	

population, the expected difference in test scores between two such examinees is 68.7 points, 68 percent higher than in the kibbutz. Thus, we find significant origin-dependence in the kibbutz but greater origin-dependence in the general population. If we subtract the difference in test scores in the kibbutz from that in the general population, we find that only a third of the advantage of having more educated parents in the city should be attributed to pecuniary factors; nonpecuniary factors that more educated parents pass on to their children without the intermediation of money account for the remaining two-thirds.[15]

CONCLUDING REMARKS

In this chapter we suggest that the degree of origin-independence of access to higher education in the kibbutz provides a useful upper bound on what public policy can achieve in this regard in the general population. Regressing psychometric test scores, used for regulating university admissions in Israel, on parents' education (and other control variables) we find, as expected, a stronger dependence on parental education in the general population than in the kibbutz. This suggests that there may be scope for improving access to higher education in the general population. However, even in the kibbutz, where investment in education does not depend on one's parents' material resources and there is a general commitment to an egalitarian ethos, test scores exhibit a significant statistical dependence on parents' education. This supports earlier findings on the importance of nonmaterial parental inputs, which "money can't buy," for children's educational outcomes.

Notes

We gratefully acknowledge, without implicating, the helpful comments and suggestions of Caterina Calsamiglia, Danny Cohen-Zada, Mark Gradstein, Caroline Hoxby, Christopher Jencks, Henry Levin, John Roemer, Michael Rothschild, David Wettstein, and seminar participants at Ben-Gurion University, Autonoma University of Barcelona, the Universities of Alicante and Bilbao, Columbia University, the NBER Education Program Meetings, and the Global Network on Inequality.

1. Betts and Roemer's (2005) quantitative analysis indicates that in the United States eliminating the statistical link between parents' socioeconomic status—as indicated by race and education—and the economic outcomes of their children would require at least a ninefold disparity between the educational resources invested in children whose parents are at opposite ends of the socioeconomic distribution. As they note, "Implementing such reforms, which allocate more money to disadvantaged types than to advantaged ones, is a remote possibility in a society that has not yet fully implemented the more moderate 'equal resource' policy" (p. 24). In related work, Roemer et al. (2003) measures the extent in which fiscal regimes of different countries equalize economic opportunity. Of course, these calculations are based on extrapolations that stray far from current practice. It may well be that full origin independence is impossible to achieve.

2. Mayer (1997:12) concluded that "once children's basic material needs are met, characteristics of their parents become more important to how they turn out than anything additional money can buy." Hart and Risley (1995) found that a child in a professional family hears more than three times the number of words per year that a child in a welfare family hears. These differences are closely linked to outcomes at age nine. Lareau's (2003) detailed ethno-graphic study contrasts the "concerted cultivation" that middle-class parents practice in raising their children to working-class parents' greater reliance on "natural growth," highlighting the advan-

tages for scholastic achievement of the middle-class approach as well as the greater stress and weaker family ties it entails.

3. Other summary statistics that have been used to characterize the extent in which achievement depends on parental background include Pearson correlations; aparametric statistics based on rank correlations, such as Kendall's *tau*; and statistics drawn from a transition matrix, such as its trace, its second-largest eigenvalue, and so forth.

4. Another interesting proxy for socioeconomic circumstances recently used to compare equal opportunity across countries is the number of books in the house, which was found to correlate significantly with PISA test scores (Schütz, Ursprung, and Woessmann 2005).

5. Jencks (1988) is led to conclude that it may not be possible explicitly to derive from first principles a consistent, *intermediate* definition of equal opportunity in education requiring less than full origin-independence.

6. Ashenfelter and Rouse (1998), Behrman and Taubman (1989), Bherman, Rosenzweig, and Taubman (1994), Scarr and Yee (1980), and Plug (2004) are examples of these studies.

7. This may be countervailed to some extent by the kibbutz's ideological commitment to egalitarian values.

8. Statistical Abstract of Israel 2007, Table 6.s 8.50 and 8.63.

9. The psychometric test is similar to the S.A.T. test in the United States. It is often taken after compulsory army service, in one's early twenties.

10. See also Beller (1994).

11. The type of institution one attends matters. Caplan et al. (2006) show that the income of university economics graduates one year after graduation is, on average, 31 percent higher than the income of college graduates; and income also increases more rapidly in the first three years after graduation university graduates. Such differences exist in almost all disciplines.

12. There are differences among kibbutzim; this describes a "generic" kibbutz.

13. As Gilboa (2004) explains in detail, because most kibbutz children leave the kibbutz and kibbutz members have little or no private assets to bequeath their children, human capital is the main channel available to parents for providing for their children's future.

14. The tests were originally calibrated so that the average would be 500 and the standard deviation 100, but there has been some change over time. The average in table 6.3 is an approximation computed by averaging over the midpoint of each category weighted by its frequency.

15. Other regressions estimated on more homogeneous subsamples of the data not presented here yielded very similar results, qualitatively and quantitatively.

7

Sociopolitical Changes and Inequality in Educational Opportunities in China

Two Different Trends, 1940–2001

Li Chunling

The distribution of educational opportunities in a population partly determines the basic characteristics of its social stratification system. As Deng and Treiman (1997) point out, "Education is the engine of social mobility in modern societies. In all industrialized or industrializing societies for which we have data, the central answer to the question 'who gets ahead' is 'those who get educated'" (391). The question of who get opportunities for education is, therefore, central to the study of social stratification: the mechanisms of selection through education are considered the most crucial and most important for differentiation of socioeconomic status (Kerckhoff 1995).

During the past sixty years, Chinese society has experienced intense sociopolitical upheavals that brought about significant changes in social stratification and education attainment. There were two different trends in the effects of education on inequality in China during this period. Before 1977, education played a very important role in the formation of an egalitarian society, and this role became more pronounced over time. Since 1978, however, the trend has altered markedly. Education has played a critical role in the transition from an egalitarian society to a socioeconomically stratified society. The problem studied in this chapter has its roots in the changes that have occurred in Chinese society since 1940 with respect to the impact of family origins and institutional arrangements on educational attainment.

RESEARCH BACKGROUND: CHINA'S SOCIAL AND POLITICAL CHANGES AND ITS IMPACT ON SELECTIVE MECHANISM OF EDUCATION

Inequalities of Educational Opportunity in Modern Societies

Despite the general impression that the selection process in the modern education system is mainly based on merit or ability, many studies indicate that characteristics of status or ascriptive attributes that have nothing to do with merit or ability still exert an important influence on educational attainment; this is especially the case with connections between family origins and educational attainment that are almost ubiquitous in all societies. With the advent of the twentieth century, one of the objectives of educational reforms carried out by many countries had been to weaken these connections, yet almost without exception these connections remain in force. The theory of cultural reproduction developed by Pierre Bourdieu (1977), a famous French sociologist, provides a valid interpretation for the way that class status is reproduced by the education system and transmitted between generations.

This state of affairs indicates that distribution of educational opportunities is still not equitable in most countries, with such opportunities biased in favor of those with a better family background. According to the view of J. S. Coleman (1988), "The impact of family background on young people's lives can be thought of as the results of three kinds of family resources: human capital, financial capital, and social capital." The education system as a sorting mechanism manifestly favors children from families of higher socioeconomic status. And this means that in most industrialized countries, education is still one of the mechanisms giving rise to socioeconomic inequality, although the intensity of this function varies from country to country. Differences between countries depend to a large extent on the features of a given education system, such as the pattern of education and the rules of selection used for school entrance. Meanwhile, cultural traditions and the mainstream ideology of any given society also may impact these national differences.

From 1949 to 1978: The Promotion of a More Equitable Distribution of Educational Opportunities

A number of cross-cultural studies have concluded that the distribution of educational opportunities, and its effect on socioeconomic differentiation in socialist or former socialist countries, is not the same as that is found in Western industrialized countries. The study of Albert Simkus and Rudolf

Andorka (1982) shows that policies adopted by socialist countries in the educational sector, such as rapid expansion of the supply of educational opportunities (especially in elementary education), reduction or exemption of tuition fees at all educational levels, and the provision of scholarships or stipends to students enrolled in higher education, greatly weaken the connection between family origins and educational attainment. Parkin (1971) also showed that some deliberate policies of socialist countries had the effect (at least at a certain stage) of biasing the distribution of educational opportunities and the pattern of education in favor of people with working-class and peasant-family background, resulting in some discrimination against those from bourgeois and professional families. There is, however, little support for the claim that educational attainment in the former socialist countries in Eastern Europe and the Soviet Union significantly differed from that in Western countries. For example, Shavit and Blossfeld (1993) compared educational attainment in thirteen countries and failed to find any systematic variation between three Eastern European countries (Czechoslovakia, Hungary, and Poland) and ten market-oriented industrialized countries.

Chinese data, on the other hand, confirm this claim. Deng and Treiman (1997) analyzed data of the National Population Census conducted in 1982, focusing on the influence of family background on educational attainment, and conclude that the distribution of educational opportunities in China was highly equitable, indicating a very weak connection between family origins and educational attainment. With the passage of time, the degree of equality tended to increase, with equality peaking during the Cultural Revolution. They explain the failure of Eastern European data to confirm the view that educational opportunities were biased toward working-class and peasant-families by saying, "Eastern Europe was not communist enough." Yet China, through a series of extremely strong measures aimed at promoting equal opportunity, succeeded in effectively cutting the connection between family origin and educational attainment, greatly reducing interclass differences in educational attainment. The earlier research conducted by William L. Parish (1984) and Martin Whyte (1981) yielded the same conclusions.

The Period from 1978 Onward: Elitism in Education and Market-oriented Reforms

The economic reform launched in 1978 brought about a series of sociopolitical changes in China. When economic growth became a priority after 1978, socioeconomic inequality between people ceased to be considered intolerable; indeed, inequality began to function as an incentive mechanism serving the needs of economic growth. With reform, the elimination of class differences was no longer viewed as one of the main functions of education. Instead, the objective was to support the selection and preparation of skilled manpower for economic growth ("realization of the four modernizations"). In the context of the "mega-trends" involving changes in ideology and in the functions of education, the educational reforms implemented since 1978 may be considered elements of two major transitions. One was the change from a popular or mass education model to an elitist one. Entrance examinations at various education levels have become increasingly strict. This has disadvantaged children from rural and poverty-stricken areas, poor urban families, and families in which parents had lower educations (often giving rise to high dropout rates). Another change involved a shift from a planned to a market-oriented educational system ("the industrialization of schooling"), which produced a great increase in tuition and fees and a significant difference in educational quality among schools in different regions and at different administrative levels. Market-oriented changes in education have led to unequal distribution of educational opportunities among students from different regions and family origins. Studies completed in recent years have showed that educational reforms have had negative effects on the distribution of educational opportunities (Zhou, Moen and Tuma 1998; Hannum and Xie 1994).

Additionally, some unusual institutions in Chinese society have impacted educational opportunities; for instance, both the household registration system and the *danwei* (work unit) system impact access to educational resources.

These major adjustments in policies have produced enormous changes in the selection mechanisms and opportunity distribution. This chapter comments on this process of change, using available data.

RESEARCH ASSUMPTIONS

Factors influencing the education attainment of an individual or the inequality of educational opportunity, as considered in this chapter, mainly involve two factors: family and institutional. Family origins include social capital (father's occupation); cultural capital (father's education); economic capital (household income); and political capital (family's class status)[1]. Institutional factors include the household registration system and the *danwei* system.

Family Origins: Social, Cultural, Economic, and Political Capital

Assumption 1: In the period from the 1940s to the 1990s, those factors relating to family origin that affected educational attainment consisted of a family's social capital, cultural capital, economic capital, and political capital. Among these factors, social capital and cultural capital played stronger roles.

Assumption 2: Family capital factors had a significant impact on educational attainment in the 1940s. Since 1949, however, when the Communist Party began to rule the country, the effects of family capital factors on educational attainment were impacted by two different trends, along with changes of the government's policies and ideology. The first trend, which occurred during the period from the 1950s to the 1970s, was one in which the effects of family capital factors were continually decreased. The second trend, occurring from the 1980s to the 1990s, involved a continually increasing impact of family capital on educational attainment.

Assumption 3: Economic capital exerted a fairly weak influence on educational attainment during the first thirty years of this period (1950s, 1960s, and 1970s); however, it significantly affected specific social groups (rural and female populations). During the latter twenty years (1980s and 1990s), there was a gradually increasing impact of economic capital on educational attainment.

Assumption 4: During the earlier thirty years, the effect of political capital on educational attainment varied significantly from that in the twenty years that followed. Family class status positively affected educational attainment—that is, those with a politically "better" class status had more or better chances of receiving education. During the last twenty years, this impact might be nonexistent or negative. Family political capital mainly affected access to secondary and tertiary education.

Institutional Factors: Household Registration System (*hukou*) and Work Unit System (*danwei*)

In addition to family origin, some social structural factors in contemporary society, such as gender and ethnicity, influence educational inequality. However, in China, the most important social structural factors affecting educational attainment are mainly those derived from special institutional arrangements. Some institutions unique to Chinese society, including the household registration system (*hukou*) and the work unit system (*danwei*), play decisive roles in the allocation of resources, and in the distribution of educational resources as well. The household registration system and *danwei* system were important parts of China's planned economy.

The household registration system divides the entire population into two status groups: one with urban household registration status and another with rural household registration. People with urban household registration status had a more advantageous position so far as the allocation of resources controlled by the government compared with those with rural household registration status. Workers in *danweis*[2] with various administrative levels or different ownerships also received different amounts of welfare allocations from the government.

Assumption 5: Household registration status immensely impacts an individual's acquisition of education in China: people with urban household registration status have much greater educational opportunity than do those with rural household registration status. During the 1950s through the 1970s, the government undertook popularization of education in the countryside, and at the same time it consciously provided opportunities for rural people to enter secondary and tertiary schools; therefore, the impact of household registration status on educational attainment tended to decline. Through the 1980s and 1990s, however, urban-rural disparities (including those in educational resources) tended to increase, leading to the gradual intensification of the impact of household registration status.

Assumption 6: The effect of household registration status on educational attainment was continually decreased during the first 30 years considered here, and then increased during the following 20 years. The *danwei* system affected individual educational attainment mainly through one's educational experiences after the beginning of employment or adult education. Adult education plays an important role in the educational attainment of a Chinese individual. During the 1950s through the 1970s, adult education programs were free, and the government, based on the state's plan, equitably allocated adult-education access to workers in all *danweis*. However, since the 1980s, tuition fees for adult education have become more and more expensive. The government no longer allocates opportunities for adult education. An individual's educational opportunities during employment, especially aimed at obtaining formal tertiary qualifications, depend to some extent on the resources of the *danwei* concerned.

Assumption 7: Education during employment is influenced by the resources of one's work unit. State-owned enterprise, party and governmental agencies, state-owned institutions, and higher level public-owned units usually control more socioeconomic resources, enabling them to provide more educational opportunities to their staff and workers, especially when it comes to gaining secondary and tertiary academic qualifications.

DATA, VARIABLES, AND METHODS

The data for this research are from a national survey that was collected in November 2001 by the SSCC project (Social Structure Change of China

Table 7.1 Distributions of sex, age, household registration, and education in SSCC data and the 2001 census (%).

		SSCC Unweighted data	SSCC Weighted data	2001 Census (aged 16–70)
Sex	Male	52.4	50.4	50.9
	Female	47.6	49.6	49.1
Age	16–20	5.4	11.2	11.1
	21–30	14.1	22.7	21.9
	31–40	25.1	26.3	26.3
	41–50	23.8	18.7	19.0
	51–60	17.6	12.5	12.8
	61–70	14.0	8.7	8.9
Household registration				
	Urban	61.5	27.1	27.1
	Rural	38.5	72.9	72.9
Education Illiteracy		8.0	8.6	8.7
	Elementary school	24.3	28.8	30.3
	Junior high school	34.2	39.6	41.1
	Senior high school	16.7	13.6	10.5
	Technical secondary school	7.0	4.3	4.4
	Junior college	6.7	3.5	3.3
	College undergraduate	3.0	1.5	1.6
	College graduate	0.2	0.1	0.1

since 1949) of the Institute of Sociology of Chinese Academy of Social Sciences. In total, 6,193 valid cases (from people aged 16 to 70) were obtained from seventy-three cities and counties of twelve provinces, through a process of multi-stage stratified random sampling. The distribution of the sample with regard to their gender, age, education, and employment status closely approximates that of the 2001 national census (see table 7.1). Hence, the data obtained are fairly representative of the population. A sample containing 5,858 people was used in our analysis (excluding current students) and the data were weighted.

Survey questions mainly involved respondents' life histories, including detailed information about education and work experiences, earnings history, and family background and migration. Table 7.2 contains the percentages, means, and standard deviations of all variables used in the analyses.

The data analysis below includes three parts. In the first part, multivariate linear regression was used to compare the impact of family origin on educational attainment during different periods, and to compare the gaps

Table 7.2 Summary statistics (percentages, means, and standard deviations) for variables in the regression analysis.

Variables	Percentage	Mean	Standard Deviation
Years of schooling	—	8.11	4.02
Father's occupation		3.22	1.01
1. Managerial and professional personnel	11.0		
2. Clerical personnel	9.2		
3. Workers	26.4		
4. Peasants	53.4		
Father's education.		2.43	1.41
1. Illiteracy	39.7		
2. Junior elementary school	13.3		
3. Senior elementary school	22.1		
4. Junior high school	13.7		
5. Senior high school and beyond	11.3		
Family annual income at 14 years old	—	1702.16	10300.08
Family's class status		1.62	1.01
1. Good	65.8		
2. Intermediate	18.3		
3. Bad	4.5		
4. Unidentified	11.4		
Household registration status in 14 years old	—	1.60	.49
1. Urban	39.8		
2. Rural	60.2		
Adult education experience during employment	—	1.28	.64
1. No	82.3		
2. Having adult education without degree	7.4		
3. Having adult education without degree	10.4		
Danwei's ownership	—	1.87	.60
1. State-owned	25.2		
2. Privately owned	62.7		
3. Other	12.1		
Danwei's type	—	2.39	.76
1. Party and governmental agencies, state-owned institutions	17.2		
2. Enterprises	26.9		
3. Self-employed	55.9		

Danwei's administrative rank	—	2.65	.66
1. Division level and higher	10.5		
2. Section level	14.3		
3. No administrative level	75.1		

generated by urban—rural and gender differences. In the second part, linear regression was used, similarly, to analyze the impact of the urban—rural divide on educational attainment in different periods and to compare gender differences. In the third part, an ordered logistic regression model was used to analyze the impact of the *danwei* system on adult educational experiences during employment.

In the multivariate linear regression analysis conducted in the first part, the years of schooling was the dependent variable, while father's occupation, father's education, household income at age fourteen, and family class status were used as independent variables. Father's occupations are divided into four categories: managerial and professional personnel, clerical personnel, workers, and peasants. Father's education is divided into five categories: illiteracy, junior elementary school, senior elementary school, junior high school, senior high school and beyond. The class status of family includes four categories: "good" (poor peasants and farm laborers, worker, the urban poor, revolutionary cadres, revolutionary soldiers, dependents of revolutionary martyrs); intermediate (middle peasants, small land-owners, collecting rentals, employees, small proprietors, small handicraftsmen, small merchants and peddlers, townspeople, petite bourgeoisie [intellectuals]); "bad" (rich peasants, landlord, capitalists, functionaries or employees of former government, reactionary army officers, counterrevolutionaries); and unidentified. The annual family income of the respondent at age fourteen is a continuous variable. In order to compare the effects of family origin in different periods, six cohorts are used based on the year of birth. The first cohort includes all people born in the period 1931–1940, who mostly received their schooling during the 1940s and early 1950s. The second cohort includes all people born in the period 1941–1950, who mostly received their schooling during the1950s and the early 1960s. The third cohort includes all people born in the period 1951–1960, who mostly received their schooling during the 1960s and early 1970s. The fourth cohort includes all people born in the period 1961–1970, who mostly received their schooling in the 1970s and early 1980s. The fifth cohort includes all people born in the period 1971–1980, who mostly received their schooling during the 1980s and early 1990s. The sixth cohort includes all people born in the period 1981–1985, who mostly received their schooling during the 1990s. However, many among the sixth cohort have not completed their education yet, so the data gathered cannot provide an accurate estimate on the impact of their family origin on their education.

The second part of the data analysis also uses the years of schooling as a dependent variable, while the household registration status of the respondent at age fourteen (urban or rural household registration status) is used as the independent variable.

The dependent variable used in the ordered logistic regression model applied in the third part of the data analysis refers to "whether having schooling or training during employment," and it is divided into three categories: (1) no; (2) yes, but without acquiring academic qualifications, (3) yes, with acquisition of academic qualifications. The independent variables include the ownership category of the *danwei*, its type, and its position in terms of its administrative rank in the hierarchical order. The system of ownership has three categories: state-owned, private or self-employed, and other. The type of *danwei* has three categories: party and governmental agencies and state-owned institutions, enterprises, and undefined work units (referring to self-employment or family-based businesses). The administrative ranks of the *danwei* concerned include three categories: division level and higher, section level, and no administrative level.

RESULTS

General Impact of Family Origin on Educational Attainment in Different Periods

Table 7.3 lists the R^2 values and the regression coefficients for the regression models of different periods. They clearly indicate trends relating to the impact of family origin on educational attainment during the period 1940–1990, when the impact gradually declined (during the earlier stage) and then gradually increased (during the later stage). The trends of changes of the R^2 values of the regression model over the years are shown graphically in figure 7.1. During the 1940s and early 1950s, 15.5 percent of the changes in the years of schooling can be attributed to the combined influence of the following variables: father's occupation, father's education, family annual income at age fourteen, and family class status; in the period spanning the 1950s and early 1960s, 16.0 percent of the changes of the years of schooling can be explained by the functions of these four variables; in the period spanning the 1960s and early 1970s, the figure declined to 13.1 percent; in the period spanning the 1970s and early 1980s, the figure dwindled to its nadir: 9.9 percent; and then, in the 1980s and 1990s, the impact of family origin

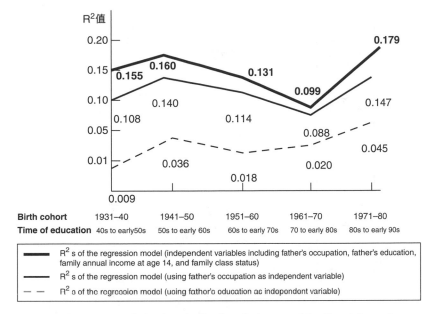

Figure 7.1 Comparison of R² values indicating the impact of family origin on the years of schooling.

suddenly rose to 17.9 percent. Whether in terms of the holistic impact of family origin or of the impact of a single factor (father's occupation or father's education), we see that from the 1940s to the 1970s, the impact of family background on educational attainment tended to decline continually, reaching its nadir during the 1970s. Thereafter, a turning point was reached, and from the 1980s to the 1990s, the effect of family background on educational attainment significantly increased, reaching a peak in the 1990s. Note, however, that a majority of the respondents born in the period 1981–1985 have not yet completed their education, hence the R² values and coefficients listed in table 7.3 provide no basis for accurately estimating the impact of family origin on their educational attainment.

The Impact of Father's Occupation (Social Capital) on Educational Attainment in Different Periods

Table 7.3 and figure 7.1 show that over the past sixty years, the father's occupational status has always affected the educational attainment of his children, with the impact increasing or declining during different periods, and with the trend of change similar overall to the holistic impact of family origin. In figure 7.1 the R² values in the regression model with father's

Table 7.3 Unstandardized OLS coefficients for the multiple linear regression of schooling's years on selected independent variables.

Independent Variables	All samples (N=5858)	Cohort born in 1931–40 (N=539)	Cohort born in 1941–50 (N=770)	Cohort born in 1951–60 (N=1158)	Cohort born in 1961–70 (N=1628)	Cohort born in 1971–80 (N=1383)	Cohort born in 1981–85 (N=382)
Father's occupation (reference groups: peasants)							
1. Managerial and professional personnel	3.431**** (.190)	5.224**** (.869)	3.897**** (.700)	3.531**** (.452)	2.583**** (.297)	3.626**** (.311)	2.051*** (.732)
2. Clerical personnel	2.434**** (.203)	3.262**** (.979)	2.883**** (.628)	2.076**** (.469)	2.038**** (.360)	2.856**** (.332)	.848* (.444)
3. Workers	1.822**** (.129)	2.093**** (.541)	2.584**** (.375)	2.529**** (.319)	2.529**** (.319)	1.320**** (.210)	1.322*** (.288)
Father's education1 (reference: Illiteracy)							
Junior elementary school	.976*** (.143)	.771 (.560)	.448 (.392)	.439 (.313)	.425 (.234)	.771*** (.271)	1.605*** (.509)
Senior elementary school	1.121**** (.115)	.688 (.440)	.927** (.354)	.362 (.265)	.520** (.197)	.801**** (.206)	.492 (.421)
Junior high school	1.604**** (.139)	.345 (.887)	.485 (.495)	.615 (.450)	.492* (.241)	1.004**** (.222)	.886* (.383)

Senior high school and beyond	2.421****	-.374	1.863	.972	1.186***	2.319****	1.260***
	(.223)	(1.511)	(1.722)	(.782)	(.367)	(.339)	(.442)
Family's class status (reference: Bad|Good)	3.588e-02	-2.255**	-1.969e-02	2.512****	-.987*	-.176	1.581*
	(.000)	(.826)	(.580)	(.544)	(.488)	(.433)	(.799)
Intermediate	-9.061e-02	-3.804****	-.845	1.855****	-1.210**	-.162	2.110*
	(.000)	(.788)	(.543)	(.510)	(.452)	(.385)	(.651)
Unidentified	.580*	-2.391*	1.465e-02	2.427****	-1.328**	.221	1.261
	(.255)	(1.041)	(.793)	(.633)	(.511)	(.409)	(.664)
Family annual income in 14 years old	1.189e-05**	-7.700e-06	4.717e-04*	2.031e-04	1.578e-04*	2.017e-06	-3.621e-07
	(.000)	(.000)	(.000)	(.000)	(.000)	(.000)	(.000)
Constant	5.931****	6.736****	5.369****	3.790****	8.046****	7.400****	6.087****
	(.226)	(.773)	(.534)	(.510)	(.459)	(.397)	(.723)
Adjusted R^2	.157	.155	.160	.131	.099	.179	.157

Note: Standard error shown in parentheses. * $p<.05$; ** $p<.01$; *** $p<.005$; **** $p<.001$

occupation as the independent variable indicate: in the 1940s and 1950s, its impact was comparatively great (10.8% and 14.0%, respectively), and then began to decline, reaching a nadir (8.8) during the 1970s, followed by a period of increasing impact, reaching a peak (14.7%) in the 1980s and 1990s. The regression coefficients shown in table 7.3 indicate that, in the 1940s (for respondents born in the period 1931–1940), the average years of schooling for children from workers' families was higher than that for children from peasants' families by 2.1 years; the average for children of clerical personnel was higher than for children from peasants' families by 3.3 years; and the average schooling years for children from managerial and professional families exceeded that for children from peasants' families by 5.2 years. In the following decades, the differences in years of schooling among people with fathers of different occupations tended to narrow. In the 1970s, the differences in average years of schooling among children from families of different occupational status declined to their lowest point: There were no major differences between years of schooling of children from the families of workers, clerical personnel, and managerial and professional personnel. However, their average years of schooling were higher than that of children from peasants' families by 2.0–2.6 years. In other words, in the 1970s, there were no major differences between the years of schooling of children from urban families with different occupational status, although real differences existed between urban and rural areas, between children from peasant and from nonfarming families. By the 1980s and 1990s, these gaps tended to widen: the average years of schooling of children from managerial and professional personnel's families was higher than that of the children from peasants' families by 3.6 years, while that of the children from families of clerical personnel was higher than that of children from peasants' families by 2.9 years. Yet the difference between the average years of schooling of children from workers' families and peasants' families was reduced to 1.3 years. Therefore, during the 1980s and 1990s children from families of higher occupational status enjoyed significant advantages in access to education.

Impact of Father's Education (Cultural Capital) on Educational Attainment in Different Periods

Table 7.3 and figure 7.1 show that the impact of the family's cultural capital on individual educational attainment was minor prior to the 1980s, but it significantly increased in the 1980s and 1990s. Note that fathers of those born in the period 1930–1950 were mostly illiterate, and hence the impact of their families' cultural capital was unlikely to be statistically significant. With respect to the three cohorts born in the periods 1931–1940, 1941–

1950, and 1951–1960, the regression coefficients of father's education are thus negligible. The impact of father's education first became significant in the 1970s, and its impact peaked during the 1980s and 1990s, as evidenced by the following data: the schooling of people whose fathers had completed upper secondary school or beyond was on average longer by 2.3 years than that of people whose fathers were either illiterate or semi-literate; the schooling of people whose fathers had completed lower secondary school was on average longer by 1.0 year than that of people whose fathers were either illiterate or semi-literate; and that of people whose fathers had completed primary school or the first four years of primary school was on average longer than that of people with illiterate or semi-literate fathers by 0.8 years.

Impact of Annual Family Income (Economic Capital) on Educational Attainment in Different Periods

Given the overall data available, the impact of a family's economic capital on educational attainment is not very significant. Only in the population sampled for people born in the 1950s and 1970s (as well as in that sampled without differentiation for respondents' birth periods) did their families' annual income exert even a weak impact. It might be said that, during the six decades under review, the impact of the family's economic capital was negligible. Empirical observation has shown, though, that since the 1990s, the impact of the family economic situation on educational attainment is increasing. Given, however, that most people affected by this are still students and have not yet completed their formal schooling, our inquiry cannot substantiate this. Although family economic capital in general has a negligible impact, analysis of some disadvantaged groups indicates significant impact, for them, of the family's economic capital on educational attainment. Comparison of urban-rural and gender disparities based on regression analysis does indicate that, for respondents, the impact of annual family income, at the time when they were aged fourteen years, is significant for rural people and females, but not for urban residents and males.[3]

Impact of the Family's Class Status (Political Capital) on Educational Attainment in Different Periods

Table 7.3 shows that the trends of the impact of a family's class status on educational attainment are inconsistent with overall tendencies relating to the impact of other family origin, moving in opposite directions during different periods. For the cohort born in the period 1931–1940, the impact of a family's class status on educational attainment was manifestly negative—that is, those born in politically "bad" or "inferior" families were likely to receive more education, while those from families of good class status received an average of 3.8 years less education. Families possessing the most economic capital, social capital, and cultural capital prior to 1949 were labeled as bad in terms of class status after 1949; however, these families were able provide more educational opportunities to their children in pre-liberation days (before 1949). By the 1950s, the function of a family's class status had lost significance, as the people from families of bad class status lost their advantage in getting education. Then, by the 1960s and 1970s,[4] the impact of a family's class became positive, as people from families of good class status enjoyed more educational opportunities. However, those getting the most education were from intermediate families rather than those of the best class status. For instance, the average years of schooling of people from families of good class status was 1.9 years longer than that of people from bad families, and the average years of schooling of people from families of intermediate and unidentified class status[5] was 2.5 and 2.4 years longer, respectively, than that of people from bad families.

A plausible explanation of these data might be the interaction of mechanisms for political screening and education selection. People from families of good class status were mostly children from families of workers and peasants, and they were in a disadvantaged position when it came to competing for educational opportunities (e.g., in sitting entrance examinations), despite the government's attempts to provide more opportunities for them by administrative means. People from families of bad class status, such as landlords, rich peasants, and capitalists (as the beneficiaries of cultural capital, economic capital, and social capital that had accumulated over a long time) were more likely to win in the competition for educational opportunities. Yet they were often excluded from access to secondary and tertiary education on political grounds. In contrast, people from families of intermediate class status (children from families of intellectuals, employees, middle peasants, small proprietors, etc.) often were more likely to obtain better educational opportunities because of the following two reasons: on the one hand, their families usually possessed a certain amount of economic, cultural, and social capital, giving them more chances in the educational competition; on the other, they were not discriminated against politically.

However, dramatic changes occurred in the impact of a family's class status on the education of the members of the generation that next followed (born in the period 1961–1970), shifting from a significant positive to a significant negative impact In other words, people from bad families were more likely to have longer schooling, with an average of 1 year more schooling than people from intermediate families and 1.2 years longer than people from good families. The resumption of national unified college entrance examinations played a decisive role in this, as the selection mechanism of higher education shifted from political to merit-based criteria. From then on, China's entire education system moved to an increasingly meritocratic and elitist criteria.

Undoubtedly, people from "inferior" status families again exhibited their advantage in such competition, while people from families of workers and peasants were disadvantaged as they lost their politically favorable treatment. Let us point out that people born in the 1960s received secondary and tertiary education in the 1980s, and the impact of a family's class status on education mainly found its expression in secondary and especially tertiary education. We can see that the impact of the family's political capital on individual educational attainment was diametrically opposite to that of the 1960s and 1970s. Note though that a family's class status affected the education of an individual born in the period 1961–1970 indirectly rather directly. Their family's class status represents the socioeconomic status of their grandfathers, and not their father's social, economic, or cultural capital. The social, economic, and cultural capital owned by a generation of grandfathers could not favorably influence its children's education (in fact, the influence might even be negative) for political reasons, but this capital could influence the education of grandchildren. The political movement was not capable of entirely cutting off the intergenerational transmission of some family capital. Politics really did attempt to disrupt the reproduction of a family's capital across generations (and it succeeded in so far as cutting the intergenerational transmission of economic capital); however, the cultural capital and social capital of a family are often transmitted through teaching by precept and example within the family, and such intergeneration connections cannot be easily severed. Once political control was relaxed, its role immediately reasserted itself. The fact that the role played by a family's political capital in the 1980s was opposite to its role in the 1960s and 1970s substantiates this point. Finally, with the advent of the 1990s, family political capital represented by class status no longer shows significant impact on individual educational attainment.

Impact of Household Registration Status on Educational Attainment in Different Periods and by Gender

Table 7.4 compares the impact of household registration status (*hukou*) on individual educational attainment in different periods and by gender. The independent variable is *hukou* at age fourteen, at a time when each boy or girl was in school. For a respondent who reached fourteen before the imple-

Table 7.4 Unstandardized OLS coefficients for the linear regression of schooling's years on *hukou* status.

Independent Variables	All samples (N=5858)	Cohort born in 1931–40 (N=539)	Cohort born in 1941–50 (N=770)	Cohort born in 1951–60 (N=1158)	Cohort born in 1961–70 (N=1628)	Cohort born in 1971–80 (N=1383)	Cohort born in 1981–85 (N=382)	Male N=2933	Female N=2926
Hukou status (reference groups: rural)									
Urban	3.110****	3.331****	4.149****	3.487****	2.987****	2.988****	1.808***	2.707****	3.548****
	(.123)	(.441)	(.319)	(.277)	(.207)	(.211)	(.168)	(.175)	(2.988)
Constant	6.804***	3.767****	5.101****	6.101****	7.381****	8.212****	8.819****	7.429****	6.164****
	(0.051)	(.200)	(.136)	(.115)	(.083)	(.088)	(.130)	(.068)	(.075)
Adjusted R^2	.098	.094	.179	.120	.111	.127	.070	.081	.123

Note: Standard error shown in parentheses. * $p<.05$; ** $p<.01$; *** $p<.005$; **** $p<.001$

mentation of the *hukou* system, place of residence at age fourteen instead was used as a criterion to differentiate farming from nonfarming household. Available data indicate that the *hukou* of the respondents did affect individual educational attainment, irrespective of the period in which they lived. With respect to the trends that developed during these periods, between the 1950s and 1970s the impact of *hukou* on educational attainment declined continually, while its impact began to rise again in the years extending from the 1970s through the 1990s. The R^2 values of the regression model over time show that the interpretive power of the impact of *hukou* on the years of schooling is rather low (9.4%) for people born in the period 1931–1940, as the *hukou* system was not implemented yet when the respondent reached fourteen. This indicates that the impact of urban-rural differences on educational attainment was not very strong, since during those years, only children from the few affluent families could have access to education, irrespective of whether they lived in town or in the countryside. However, the average years of schooling varied a great deal for rural versus urban residents, with urban people having an average of 3.3 years more schooling than did rural people.

The impact of *hukou* status on educational attainment for people born in the period 1941–1950 quickly rose (to 17.9), with people from urban households receiving an average of 4.2 years more schooling than people from rural households. For people receiving education in the 1960s and 1970s, the impact of *hukou* status tend to decline gradually, with the R^2 value declining to 12.0 percent and 11.1 percent, respectively; meanwhile, the difference in the average years of schooling between people from urban and rural households declined to 3.5 years and 3.0 years, respectively.

In the years from the 1980s to the 1990s, the impact of household registration status tended to increase, with the R^2 value rising to 12.7 percent; however, there was no significant enlargement in the gap between the average years of schooling of urban people and that of the rural people (3 years). This indicates that, since the 1980s, the impact of *hukou* status on educational attainment has increased, while, because of the increased supply of educational opportunities, the gap between the average years of schooling of rural and urban residents has not widened. In the meantime, the data of table 7.4 indicate that the impact of household registration status on the education of females was greater than the impact on education of males. *Hukou* status could explain 12.3 percent of the urban-rural gap in average years of schooling of females, but could only account for just 8.1 percent of the urban-rural gap in average years of schooling of males. Female, urban household residents averaged 3.6 years more schooling than females from rural households, while the gap was only 2.7 years among males.

Impact of the Ownership System, Type of Danwei, and Administrative Rank of Danwei on Adult Educational Experiences

The three ordered logistic regression models shown in table 7.5 were used to examine the influence of the ownership system of a given *danwei*, its type, and its administrative rank on adult educational opportunities. The data given by model I and model II indicate that in both cities and townships (towns), a *danwei's* ownership and type both influenced adult educational experiences, whether respondents have had opportunities to attend school or studied otherwise since starting work. In cities, the percentage of employees of state-owned and otherwise-owned *danwei* (including collective, Sino-foreign joint ventures, co-production, solely foreign-owned, and mixed-ownership enterprises) who have had adult educational experiences or formal qualifications, including degrees, was 2.5 and 2.0 times higher, respectively, that of the employees of private-owned *danwei* or the self-employed; meanwhile, staff members and employees of party and governmental agencies and state-owned institutions had 4.2 times as much opportunity as did the self-employed (people without a definite *danwei*); and employees of enterprises had 1.5 times as much opportunity as did those people without a definite *danwei*.

In townships and rural towns, the likelihood of enjoying adult educational opportunities was 11.7 and 11.1 times greater, respectively, for employees of state-owned and other ownership *danwei* that for the employees of private-owned *danwei* or the self-employed; adult educational opportunities enjoyed by employees of party and governmental agencies and state-owned institutions were 4.0 times greater than for the self-employed but the likelihood of enjoying adult educational opportunities was only half as much as that enjoyed by self-employed.

Model III was used to see whether administrative rank of a given *danwei* among public-owned units had any impact on the adult educational experiences enjoyed by its employees. The impact was, in fact, significant: the *danwei* with an administrative rank can provide more adult educational opportunities to its employees; however, the gaps between units of different ranks were not large. The employees of units at the division level or higher and the section level both enjoyed 1.8 times as many adult educational opportunities as the employees of units without administrative rank.

CONCLUSION AND DISCUSSION

In the period 1940–2001, education in China developed rapidly, leading to a quick expansion in the availability, and a gradual extension of the duration, of schooling. Based on the data of this inquiry, the average length of school-

Table 7.5 Coefficients for the ordered logistic regression of adult education on ownership, type, and administrative rank of *Danwei*.

Independent Variables	Model I (Urban) Coefficient	Odds ratio	Model II (Rural) Coefficient	Odds ratio	Model III (Public-owned *danwei*) Coefficient	Odds ratio
Ownership (reference group: private and self-employed)						
State-owned	0.9166****	2.5	2.4560****	11.7		
	(0.1890)		(0.4417)			
Other	0.6800***	2.0	2.4054****	11.1		
	(0.1939)		(0.2944)			
Type (reference group: self-employed)						
Party & governmental agencies/state-owned institutions	1.4448****	4.2	1.3763***	4.0		
	(0.2152)		(0.4372)			
Enterprises	0.4123*	1.5	−0.7766*	0.5		
	(0.1833)		(0.3904)			
Administrative rank (reference group: no administrative level)						
Division level and higher					0.5861****	1.8
					(0.1471)	
Section level					0.5947****	1.8
					(0.1388)	
Intercept 1	−2.7361****		−4.3124****		−1.4924****	
	0.1239		0.1819		0.1175	
Intercept 2	−2.0824****		−3.5575****		0.8961****	
	0.1174		0.1485		0.1129	
−2 log likelihood	3050.369		791.440		2506.949	
X²	313.7376****		178.0680****		22.0164****	
Degree of freedom	4		4		2	
Number of sample	2136		1950		1385	

Note: Standard error shown in parentheses. * p<.05; ** p<.01; *** p<.005; **** p<.001

ing for people born in the period 1931–1940 was 4.5 years; the average length for people born in the period 1941–1950 was 5.9 years; that of those born in 1951–1960 was 6.7 years; for those born in 1961–1970 was 7.9 years; for those born in 1971–1980 was 8.8 years; and for those born in 1981–1985 was 9.6 years (since some of this last group have not yet completed their schooling, this number should increase). Other statistics also show a consistent growth in the rate of graduation from primary and lower secondary schools to higher level schools and a consistent growth of tertiary enrollments since 1949. But along with the sustained growth of educational opportunities, we have not witnessed sustained and steady progress toward a more equitable distribution of educational opportunities.

As indicated in the data analysis provided in this chapter, the trends of development toward greater equality in educational opportunities were severed into two stages of development that move in diametrically opposite directions. The first stage extended from the 1950s to the 1970s, and it was characterized by the phenomenal growth of educational opportunities, as well as the movement toward a more equitable distribution of educational opportunities. The second stage extended from the 1980s to the 1990s, and it witnessed both the expansion of educational opportunities and the growth of educational inequality. The turning point of these stages of development came with changes in social, political, and economic conditions, as well as with changes in government policies: a theme that this chapter addresses.

The fluctuating influence of family origin on educational attainment demonstrates the strong effect that changes in state policy and ideology have had on the mechanism of distribution of educational opportunities in China. The dramatic changes during different periods, with respect to the impact of a family's class status on educational attainment, provide strong evidence of this pattern. The influence of institutional partition or segmentation (as seen in the *hukou* and *danwei* systems) on educational attainment reflect the ways that government policies have adjusted institutional arrangements to meet the needs of the new market economy, as well as to exercise important influence on the allocation of resources under these new circumstances. The waxing or waning of the degree of inequality, when it comes to the distribution of educational opportunity, is thus closely linked to state policies. The rapid increase of educational inequality over the past two decades is to a large extent the consequence of governmental policies.

We should no doubt affirm the achievements of educational reform during the past two decades, including the expansion of availability, selection and training of elites, and the pursuance of higher cost-effectiveness; however, we cannot overlook educational inequalities that have accompanied these trends. It is, therefore, imperative for us to reappraise and reflect on some of the priorities of educational reforms and the specific strategies that followed. However, this problem has not attracted enough attention from policymakers in the educational sector. As matters stand, inequality in the distribution of educational opportunities is still increasing, and the elitism and market-orientation of the educational system are likely to continue to develop. From the mid-1990s onward, the expansion of the scale of higher education through the recruitment of more new entrants each year has somewhat counteracted the trend of increasing elitism, but the commercialization of the entire education system is gaining great momentum. Our findings show that this trend has had the greatest impact on children, especially girls, in poverty-stricken areas, while existing educational inequality has seriously impaired their chances of personal development and upward mobility.

Notes

1. Each family's class status was determined by the government according to certain political criteria during the 1950s and 1960s. Status was divided into three categories: good class status (such as manual workers, poor peasants, and communist cadres); bad class status (such as capitalists, landlord, rich peasants, and former government officials); medium class status (such as professionals, clerks, and medium-rich peasants). The government gave preferential treatment when it came to the distribution of educational and job opportunities to people from the families of good class status, while discriminating against those from families of bad class status.

2. *Danwei* (单位) refers to work units such as factories, companies, schools, and government departments.

3. The table providing the results of the regression analysis used for comparing the disparities brought about by urban-rural and gender differences is omitted here, owing to limited space.

4. The impact of a family's class status on educational attainment is mainly manifested in secondary and tertiary education, and individuals born in the period 1951–1960 mostly received their secondary and tertiary education in the late 1960s and 1970s; those born in the period 1961–1970 mostly received their secondary and tertiary education in the late 1970s and 1980s.

5. "Unidentified class status of a family" usually refers to situations of neither very good nor very bad class status, and these respondents often failed to remember or clarify it. Besides, younger people born since 1971 are not well aware of their families' class status.

8

Middle-class Losers?

The Role of Emotion in Educational Careers in Hong Kong

Yi-Lee Wong

In addition to an introduction of free basic education, the last century has seen a continuous expansion of education at all levels, in many countries (e.g., Schofer and Meyer 2005; Torres and Antikainen 2003). However, despite this continuous educational expansion, it has been well documented for many industrial-capitalist societies that class differentials in educational attainment remain (Shavit and Blossfeld 1993). It is true that sociologists and education researchers do not agree on whether the observed class gap in educational attainment has been narrowed or widened (e.g., Moore 2004). Neither do they have consensus on how the observed class gap should be interpreted (e.g., Marshall, Swift, and Roberts 1997; Saunders 2002). But, most sociologists agree that some classes benefit from the educational expansion more than do others.[1] In particular, in many industrial-capitalist societies, children of a relatively advantaged class background, usually labeled as the middle class, are more likely than their relatively disadvantaged class counterparts, usually labeled as the working class, to take up new places created by an educational expansion (e.g., Halsey, Heath, and Ridge 1980).[2] That is to say, on the one hand, the working class benefits from an educational expansion in absolute terms in a sense that, without the expansion, it would have been impossible for them to receive a primary or secondary or even tertiary level of education, while, on the other hand, the working class still lags behind relative to its middle-class counterparts.

Over the last few decades, a lot of attention has been directed to the observed patterns of educational inequality and, indeed, considerable efforts have been made with a view to explaining the patterns (e.g., see the summary in Moore 2004, chap. 1). A number of accounts, somewhat competing, have been put forward to explain why the middle class is more capable than its working-class counterpart of taking advantage of an educational expansion: some focus on class differences in various kinds of parental resources (e.g., Lynch and Moran 2006); some highlight class differences in children's motivation or educational aspirations (e.g., Lewis 1959; cf. Nash 2002); some refer to class-specific values or culture (Willis 1977; Kohn 1977; cf. Bourdieu and Passeron 1977); and some suggest class-specific sets of costs and benefits in understanding class-specific perceptions about risk of different educational options (e.g., Nash 2006; cf. Boudon 1974). No doubt, these attempts are all important contributions to our understanding of the observed patterns; and each has rather different implications for educational policies if a class gap is to be narrowed.

Some efforts have also been made to examine the instances of so-called working-class winners—those working-class students who succeed in taking advantage of an educational expansion by becoming highly educated; their successes are found to be a mixed blessing in that these "winners" somehow feel that they are caught between the two classes (e.g., Jackson and Marsden 1962). However, the following instances do not seem to receive the same level of attention: given their advantaged background, having higher chances of staying on in education, some middle-class children still fail to grasp a newly arisen opportunity to fill new places provided by an expansion; how would this so-called failure impact on the middle-class children? Sociologically speaking, what can we learn from the instances of so-called middle-class losers?

The focus of this chapter is on some so-called middle-class losers: seventeen students of a middle-class origin selected from a qualitative study of community-college students in contemporary Hong Kong. They all failed in their previous attempts to follow a so-called traditional route to a local university—passing the required local public examinations—and chose an unconventional alternative that became available in Hong Kong in 2000, studying for an associate degree in community college, in the hope that they would transfer later to a university. Examining their subjective accounts of educational achievements and failures, I shall explore the role of emotion in their educational careers in order to see what we could learn from them in understanding educational inequality. In what follows, I first provide a brief overview of the background of this qualitative study: the education system in contemporary Hong Kong, highlighting the emergence of the community college in the year 2000. Second, I describe the design of the qualitative study and discuss its major limitations. Third, I highlight that the community-college students of the qualitative study, including the seventeen discussed in this chapter, saw themselves as losers in the education system, feeling ashamed of their academic failures. Fourth, referring to the narratives of seventeen middle-class community-college students, I discuss their feelings of shame, guilt, and agony, and I explore the roles these feelings play in the students' educational careers. I end this chapter with a special note that emotion is an important but underexplored area in the study of educational inequality, and I offer three suggestions for further investigation.

THE EDUCATION SYSTEM IN CONTEMPORARY HONG KONG

In Hong Kong, except for pre-school nursery education, education at all levels is basically provided by the Hong Kong government (cf. Post 1993). As shown in figure 8.1, in order to stay on in education, students have to go through a number of centralized allocation schemes and public examinations, although some schemes and examinations have been abolished or reformed throughthese years.

Presently, a nine-year basic education—six years of primary education and three years of junior secondary education—is free and compulsory to all students. Since 1983, all school-age students (aged six) have to join the centrally administered Primary One Admission Scheme (POAS; e.g., Sweeting 2004). At the end of primary education, every student at the age of eleven has to join the Secondary School Placement Allocation Scheme (SSPAS), so that he or she will get allocated to a secondary school. After studying in a secondary school for three years, students will have completed a nine-year basic education. After that, students who want to continue their education may stay on for two years so as to prepare for the Hong Kong Certificate of Education Examination (HKCEE),[3] taken at the age of sixteen. The results of this public examination determine whether a student can get a place in secondary form six; presently, only about 40 percent of them can get a place in a two-year course preparing them for the public examination—the Hong Kong Advanced Level Examination (HKALE)[4]—taken at the age of eighteen. Then, about 50 percent of students who take the HKALE can get a place in a local university. Taken all together, the current policy is to maintain the proportion of students of the relevant age group getting a first-year first-degree place at 16 to 18 percent.

Over the last five decades, the provision of local education for the population has been improved in two significant ways. First, the passing of the acts of free, universal, and compulsory six-year and nine-year education, in 1971 and 1978, respectively, makes a basic education readily available to everyone. Second, the system of education in Hong Kong has become less elitist: an increase in the number of local degree-granting institutions—from one university before 1963, dramatically increasing to seven universities in 1992 and to twelve degree-granting institutions in 2007—allows a greater proportion of students of the relevant age group (from about 2% in the 1960s to 16 to 18% since the mid-1990s) to receive a tertiary education. The improvement

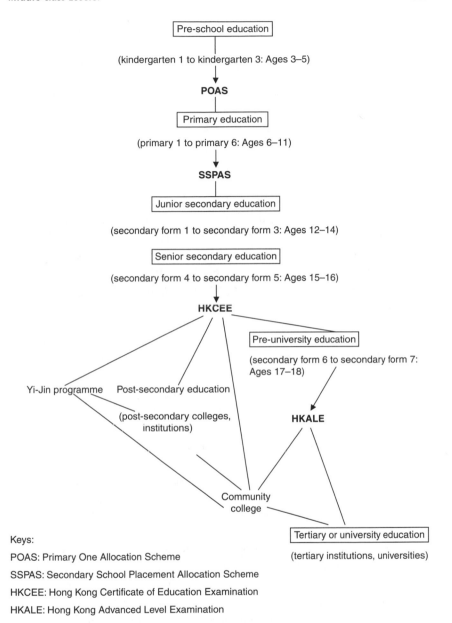

Figure 8.1 The present educational system in Hong Kong.

Keys:

POAS: Primary One Allocation Scheme

SSPAS: Secondary School Placement Allocation Scheme

HKCEE: Hong Kong Certificate of Education Examination

HKALE: Hong Kong Advanced Level Examination

can be seen from general statistics. In 1961, nearly 80 percent of the population aged fifteen and above had, at most, a primary education (about 30% having no education), whereas only about 4 percent had a tertiary education (including a nondegree education); in stark contrast, in 2006, only about 7 percent of the population aged fifteen and above had no education, whereas over 70 percent had at least a secondary education (about 23% having a tertiary education; Hong Kong Census and Statistics Department 1971, 1981, 1991, 2001, 2006).

Despite improvement in the provision of higher education, by design over 80 percent of students of the relevant age group cannot get a place in local universities. In the 1980s and early 1990s, when the economy was doing very well, these young people were easily absorbed by the labor market. However, the economy has been doing poorly since the mid-1990s, especially after the 1997 Asian financial crisis. An increasing number of young people could not stay on in education and also could not get a job (equivalent to NEET—not in education, employment, training—teenagers in Britain). The government was under great pressure to handle this increasing number of young people. The Yi-Jin program, designed for those who failed all subjects in HKCEE, was introduced in the late 1990s. In addition, the government, while seeking to maintain the proportion of the relevant age group getting a first-year first-degree place at the 16 to18 percent level, sought to increase the proportion of the relevant age group getting a post-secondary education, from the existing 34 percent to 60 percent in ten years (Hong Kong Education Commission Report 2000:3–4). In response, three local universities launched self-financing community college programs in 2000, offering a variety of subdegree programmes. Since then, community college and the subdegree program (the associate degree program in particular) has become a booming market: over the last seven years, from 2001 to 2007, the number of institutions providing subdegree programs (many of them community colleges) has increased from eleven to twenty, and the number of associate degree programs offered has increased nearly ten times, from 16 to 148 (Hong Kong Education Bureau 2010). In competing for students, community colleges promote themselves as providing an alternative route for students who fail the HKCEE or HKALE and cannot get into a university, local or overseas, although in reality fewer than 3 percent of community college students have successfully transferred to local full-time degree programs (e.g., Mingpao 2007). The community college is a concept new to Hong Kong, borrowed from the United States. Beginning in 1901 in the United States, community colleges were open to all who could pay a low tuition fee; what a community college seeks is not only to prepare students to transfer tofour-year colleges after two years of studies but also to offer nontransfer courses, including vocational courses or courses for personal interests and development (American Association of Community Colleges 2010). Their counterparts in Hong Kong are different in at least three respects: admission, tuition, and function. Community colleges in Hong Kong are not open to all (also see figure 8.1), since they have adopted certain entry requirements.[5] Doing a subdegree program in a community college in Hong Kong is not cheap; the annual tuition is at least the same as for obtaining a local first degree—about HK $40,000 (about US $5,100) a year, depending on the program and the policy of the institution[6] In contrast to viewing the community college as a multifunction tertiary institution, as is the case in the United States, the majority of Hong Kong's community college students enroll because they want to transfer to a local university, and therefore most of them are full-time students of the relevant age group rather than mature students (Ng and Cheng 2002).

RESEARCH DESIGN

Students studied for this chapter were selected from a qualitative study of fifty-two community college students in contemporary Hong Kong. Those fifty-two students were recruited and interviewed between December 2005 and June 2006. As I was teaching a semester course of Introduction to Sociology to students in various associate-degree program—mainly associate degrees in business administration and associate degrees in the arts—in the 2005–2006 academic year, at the end of each semesters (mid-December and mid-May, respectively), I announced the plan to recruit students for my project, entitled "Educational Inequality in Contemporary Hong Kong" Interested students then left their English names, instead of their Chinese names (so that I could not identify them) and contact information. Out of ethical concerns, I contacted these students after our professional relationships had ended.[7] We fixed the time, date, and place for taped interviews. Though sixty-five students had left their contact information, owing to time constraints I interviewed only fifty-two.

Most interviews were conducted in open areas close to the community college and some took place in a cafeteria. Then I used the Goldthorpe class scheme (Erikson and Goldthorpe 1992:39–42) and followed the dominance method to classify students in terms of class origin.[8] For present purposes, I focus on seventeen community college students of middle-class origin:[9] eight of them whose father or mother had a class I or class II job (a professional, managerial, or administrative job), six of them whose father or mother had a class IIIa job (a clerical job), and three of them whose father had a class IVa job (a self-employed manager running a small business). Ten students were female and seven male; they were all born in Hong Kong.

Consistent with the fact that most community college students are students of the relevant age group, rather than mature students, their ages ranged from twenty to twenty-four, with the average being twenty-one.

The interview was semi-structured. Before taping, I collected background information from the students, including their personal details and demographic characteristics, occupations, and educational attainments of their parents and siblings. During the interview, each student was asked to talk about five main areas: current situation (including educational aspirations and immediate and future educational and career plans); educational experiences (including perceptions of teachers and classmates at different stages); relationships with parents (including perceived parental aspirations and parental support received throughout his or her educational career); evaluation of him or herself and classmates as students; evaluation of the existing education system; and evaluation of Hong Kong as a place for people's development.

At the end of the interview, students were also asked why they agreed to participate in this research project and whether they would be interested participating in any follow-up studies. The duration of the interviews ranged from forty-five minutes to two hours, an average being about an hour. My conversations with students sometimes continued after the taped interview; in fact, it lasted for another hour in a number of cases. On some occasions, I even had to take up the role of counselor handling their emotional issues. Then, between June and September 2006, all interviews were transcribed and translated from Cantonese, the major local dialect in Hong Kong, into English. The interviews were analyzed along several themes, such as student educational aspirations, parental assistance, student feelings toward their educational careers and their parents, and so on. The theme of feelings of shame, guilt, and agony emerged in these analyses of *how* these students talked about their educational experiences. In this chapter, I report on the narratives of seventeen middle-class students on their educational experiences: *how* they talked about their educational achievements and failures.

Before moving on to discuss the data, I caution readers that this is an exploratory study of a small, nonrandom sample of self-selected community-college students. Statistical representativeness, reliability, and validity of results are issues. As for statistical representativeness, I did not use a sampling frame to recruit a statistically representative sample, but basically used convenience sampling to recruit a group of self-selected students. While this sample is not statistically representative, it is biased toward a particular group of students because of the research topic (on educational inequality) and the context of recruitment (confining to students taking the course of sociology being taught by me). This bias is reflected in students' responses to the question of why they had agreed to join this research: nearly half of them wanted to help me, some were interested in the topic of educational inequality, and some stated clearly that they wanted to voice their discontent with the education system.

The fact that these students trusted me as their former teacher made it easier for them to share their feelings with me. In this study, the main thrust of their accounts was their reflections on their educational careers and their evaluations of what they did and what their parents did for them. (As for the part about their parents' expectations of them and what their parents did for them, I did not interview their parents for cross-references and so the students were the only source of information.) In a way, one could doubt the reliability of these results. In addition, as expected, in these self-reported accounts students were reconstructing their experiences and unavoidably this made them look more coherent and logical than they actually were. Furthermore, in portraying themselves to a researcher, who was also their former teacher, the students might have presented themselves in a way that they thought would appeal to me as researcher/teacher. In this sense, also, one could doubt the validity of the results.

To reiterate, what I do in this chapter is to draw upon the rich details of students' narratives in order to determine what we can learn from these so-called middle-class losers and to explore the role of emotion in their educational careers. Readers should bear in mind the limitations of the results of this study; yet, I argue that these limitations do not make the students' accounts, however distorted or statistically unrepresentative, less useful in providing new lines of inquiry for the study of educational inequality.

TAKING AN UNTRADITIONAL ROUTE TO HIGHER EDUCATION

Before the year 2000, when a student failed at any stage in the system, there were only two choices: either to repeat or to quit. It is true that the main idea of setting up the community colleges was to provide more students with a postsecondary education, not to offer students an alternative route to a local university. Yet nearly all students who study in a community college do not take their subdegree offered there as a final degree but, rather, as a springboard to a university, preferably a local one. The same is true of all fifty-two community-college students in this study.

Aspiring to a higher qualification, the fifty-two students all bought into the achievement ideology. This attitude was reflected in how they evaluate Hong Kong as a place for people's development and how they explain one's success in Hong Kong. When asked "who are successful in Hong Kong and what makes them successful?" some students cited their parents or friends, but most cited a Hong Kong tycoon—Ka-Shing Lee (who was listed as one of the top ten richest people in the world, at least over the last decade)—and some famous public figures, including the current chief executive and senior secretaries in the government. Despite this slight variation in the people the students cited, their reasons for doing so were more or less the same: those people were successful because they were all self-made individuals who started from scratch and made their way all by themselves.

And when asked why these people could succeed, most students invariably referred to three individual characteristics: talent, capability, and diligence. In short, all fifty-two community college students embraced the Hong Kong dream: a common belief shared by most Hong Kong people that Hong Kong is a land of opportunities, and everyone can succeed if she or he is talented and diligent; that is, they endorse the meritocratic principle in explaining success, success being equal to a combination of talent and effort.

In embracing an achievement ideology and having a strong belief in the meritocratic principle, the students saw it necessary for an education system to play the roles of differentiation, allocation, and selection; the following quotations are typical examples of their views on the role of education in Hong Kong:

> "Education is a device differentiating talented or hardworking people from the rest."
> "Education is to allocate students to different jobs."
> "Education is to get rid of bad students or those who don't like studying."

The students believed that the education system in Hong Kong is basically fair and just in this process of differentiation, allocation, and selection, especially when the process is enhanced through a series of public examinations applying the same standards openly to everyone and cheating was seriously guarded against. However, at the same time, in their evaluation of the education system, students expressed a taste of bitterness or anger. While endorsing that education should play the roles of differentiation, allocation, and selection, these students felt that the education system in Hong Kong is too cruel, as implied in the metaphors used in the following quotations:

> "Education is like a sieve, a tournament, a very crude tournament with only very few winners and a lot of losers."
> "Education determines the life and death of students although it is efficient for administrators to classify, rank, or label students."
> "Education is a means to order people: we are constantly ranked. Schools of different bandings are ranked in a league table; students in the same school are allocated to elite class and non-elite classes; and students in the same class are still further ranked every semester."

Despite considering social competition through education to be cruel, all fifty-two students were willing to play by these rules: they used a socially acceptable institutional means, albeit an untraditional one, to achieve a goal commonly seen as socially desirable. In doing so, the students adopted the mainstream perspective to evaluate themselves and their classmates as students. This led them to formulate some self-defeating views of themselves, as the following quotations show:

> "I am not successful. Successful students could get into a very selective department at university. If it is not difficult but easy to get into a department, then that student is not that successful."
> "If I am good, I would not have been here."
> "Studying here means that I am not capable."
> "Successful students won't take this route to university."

Some students mentioned that whether they could be seen as successful or not depended on the definition of "successful student." They were ambivalent about how to judge themselves. But, all fifty-two students were certain that they were losers in the existing education system. We could argue that perhaps, because these students do not want to be seen as bad losers, they did not want to blame the system (at least in the presence of the researcher) in explaining their failures; rather, they lay the blame on themselves. Yet, what could not be denied was that their self-critical view of themselves revealed their acceptance of the rules of the system for deciding winners and losers, and thus of its standards for judging each contender. Their acceptance became particularly obvious in how they evaluated their classmates. Without exception, all fifty-two students referred to performances at public examinations as major yardsticks to evaluate their classmates. Using Bourdieu's (1984) phrasing, the students were using the mainstream standards to judge themselves as well as other students; therefore, they felt ashamed of their academic failure. This echoes Sayer's (2005) insights: a particular feeling about a given system of inequality or injustice reflects a specific attitude toward the system. For example, Willis's (1977) "working-class lads" or MacLeod's (2004) "Hallway Hangers" did not feel shameful about their so-called academic failure because from the start they did not buy into the achievement ideology. In contrast, the community college students felt so shameful about their failure precisely because they believed so much in the achievement ideology but failed to live up to that standard (failing the rather fair and just public examinations).[10] In other words, those students who do not accept the achievement ideology would probably choose to drop out when they could not stay on and might not choose the option of doing an associate degree in a community college; and perhaps they would not feel ashamed of their so-called academic failure. In short, despite their academic failures, all fifty-two students of the qualitative study did not challenge the education system; rather, they internalized the blame.

MIDDLE-CLASS LOSERS

The seventeen middle-class community college students realized that they were more advantaged than most other students in the education system because of their relatively comfortable family backgrounds. They all described in detail what their parents had expected of them and how they used various kinds of resources for them at each stage of their educational careers. In order to give them a head start, in many cases the parents had worked the education system—the POAS—such as moving to a better catchment area[11] or using relevant social connections to get them into an elite primary school. And, without exception, all their parents provided them with academic assistance (sending them to cram schools and/or employing private tutors) and sent them to extracurricular activities that counted in the system (such as learning to play various musical instruments, especially piano) so as to work the SSPAS in the hope that the students would get into an elite secondary school. Indeed, nearly all of them studied in elite primary schools; and all except five studied in elite secondary schools. Failing to pass the HKCEE or HKALE examinations, the seventeen middle-class students got their parents' support in taking up a newly available, though expensive, option—taking an associate degree at this community college—in the hope that they would eventually receive a university education. And in eight cases, it was their parents, rather than the students themselves, who chose this newly available option. In short, the parents of the seventeen middle-class students here were as well informed about how to work the education system and were strategic in using various kinds of resources for their children's education, as are many other middle-class parents (e.g., Laureau 2000; Ball 2003; Devine 2004).

What the parents of seventeen students did for them actually echoed what I reported on the strategies of Hong Kong middle-class parents for their children's education in a previous study (Wong 2007). But there were two major differences between the middle-class community college students here and the children of the middle-class respondents in my previous study: first, the former failed to get into a local university despite their parents' strategies for their education, whereas quite a number of the latter succeeded; second, community college was an option for the former but it was not for most of the latter because they completed their formal education long before the year 2000.

Feeling Ashamed: Deviating from the Norm

Although by design over 80 percent of Hong Kong students of the relevant age are doomed to fail to get a place in a local university, none of the seventeen middle-class students referred to this structural design. As discussed above, they believed that the public examinations were more or less fair, and that the most important factors leading to one's success were individual talent and effort. So, in explaining their academic failures, what all these students referred to were their laziness and academic inadequacy. However, in reality, many of them did work very hard. This fact, then, reinforced their view that perhaps they were lazy, but the major reason for their failure was that they were too academically inadequate to pass the required public examinations.

What made them feel particularly ashamed was the fact that they failed in spite of what their parents did for them. As just described above, they knew very well that their parents were strategic about their education and had done a lot to promote their educational success. Given these efforts, in their accounts they expressed a particularly strong sense of shame about their academic inadequacy. What strengthened their feelings of shame was the fact that in their social circle they were one of the very few who failed to do well academically. And they felt very bad about deviating from their perceived norm, as Brenda expressed:[12]

> All uncles and aunts from my mother's side and my mother graduated from the same (elite) secondary school as mine. My sister and I also studied there....They all got into university. I am the only one who fails to do it....Students from my school can't be bad....All my secondary-school classmates did so well at HKCEE and I was the only one who did it so poorly! I was the only one in my class who failed to stay on to do HKALE. I feel really bad about it!...Somehow, I feel ashamed whenever classmates here ask me which secondary school I went to. I don't want to tell them. I don't want to see their surprised looks: how come students from my secondary school would end up in this community college?

As Brenda provided rather detailed information in her comparisons commenting on her academic ability, let me use her case for further elaboration. In making a judgment about her academic ability, Brenda referred to three major groups for comparison: first, her closest family members (her mother and elder sister); second, her peers (especially her secondary-school classmates); and third, her relatives (especially her cousins). In comparing herself with her academically capable mother and elder sister, she highlighted changes in the education system. Brenda believed that the education system was previously more competitive and selective than it is currently, and that it was more difficult for her mother or elder sister to stay on to do HKALE than for her to do the same. Despite that, the fact that her mother and elder sister succeeded whereas she failed made her feel very strongly that she was academically inadequate.

It is suggested that working-class children have low educational aspirations partly because they lack role models (e.g., MacLeod 2004). In stark contrast, the seventeen middle-class students here perhaps have too many role models. Their role models probably played a part in leading them to have high educational aspirations. But, seemingly at this stage, their role models are one major source of the students' pressure and negative feeling about their academic adequacy.

What made this negative feeling even stronger was Brenda's comparison of herself with her secondary-school classmates. Studying in the same class of the same elite secondary school where the majority of its students could get into a local university, Brenda was one of the very few who failed to stay on to do HKALE. Before taking the HKCEE, Brenda believed that she was entitled to stay in the same "habitus," in Bourdieu's (1984) words, as her secondary school classmates; but then she was dislocated, so to speak, to a community college. Brenda and some other students who were also graduates of elite schools explained that they were under constant pressure throughout their secondary-school years: they were continuously compared, day after day, term after term, year after year, with a group of very capable peers, and they rarely had a sense of achievement there. This echoes local journalism reports that whereas problematic students in low-end schools usually have behavioral problems, their counterparts in elite schools usually have emotional and psychological difficulties (e.g., Mingpao 2007).

In stark contrast, when studying at a community college, those elite-school students actually had a sense of achievement and superiority. That is, compared with some of her community college classmates—those ordinary-school students—Brenda somehow felt superior. But, this did not boost her confidence; as Brenda noted, she felt superior not because she was good but just because her present reference group was so incapable. And, Brenda was not at ease mingling with them, telling me that those ordinary-school students, her current classmates, were not her "people." In other words, her dislocation posed a challenge to Brenda's sense of belonging. And, in coping with this challenge, Brenda, as well as some elite-school students, sought to distinguish herself from her community college peers by stressing the differences between elite-school students and ordinary-school students, such as their abilities, language skills, and general attitudes. Put simply, a newly gained sense of superiority did not make Brenda feel better about herself; rather, it served to remind her that she was dislocated, and together with her dislocation it served to pose a challenge to her sense of belonging.

Brenda's negative feeling was further reinforced by her comparison with her relatives during family gatherings. In particular, Brenda felt the pressure of being compared with her cousins: all her cousins were doing a bachelor's degree in a local university. Brenda highlighted to me: "I hate those gatherings! I am ashamed of being asked constantly what an associate degree is and what the degree will lead me to.... I don't want my mother to lose face! But I guess I already did."

In a sense, family gatherings are taken as battlefields for status competition; Brenda felt that because of her academic failure and dislocation, her mother was losing in this competition. Taking all these comparisons together, wherever she was (at home, at community college, or in family gatherings), Brenda was constantly reminded that she was deviating from the norm; and, these reminders were mutually reinforcing strengthening Brenda's feelings of shame about her academic inadequacy.

Feeling Guilty: Letting The Parents Down

Understanding very well that their parents had such high expectations of them and had planned and done so much for them, these students not only felt ashamed of their academic failure but also felt guilty about letting their parents down. Some even highlighted that they had been disappointing their parents throughout their educational careers, as Ann recalled.

> My mum sent me to an elite primary school. I did quite well only at the primary level; that was why I could get into an elite secondary school....I didn't do well since secondary form one; I wasn't ranked top there....My mum had been anxious about my academic performance, sending me to cram schools and employing private tutors for me....But what she did for me was fruitless. I didn't do any better; I was still ranked quite low....I knew my mum was angry and deeply disappointed with me, year after year. And, finally I failed HKCEE....It was my mum who suggested to me that I should try community college....I don't think my mum now would have hope for me any more because I have disappointed her so many times.

Like Ann, Cindy also felt guilty about failing to live up to her parents' expectations of her. Cindy somehow felt that her parents were just wasting their resources on her, as she elaborated:

> My parents spent a lot of money on my education....They forced me to learn the piano. I don't like it. But my parents insisted that I had to take the lessons because they thought that would be good for my future....They believed that this would increase my chances of getting accepted to an elite secondary school and thus passing HKCEE....I think they are just wasting their money.

In response to their parents' high expectations of them, the seventeen middle-class children did try hard in order not to let down their parents; but apparently, however hard they tried, they still failed to achieve what their parents had expected of them. In other words, all the students have repeatedly gone through the following cycle: doing not so well in one test/examination and thus disappointing their parents, then parents' giving them encouragement and doing something for their academic performance and students trying harder, and students' doing not so well in the following test/examination and thus disappointing their parents again. This seemingly endless cycle of getting parental encouragement and feeling their parents' disappointment somehow plays a role in reinforcing the students' sense of shame and guilt: their constant failing to live up to their parents' expectations not only reinforces their feelings of shame but also makes them feel guilty about disappointing their parents on a regular basis. Their sense of guilt echoes the finding of a longitudinal study in the U.K. on middle-class children: despite their parents' strategies for them, middle-class adult children do not do particularly well; they feel guilty about wasting their parents' investments in them (Power et al. 2003).

Yet there seems a subtle difference in this sense of guilt between those students whose parents chose the option of community college for them and those who chose this option for themselves. Most of the former (such as Alex, Ann, Cindy, Doris, and Larry) somehow felt that whatever route they took, they just could not get into a local university. Given that the option of community college is so expensive, these students felt that, but for their previous failures in the public examinations, their parents would not have wasted so much resources to opt for such an expensive alternative to support them staying on in education. Their guilt is more about their previous failures that led to the current consequence.

In contrast, the guilt of those who chose this option for themselves is about both: their previous failures and their decision of doing an associate degree. Given the newness of community college, most of them (such as Amy, Daisy, David, Debbie, Irene, Julie, and Nancy), as with many community-college students, were concerned that they might not get transferred to a local university after completing their associate degree programs. Since they made such a decision and asked their parents to support that decision, they somehow felt that they were accountable to their parents; they were anxious about the possibility that they had to disappoint their parents again. Perhaps, this difference somehow reflects that these two groups of students had rather dissimilar educational aspirations. But, the latter group of students were concerned with convincing their parents that their decision was justified and their concern somehow reinforced their feelings of guilt; in contrast, there was also a sense of anger in their feelings of guilt for the former group: they were somehow angry with their parents for making that decision for them.

Feeling Agonized: Imagining a Different Outcome

Feeling academically inadequate, all seventeen students blamed themselves for their academic failures and also for letting down their parents. However, at times, they also blamed their parents for their academic failures: they sort of imagined that if their parents had used different strategies for them, they would not have ended up in a community college. Some students somehow felt that their parents were perhaps being counterproductive at times, giving them too much pressure. For example, both Ann and Cindy, despite feeling so guilty about disappointing their parents, questioned whether their parents had to be so pushy. Alex and Fred expressed a similar doubt toward their parents' pushiness. As Alex articulated, in freeing him from all kinds of obligations or worries, and asking him to focus only on his academic work, his father was giving him not assistance but great pressure.

> I told my father that I wanted to gain some work experience and asked him for permission to take up a summer job.... But, he never wants me to take up any job, even a part-time one, or other voluntary activities but asks me to just focus on my studies. He said that I would have plenty of opportunities to work later on and that I should just devote all my time and energy to my studies.... But he never understands that I need breaks and I can't study all the time.

This echoes Devine's (2004) speculation: middle-class parents' strategies could be counterproductive, placing too much pressure on their children, leading them to do more poorly than they would otherwise have done without such pressure (cf. Laureau 2000). Indeed, how they should manage their time was a common topic over which seventeen students and their parents often argued and disagreed. In addition to blaming their parents for being too pushy, some of these students wondered whether their parents had chosen a wrong strategy for them. For instance, both Ann and Brenda, while feeling so ashamed of their academic performance, were somehow angry about their mothers' refusal to sending them abroad right after they failed HKCEE; that option, they believed, would have been a better strategy than sending them to this community college.

Whereas some students found their parents too pushy, others felt that their parents were too carefree. Knowing that many middle-class parents were very pushy (cf. Laureau 2002), Keith and Larry criticized their parents for being "atypical" middle-class parents, and considered that their parents should have been more strategic or should have done more for them. In other words, despite realizing that their parents had done a lot for their education, they were still angry with their parents, questioning why they did not do more or did not do something different for them, as in the case of Keith.

> I studied in an elite primary school; I got there because my mother was an alumna and this gave me some points at the POAS....I was then allocated through the SSPAS to a band-five secondary school.[13] I asked my mum if she could do anything about it. But she said: "It is okay to have a place to study and what the fuss are you making?"...A normal middle-class mother would do her best to get her child to a good school. But my mum didn't. She didn't do anything for me....She is just an atypical middle-class mother!...I wished my parents had been as pushy as other middle-class parents and had done more for me....If my mother had got me into an elite secondary school, I would not have failed HKCEE and would not have studied here.

Similarly, despite the fact that his parents used their social connections to get him out of a less desirable into a more desirable secondary school, and despite the fact that his parents let him retake HKCEE three times, Larry was still dissatisfied with the fact that his parents did not push him even more, so that he would have had clearer goals earlier on.

> My parents suggested that I join Yi-Jin programme after I failed HKCEE (the third time). And then they supported me here doing a pre-associate degree and then an associate degree....I didn't do well at school....Looking back, I think, I didn't sense I was "at risk"; I just spent all my time playing TV games and hanging around. My parents discussed with me about my educational plans. But they never pushed me....I wished my parents had pushed me more and planned more for me so that I could have had clearer goals and would have understood the importance of hardworking earlier on. And I would not have wasted so much time finding my way.

What the anger of these students revealed was that their relationships with their parents were quite strained at times. Throughout the process of negotiating or fighting, so to speak, with their parents, seventeen students mentioned that their parents at times voiced their dissatisfaction with their not working hard enough. In many cases, their parents actually warned them that they should learn from their past failures and work harder at community college.

Their parents' remarks about them being lazy seem to have an effect on them. On the one hand, this reinforced the students' feelings of shame about their previous academic failures and their feelings of guilt about letting their parents down, and thus made them blame themselves even more for their failures. However, on the other hand, some students felt that in making this remark their parents did not seem to appreciate that they had worked hard before; this made the students angry and thus place some of their blame on their parents for their failures.

Signaling to Their Parents for More Effective Educational Strategies or Different Options

In explaining their academic failures, these students immediately blamed themselves, feeling ashamed of being academically inadequate and also guilty about disappointing their parents; yet at the same time, they somehow blamed their parents, feeling angry with them and imagining that if their parents had done more or differently for them, they would not have ended up studying in a community college. In brief, feeling frustrated about their academic failures, these students were ambivalent and did not know where they should lay the blame. Their feelings of shame could be damaging to their confidence in their academic ability. Their feelings of guilt could further reinforce their sense of academic inadequacy. And, their feelings of agony could strain parent-child relationships. In short, these feelings are their expressions of their frustrations regarding the education system and their academic setbacks; and in one way or another, these feelings could adversely affect these students' academic performance.

Nevertheless, these feelings, however destructive they might seem, could serve some role in parent-child negotiations regarding educational options. Just as Ball, Maguire, and Macrae (2000) argue that the way secondary-school students make educational decisions is a rather messy process, instead of a rational one, likewise the way parents and children negotiate different educational/career options could also be seen as a complicated and emotionally charged process, rather than a series of straightforward and rational discussions. In negotiating with their parents, these seventeen middle-class students are communicating their desires not only through their texts but also through their emotions, of various kinds. In other words, students' feelings, however destructive they might seem, could serve as a signal for their parents to rethink or re-evaluate what they have done for the students' education, and then to opt for a more effective strategy for the students' education or for a totally different option. Indeed, some of their parents have plan Bs for them.

Two types of plan B could be identified. The first is another strategy for education: sending them to a degree program outside of Hong Kong. Having negotiated with their parents that they wanted to study abroad, Ann, Brenda, and Daisy said that finally their parents agreed with their views and were planning to send them abroad for a degree program in the United States the following year. This is in line with the finding that sending children to the West for higher education is quite a common strategy of middle-class parents in eastern Asia (cf. Waters 2006). In contrast to these students, Doris's mother considered a degree from China more worthwhile than a Western degree in Hong Kong, and thus had already enrolled her in a degree program there for the next year. This is consistent with a recent report from the latest Hong Kong census that reported that the number of students getting a degree in China has been on the rise in the last five years (Hong Kong Census 2006).

The second type of plan B is a career strategy: getting them a relatively advantaged job. Larry said that his father was finally convinced that Larry was not an academic type and therefore would arrange for him to work as a junior agent in the coming year in the company where Larry's father was a managing director. Similarly, Julie made clear her desire to her parents to become a businesswoman; her parents not only supported her trip last summer to Taiwan to see if there were any opportunities to start a trading business there but also agreed to give Julie some start-up capital to run a small business later on. These two cases provide illustrations for Goldthorpe's (2000) speculation that when middle-class parents fail to secure their children a higher qualification, strategies for getting their children a relatively advantaged job would come into play.

While more effort is required to explore further what types of plan Bs that middle-class parents would and could offer their children in guarding them against downward mobility, the following also deserves more of our attention. To reiterate, community college is new to Hong Kong. In theory, academic results obtained at a community college should be one major consideration in students' applications for transfer to any local degree program. But in reality, as many community college students and teachers have noticed, given the newness of community college, especially when there is no governmental regulation of its academic standards, local universities do not know how to make sense of the academic results of community college students.[14] And therefore, in selecting community college students, local universities do not pay much attention to their academic results and still refer to earlier results of public examinations, especially HKALE; they also take account whether students are graduates of elite secondary schools. Although so far only 3 percent of community college students have successfully transferred to local degree programs, six of seventeen students here (over 35%!) were offered a place in a local university for the year of 2006–2007. This overrepresentation of middle-class students in successful transferrals has in part to do with the small size of this study, for every student in this small sample is counted as 6 percent. And this result also has in part to do with a self-selection bias; the study might somehow attract those students who have a higher chance of getting transferred.

But my point here is this: middle-class students might well be considered to be losers at this stage, failing to get into a local university through HKALE; yet, as most of them are graduates of elite secondary schools, they might still be advantaged vis-à-vis their working-class counterparts in using community college as a springboard to a local degree program. In other words, the class differentials in taking community college as a route to a local university would be an important area for further examination in explaining educational inequality.

CONCLUDING REMARKS

What I sought to do in this chapter was to explore what we could learn from seventeen so-called middle-class losers. As expected, their parents were, and still are, strategic about their education. What their parents did in promoting the educational success of these students did not differ from what many other middle-class parents in Hong Kong have been doing. But, because of government policies—fewer than 20 percent of students in the relevant age group being allocated a place in a local university—it was not surprising that these students' parents, however strategic they were, failed to secure them places. Mobility researchers have found that given a level of academic ability, middle-class students have higher chances than their working-class counterparts of staying longer in education, getting a relatively advantaged job, and ultimately staying in the middle class (e.g., Savage and Egerton 1997; Marshall et al. 1997), and have speculated that that is because middle-class parents will use more effective strategies for their children when their earlier strategiesfail.

However, what is missing here is the link between middle-class students' failing at one stage and succeeding in staying at another. The accounts of seventeen middle-class students here somehow could provide such a link. Their emotions serve as a mechanism through which the students communicate their frustration and different desires to their parents, and thus signal to their parents that they should opt for other or more effective strategies. Indeed, some of the parents planned to enable their children to obtain a higher qualification outside of Hong Kong, while others planned to get them a relatively advantaged first job. In other words, it is still too early to judge whether seventeen middle-class students, as well as other community college students of middle-class origin, are really losers: even failing to get transferred to a local university, they might still have good chances of getting a relatively advantaged qualification (outside of Hong Kong) and thus a middle-class job later on; in short, they still have good chances of avoiding a relatively disadvantaged job.

In explaining class differentials in educational attainment, sociologists have drawn on a number of different insights and referred to class differences in parental resources of various kinds: children's upbringing (or habitus), children's educational aspirations/motivation, children's perceived educational opportunities (including perceived risk in pursuing different educational options), and effectiveness of parental strategies for securing children a higher qualification. This exploratory study of seventeen middle-class students is consistent with all these explanations: their parents have an abundance of resources and are strategic in promoting their children's educational success, while the students have high educational aspirations. But, what this exploratory study adds is that the emotional aspects of class and social mobility, in addition to the material or cultural factors, are equally important for understanding educational inequality and thus social inequality.

Just as the working class has hidden injuries of class (Sennett and Cobb 1972) and some working-class "winners" are ambivalent, feeling guilty about leaving their families behind (Jackson and Marsden 1962), so the middle-class "losers" here are tremendously ashamed of themselves, struggling to remain in a relatively advantaged class. This suggests that as long as the society remains highly stratified or unequal, even with some kind of justification (if not a myth) that promises social mobility, emotions accompanying class positions and various types of social mobility seem more negative than positive. In other words, in an unequal system, perhaps not many people are genuine winners, at least in emotional terms.[15]

What this exploratory study also suggests is that the emotional aspects could somehow provide an additional, if not new, mechanism for explaining class differentials in educational attainment. This chapter focused on the middle class: seventeen middle-class students. But, as mentioned at the outset, their working-class counterparts in the same qualitative study also feel ashamed of their academic failures. What is not reported in this chapter are working-class students' feelings of guilt and agony, and the class differences in expressing these emotions. In future research,I shall examine how middle-class and working-class students differ in expressing their shame, guilt, and anger, and thus explore further the roles of these feelings for different classes in educational inequality.

Given the small number of cases in this exploratory study, my results should be treated as tentative and more work is needed. At least three dimensions need to be explored further. The first is the gender dimension; all students feel so ashamed of their academic failures, yet apparently, female students compared to their male counterparts express guilt more than anger, whereas male students express anger more than guilt. More work is required to investigate how the two genders differ in expressing their shame, guilt, and anger. The second dimension is the impact of students' emotions on their academic performance. As suggested above, these feelings might affect adversely students' academic performance, and so it might be worth examining the respective impacts of shame, guilt, and anger on students' actual academic performance. And the third dimension is parents. In reporting the process of negotiation between parents and children, I focus on one side of the story: children. An examination of the other side—parents and their emotions—would probably provide further insights into the mechanisms operating through the emotions that lead to the observed educational inequality. That would provide a more comprehensive picture of parent-child negotiations and a better understanding of the roles of their respective emotions in their negotiations. This, in turn, would shed light on the emotional aspects—an underexplored area—of understanding the observed class gap in educational attainment.

Notes

1. A number of debates over class go on, such as how the concept of class should be defined, operationalized, or measured; how class should be approached; and whether the concept of class, compared with race and gender, is still relevant in the study of social inequality in general and educational inequality in particular, especially in the case of the United States (Van Galen and Noblit 2007). See Crompton (1998) and Savage (2000) for a useful summary and review.

2. In this chapter, I take class as a relational concept, in that the middle class and the working class refer to the relatively advantaged and the relatively disadvantaged, respectively.

3. The syllabus of each subject for HKCEE is covered in secondary forms four and five.

4. The syllabus of each subject for HKALE is covered in secondary forms six and seven.

5. But in reality, community colleges are accused to paying no attention to those minimum entry requirements and caring only about the number of students that they could recruit (e.g., Mingpao 2007).

6. For example, one community college charged HK $50,000 a year for the year 2005–2006, and announced in late 2006 that they would increase the tuition fee to HK $70,000 for the year 2006–2007, and to HK $80,000 for the year 2007–2008 (Mingpao 2006).

7. I contacted students from the first semester in early February 2006, after they obtained their examination results for the semester, and I interviewed them between mid-February and late March 2006. As I left for Japan for a new position in mid-June 2006, I contacted students from the second semester on June 1, 2006 and interviewed them between June 3 and June 10, 2006.

8. Refer to Erikson and Goldthorpe (1992: 265–266) for the two criteria of dominance: those of work time and work position. The first is that employment dominates nonemployment and full-time employment dominates part-time. The second is that in references to the hierarchical dimension of the scheme, a higher level employment should dominate a lower-level one.

9. As I take the middle class as a relatively advantaged class background, the middle class in this chapter is used in a broad sense of the Goldthorpe class scheme; that is, in addition to classes I and II, I also include class IIIa and class IVa. Like

many industrial-capitalist societies, professional, managerial, and administrative jobs (classes I and II) are more advantaged than other jobs. A clerical job (class IIIa) was relatively advantaged in the 1960s and 1970s, and equivalent to an administrative job nowadays and thus remained as a relatively advantaged class origin in the Hong Kong of the 1990s and 2000s. Running a small business is more advantaged than most of the self-employed in Hong Kong. And, as I argued elsewhere (Wong 2004), in Hong Kong running a small business (class IVa) is one major pathway to becoming a manager.

10. I do not mean to argue that buying into the achievement ideology would definitely lead those who fail to live up to the ideology to feel ashamed. But, rather, a person's feeling of shame could be used to infer that the person buys into the achievement ideology.

11. Some students also mentioned that their parents used faked addresses in working the POAS in order to get registered in a so-called good catchment area.

12. The names of students in this chapter are fictitious.

13. Secondary schools in Hong Kong were classified into five bandings according to students' academic performances; students of band-five schools were generally labeled as "garbage" students. The Education Department somehow believes that this label would vanish with the change of this five-banding system into a three-banding one (e.g., Sweeting 2004).

14. Local universities also anticipate that community colleges might inflate their students' grades in order to help their students get transferred, and thus increase the colleges' rates of transferral.

15. In reporting some negative feelings of so-called winners of the education system in her study in the United States, Brantlinger (2007:247) argues that, given the existing capitalist system and social class relations, "frustration, anger, and violence toward others and self are endemic to winners and losers in the hierarchical forms of schooling"; she even concludes that no one is a winner in this system.

9

The Afterlife of NEETs

Karen Robson

In the last two to three years, the acronym NEET, for "not in education, employment, or training," has cropped up in policy discussions surrounding young people's transition from school to work, particularly in the United Kingdom. This new category of young people refers to those who are not just *economically* inactive but also seemingly completely inactive, occupying an unconstructive (and potentially threatening) position on the social topography.

The NEET acronym became popular in political discourse after publication of the Social Exclusion Unit's report in 1999, wherein the group was defined. Shortly thereafter, this became the term used by civil servants and politicians to discuss this subgroup of young people. In 2005, a report from the U.K. Department for Education and Skills shed further publicity on the topic (DFES 2005), indicating that numbers of NEETs in the U.K. remained "stubbornly" at 10 percent over the previous decade. The group made further news when a report released by the Prince's Trust (2007) gave figures about the costs of NEETs to society, including the potential social-welfare benefits that would be paid out over a lifetime.

Viewing NEETs solely as a drain on society, however, interprets NEET status as an active choice that young people are making about their lives—a "career choice" of sorts. A sociological perspective (and decades of social mobility and stratification research), however, recognizes its structural roots in society and ascribed characteristics, like race, gender, and class, all of which interplay to determine life chances. As Colley and Hodkinson (2001:345) argue, there is little to be gained by "locating the causes of non-participation (solely) within individuals and their personal deficits." Similarly, Yates and Payne (2006:329) argue that NEET as a concept itself is problematic, in that it defines young people by "what they are not" instead of considering that these young people come from varied difficulties and situations.

AN OVERVIEW OF THE LITERATURE

It should be mentioned that the category of NEET has virtually usurped discussions of "youth unemployment" in the U.K. literature prior to the late-1990s examined "early school leaving" and "youth unemployment," but for the most part these problems have been collapsed into a larger category of disengaged youth—that is, NEETs.

The Correlates of Being NEET

In the past few decades, the transition between school and work has become increasingly diversified, such that it is no longer a standardized experience. As well as becoming prolonged (i.e., extended periods spent in education), the school-to-work transition is characterized by a remarkable person-specific trajectory. As social contexts change, each cohort experiences different sets of obstacles and opportunities that shape individuals' futures (Bynner and Parsons 2002). Other researchers have referred to this de-standardized process as "yo-yo" transitions (EGISR 2001; Walther et al. 2002), whereby the prolonged transition from youth to adulthood is fragmented into "uncertain perspectives," requiring young people to make individual decisions about their futures (as opposed to previous generations, which had more homogeneous status passages), and these decisions are also of increased importance to their futures.

Although research is not the focus of this chapter, it should be noted that a body of work has examined the factors associated with becoming NEET. There is a common assumption in the U.K., particular in policy arenas, that while NEETs come from diverse backgrounds, they share "low levels of aspiration and little motivation" (Popham 2003:8). However, Bynner, Joshi, and Tstatsas (2000) and Bynner and Parsons (2002) have identified several risk factors of becoming NEET in the U.K. Using data from two British birth cohorts (the National Child Development Study of 1958 and the British Cohort Study of 1970), they have found that family socioeconomic background (i.e., class), parental education, parental interest in the child's education, area of residence, and the child's educational attainment were all strong predictors of later-life NEET status. Additionally, research undertaken by the U.K. Department for Education and Skills (now the Department for Children, Schools, and Families) found ten factors associated with being NEET: no educational qualifications, school exclusion, previous truancy, low skill occupation of parents, living in a household where neither parent worked full time, being a teen parent, living outside the family home, having a health problem or disability, or having parents living in rented accommodation (DCSF undated:7). Clearly these ten factors point to young people who have had negative experiences in their early education experience and have come from lower socioeconomic backgrounds.

In terms of later-life outcomes associated with being NEET, there is fairly little published British research. Through analysis of British birth cohort data, Bynner and Parsons (2002) found that the later-life consequences of NEET varied according the sex. For males, the main consequences were poor labor-market experiences. For females, however, the vast majority of whom were teenage mothers, negative mental health outcomes (depression and low self-esteem) were also observed.

NEET in an International Perspective

The NEET phenomenon has drawn research and policy interest not only in the U.K. but also in Japan (Inui 2005; Yuji 2005) and to some extent, by European policymakers (Walther and Pohl, 2005).[1] As well, research in Sweden by Franzen and Kassman (2005) has found that economic inactivity in young adults (early twenties) was strongly associated with economic inactivity seven years later, and was particularly strong for immigrants and those with low levels of education. The authors argue that early inactivity is the first step in a marginalization process.

Of particular relevance to the current study is the work of Walther and Pohl, who examined NEETs in a European context, using European data sources, particularly the European Labour Force Survey database. They note that there are no reliable data on this group of young people, as they are often placed into the broader "economically inactive" category. This is problematic because this latter group also includes those with domestic responsibilities and those who are in mandatory national service. To add to the complexity, many definitions of "economic inactivity" include those who are in full-time education (Eurostat 2004).

Walther and Pohl (2005) divided countries into very high, high, medium, and low levels of NEET. The U.K., Poland, and Spain were categorized as high, with rates between 6 and 10 percent, while medium rates (between 3 and 6%) were found in Finland, Austria, Greece, Slovakia, and Italy. Denmark and Slovenia had low rates—less than 3 percent. The authors examined national policies that contributed to the NEET rates in each country, finding that in countries with very high and high NEET rates, ineligibility for benefits and a feeling of abandonment, as well as the presence of an informal economy and a lack of trust in government employment services, were the driving forces behind this phenomenon.

Other authors have found that the persistence of being in NEET status in Organization for Economic Co-operation and Development (OECD) countries was particularly strong in Italy and Greece (Quintini, Martin, and Martin 2007) and that low educational attainment was strongly associated with NEET status.[2]

THEORETICAL FRAMEWORK

Forms of Capital

In a similar vein to the work on NEETs conducted by Bynner and associates (Bynner 2005; Bynner and Parsons 2002; Bynner et al. 2000), the route to adulthood is conceptualized here as one during which various investments are turned into forms of capital. Bynner (2005) adopts Côté's (1996) idea of "identity capital," whereby individuals succeed (or do not succeed) in the labor market owing to their stocks of educational, social, and psychological characteristics and resources. In this particular analysis, the forms of capital as defined by Bourdieu (1986) are the focus, particularly economic and social capital. According to Bourdieu, it is the possession of these forms of capital (and their combinations) that defines a person's place on the social topography.

There are various mechanisms that can hinder the acquisition of the forms of capital, and NEET status is understood here as a personal characteristic that acts to inhibit further acquisition of economic and social capital. Of course, it is recognized that other factors play a role in getting a young person to the NEET status in the first place. According to previous literature, young people in the U.K. come disproportionately from disadvantaged families, and therefore have hampered economic and social capital "stocks" from the outset. But the objective in this chapter is to examine whether NEET status impacts not only later-life economic correlates (to which previous research has already pointed) but also the social domain. In a similar vein, Raffo and Reeves (2000), in particular, theorize about the role of social capital in the social exclusion of young people in their transition from school to work. Through qualitative research on marginalized British youth, these researchers have provided evidence of how limited or culturally inappropriate social resources limit the later-life chances of at-risk young people.

Cross-National Comparisons

A popular way of contextualizing country differences is to use Esping-Andersen's (1999) framework, which groups country regimes according to their type of welfare capitalism. As cross-national (social) research has grown over the last decade, primarily owing to the increased availability of large-scale cross-national data sets, a growing number of alternative frameworks are being suggested to account for country differences that emerge in the data. While the Esping-Andersen framework may be the most widely used, much cross-national research has found that country differences do not fit so neatly into the regime types he described (for an overview, see Bambra 2007). It is of great importance that any framework used to interpret country differences takes the culture, history, and political context of those countries into consideration, as the differences that young people experience from country to country surely are driven by a variety of conditions.

An interesting variant on regime theory offered by Walther and associates (Walther 2006; Pohl and Walther 2007) is of particular relevance to the topic of this chapter. Walther and associates suggest a typology that groups countries into "youth transition regimes" that take the economic, institutional, and cultural specificities of young people's school-to-work transitions into account. Walther and associates start first with Gallie and Paugam's (2000) modification of the Esping-Andersen model to make the model more conducive to studying unemployment in Europe. The four different transition regimes and their characteristics are displayed in table 9.1.

It should be noted that the countries in table 9.1 essentially break into the same groupings as in the Esping-Andersen framework, but the reasoning for their grouping is much more relevant to the subject matter addressed here. The column labeled "school" breaks the regimes into "selective" and:"not selective." "Not selective" here refers to the extent of a fairly standardized delivery of a comprehensive curriculum until the end of compulsory schooling, and it characterizes three of the four regime types. It is only in the employment-centered regime that schooling is classified as selective, which serves to "allocate the younger generation occupational careers and social positions in different segments" (Walther 2002).

In terms of "Training," each regime is characterized by its own specific training characteristics. "Flexible standards" are those that have been implemented by national frameworks but are flexible enough to allow for individualized routes; while in the employment-centered regimes, standardized training is highly formalized and regulated. In the liberal regime, "flexible, low standards" refers to a highly differentiated training phase, with a large number of vocational and academic options. For the subprotective regimes, "low standards" and "coverage of training" refer to vocational and training programs that are only weakly developed and are limited in delivery.

Each transition regime is also characterized by its social security, employment regime, and rates of female employment. Where young people are not entitled to social benefits, the family is expected to be the provider of social security. On the other end of this spectrum is the collective orientation toward social responsibility (i.e., universalistic regime). An open

Table 9.1 Transition regimes.

Regime Type	Countries	School	Training	Social Security	Employment Regime	Female Employment	Concept of Youth	Concept of Youth Employment	Concept of disadvantage	Focus of transition policies
Universalistic	Denmark, Sweden	Not selective	Flexible standards	State	Open, low risks	High	Personal development and citizenship	'not foreseen'	Mixed (individualized/structure-related)	Education, activation
Employment-Centered	Germany, France, Netherlands	Selective	Standardized	State/family	Closed, risks at the margins	Medium	Adaptation to social positions	Disadvantage (deficit model)	Individualized	(pre-)vocational training
Liberal	UK, Ireland	Not selective	Flexible, low-standards	State/family	Open, high risks	High	Early economic independence	Culture of dependency	Individualized	employability
Subprotective	Italy, Spain, Portugal	Not selective	Low standards and coverage	Family	Closed, high risks, informal work	Low	Without distinct status	Segmented labour market, lack of training	Structure-related	'some' status: work, education or training

Source: Walther 2006: 126.

employment regime with low risks is characterized by an extended public sector with broad access, while an open employment regime with high risks is one that is fluid with many access options, but also potentially precarious. Closed employment regimes are those which are highly regulated. In the case of the subprotective regime, much employment is also found in the informal sector as well.

The final four columns focus on the regimes' orientations toward youth and the resulting youth transition policies that are found in each. As indicated in table 9.1, each regime has a distinct concept of youth. In the universalistic regime, youth is regarded as a time for young people to development themselves as individuals and as citizens, while in the liberal regime, young people are expected to focus on carving out their own independence as a matter of priority. In the employment-centered regime, youth is considered a time of adapting to the social position, while in the subprotective regimes, this time does not hold any particular status. This idea of youth is associated with concepts of youth unemployment, ranging from "not foreseen" in the universalistic regime (i.e., young people who are not working are expected to be in training) to a deficit model (employment-centered regime) that regards youth unemployment as an indicator of some shortcoming (i.e., in training or preparation) of the individual. The culture of dependency approach in the liberal regime is associated with a focus on getting youth back into the labor market as quickly as possible, often with unreliable standards of quality in training and preparation. In the subprotective regime, lack of training and a segmented labor market fuel a high rate of youth unemployment. The concept of disadvantage in these regimes varies from blaming the individual (employment-centered and liberal) to the structure (subprotective), or a combination of both (universalistic).

How countries create policies that address youth- transition issues clearly arises from their various orientations, as addressed above (as well as others). In a general sense, universalistic regimes focus on education programs and the concept of supportive "activation"—that is, young people are entitled to a variety of entitlements that will train and prepare them for the labor market. The employment-centered model focuses on pre-vocational training to give young people the necessary skills required for entrance into the highly regulated workforce. In liberal regimes, the focus of transition policies is on overseeing job-search activity in order to maximize the employability of the individual, while in subprotective regimes the policies surround youth transitions, according to Walther (2006:129), "can be characterized by the discrepancy between comprehensive reform plans and the heritage of structural deficits in implementing these reforms." Clearly, these regime types overlook the details specific to every country in the desire to achieve parsimony; this is the case with any regime theory. It does, however, give a framework around which to build an understanding of how country differences impact NEET outcomes, while the findings in some countries should be expected to be rather similar.

RATIONALE OF CURRENT STUDY AND HYPOTHESES

The overview of the above literature points to a lack of understanding about how individuals become NEETs and the later-life outcomes associated with this labor-market status. While some U.K. researchers have been interested in these topics, the issue of measurement has been raised. A lack of consensus on what NEETs are and how they should be defined makes the results of the research difficult to compare. The work by Bynner and associates, while reflecting a longitudinal approach, can really only tell us about NEETs from certain birth cohorts. As the literature review argues, the transitions from school to work have increased in complexity, and the experiences of new cohorts of young people are certainly different from those born in earlier decades. A related concern is the prevalent focus on NEETs in the U.K. policy arena and the seeming lack of discussion about this group of young people in other countries. Is it the case that there are more NEETs in the U.K., or that being a NEET in the U.K. is more detrimental than in other countries?

The existence of longitudinal panel data from a variety of countries allows for cross-national comparisons of NEETs and their correlates. It is expected that NEET status will be particularly high in the U.K., and that the southern European countries (particularly Greece and Italy, as identified by Quintini et al. 2007) will also have high rates. Unfortunately, retrospective detailed information about the young person's family of origin is not available in the data set examined here, so the predictors of becoming a NEET cannot be properly examined. The focus here is, therefore, on later-life associations, which are directly observable in the data.

Transition regime theory suggests that different countries have different ways of dealing with youth transitions. It is hypothesized that the risk associated with recurrent NEET status would be highest in the subprotective countries, where there are fewer safety nets. In the liberal countries, it is expected that extended spells would be curtailed by policies designed to get young people back into the labor force. Universalistic nations should have the least problem with NEET recurrence. It is less clear how recurrent NEET status should be hypothesized to act under employment-centered regimes if the orientation toward unemployment is that NEET status lies within deficits of the individual.

In terms of economic-capital outcomes, given the varied orientations to benefits systems and the focus of blame on youth disadvantage, it is expected that NEET status would impact economic capital outcomes the most in the subprotective regimes (with the least protective forces or interventions in place), followed by the liberal and employment-centered regimes, and the least in the universalistic regimes. With regard to social-capital outcomes, the importance of the "informal" sector in the subprotective regimes suggests that NEET status may more greatly impact social-capital development in cultures where social networks are of greater importance to successful youth transitions.

DATA, METHODS, AND ANALYTIC STRATEGY

Data for the analyses come from the European Community Household Panel (ECHP), which is a harmonized sample survey organized and largely funded by Eurostat, covering most member countries of the European Union during its data collection phases (1994–2001). In each country, an initial sample of households was selected, with all adults in each selected household being interviewed. Respondents aged seventeen and over were interviewed (although in some cases, sixteen-year-olds were interviewed as well). Data were also collected about the children in each household. In each subsequent year, original sample members were re-interviewed, thus making it possible to study changes in individuals and their families over time.

Owing to the nature of the subsample of interest, in the analyses that follow the data are restricted to individuals who were between sixteen and twenty-four years old during the survey years. The countries included in the analyses reflect those subsamples of young people that were large enough to facilitate panel analysis of the predictors and outcomes of inactivity in the labor force over time (and, unfortunately, do not reflect any country illustrative of the universalistic regime). Although fifteen countries were included in the final years of the sample, the analyses here are limited to the U.K., France, Germany, Spain, Portugal, Italy, and Greece. In all countries apart from the U.K. and Germany, the sample was selected and first interviewed in 1994. In the U.K. and Germany, data from existing household panel surveys (the British Household Panel Study and the German Socioeconomic Panel, respectively) were transcribed into the common ECHP format so that they could be analyzed alongside the new surveys.

Not in Employment, Education, or Training:
Measurement Considerations

The main objective of this chapter is to identify and analyze the covariates of a particular form of economic inactivity. It should be noted that there is no agreed labor-market definition of NEET (in terms of measurement), neither within the U.K. nor internationally (Furlong 2006). As such, the measurement of economic inactivity in the way that it is intended for the NEET group is of core concern. Quentini, Martin, and Martin (2007) have also examined the NEET group within the ECHP, but they have included the unemployed among the economically inactive. According to the ILO and other sources, one of the criteria for being unemployed is that the respondent is actively seeking work. This runs contrary to the discourse around the NEET literature (and media hype) which in no uncertain terms labels this group as not looking for work.

It should be noted that the ECHP collected a variety of methods for recording economic activity. There are two general ways of assessing main economic activity: self-defined status, and the official International Labour Organisation (ILO) definition. Although there is high correlation between the measures, there is noticeable incongruence between self-reports of unemployment and ILO classification of unemployment. The official ILO definition of "unemployed" requires that the person be actively seeking work and be available to start a potential job within two weeks. This incongruency between self-definition and official measures in the ECHP has been reported by Richiardi (2002). One possible explanation for this discrepancy is social desirability, with people preferring to be viewed as unemployed rather than as inactive. For purposes of this chapter, the ILO definitions of labor market activity have been preferred, although exceptions have been made in the case of the U.K., where reporting systems were slightly different from those of other countries.

Individuals were classified as working if their ILO status was defined as currently working or normally working. The category of "training or education" was created for those whose ILO status was inactive but their self-reported status was "education or training" or "spec train scheme 15+ hrs." The unemployed were denoted by the ILO classification of unemployed, except in the case of the U.K., where it was measured by self-defined unemployed status and ILO as inactive (owing to the absence of an ILO-defined measure of unemployed in the data set). The final category of "inactive other" was created for all others who were inactive according to the ILO definition of inactive (including those who self-defined as unemployed), but were not in education or training. Owing to the slightly different coding scheme in the U.K., this last category was assigned to those who self-defined as "other inactive," which excluded those who were in education or employment for fewer than fifteen hours a week or in famil- care roles. People in compulsory national service were included in a separate category.

While the reporting differences for the U.K. versus other countries possibly call into question the direct comparability of the categories created here, it should be noticed that the inactive category here was created to be as conservative as possible—that is, to only include people who were most likely to fit the commonly understood definition of NEETS. The restrictions imposed here, particularly the elimination of "unemployed" young people from the analyses, allow the focus of the forthcoming analyses to be on the truly inactive segment of the youth population. The techniques described above left a sizable group of young people still to be analyzed. Table 9.2 displays the number of NEETs identified per year and by country. The minimum cell size observed here is 31 (France, in 2000), with rather large numbers (i.e., in excess of 200) observed in Italy. Table 9.3 reports the percentage of NEETs by the sixteen- to twenty-four-year-old age group, per country. The OECD has not collected official NEET figures until quite recently, so it is not possible to compare these figures with official numbers. It should be noted, however, that as expected, the U.K. rate is consistently the highest of all countries considered here.

Table 9.2 NEET observations per year, by country.

	France	Germany	UK	Italy	Greece	Spain	Portugal
1994	34	50	125	122	43	121	93
1995	100	75	129	231	85	152	104
1996	87	75	119	223	66	126	131
1997	52	68	109	175	52	91	93
1998	32	62	117	121	94	74	106
1999	32	56	111	118	112	50	95
2000	31	68	105	105	82	44	80
2001	35	58	107	101	68	57	64

Table 9.3 NEETs as a % of the 16–24 age group, by country.

	France	Germany	UK	Italy	Greece	Spain	Portugal
1994	0.016	0.032	0.098	0.042	0.028	0.041	0.052
1995	0.049	0.047	0.103	0.082	0.052	0.055	0.055
1996	0.044	0.049	0.093	0.081	0.042	0.048	0.069
1997	0.030	0.047	0.086	0.072	0.035	0.034	0.049
1998	0.024	0.044	0.098	0.055	0.070	0.032	0.058
1999	0.027	0.039	0.100	0.058	0.088	0.024	0.054
2000	0.023	0.049	0.097	0.056	0.067	0.023	0.049
2001	0.027	0.045	0.104	0.063	0.056	0.033	0.042

Control Variables

Gender was dummy-coded so that "male" was equal to 1. Household composition was measured using a modified variable that was already presented in the ECHP (sociological household typology) and reclassified into the following: young person living alone, couple without children, couple with at least one child, young person living with one's parents, and other households (to reflect the majority of household types these young people lived in at the time of the survey). As there were too few single parents in the sample to constitute an analyzable group, they were grouped into "other households." It should be noted that the survey contains no information about the households in which the young people grew up.

Outcomes of Interest

NEET status was examined to see how it influenced NEET status in successive years and how this differed by country. Thus, NEET status in $t+1$ and $t+2$ were examined in the forthcoming analyses. It was possible to examine successive years, but the sample size becomes much smaller and less comparable.

Economic-capital outcomes were measured by whether or not young people had low educational attainment and whether or not they were in households that were in the lowest quintile of household income. Low education was measured with a dichotomous indicator denoting the highest qualification, as the International Standard Classification of Education (ISCED) was level two or below. In all countries in the analysis, ISCED level two refers to the end of compulsory education. Individuals with qualifications higher than level two were coded zero. A variable measuring the quintile of household income was created separately for each country, which was equivalized by household size and standardized by the purchasing-power parity of each country.

Social-capital outcomes were measured using two indicators: whether or not the respondent was a member of a club, and how often the respondent met friends. Club membership was measured in the questionnaire by the question, "Are you a member of any club, such as a sport or entertainment club, a local or neighborhood group, a party, etc.?" to which the respondent was able to answer yes or no. A dichotomous indicator where 1 was equal to yes and 0 was equal to no was created. The extent to which individuals met friends was tapped through the questionnaire item, "How often do you meet friends or relatives not living with you, whether here at home or elsewhere?" and the response categories were: "on most days," "once or twice a week," "once or twice a month," "less often than once a month," and "never." The categories were reverse-coded so that higher numbers were associated with greater frequency of contact with friends. It should be noted that in France, only the response categories of "often," "sometimes," and "rarely" were offered, and therefore comparisons on this variable need to be made with caution.

Analytic Strategy

As described above, the ECHP was an annual longitudinal panel study in which data are available for a range of up to eight years for several countries—indeed, all the countries that were included in the analyses that follow. The analyses pooled all waves of data, although they were carried out separately for each country (to aid in the interpretation of the results of country differences). As such, several observations per case are included; as well, the observations themselves are not independent in the sense that there are repeat individuals over the waves of data. This situation presents a problem with various regression techniques, which assume the independence of both the observations and the error terms. There are various solutions to this problem (see, for example, Wooldridge 2002). I have chosen to use random effects models (both logit and regression), which are couched in the assumption that there are no correlations between the unobserved effect and all independent variables (Greene 2003; Rabe-Hesketh and Everett, 2004).

To model the assumption that there are causal effects between the variables examined here, particularly for the long-term associations between NEET status and later-life outcomes, time series indicators were used in the estimations. Thus, when estimation all of the outcomes examined here were made, their status at $t+1$ and $t+2$ were the dependent variables of interest. In addition, baseline characteristics at previous years were controlled for such that the effects of being NEET were not overstated. For example, when examining the association between being NEET in t and low education in year $t+2$, education in year t and $t+1$ were included in The estimations, as well as controls for age, gender, household structure, household income, and wave of survey.

RESULTS

NEET Persistence

Table 9.4 displays the results of six separate estimations of later-life NEET status. The coefficients of interest (NEET in year t) are all statistically significant in all countries for predicting NEET in $t+1$ and $t+2$. The impact of NEET status in year t is strongest in all countries from t to $t+1$; however, this drops off dramatically in $t+2$ for all countries with the exception of Spain. The decrease in the size of the coefficient is particularly noticeable in the U.K., where it drops from 1.713 to 0.449.

Table 9.4 Being NEET in successive years: results of random effects logistic regression.

Random Effects Logistic Regression Coefficients

	France	Germany	UK	Italy	Greece	Spain	Portugal
NEET in t+1							
NEET in year t	2.021***	2.008***	1.713***	1.790***	2.164***	1.884***	2.762***
	(0.262)	(0.170)	(0.126)	(0.101)	(0.142)	(0.136)	(0.128)
N	8276	7788	5790	13058	7465	13055	9940
Rho	0.043	0.085	0.069	0.087	0.084	0.094	0.079
Likelihood Ratio	202.2	328.7	364.9	479.5	323.7	321.3	570.5
Chi-Square							
NEET in t+2							
NEET in year t	1.274***	0.949***	0.449*	1.126***	1.258***	1.608***	1.523***
	(0.290)	(0.254)	(0.184)	(0.129)	(0.197)	(0.188)	(0.183)
N	5139	5081	3806	9002	4831	8846	6785
Rho	0.0214	0.0154	0.072	0.0223	0.0162	0.0325	0.0153
Likelihood Ratio	160.8	245.2	182.2	415.2	310.6	269.8	505.7
Chi-Square							

$*p < 0.05$, $**p < 0.01$, $***p < 0.001$

Standard errors in parentheses. Controlling for NEET in previous years, sex, age, household income, household structure, and wave of survey.

Economic-Capital Outcomes

In terms of low education in the year after the first observed NEET status, being NEET in year t was found to be a significant predictor in all countries except in the U.K. (see table 9.5). Unlike other countries, in the U.K., being NEET in year t was found to be *negatively* associated with low education in $t+2$, while it dropped from statistical significance in France and Greece. While the results for France and Greece dropped from statistical significant in $t+2$, the size of the coefficient increased in a positive direction for Germany, Italy, and Spain. In terms of being in the lowest quintile of household income, being NEET in year t was a significant predictor in Germany, Greece, Spain, and Portugal in $t+1$ and $t+2$. The coefficients decrease in size somewhat for all countries from $t+1$ to $t+2$. The U.K. had significant results only in $t+2$.

Social-Capital Outcomes

Table 9.6 reports the results of the random effects regressions for social-capital outcomes in $t+1$ and $t+2$. NEET status in year t was significantly and negatively associated with club membership in Greece, Spain, and Germany. In the results for $t+2$, Germany and Greece dropped from statistical significance, while the Italy achieved statistical significance and the coefficient for Spain increased in a negative direction. In terms of meeting friends, the effect of being NEET in t was statistically significant and negative in France, Germany, Italy, and Greece. In the U.K., however, the effect was positive. There was no statistically significant effect of being NEET in year t on the frequency of meeting friends in $t+2$ for any countries considered here.

DISCUSSION

A transition regimes theory developed by Walther and associates was proposed as a framework for developing hypotheses about the later-life associations of having been NEET, along with a capitals framework for understanding the different facets of stratification. Table 9.7 summarizes the statistically significant findings of the full estimations organized by regime type.

It was hypothesized that the risks associated with recurrent NEET spells would be highest in the subprotective countries. Indeed, in all four of the subprotective countries, NEET in year t was a statistically significant predictor of NEET in years $t+1$ and $t+2$—but this result was found also in the U.K. and Germany. If we look at the size of effects year on year, however, the percentage decrease in the size of the coefficients is the least in the subprotective

Table 9.5 Economic capital in successive years: results of random effects logistic regression.

Random Effects Logistic Regression Coefficients

	France	Germany	UK	Italy	Greece	Spain	Portugal
Low Education in *t+1*							
NEET in year *t*	0.785***	0.742**	−0.261	0.425***	0.559**	0.893***	0.994***
	(0.219)	(0.228)	(0.134)	(0.126)	(0.176)	(0.169)	(0.219)
N	8623	7955	5930	13228	7695	13179	10065
Rho	0.0124	0.0114	0.0123	0.0117	0.0137	0.0117	0.013
Likelihood Ratio Chi-Square	3002.1	2038.2	1325.7	4148.9	2354.4	5059.4	2593.4
Low Education in *t+2*							
NEET in year *t*	0.49	1.100***	−0.773***	0.917***	0.441	1.090***	0.782***
	(0.257)	(0.280)	(0.219)	(0.159)	(0.239)	(0.205)	(0.236)
N	5596	5293	3994	9214	5103	8990	6929
Rho	0.0144	0.0123	0.017	0.0147	0.0133	0.0128	0.0139
Likelihood Ratio Chi-Square	1570.1	1263.8	787.3	2341.9	1448.8	2791.8	1651.2

Lowest Quintile in *t+1*

NEET in year *t*	0.297	0.538***	0.0763	0.195	0.481***	0.570***	0.703***
	(0.179)	(0.159)	(0.134)	(0.106)	(0.144)	(0.125)	(0.128)
N	8590	7895	5862	13071	7617	13090	10046
Rho	0.0149	0.0144	0.0588	0.0276	0.0522	0.0366	0.0143
Likelihood Ratio Chi-Square	1521.8	1545	768.6	2502.1	1061.1	1858.4	2197.4

Lowest Quintile in *t+2*

NEET in year *t*	−0.148	0.416*	0.546***	0.0406	0.429*	0.482**	0.518**
	(0.248)	(0.205)	(0.150)	(0.136)	(0.184)	(0.161)	(0.161)
N	5554	5229	3909	9001	5010	8869	6904
Rho	0.0133	0.014	0.0397	0.0136	0.0137	0.0133	0.0138
Likelihood Ratio Chi-Square	925.4	1009.6	476.8	1980.8	818.1	1519.5	1410

*$p < 0.05$, **$p < 0.01$, ***$p < 0.001$
Standard errors in parentheses. Controlling for economic capital in previous years, sex, age, lagged household income, household structure, and wave of survey.

Table 9.6 Social capital in successive years: results of random effects logistic regression.

Random Effects Logistic Regression Coefficients

	France	Germany	UK	Italy	Greece	Spain	Portugal
Club in t+1							
NEET in year t	-0.413	-0.448*	-0.0107	-0.0765	-0.687**	-0.477**	-0.324
	(0.237)	(0.218)	(0.155)	(0.109)	(0.265)	(0.153)	(0.195)
N	8623	7955	5930	13228	7695	13179	10065
Rho	0.126	0.082	0.208	0.096	0.095	0.170	0.094
Likelihood Ratio Chi-Square	1158.5	705.2	667.3	1489.9	502.7	903.4	1575.6
Club in t+2							
NEET in year t	-0.544	-0.038	-0.084	-0.309*	0.0142	-0.651***	-0.271
	(0.316)	(0.245)	(0.133)	(0.130)	(0.263)	(0.194)	(0.229)
N	5596	5293	3994	9214	5103	8990	6929
Rho	0.017	0.012	0.011	0.015	0.089	0.013	0.015
Likelihood Ratio Chi-Square	1252.7	763.1	592.3	1596.3	408	1468.9	1398.6

Meet Friends in t+1

NEET in year t	−0.083**	−0.098*	0.064***	−0.136***	−0.069*	−0.017	−0.056
	(0.029)	(0.050)	(0.024)	(0.025)	(0.034)	(0.025)	(0.036)
N	8582	5724	5614	13200	6089	12441	9783
Rho	0.086	0.095	0.049	0	0.185	0	0.083
Likelihood Ratio Chi-Square	685.6	86.86	492.5	1511.2	284.8	220.8	2718.9

Meet Friends in t+2

NEET in year t	−0.031	0.034	0.049	−0.055	−0.038	−0.029	−0.056
	(0.039)	(0.059)	(0.030)	(0.030)	(0.042)	(0.032)	(0.041)
N	5563	3524	3753	9187	3588	8287	6650
Rho	0.122	0.144	0.111	0.0434	0.221	0.0832	0.13
Likelihood Ratio Chi-Square	417.2	556.7	207.7	981.9	272.7	85.84	2290.9

$*p < 0.05$, $**p < 0.01$, $***p < 0.001$

Standard errors in parentheses. Controlling for social capital in previous years, sex, age, lagged household income, household structure, and wave of survey.

Table 9.7 Outcomes by transition regimes.

Regime Type	Countries	NEET t+1	NEET t+2	Low Education t+1	Low Education t+2	Low HH Inc t+1	Low HH Inc t+2	Club t+1	Club t+2	Meet friends t+1
Emp cen	France	2.021	1.274	0.785						-0.083*
	Germany	2.008	0.949	0.742	1.100	0.538	0.416	-0.488		
Liberal	UK	1.713	0.449		-0.773		0.546			0.064
Sub-protec	Italy	1.790	1.126	0.425	0.917				-0.309	-0.136
	Greece	2.164	1.258	0.559		0.481	0.429	-0.687		-0.069
	Spain	1.884	1.608	0.893	1.090	0.570	0.482	-0.477	-0.651	
	Portugal	2.762	1.523	0.994	0.782	0.703	0.518			

*Response categories different in France.

countries. From $t+1$ to $t+2$, for example, the coefficient for Spain is still 85.4 percent of its original size, with corresponding figures of 62.9 percent for Italy, 58.1 percent for Greece, and 55.1 percent for Portugal. The hypothesis that recurrent NEET status would be least pronounced in the U.K. was partially supported by the large drop in the coefficient from $t+1$ to $t+2$ (the largest decrease overall, going to 26.2% of its original size). The effects for Germany and France did somewhat occupy a middle position between the U.K. and the subprotective countries.

In terms of economic-capital outcomes, it was hypothesized that NEET would impact strongest the economic-capital outcomes in the subprotective regimes. Some support is found for this hypothesis in table 9.7, where NEET status predicts low education and low household income in $t+1$ and $t+2$ in both Spain and Portugal. Similarly, for Greece, low education in the year following NEET status was observed, as well as low household income in both years. For Italy, household income was not affected, but low education in both years was. It should be noted, however, that similar results were also found in Germany, while the results for France were rather different from those of its regime-mate. The results for the U.K. were surprising, with low education being negatively associated with NEET status—the reverse relationship that was expected, suggesting that there may some validity issues with the NEET definition or that the U.K. is particularly effective in retraining NEETs. However, with regard to household income, the failure of NEET status in year t to achieve statistical significance in $t+1$, but to then achieve significance in $t+2$, suggests that there is a lagged negative effect of having been NEET.

Owing to the importance of the informal section in the subprotective regimes, it was hypothesized that NEET status may impact more greatly the social networks and the sorts of benefits associated with knowing people. There is support for this hypothesis, with club membership being negatively associated with NEET status in $t+1$ in Spain and Greece, and in $t+2$ in Italy and Spain. Further, the frequency of meeting friends in $t+1$ was negatively associated with NEET status in Greece and Italy. Interestingly, the coefficient for meeting friends was positive in the U.K., suggesting that NEET status adds to the socializing potential of young people. In the context of British policy understanding of the NEET phenomenon, however, this is probably to be expected, as young people may be engaging in development of negative social capital by fraternizing with individuals who reinforce their NEET identity (Wacquant 1998).

Alternative Explanations

While there has been support for the transitions regime framework, it has been far from perfect, particularly regarding the rather large discrepancies

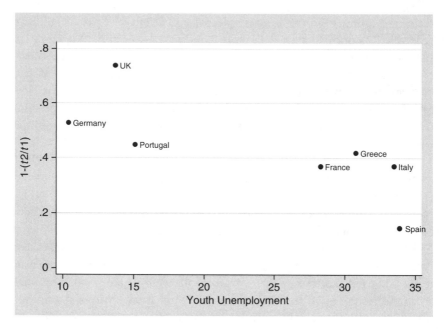

Figure 9.1 Change coefficients by youth unemployment, 1997.

Source: United Nations. *Human Development Index*; http://hdr.undp.org/en.

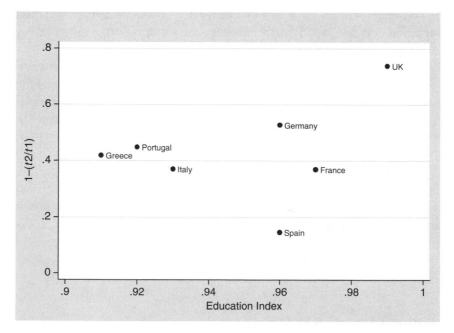

Figure 9.2 Change coefficients by education index, 2000.

Source: United Nations. *Human Development Index*; http://hdr.undp.org/en.

between predictors and outcomes in France and Germany. It is perhaps useful, then, to think about what other macro features of countries may be driving the differences that have been observed between countries.

If we focus on the outcome of recurrent NEET status, it is possible that these coefficients are related to macro-economic phenomena occurring within each country. There are many possible correlates that may be driving the differences between the coefficients observed between the countries, such as local youth unemployment rates, literacy rates, and opportunities for training and postsecondary education.

If attention is turned to the reduction in NEET rates from $t+1$ to $t+2$, then $1-(t+2/t+1)$ can be considered the percentage decrease in the coefficients between $t+1$ and $t+2$. The larger the number, the more effective the country in question has been in reducing long-term NEET status. These figures can then be cross-tabulated with macro data figures in each country to observe if there are any associations. Figure 9.1 displays the plots between the decrease in risk of being NEET from $t+1$ to $t+2$ with the youth unemployment rate in each country in 1997.[3] Figure 9.2 uses the education index as the variable on the horizontal axis. The education index is a component of the Human Development Index based on adult literacy and school enrollment data (http://hdr.undp.org/en/media/Fu_HDI.pdf [accessed May 31, 2010]).

In figure 9.1, large decreases in the coefficients observed in the U.K., Germany, and Portugal are associated with the lower rates of youth unemployment. Conversely, the small changes observed in Spain are associated with the high rates of youth unemployment.

In figure 9.2, a similar trend, albeit not as strong, is observed. Countries where the change was the greatest are generally associated with higher education index values. Examined from this perspective, there is also some clustering by regime type among Greece, Portugal, and Italy, as well as in Germany and France.

Limitations

It needs to be emphasized that these data cannot distinguish between voluntary and involuntary NEET status. Previous qualitative research on NEET youth in the U.K. found that voluntary NEET status "is not associated with being from either disadvantaged or more privileged backgrounds: their current status is a product of a range of structural and institutional influences that have shaped their decision-making" (Pemberton 2007:15). The measurement of NEET here, therefore, combines people who are very disadvantaged with those who are working to develop skills through unpaid means, traveling for leisure, engaged in voluntary work, or simply taking a break (Furlong 2006). As argued by Furlong:

[t]he usefulness of NEET as a category is therefore compromised through the ways in which disadvantaged people who may lack the resources to navigate transitions or exercise choice are combined with more privileged young people who are able to exercise a significant degree of choice regarding the ways in which they manage their lives. (2006: 557)

There is clearly a difference between those who choose to become NEET and those who arrive in the status through the interplay of institutional, structural, and individual factors (Bynner 2005). It may be most problematic in the U.K., owing to popularization of the "gap year" that many young people take between finishing secondary school and starting post-secondary education. Clearly, NEET is a culturally and even person-specific phenomenon.

CONCLUSION

Some support was found for the notion that recurrent NEET status would be differentiated by regime type, with the strongest incidence of recurrence found in the subprotective countries. Additional analyses using macro data found that, to some extent, the youth unemployment rates and education indices of the countries were of additional assistance when interpreting the differences among countries, and that the NEET situation in each country is associated with the countries' economic situation and orientation toward education of young people.

With regard to economic capital outcomes, some support was also found for the prediction that economic-capital outcomes would be most impacted in the subprotective regime. However, there was little similarity in outcomes between the employment-centered regime countries (France and Germany); and in the U.K., NEET status was found to be negatively associated with later-life low education. The hypothesis that predicted that social-capital outcomes would be strongest in the subprotective countries was also supported, while in the U.K., being NEET was positively associated with the frequency of meeting friends.

The transition regime framework has been a useful tool for establishing a prior hypotheses and theorizing about where the differences observed in these analyses point. However, there were rather notable deviations in how the individual countries performed, particularly between the regime-mates of France and Germany. It is thus necessary to examine other factors, such as macro-level indicators, to understand how this form of youth social exclusion is situated within the country's individual context.

The validity of the measurement of NEET has been called into question by other authors mentioned earlier in this chapter and with regard to the counterintuitive findings that were discussed earlier. If it is the case that

NEETs are such a heterogeneous group (at least in the U.K.), then more appropriate definitions and measures must be created to capture this economic status. While these data stopped being collected in 2001, they provide a historical snapshot of how NEETs have fared in terms of human- and social-capital outcomes over part of the life course. More current data, particularly the EU- Statistics on Income and Living Conditions (the predecessor of the ECHP, currently released only in two waves and with limited countries and access), will allow researchers to examine this research question with a more recent European samples.

Notes

1. In terms of Japanese research, however, the discourse of NEETs is framed around individuals who are withdrawing from society, rather than any perceived *threat* to society.

2. It should be noted that Quintini, Martin, and Martin (2007) conducted their analysis on the same data as will be analyzed in the estimations that follow. It is important to note, however, that Quintini et al. include in their estimations unemployed youth and those in military service. It will be explained later in this chapter that the operationalization of NEET used in the estimations that follow exclude these two groups.

3. Data for 1997 were used, as it was a year that was the midpoint in years of the panel data under consideration. In no country were there substantial year-on-year differences that would make the choice of 1997 particularly biased.

10

Overeducation and Social Generations in France

Welfare Regimes and Inter-cohort Inequalities in Returns to Education

Louis Chauvel

This chapter presents a comparative theory and an empirical analysis of inequalities in economic opportunities and returns to education across birth cohorts. It focuses on the consequences of economic slowdowns in different types of welfare regimes and analyzes how discontinuities in economic trends produce diverse effects on the balance between birth cohorts. Here, I analyze how these changes configure divergent birth-cohort life chances and, *in fine*, create different conditions for the emergence of social generations (Mannheim 1928/1990).

A comparative theory of welfare regime—specific responses to economic fluctuations, based on Esping-Andersen's (1990, 1999) typologies, offers a general framework for the analysis of inter-cohort inequalities both in terms of cohort opportunities and life chances and in regard to the valorization of education. A set of methodological tools is presented and tested on the French case, an extreme situation with strong inter-cohort inequalities and social-generation fractures. Finally, an empirical comparison of four countries—Denmark (DK), France (FR), Italy (IT), and United States (US)—based on the Luxembourg Income Study data, illustrates how different welfare regimes produce alternative distributions of economic resources to birth cohorts and valorize differently their educational investments.

The main finding is that conservative (FR) and the familialistic (IT) welfare regimes are marked by strong inter-cohort inequalities at the expense of younger social generations, while in contrast social-democratic (DK) and liberal (US) systems show less inter-cohort redistribution of resources. As far as education goes, while there is no clear decline in the return to education in the latter countries, the former nations show strong drops in the value of intermediate levels of education. This means that national trajectories of social change have diverged, and we should anticipate the long-term consequences of these divergences.

DIFFERENT RESPONSES OF WELFARE REGIMES
TO ECONOMIC STRESSES

In previous research analyses (Chauvel 2006, for a France–United States comparison), I documented differences between the French and the American responses to the economic downturn of the 1970s. My objective was to examine the concept of social generations as it relates to the distribution of well-being, and to compare the dynamics of American and French welfare regimes. The French case is characterized by strong generational imbalances, in the context of economic fluctuations from the *Trente glorieuses* (1945–1975) [the thirty boom years] to the *Croissance ralentie* (1975–present) [the growth slowdown],[1] I documented the existence of a generational rift (*fracture générationnelle*) in France between the generations born before 1955 (the early baby-boom generations and the previous ones, who benefited most from the economic acceleration of the postwar period) and those born after 1955 (who are facing an economic slowdown, high youth unemployment, and the resulting social problems). Thus, we find an *insider-ization* of older generations and an *outsider-ization* of younger ones. That *fracture générationnelle* is often denied by policymakers and in the public debate; however, the long-term implications of these generational dynamics could have major consequences for the stability of our welfare state. Furthermore, if we see in France the emergence of strong inter-cohort inequalities at the expense of young adults, the American reaction to the same stresses (economic slowdown and increasing competition) has been different: although inequalities between cohorts are less visible, an increase in inequality within cohorts is obvious. Moreover, when we include the problem of education and its returns in socioeconomic terms, the contrast between France and the United States is clear. For intermediate levels of education—the end of secondary school or "short tertiary" (limited college), we observe a strong cohort decline in the return to education in France. With the same level of education and with the same age or experience, new French birth cohorts find lower positions in the socioeconomic hierarchy than do the previous cohorts. In the United States, such changes are quite unclear.

My aim in this chapter is to generalize these results, developing a framework for an international comparison based on the Esping-Andersen (1990) trilogy of welfare regimes, completed by the post-Ferrara (1996) controversy, since I include the fourth Mediterranean "familialistic" model. My argument is that, in the intrinsic logics of different welfare regimes, the probable set of socioeconomic responses to contemporary common challenges or stresses (economic slowdown, social distortions in the face of globalization, obsolescence of unqualified or industrially qualified labor, etc.) could be significantly different. As a clue to these differences, we notice strong cohort-specific scarring effects in France and in Italy, whereas these are unclear in Nordic countries and almost nonexistent in the Anglo-Saxon or liberal welfare regimes. We develop a welfare regime—based theory of comparative differences in inter-cohort inequalities, in intra-cohort changes in stratification, and in terms of return to intermediate levels of education. In this chapter, the empirical aspect of intra-cohort inequality will be less developed, even if the results are interesting for the academic debate on life course and welfare regimes (see Mayer 2005:34).

The theoretical aspect of these comparative analyses of welfare regime responses to economic fluctuation is based on the standard Esping-Andersen's typology of welfare regimes (1999). Four regimes are presented here: the corporatist (or conservative), liberal, universalist (or social democratic), and familialistic. What are the ideal-typical responses of these regimes to economic downturn in terms of youth opportunities, protection of different age groups, and earnings return to education?

Corporatist Regimes

Since it is based on the long-term loyalty of employees and the recognition of institutionalized social rights of protected social groups, the probable response of the corporatist regime (including France) to economic slowdown, international competition, and economic shortage of the welfare regime as such (as a redistributive agency, as a ruler of the labor force, and as an employer) will be: a more expensive protection of insiders (the stable workforce with higher seniority and high rates of trade-union memberships) at the expense of young adults who are completing their education, and of women, and immigrants, all of whom have fewer opportunities to defend their interests.

Youth unemployment results from the scarcity of (decent) jobs in the labor market. The lack of investment in new jobs, combined with the difficulty of competing with protected insiders, and the resulting exacerbation of intra-cohort competition among the young for rare positions generate a decline in wages and specific renegotiations and retrenchments of the social rights of younger social generations. If seniors are victims of early retirement, they also benefit from better income protection and greater access to comfortable pensions and/or acceptable conditions of pre-retirement (better than the usual unemployment protections for younger adults). The social generations of seniors are more equal (in intra-cohort terms) because they are the homogeneous cohorts of the "wage earner society" (Castel 2003) of the golden period of the 1960s–1980s (seniors' intra-cohort inequality declines), with better pension plans developed for all (seniors' relative income increases); conversely, the new cohorts of adults face a stronger polarization between winners and losers (Brzinsky-Fay 2007; Bell et al. 2007).

Another aspect is the declining value of education. Because of massive risks of unemployment, the young and families tend to prefer longer education, in a system which is massively subsidized by the state. This means a massive increase in the access to (postsecondary) education of young cohorts (Van De Velde 2008), combined with a lack of improvement in labor-market entry. As a consequence, young cohorts face a trend of strong educational inflation, indicated by a decline in the earnings value of educational credentials, particularly from less selective institutions (Duru Bellat 2006), whereas elder cohorts remain protected against this inflation because they are not in competition with the younger ones.

Liberal Regimes

The liberal regime (including the United States) is characterized by another set of likely answers to the same challenges. Because of the market orientation of this regime, the response to economic shortage is welfare-state retrenchment, including a limitation on redistributions to worse-off populations, stronger market competition, and dismantling former social rights considered to be rent-economy devices and distortions for market equilibrium. The logic of this is intensified competition between juniors and seniors (who have less intangible rights), which reduces the better positions that seniors previously obtained in the context of affluence. The consequence is reduced inter-cohort inequality (the new cohorts benefit relative to the seniors). However, this enhanced competition means stronger intra-cohort inequalities.

In terms of the value of educational credentials, no clear change is expected, for a number of reasons: first, lifelong education is more usual in the United States than in continental Europe, and there are less cohort contrasts in terms of educational investment; second, since education is a costly semi-private investment, the returns to education are more stable, since investment will decline if returns weaken; third, because of stronger inter-cohort competition, major contrasts do not exist in the value of credentials and degrees across cohorts.

Universalistic Regimes

The universalistic regime (including Finland) is defined by a collective vision for long-term stability, progress, and development for all, with a strong sense of collective responsibility. Successfully integrating newer cohorts is considered to be a national priority, since a failure in the early socialization of young adults is seen as a massive problem for the future development of society. High rates of youth unemployment and earnings declines among young adults could accompany long-term risks of anxiety, and loss of self-esteem among the young, increasing suicide rates, or a decline in the fertility index. Indeed, in universalistic regimes, the social cost of a failure in the process of integration and socialization of the young is viewed as unacceptable. More generally, greater control over the social risks across the complete life course is a central dimension of the Nordic welfare state model. It means that important changes in inter-cohort inequalities will be collectively controlled and balanced by public policies.

In terms of education, the global context of competition and massive pressure on lower and, now as well on intermediate, levels of skills, and additionally, the problem of old age and the need to maintain elders in the workforce in better conditions, are all constraints that demand a better distribution of skills among age groups and a commitment to flexicurity shared by individuals and collective society. The consequence is a stronger control in universalistic regimes, relative to the two previous models, of both intra- and inter-cohort inequalities. When considering the value of education, its collective control (involving a balance between public investment and subsidization of education, as well as incentives to avoid over-education) must avoid major changes in the scarcity or abundance of each level of credential or degree. As in the liberal regime, flexicurity and policies of inter-job mobility reduce the contrasts between age groups, avoid excessive protections of some cohorts at the expense of others, and limit the situations of cohort-rents.

Familialistic Regimes

The familialistic regime (including Italy) shares many aspects of the corporatist model, but families are here a legitimate institution in the redistribution of resources, both culturally and for the regulatory activities of the state. More precisely, in this regime, some sectors of the economy are strongly protected (mainly the core sectors of the public economy and of large private companies such as banks and insurance), with most of their labor regulations based on seniority rights. Meanwhile, in most mid- and small-sized companies, regulation is based primarily on family interconnections, where both localism and the long-term loyalty of workers are fundamental institutions.

In the context of post-affluent societies, and of scarcity of jobs, housing, and other resources, parents of young adults are expected to offer them help and protection, and most families act in conformity with these social pressures. The consequence is a trend toward increasing dependence of young adults on their parents, up through age 35 or even beyond this age, in a context of declining levels of wages and standards of living for new entrants into the labor market. Consequently, seniors exert political pressure so as to obtain better pensions, in order to be able to support their own children. The context of economic dependency generates stronger constraints on young families, increases the social pressures on women to choose between work and children, and is accompanied by a strong decline in the fertility rates, which creates a paradoxical context of familialism without families. This becomes a major problem in terms of the long-term sustainability of pensions and the welfare regime (shorter and less affluent careers of juniors, generational collapse of one-child families, etc.). Conversely, the decline of incomes for young families is offset by the reduction of family size.

In this familialistic regime, national homogeneity may be weaker compared to other regimes, since inter-provincial imbalances (strong unemployment rates in some localities might accompany workforce shortages in others) are structural traits of a labor market where localism and strong ties are important aspects of social regulation, implying less geographic mobility. Another dimension is a strong development of mass tertiary education, which generates a strong tendency toward over-education or credential inflation. Dependent young adults having parents with poor family interconnections and social capital (parents who therefore cannot find a job for their children) continue on to later and later stages of education, sometimes in sectors where the job market for educated young adults is quite narrow. As a result, unemployment rates by level of education can be flat or even increasing. Such a dynamic may create a strong decline in the value of a diploma.

While the welfare regime dynamics and transformations are central issues, other factors may also influence outcomes. These include:

- Economic acceleration. Even in the short term, a better economic situation might diminish pressure for welfare retrenchments.
- Quality of the transition from school to work. Close relations between the educational system and the labor market, organized internships, strong network of alumni, and the like. limit the risk of outsiderization of young adults.
- Shape of demography. A boom in fertility rates may generate, twenty or twenty-five years later, a phenomenon of overcrowding in the labor market (Easterlin 1961; Easterlin, Schaeffer, and Maucunovich 1993).

The combinations of these factors are much more complex than expected. Because of the diversity of potential configurations, we should expect that the welfare-regime explanation outlined here is only part of the real history of each nation. Although each welfare regime offers its own strong constraints, historical configurations (demography, level of development and opportunities for growth, etc.), and achievements of social policies (educational booms, structural reforms on the labor market, etc.) could also be important explanatory factors.

DEFINITIONS AND TOOLS OF GENERATIONAL RESEARCH

The use of *generations* in European social science is less narrowly defined than in the American academic context. For American sociologists, *generation* refers to the sociology of kinship and to family issues, while *cohort* (or *birth cohort*) refers to people born in the same year (Ryder 1965). Therefore, in American academic journals, the expression "social generation" is quite uncommon (except in the discussions of Karl Mannheim's theories). If some economists in the American tradition (Easterlin 1966; Auerbach, Gokhale, and Kotlikoff 1994) write about generations and generational accounting, the birth cohorts they consider also are engaged in kinship relations of generational transmissions (gifts, education, legacy, etc.). The European tradition is different. Here (Mentré 1920; Mannheim 1928/1990), "social generation" is defined as specific groups of cohorts exposed to a common pattern of social change and/or sharing collective identity features such as ethnicity, gender, or class.

Historically, four definitions of *generation* exist (Mentré 1920). The first one is less important to our argument: *genealogical generation* pertains to the sociology of family and kinship. The three others relate respectively to demographic, social, and historic generations. A *demographic generation* is identical to a birth cohort—that is, the group of individuals born in the same year. This is the most neutral clustering criterion, and it assumes no common trait. Conversely, a *historical generation* is a set of cohorts defined by a common culture, shared interests, consciousness of the generation's specificity and its historical role, and occasionally, its conflict with other generations. A historical generation may define itself by the time of its coming of age in history; a decisive example is the so-called *génération 1968*, which refers to the first cohorts of the baby boom (born between 1945 and 1950). The *génération 1914*, the generation of young adults of the First World War, is another dramatic example. *Social generation* is defined as a link between these two polar definitions. In the empirical social sciences, we first look at demographic generations, then we define historical generations from the results of sociological analysis, assessment and interpretation of the diversity or homogeneity of cohorts, and their objective and subjective identities and consciousness.

First, we must look at socialization in general, without delving into a systematic theorization. During youth, between the end of school and the stabilization of adulthood, there is a specific period of transitional socialization, which is a pivotal point in the formation of individuals' choices for the future; in a short period, usually some months, the potentialities offered by family and education turn into concrete positions from which people will construct their life courses. That individual process has collective consequences when a cultural or historical polarization has a socialization effect on most individual members of the new generation (Mannheim 1928/1990).

For people at age 20, collective historical experiences such as May 1968 or July 1914 could form durable opportunities or scars, since these people face a major transition in their lives within a dramatic social or historical context. In contrast, children cannot completely participate yet, and older people might be less affected, since they are already influenced by other experiences accumulated in other historical contexts (Ryder 1965). This transitional socialization is not necessarily sufficient to create or promote durable generational traits; they need a continuous process of collective recall to reinforce the social generation's identity, which would progressively vanish otherwise (Becker 2000).

A major problem in generational social change analysis is the intersection of three social times: age, period, and cohort. The most common time is *period* and pertains to the succession of historical epochs; the second time relates to *age* and the aging process; the third one is the *time of generations*, which consists of the continuous process of replacement of older cohorts by new ones. These three times are organized in a two-dimensional plane (see figure 10.1) that implies a profound indeterminacy.

In any given period, different age groups coexist (defined by age thresholds, age status, and roles); however, they also represent different generations that have been socialized in different historical contexts. When we compare different age groups at a given date (period), we cannot know *a priori* whether their differences result from age or from generation. In year 2008, on the Lexis diagram, for example, if the age group at age 60 (born in 1948) is at the top of income scale, we do not know whether it is an age effect (any cohort will enjoy better income at age 60 than when younger) or a cohort effect (the 1948 cohort has faced the best career opportunities of the twentieth century since its entry into the labor market). Age-period-cohort models have been developed to reveal generation effects, which can be discerned when specific traits appear in the life line of specific cohorts (Mason et al. 1973).

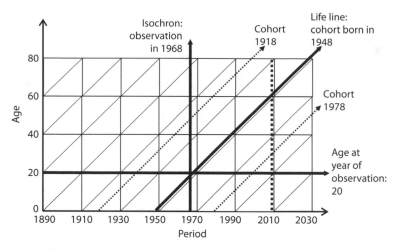

Figure 10.1 Lexis diagram of social change: age, period, time of generation.

Note: A synthetic view of the interactions of social times: when we cross periods (horizontal) and age (vertical), the time of cohorts appears on the diagonal ($a = p - c$). In year $p = 2009$, people at age 61 are born in 1948; they were 20 in 1968. At each period, young and old age groups are also different birth cohorts for whom socialization occurred in different contexts: the 75-year-old age group of 2009 (born in 1935) is also the "welfare generation" that has had abundant access to public pensions and health systems, while the same age group in period 1968 is the remains of the "sacrificed generation" born in 1894 (20 years old in 1914).

It is possible to mobilize Mannheim's theory of early adulthood socialization, where the newer generation, which has just experienced its transitional socialization, is generally reacting strongly to new trends. In periods of sudden social change, the newer cohorts are the most influenced by the discontinuities of history because they are the first to experience the new contexts of socialization that previous cohorts could not anticipate and in which they do not participate (Mead 1970). More precisely, during an economic acceleration, the young generation of adults generally do better than the older ones because they can move easily to better positions; conversely, during an economic slowdown, the newcomers are generally more fragile because they have less room in the social structure and no past accumulation of human or social capital, nor do they possess social rights to smooth the downward shock they face. We can expect such fluctuations in the distribution of well-being by cohorts, with a succession of sacrificed and elect generations emerging over time; and if the effect of socialization is strong and durable, each generation retains the consequences of its difficult or favorable entry. These fluctuations in the distribution of well-being before any redistribution could correspond to even stronger inequalities after redistribution, since the generations marked by prosperity tend to accumulate larger contributive social rights than do the generations marked by deprivation.

THE MULTIDIMENSIONAL *FRACTURE GÉNÉRATIONNELLE* IN FRANCE

In terms of inter-cohort inequalities, France offers empirically a clear, and extreme, model of this phenomenon. In France, convergent evidence shows how the economic slowdown has provoked a dramatic multidimensional *fracture générationnelle* since the late 1970s (Chauvel 1998, 2002: preface, 2003). This portrait is grim, but it is founded on strong empirical evidence, with alternative sets of microdata offering similar and convergent results, confirmed by various authors (Baudelot 2000; Koubi 2003; Peugny 2009). Three principal topics are highlighted here: first, the economic marginalization of new entrants into the labor market and its direct effects on social structure; second, the long-term consequences of this deprivation in terms of socialization and life chances; and finally, the consequences, which we evaluate in terms of life styles or political participation.

The Economic Decline of Youth

The first aspect of the dynamics of social generation in France is the change in the cohort distribution of economic means. A large income redistribution occurred between the 1970s and the present. In 1977, the earnings gap between age groups 30–35 and 50–55 was 15 percent; the gap is now about 40 percent. During the *Trente glorieuses*, the young wageearners generally began in the labor market with the same level of income as their parents had achieved at the end of a complete career. In contrast, for the last twenty years, we have observed the stagnation of the wages of the young, while wages for older people have grown by 20 percent or more.

Here is a new difference between age groups, with consequences that are not completely understood by contemporary social sciences. Yet, this is not simply a change affecting the relative position of age groups: members of the older generation (who are now, roughly, age 55) were relatively advantaged in their youth when compared to their seniors, and they are also relatively advantaged now, when as seniors they are compared with their young successors. The generational gaps result from double gains and double pains.

How can we explain this increasing gap? This is a consequence of a changing collective compromise that occurred during the mid-1970s and early 1980s. This transition in the social value of generations brought about a change from a relative valorization of newer generations (which were viewed as a positive future to be invested in) to a relative valorization aimed at protecting adults' and seniors' stability, even at the expense of the young. The main factor in this redistribution of well-being concerned unemployment. High unemployment rates were socially acceptable for young French workers, provided that adult employees with dependent children could avoid these difficulties. In 1974, the unemployment rate of those who had left school within the past twenty-four months was about 4 percent; by 1985, those who left school recently had an unemployment rate of 35 percent, which remained steady through 1996; in 2002, at the end of the recent wave of economic recovery, this rate still was close to 18 percent. The unemployment rate of recent school-leavers is strongly reactive to the current economic situation, whereas for the middle-aged and seniors, the rates remain more stable. Therefore, an economic slowdown has serious consequences for younger adults, and economic recovery first benefits new entrants in the labor market.

An unexpected consequence of this collective compromise for the protection of adults at the expense of newcomers is the lack of socialization of the new sacrificed generations: even if they are now adults, with dependent children of their own, their unemployment rates remain much higher, while their earnings are abnormally low when compared to other age groups, because of a kind of "scarring effect." At the end of the 1980s, the unemployment rate of this group at age 40–44 was still about 4 percent and is now over 8 percent. (The age compromise for the protection of adults with dependent children is no longer evident.) This scarring effect is even clearer concerning earnings: the cohorts of new entrants in the labor market in a time of downturn must accept lower wages; conversely, for young workers, a strong economy allows them to negotiate better earnings. After this entry point, the earning gaps persist because of the lack of a catch-up effect on earnings (Chauvel 2003: chap. 3): some generations are about ten points above or below the long-term trend because of the point of time at which they entered the workforce, and after age 30, the relative benefit or handicap remains stable.

A complementary factor relates to the dynamics of occupational structure and the stratification system. In France, as in the United States (Mendras 1988; Bell 1973), the standard hypothesis of stratification change suggests that the long-term educational expansion of the twentieth century, and the emergence of a knowledge-based society, has stimulated the enlargement of the middle and upper middle classes; thus, the newer generation might automatically have benefited from the expansion of the occupational groups of experts, managers, or professionals (*cadres et professions intellectuelles supérieures*, in French[2]), to whom we often add middle management and lower professionals in the private and public sectors (such as school teachers and nurses) who exemplify the new technical middle class and whose social hegemony was predicted in the seventies (*professions intermédiaires*, in the official French nomenclature of occupations).

At the aggregated level, the expansion of these middle and higher occupational groups in France seems to support this idea: for the aggregated age group 30–54, the rise is from 12.5 percent of the total population in 1970 to 31.5 percent (figures 10.2a and 10.2b). However, when we make a distinction between age groups, the dynamics are much more complicated: at age 30, the percentage of those in middle and higher white-collar occupational groups jumped from 13 percent in 1964 to 24 percent in 1975, reaching 26 percent in 1980. In the earlier period, the trend strongly accelerated for these "juniors," but stalled after 1980: there was only a four-point increase

(a)

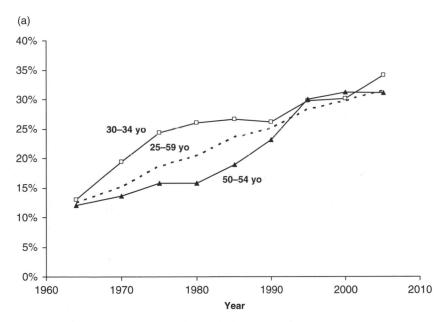

Figure 10.2a *Cadres et professions intellectuelles supérieures* plus *professions intermediaries*, in two age groups, by year.

Note: In 1980, 26% of "juniors" (age group 30–34) are in the middle or higher occupational groups, whereas 16% of "seniors" are in that group. In 1995, the proportions are, respectively, 29% and 30%. For the average labor force, the trend is linear, but not for the age groups. Here, therefore, is implicit cohort dynamics.

Source: Enquêtes *Emploi* 1970–2005 and *Formation-qualification-professionnelle* 1964. INSEE; archives CMH-Quételet.

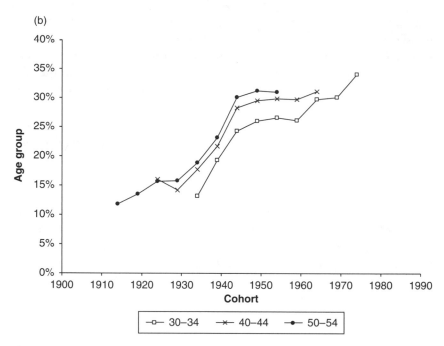

(b)

Figure 10.2b *Cadres et professions intellectuelles supérieures* plus *professions intermédiaires* in two age groups, by cohort.

Note: Same data as figure 10.2a, but with different age groups and cohort on horizontal axis. See the generational boom in access to middle-class positions for cohorts born in 1945–1950 and the following stagnation. The cohort diagram is a strong instrument for analysis of cohort effects, by comparing the achievements at the same age of different cohorts. If curves are linear, cohort shows stable progress; if there are accelerations and decelerations affecting the same cohorts, we can analyze long-term cohort effects. Since the opportunity for growth is neither similar nor linear from one cohort to another, some benefit from better careers than do others. Generational history is not linear.

Source: Enquêtes *Emploi* 1970–2005 and *Formation-qualification-professionnelle* 1964. INSEE; archives CMH-Quételet.

in the two decades between 1980 and 2000, compared to an eleven-point increase from 1964 to 1975.

In the middle of the boom years known as the *Trente glorieuses*, France experienced a dramatic expansion of the public sector and high-tech large companies (Airbus, France Télécom, civil nuclear electricity planning, health system, universities and research centers, etc.), creating strong demand for highly qualified employees with higher education. The first cohorts of the baby boom (the 1945 cohort, which was 30 years old in 1975) were surely not a sacrificed generation, since they enjoyed longer education in the context of a dynamic labor market and did not face the diminishing returns on education that subsequent cohorts have faced. In 2000, twenty-five years later, the portion of 30-year-olds in mid-level and higher white-collar occupational groups is quite similar and stable (26%), compared to 23 percent in 1975 and 24.5 percent in 1980. In this respect, the cohort born in 1970 has experienced no clear progress. However, during the 1990s, the expansion for seniors (who were the juniors of the 1970s) is apparent. Thus, the expansion of mid-level and higher occupational groups across generations is not linear. The apparent linear growth results from the inappropriate aggregation of a strong expansion—for the early baby boomers—and of a strong slowdown for the succeeding generations.

When we shift from occupations to incomes (figure 10.3), the findings are similar: whereas the standards of living (here in terms of disposable incomes after taxes and benefits per consumption unit, relatively to the national average) were comparable or even flat from age 25 to 55, there is

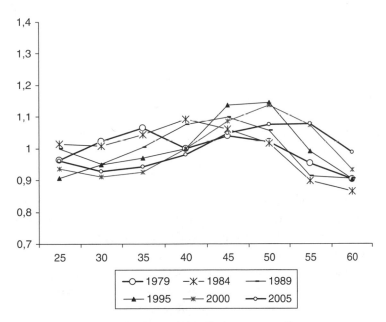

Figure 10.3 Relative income (radi), 1979–2005, by age group.

Note: Relative adjusted disposable income (radi), as follows: radi = 1 relates to the 30- to 64-year-old average of the period; periods 1, 2, 3, 4 relate to data for 1985, 1990, 1995, 2000. On the figure, age 30 pertains to the group age 30 to 34. Population: any individuals characterized by their household's radi.

Source: LIS project microdata, plus *Budget des ménages*, 2000–2005, for the latest period.

now a huge contrast between age 30 and age 50. These age transformations hide stable long-term inter-cohort inequalities.

Scarring Effect

These evolutions would have had no significant social impact if, for the new generations, the early difficulties had no permanent effect. If the new entrants into the labor force in a period of scarcity could catch up after their early difficulties, the problem would be anecdotal or residual. The assessment of the long-term impact of these early difficulties is central to the interpretation, however; if young, deprived generations do not catch up, a kind of long-term *hysteresis* effect appears that we can call a "scar" or "scarring effect," since the handicap seems enduring. The age-period-cohort analysis shows that cohorts who experienced a difficult entry because of a context of recession continue to suffer from a relative delay in upward mobility when they are compared to the average situation. In contrast, those with a favorable entry in a period of expansion continue to benefit from a relative advance. The relative position of a collective cohort at age 30 is rapidly crystallized, and there does not appear to be a substantial catch-up effect later on (see figure 10.2b).

How can we explain the absence of generational catch-up dynamics? Those who had benefited from a period of entry marked by a strong demand for skilled jobs experienced faster career and earlier labor experience at higher levels of responsibility, with better wages. These individuals (and the cohort they constitute at an aggregated level) retain the long-term benefits of the early opportunities they enjoyed, which will positively influence their future trajectory at any later age. For those who entered the labor market under difficult economic conditions, the periods of unemployment they faced, the necessity to accept less qualified jobs with lower wages, and the consecutive delays in career progression, imply negative stimuli for their own trajectories (decline in ambition, lack of valued work experience) and could appear as a negative signal for future potential employers. The hypothesis we present here for France is that cohort-specific socialization contexts imply long-term opportunities and life chances for individuals and for their cohorts; when the difficulties disappear, the cohorts who faced these problems will continue to suffer from long-term consequences of past handicaps.

In more concrete terms, the cohorts born during the 1940s, who benefited from the economic acceleration of the late sixties, were relatively privileged compared to the previous cohorts when young, and they are relatively advantaged when compared to the newer ones, because of the lack of progress for the young from 1975 to the present. We can generalize from this observation: the cohorts who entered the labor force after 1975, experiencing an economic slump and mass unemployment, have been the early victims of the new generational dynamics, and they retain the long-term scars of their initial difficulties in the labor market.

An important point we cannot develop at length here is the consequences of educational expansion. If the level of education has increased in the cohorts born from 1950 to 1975, that positive trend also was accompanied by a strong social devaluation of qualifications and educational credentials (Chauvel 2000). More specifically, the first cohorts of the baby boom have benefited from an expansion of education at a time when the rewards for education remained stable: even if there were twice as many *Baccalauréat* recipients in the 1948 cohort as in the 1935 one, their likelihood of access to higher social or economic positions did not shrink. On the other hand, the generations that followed had to deal with a strong trend of devaluation in terms of the lower economic and social returns to education. The first consequence was a rush to the most valued and selective credentials (in the *grandes écoles* of the elite, such as *Ecole Polytechnique, Ecole Nationale d'Administation, Sciences-Po Paris*), whose value remains stable but whose population becomes more and more selective and may be discriminatory in terms of social origins. The second consequence is a strong devaluation of less prestigious universities, which are less exclusive but have much smaller per capita endowments in comparison to the *grandes écoles*. In the same way, the best secondary schools become more selective, with major consequences in terms of urban segregation. In the French case, the school system was traditionally the central institution of the republic and at the heart of its idea of progress, providing the strongest support for French-style social democracy and meritocracy. The collapse in the value of intermediate-level educational credentials (figure 10.4) implies a destabilization of this myth and a pessimistic outlook on progress—developments that we can expect to have political consequences.

Now that we are nearing the end of this long-term slowdown, which began twenty-five years ago, we can compare two social and genealogical generations.[3] For the first time in a period of peace, the youth of the new generation are not better off than were their parents at the same age. In fact, the 1968 generation, born in 1948, are the children of those born in 1918 (who were young adults in World War II and who worked in difficult conditions at the beginning of the *Trente glorieuses*). The condition of the baby boomers was incomparably better than that of their parents. But the following genealogical generation, born around 1978—who are now between 25 and 30 years old—faces diminished opportunities of growth, not only because of an economic slump but also because of their relatively poor outcomes in comparison to those of their own parents, who did very well.[4]

We now observe rising rates of downward social mobility connected to the proliferation of middle-class children who cannot find social positions comparable to their parents'. This *déclassement social* goes with a strong effect of *déclassement scolaire*—that is, a steady decline, from one cohort to the next, of the social prestige of occupations corresponding to any given level of education. The cohort analysis of this decline shows that cohorts born before 1950 do not participate in this *déclassement scolaire*, since they enjoyed high status at age 25 and they continue now to benefit from it. The cohorts facing lower positions at age 25 are almost unable to catch up from early difficulties in the labor market. An important aspect is the cohort impermeability of the process: those who acquired their status in better situations are able to retain their early advantages, when others suffer from a lack of resilience long after their entry into the labor market.

Consequently, France offers an ideal example of the problematic dynamics of a corporatist regime, since the nation is unable to distribute benefits to its young adults. It sacrifices the interests of large fractions of its population, and it is unable to organize its own transmission to newer generations. We next address the lack of intergenerational sustainability, since such

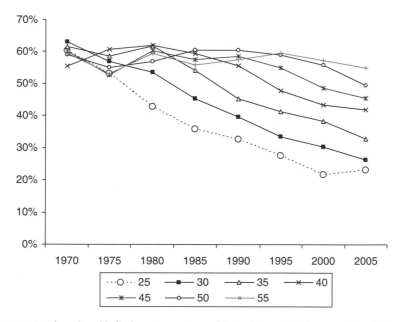

Figure 10.4 Educational inflation: Percentage of baccalaureat holders accessing higher or lower service-class positions (*cadres et professions intermédiaires*), by age group.

Note: And no more = validation of the end of secondary education.

Source: *Enquêtes Emploi 1970–2005*. INSEE; archives CMH-Quételet.

welfare regimes support the social rights of earlier cohort generations while depriving newer generations of its benefits.

IS FRANCE AN EXCEPTION? AN INTERNATIONAL COMPARISON OF COHORTS

This question is very interesting indeed, since with France we have a country presenting in many respects highly specific traits. France is defined by a homogeneous culture—notably by a political culture that rejects free-market discipline. It is homogeneously governed by a centralized system of governance that tends to reproduce, for long periods, similar and erroneous diagnoses and decisions throughout the nation. The political culture is characterized by stop-and-go policies of alternating periods of excessive investment and of scarcity, which tend to create backlashes and counterbacklashes. France is also a country where the first years on the labor market are of strategic importance when it comes to the future life chances of individuals: early successes or early failures become, respectively, positions of rent or conversely lifelong handicaps. France may be unusual in its experience of exceptional inter-cohort inequalities. More decentralized countries (such as the United States or Italy) could blur these fractures; more responsible political regimes could avoid stop-and-go policies or more rapidly diagnose previous mistakes and take steps to counteract them. Societies where the life course is characterized by more instability or by less conservative processes than in France might be more open to the redistribution of opportunities between cohorts.

A solution to test this idea of a possible French exceptionalism is to compare the dynamics of incomes over the life course in different nations. Four countries are considered here: France, Italy, Finland, and the United States, one country for each type of Esping-Andersen welfare regime. The four countries are characterized by (approximately) similar levels of development, and the trends are roughly parallel, even though the American economy was the first to stagnate in the 1970s and it managed to outperform others during the 1990s.

The four selected countries have microdata available in the Luxembourg Income Study Project (LIS 2010), but other countries could have been selected with similar results. Since in this chapter the major concern is with consumption, the focus is on household-level standards of living and not on personal earnings; here, we focus less on economic rewards from occupations than on life chances in terms of access of different cohorts to commodities. The LIS project data offer the possibility of computing adjusted disposable income (total net income after taxes and transfers, adjusted by household size, where the equivalence scale is the square root of the number of residents of the household) in order to compare the living standards of age groups at four different periods—around 1985, 1990, 1995, and 2000.

The main results of the comparison of the relative adjusted disposable income (radi) in figure 10.5 are:

- In 2000, the shapes of the age distribution of the average radi are similar, with an ascending slope to age 55 and a declining standard of living after (decline of earnings or retirement).
- From 1985 to 2000, except in the United States, we note a general increase of seniors' income, more modest in Finland and very significant in France.
- France and Italy are characterized by a strong relative decline of the age group 35–39; the French dynamics pertain to a very clear cohort wave (there is a progressive shift of age at maximum income from ages 40 to 50).
- In Italy, the decline of radi at age 30 is less significant, but note that at age 30 most Italians are not head of their own households, and most of them continue to nominally benefit from the affluence of their own seniors.

The main point is that France and Italy show profound redistributions of living standards to the profit of seniors and at the expense of younger middle-aged adults, whereas Finland and the United States face no massive transformations. (There is a slight improvement for Finnish seniors; however, its relative consequences are shared by all the other age groups.) Although both the Nordic and liberal welfare regimes aim to erase inter-cohort inequalities, the corporatist and the familialistic regimes generate visible imbalances between age groups, and the age groups relating to the part of the life course when young families appear are marked by profound transformations.

In France, while the gap in 1985 between the 55-year-old and the 35-year-old age groups was 15 percent, the gap is + 16 percent in 2000—that is, we have a redistribution of 31 points. In Italy, the numbers are, respectively, 8 and +22 percent, with a redistribution of 30 points. These implicit redistributions between age groups are not negligible; here is the evidence of the stability of both the Nordic and the liberal regimes in terms of inter-cohort inequality and of the strong inter-cohort inequalities created inside both the corporatist and the familialistic regimes.

If the inter-cohort inequality dynamics affect different shapes inside the different welfare regimes, intra-cohort inequality matters, too. In terms of contrasts between the top and the bottom of the standard-of-living

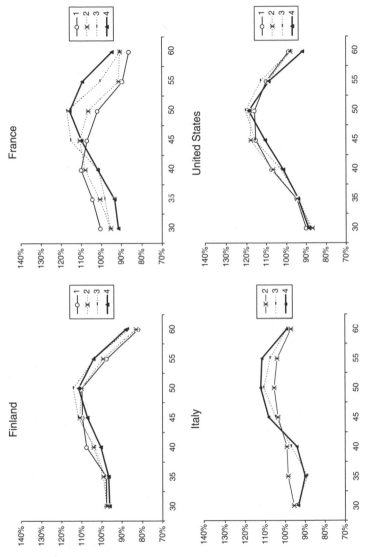

Figure 10.5 Comparison of relative income (radi) by age group, for 3 periods.

Source: LIS project microdata and the author's calculation. Relative adjusted disposable income (radi); radi = 1 relates to the 30- to 64-year-old average for the period; periods 1, 2, 3, 4 relate to LIS data for 1985, 1990, 1995, 2000. On the figure, age 30 pertains to the group age 30 to 34. Population: any individuals characterized by their household's radi.

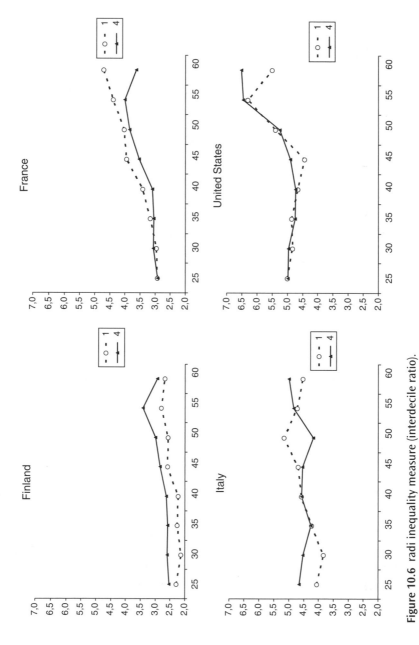

Figure 10.6 radi inequality measure (interdecile ratio).

Source: LIS project microdata and the author's calculation. See figure 10.5. Periods 1, 2, 3, 4 relate to LIS data for 1985, 1990, 1995, 2000.

distribution, the cohort dynamics are significant. We measure here the intra-cohort inequality with the interdecile ratio D9/D1, or the ratio between the income of the richest 10 percent and the income of the poorest 10 percent (figure 10.6).

The most noticeable results are:

- The spectrum of inequality measures is well known: the United States is the most unequal country, with Finland being the most equal; Italy is closer to the United States and France is closer to Finland.
- In Finland, the situation is stable.
- In France, we have a decline in seniors' inequality: in the eighties, the older the cohort, the stronger the intra-cohort inequality; meanwhile, the former older cohorts have been replaced by younger ones that are more egalitarian. However, the youngest cohort does not improve its degree of intra-cohort equality.
- The United States faces stronger intra-cohort inequality for seniors (the young being more egalitarian, and inequalities seeming to increase with age), and this structure of increasing inequality among older groups is growing (the contrast between juniors and seniors is deeper nowadays).
- Italy is more unstable, but younger cohorts face stronger intra-cohort inequality in 2000 than in the mid-1980s, when it is the opposite at age 50. The younger Italian cohorts are visibly challenged: They are relatively poorer (see figure 10.5), more unequal, dynamically facing pauperization and increasing inequality. Moreover, a deeper analysis (Chauvel 2007) shows that these elements are even more severe when we include a demographic argument: the situation of young Italian adults is difficult, and so their answer to this challenge has been a decline in their fertility. Fewer children mean higher standards of living (because the income is shared between fewer consumption units). If the fertility rate of contemporary young adults had remained unchanged when compared to the 1980s, their economic difficulty would be even more pronounced.

In France, and in Italy, the conditions and the standards of living of younger cohorts are destabilized: the young experience dynamics that are significantly less propitious than those of their elders. This means a rupture in the welfare regime that is not sustainable, since the socialization of newer cohorts differs from that of previous cohorts, at the expense of newer cohorts. Conversely, no radical changes appear in either the Finnish or the American dynamics: these are stable welfare regimes with no clear rupture in the process of socialization of different cohorts. The strong social protection in Finland remains a collective good shared by all age groups, and the American inegalitarian system remains almost the same for the period 1985 to 2000. (If we turn instead to the previous period of Reaganomics, the rupture of regime was obvious, but it is now a matter of long-term historical change.)

WELFARE REGIME AND RETURN ON EDUCATION

Credential inflation is defined here as the decline in the nominal value of educational qualifications (in terms of access to income) that new cohorts experience, when compared to the income achievements of elder cohorts at the same age. It does not mean simply that the younger are in a lower position than their elders, since this could affect their life course. More subtly, it may not simply be a shared downward shift—one that is shared in parallel by all age groups—because it might be the result of a long-term increase in educational attainment. If this downward shift is equally shared, however, there is no specific downturn for younger birth cohorts. Thus, we search for specific patterns indicating a lack of parallelism in the changes by age group.

We focus here on the intermediate levels of education (graduation from secondary education, and no more), which are known in France to be notably more responsive to the effects of educational expansion (Duru-Bellat 2006). We assess the consequence of the educational expansion and the diffusion of credentials on the mid-educated lower middle class. Moreover, to have a comparable scale across years and countries over a relatively long period, we analyze the average position of this mid-educated group compared to the average national population during the considered period. The idea of educational credential inflation goes with the hypothesis that the average mid-educated population, compared to the total population, is declining from period to period and from older to younger cohorts; however, for the purpose of this inter-cohort comparison, we are more interested in nonlinear or at least nonparallel changes. What are our main findings? See figure 10.7.

- Everywhere, from the first period to the last one (mid-1980s to around 2000), and from the oldest to the youngest age groups, we measure a dynamics of decline in the relative position of the mid-educated group compared to the average population. In the long term, it results from a mathematical relation: the larger the mid-educated group, the lower its relative position to the total average. Within these long-term dynamics, new young age groups consistently arrive too late, but they will be followed by even younger groups likely to be even closer to the bottom.
- However, the most important elements reside in the nonlinear or nonparallel evolutions. The French case is typical: there, the older age

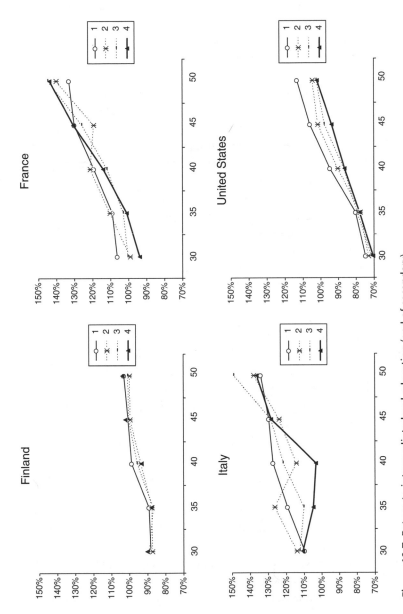

Figure 10.7 Return to intermediate-level education (end of secondary).

Note: 1 = nat. median radi.

Source: LIS project microdata and the author's calculation. See figure 10.5. Periods 1, 2, 3, 4 relate to LIS data for 1985, 1990, 1995, 2000.

groups maintain or increase the relative value of their educational position (the 50-somethings of 2000 are the first cohorts of the French baby boom, a cohort that in France enjoyed a boom in access to the end of secondary and beginning of tertiary education. Meanwhile, the new cohorts of 30-somethings face a clear decline in their position).

- The American case is interesting, since the situation is quite the opposite: the 40- or 50-somethings are experiencing a decline in their position, whereas the younger age groups are in a stable position; these cohorts were the young generations of the American baby boom, which faced a less pleasant situation than did the French one (Vietnam war, entry in the economic slowdown of the late 1960s, and later). They were also the mid-aged adults who experienced the strong reforms of the 1980s, and were the targets of the restructuring and downsizing by American industry (Newman 1999).

- In Finland, the trends are less visible, even though the mid-aged population of the survey in 2000 shows a visible but modest decline.

- Italy is the most significant case where the mid-aged population faces a strong decline, similar to the observations of figure 10.5: when they stay home (in the house of their parents), the young lower-middle-class Italians risk no *déclassement;* but when they enter adulthood as independent workers and parents, their situation appears exceptional in the comparison. More precisely, this decline hides an even deeper change, since the decrease in the Italian fertility rates (with .4 children fewer in fifteen years for the middle-aged households) expresses an even stronger downturn. In this case, we measure significant nonlinear changes where the issue is not a polarization between the young and the seniors, but between the last cohorts of affluence, who are close to retirement, and the first cohorts of the economic slowdown, which are middle-aged today.

These nonlinear changes, when they are substantial (in France and in Italy), suggest that some cohorts are about to avoid a process of educational or credential inflation that other cohorts are facing. These changes show that the populations of some welfare regimes are at risk from stop-and-go policies. In these countries, the contrast between close birth cohorts could become generational fractures, objectively speaking, even if the translation of these fractures in terms of social generations and of generational conflict will not simply be automatic. Conversely, the logics of other welfare regimes (the liberal and the social democratic) aim to limit shocks, to soften cohort fractures, and to smooth strong contrasts between close age groups. It is clear that the positive aspect of the social-democratic regime is to maintain economic inequalities inside acceptable limits (despite their recent increase), even if other challenges exist (problems of declining social homogeneity, of responsibility and incentives to work in a very equalitarian country). The liberal regime presents more risks of conflict and of social difficulties connected to traditional (hierarchical) inequalities; however, it shows lower risks of fracture between birth cohorts than is the case in continental Europe. In the United States, the generation X seems to be less affected by concrete generational situations than in continental Europe.

WELFARE REGIME RUPTURES AND BALANCE BETWEEN SOCIAL GENERATIONS

The main conclusion here is that the responses of the different welfare regimes to the economic slowdown of the post-1970s period have differed substantially. The Finnish model of welfare faced the challenge with a universalistic objective of stabilization and protection of all age groups equally; the young adults are not the specific victims of any kind of retrenchments in this model. At the opposite part of the inequality spectrum, the United States did not diverge from its principle of market competition, and both the young and elders face similar challenges when it comes to their life course. In those countries, the value of education in terms of economic position is less obviously destabilized than in continental Europe.

Conversely, the French and the Italian responses to the new economic challenges, with stronger protections and more affluent positions of seniors, and greater difficulties for the younger cohorts (lower relative income, difficulties in gaining access to economic independence and in entering the job market, and in Italy, stronger inequality and difficulties in mid-life), creates a paradoxical situation where social democracy seem to improve the conditions of older cohorts while the younger cohorts are destabilized and continue to destabilize, even at age 40, when new generations appear and are ready to be socialized. There, the declining value of education when it is compared to the socioeconomic positions of former cohorts (the *déclassement scolaire*) also fuels a pessimistic feeling about a future in which there is a strong risk of destabilization of cultural and political participation. This could partly explain the high level of French pessimism and the feeling expressed by young adults of a double victimization: viewing themselves, that is, as victims of a fake liberalism, which gives freedom to those who have the economic means and a fake socialism that has forgotten the young.

The central point of my conclusion pertains to the long-term sustainability of welfare regimes. To be stable in the long term, a social system must arrange its own reproduction from one generation to the next, and the reproduction of the capacity to create new periods. In France and in Italy, today's seniors benefit from a large welfare state, but the vast social rights they were able to accumulate was the consequence of their relatively advantaged careers; I assert that the new generations, when they become seniors themselves, will not be able to benefit from the same rights, and the large size of the present welfare state will automatically erode with cohort replacement, since the reproduction of the welfare regime is far from certain.

In France, where the generational dynamics of the different social strata are parallel, if not similar, the major problem is not generational inequalities but the fact that newer generations heavily support a welfare system that could collapse before they benefit from it. The problem is not stagnation but lack of preparation for the long term, at the expense of the most fragile population: the young and the recently socialized generations. Herein lay the problem of sustainability for the current welfare regime: it appears large, strong, and durable, but its decline is almost certain; the security it offers to seniors is often at the expense of young cohorts facing radical uncertainty.

In the United States, the case is more complicated. For the young generations, the highest classes enjoy exceptionally better positions while the middle classes see their fortunes stagnate, and the poor are subjected to relative, if not absolute, deprivation. For the moment, this regime is stable and seems durable. At the opposite end, the Finnish case shows that the high standards of protection, equality, and solidarity can be intergenerationally stable too, since newer cohorts benefit from similar conditions and rights as their elders.

The key question is, will the younger generations in France or in Italy continue to tolerate a system where their social condition is devalued compared to older generations, with no clear prospects for improvement? For the moment, these intergenerational inequalities are accepted, since they are generally unknown—their social visibility is low and their political recognition null. These examples of the corporatist and familialistic impasse show that if we want social solidarity across age cohorts, there is no other way than via a universalistic model (similar to the Nordic one) that supports equally the young, the middle-aged, and the old in a long-term perspective of socialization. In terms of consumption, these results give a better understanding of differences in the national life courses from the perspective of people's standards of living. In France, compared to the United States, the young generation faces real difficulties; at the opposite end of the age spectrum, today's seniors benefit from a specific economic boom and from economic homogenization (more equality). Along these lines, in France, seniors appear attractive targets for the marketing of products, while the young are often framed in terms of social problems.

The Italian situation is similar, but the demographic collapse of young generations of adults (who are less numerous with fewer children) and their increasing degree of familialistic dependence combine to reduce the extent to which the social problem is immediately visible; however, this problem will inevitably present itself, raising questions about who will care for elders. Conversely, Finland seems to be a stable model of development of a universalistic solidaristic regime of collective improvement. The social problems that appear elsewhere (a widening gap between the rich and the poor, accumulation of social problems for the newer generations, destabilization of the young and educated middle class, etc.) seem to be relatively less pronounced, and the general atmosphere is more propitious to socially homogeneity, with the development of a wageearner middle class in a knowledge-based society. While recognizing that there are limitations to the welfare regime model, this analysis suggests that the universalistic welfare regime is sustainable and maintains its own capacity for long-term development.

The real problems are elsewhere. The French and the Italian cases are more problematic, with clear signs of failures in the socialization of the new generations. In this respect, we will have to extend the comparison. If Germany tends to offer more optimistic prospects (if we overlook demography), the case of Spain could be also very interesting: there, the *mileuristas* (young university graduates earning less than 1,000 euros a month, which leaves them less affluent although better educated compared to their parents) present a problem of major importance for the future of social development. In many other countries, the same kind of analyses could be useful; for example, in Argentina, where public universities have offered for the last twenty years more young graduates than the economy could absorb, and in Japan, where the post-1990 economic slowdown has produced consequences including a failure in the socialization of younger adults and an emergence of new social problems involving *hikikomori* (ひきこもり), young eternal adolescents preferring videogames to real life; *freeters* (フリータ, or *furita*), who are new cohorts of nonlabor force nonstudents living with the support of parents; or parasite singles (パラサイトシングル, or *parasaito shinguru*), who live for years or decades in their parents' homes. Problems connected with overdevelopment can be observed now in Taiwan, and even might emerge now in urban China, where some young graduates of prestigious universities prefer to stay with uncertain or poor social status in Shanghai or Beijing, rather than accept better positions in mid-sized cities (cities of perhaps 5 million inhabitants) in continental China. This problem will be one of the most frustrating confronting longtime and newly developed societies in the twenty-first century.

Notes

I wish to acknowledge the useful discussions, comments, help, and support I received from Riitta Jallinoja, Ian Rees Jones, JP Roos, Pekka Sulkunen, Aurélie Mary, Enzo Mingione, Katherine S. Newman, and Paul Attewell.

1. France and the United States both experienced a period of postwar affluence: the American "Golden Age of capitalism" (Maddison 1982) and the French *Trente glorieuses* (Fourastié 1979), which contrast with the subsequent period of economic slowdown and diminished expectations (Krugman 1992). See, notably, Chauvel 1998/ 2002.

2. The French representation of the social stratification system in terms of occupation is different from the American one; the French tradition is very strong and contributes to a declining but still central "classist" vision of French society, shared by most social scientists, the media, and social actors. In this respect, the contrast with the United States is dramatic. See also Szreter (1993), who develops a comparative view of the difference in the representations of middle-class occupational groups.

3. During the twentieth century, an average age gap of about thirty years separated parents and their children.

4. These parents are about to help their children in different ways with the intensification of *solidarités familiales* (transfers and transmissions between generations, both financial in kind and cultural and material) that Attias-Donfut (2000) describes; but at the collective level, the first and the most efficient *solidarité* would consist of a redistribution of social positions.

11

Education and the Labor Market

The Case of Poland

Pawel Polawski

THE CONTEXT FOR THE DEBATE ON EDUCATION

Various arguments are offered to support greater investment in education, along with higher levels of education for more people. One common assumption holds that widely accessible educational opportunities are the remedy not only for income inequalities but also for failures of governance. After all, the legitimacy of any political system is enhanced by an increasing number of actors becoming engaged in the process of governing, and by the development of various forms of participatory democracy or, in a different convention, of deliberative democracy (Dryzek 1990; Hirst 1994). These depend on the enrichment of a knowledge base that supports policy decisions (Kooiman 1993), and consequently along with this, on a well-informed and properly educated populace. The notion of empowerment (whose elements are introduced to schools through, for example, civil rights classes) is nothing but a democratizing strategy, based on an assumption that knowledge guarantees wider participation in public life. Civil education plays an essential role in this process by teaching people how to formulate their objectives, articulate their self-interests, and gain information regarding individual entitlements and how to achieve them. It is also assumed that the better educated people are, the more conscious and active they will be (Hall and Taylor 1996). This suggests that those who are, relatively speaking, highly educated will not only be more efficient in dealing with formal and informal rules of social life, but that they will also tend to be more often actively involved in many aspects of public life—in short, that they will try to influence administrative decisions and participate in national elections (Czapinski and Panek 2007). The educated citizen is a conscious citizen and therefore a more valuable one.

The very notion of democratization places an emphasis on such functions of education as legitimizing and stabilizing the political order. It's worthwhile to recognize that this kind of thinking is not only present in politics but also has its history in sociology, as exemplified by what Ernest Gellner has stated in *Nations and Nationalism* (1991). Among other matters, he writes about how educational systems have influenced the character of nation-states during the process of their development. Gellner's arguments deal with, first, the role of general education in the process of widely circulating the ideas that help transform the State into what is described usually as the Nation; and second, the need for standardization of school training, along with limited specialization at the primary school level, within a mobile industrial society. Whereas the ideological function of education in Gellner's analysis is latent, it has since become manifest, and some references are made to it, for instance, in the name of social dialogue.

The most often used argument for increasing the level of education, which has solid support in available data, refers to the concept of human capital and the economic functions of education. It has been assumed after Becker (1975) that human capital is a basic factor of economic growth, and the increased competitiveness of individual companies and the economy as a whole. Rhetorically, the European Union (EU) views the profits derived from higher education in the context of human capital; this can be seen clearly in EU documents and strategies. At the summit in Lisbon 2000, for example, it was agreed that the most important aim of the union was to strive to achieve a more dynamic and highly competitive economy for its member states, while improving labor market conditions as sketched out in a "better jobs" campaign; and, at the same time, maintaining tight social cohesion. (In EU documents, the idea of social cohesion is somewhat hazy.) The general objectives are to be achieved by increasing investments in human resources; reducing the number of young people between ages 18 and 25 who end their education at a secondary school level; transforming schools into local, commonly accessible "educational centers"; developing and carrying out active policies in the labor market; encouraging the notion of lifelong learning; and improving the educational system so as to produce a more flexible workforce. Similar plans and objectives are included in the strategies of the EU members: in Poland, for example, this is known as the Human Capital Operational Program.

What we call *human capital* should enhance individual opportunities. It seems that this is the case if the basic factor of human capital's quantity is education, measured either in years of learning or by the level of educational degree attained. Indeed, the correlation between the level of educational attainment and the income, or the unemployment risk, is universal. For example, comparative data demonstrate throughout OECD countries that the higher an individual's level of formal education, the higher his or her earnings, the lower the risk of unemployment, and the fewer expected years of unemployment during the course of a working lifetime (OECD 1998:110). Consequently, we tend to place the blame for individual failure on personal faults. The most obvious fault is inefficiency in dealing with the labor market, along with a lack of qualifications necessary to obtain success in this market. So, achieving a higher level of education and the necessary qualifications seems to be a universal remedy for personal troubles and, along with them, social and economic problems. There is evidence that investing in education pays: in OECD countries, the rate of return to tertiary education ranges between 5 and 15 percent, and the average return is slowly increasing (Boarini and Strauss 2007).

However, it is quite possible that these arguments for increasing the level of education (especially in terms of public policy and the labor market) may not fit current economic realties. The production of well-educated graduates with suitable credentials can sometimes be higher than the demand for them, resulting in a relative decline of opportunities for a highly qualified labor force. The particular educational courses offered may not meet employers' needs.

Peter M. Blau (1994) discusses the paradoxical pursuit of education, which is what happens when the level of education in the prevailing population does not necessary mean relatively higher earnings and better life-chances for everybody:

> Since educational qualifications contribute to occupational achievements in industrial societies, individuals have incentives to improve their career chances by acquiring as much education as possible. Aggregate occupational opportunities, however, as distinguished from the comparative occupational chances of individuals, depend largely on the occupational services in demand in the labor market. The pursuit of superior education by many persons to improve their occupational chances raises the level of education in the population. But a higher prevailing level of education in a country has little effect on occupational opportunities, which are exogenously determined by economic demand. Consequently, fewer positions are available for qualified candidates; there is more competition for available opportunities; and returns to education decline. Since the best educated candidates continue to have the best chance to obtain any given position, it continues to be rational to pursue superior education. (Blau 1994:103)

Statistics show that the phenomenon of overeducation is common in highly developed countries. For example, Groot and Van den Brink (2000) state that roughly one-fourth of employees in twenty-five industrial countries can be considered overeducated; this means that they work at positions for which their qualifications are not required. Other data (Belfield 2000:37) indicate that in

European countries, the magnitude of overeducated people ranges between 15 and 30 percent. Furthermore, the rate of return to education is about 50 percent lower for those employees whose job doesn't require their skills than it is for those who work in jobs appropriate for their qualifications (Duncan and Hoffman 1981; Sicherman 1991). On average, education gives an advantage, but for some employees that advantage is smaller than for others.

In Poland, and most likely in other postcommunist countries as well, the phenomenon of overeducation is relatively new. During the 1990s, people noticed the correlation between higher education and higher earnings, along with lower unemployment rates for more educated workers. Simultaneously, there was an intensive promotion of higher education, with campaigns to convince people that school qualifications and other training programs would create personal prosperity now and in the future. In Poland, as a result, the educational achievements of the labor force have increased rapidly since the beginning of the 1990s. The education level of the population has improved to include, for example, higher enrollment rates in secondary education and a significant increase in the percentages of the population with a college and university degree. Moreover, it seems that education reforms and privatization have at least partly counteracted past inequalities in access to educational institutions. Although these reforms have been somewhat effective in fighting educational inequalities, they have, however, also created selection mechanisms and barriers in the labor market.

The following chapter offers, first, a description of changes in Poland's educational system during the past decade; and second, a discussion of the impact of these reforms on workers' skills, as well as on the role of educational credentials in the labor market. The analysis is based on secondary data drawn from official statistics and reports concerning implementation of the reforms. Additionally, I will dispute the argument that what has happened in Poland is an example of what the sociologist R. K. Merton terms "unanticipated consequences": we are increasing the level of human capital in the population in order to give people equal chances, but by increasing the general level of education, we are disadvantaging some people in the labor market. Even if we haven't yet produced overeducation, certain conditions are ripe for it.

THE "EDUCATIONAL MIRACLE" AND ASPIRATIONS OF POLES

One of the characteristics of Polish society during the era of Real Socialism was a phenomenon known as the "decomposition of social stratification components" (Slomczynski and Wesolowski 1974; Wesolowski 1980). In capitalist societies, three dimensions of inequality—education, earnings, and occupational prestige—tend to be highly correlated. But in communist Poland, these dimensions were not aligned. Those who had the most education did not tend to earn more than those with less education. For example, in 1981, the average earnings for employees with a tertiary education amounted to 94 percent of the average earnings for all workers in Poland; only 60 percent of employees with tertiary education had higher earnings than the average salary in Poland (Wesolowski and Mach 1986; Mokrzycki 1997). In other words, education didn't pay, at least not when measured in terms of earnings.

Education's lack of fit with earnings and occupational prestige lasted until the beginning of the 1990s. Meanwhile, the proportion of Poles with higher education remained relatively low. This was caused by the structure and capabilities of the educational system, which effectively limited the number of students. In 1990, at the beginning of the transformation, only 7 percent of Poles had a tertiary education, compared to a 20 percent average at that time for the countries of the European Union. There were just over 40,000 students at the Polish universities. All of the universities were public except the Catholic University of Lublin, which was financed by the church.

In 1990, as a result of political reforms and according to the logic of the free-market economy, a recomposition of the social structure began. Among other matters, it involved aligning employees' level of income to their education and professional position (Pohoski 1995:365–366; Domanski 1997). As a result, gaps developed in the earnings of educated employees compared to manual workers—differences that favored the former group. At the same time, in 1990, Parliament enacted a new education law for tertiary education that facilitated the establishment of private educational institutions, with the state administration controlling accreditation and supervising the quality of the new private colleges and universities, which would receive limited funds from the public finances.

These changes resulted in a rapid expansion of tertiary educational institutions. Between the years 1990 and 2000, the number of tertiary instiutions in Poland quadrupled, from 112 to 441 (see table 11.1). The number of students increased almost fivefold, from 403,000 in 1990 to nearly 2 million in 2006. The percentage of those in higher education is now almost 50 percent—that is, roughly half of the population of an age appropriate to attend college or university (aged 18 through 25) is enrolled. The net coefficient (the proportion of people aged 18 through 25 who are students) amounted to 38 percent in 2006, while it was only 9.8 percent in 1990.

It's also important to note that this educational boom in Poland has been financed out of tuition and fees. A significant number of students have been paying for their own education, which wasn't the case prior to the transformation. Yet commercialization has led to more than just the

Table 11.1 Tertiary schools and students by type of institution, 1990–2007.

Type of institution	Institutions				Students (in thousands)				Graduates (in thousands)			
	1991	1999	2004	2006	1991	1999	2004	2006	1991	1999	2004	2006
	112	277	420	441	407,9	1 421,3	1 912,8	1 927,7	59,0	212,9	381,5	391,7
Universities	11	15	17	18	141,1	410,8	554,9	550,5	19,3	67,8	110,1	115,9
Technical universities	30	23	22	22	84,0	289,3	340,2	318,9	11,7	34,3	57,1	55,7
Agricultural univerities	9	9	9	8	36,4	78,0	107,6	92,0	6,0	12,1	17,9	16,6
Universities of economics	5	94	93	95	24,0	332,1	387,9	406,2	3,1	44,2	100,2	88,0
Teacher tertiary schools	10	19	17	17	47,6	137,6	133,8	117,4	8,4	29,9	33,9	32,7
Medical universities	12	10	9	9	38,7	28,1	44,5	53,1	5,6	4,4	6,0	9,9
Maritime tertiary schools	3	2	2	2	2,5	8,6	12,1	10,5	0,3	1,3	2,5	2,4
Academies of physical education	6	6	6	6	14,6	20,9	27,0	29,0	2,4	4,9	4,8	5,7
Academies of fine arts	17	21	22	21	8,2	12,0	15,1	14,9	1,3	1,7	2,5	2,8
Theological tertiary schools	7	14	14	14	6,7	9,1	10,4	10,7	0,9	1,3	2,0	2,7
Other tertiary schools	2	25	28	36	4,1	65,8	72,2	80,0		9,6	17,1	17,4
Nonuniversity tertiary schools		39	181	193	0,0	29,0	207,1	244,5	1,3	1,3	27,4	42,0

Source: GUS 2007; own calculations.

establishment of numerous new colleges. After 1990, private but also public colleges developed a system of charging for extramural and evening education. Now, about one-third of all students are learning in private institutions, and about 50 percent of all students are in the extramural or evening system. (This compares to only 20 percent in 1990.) Available statistics indicate that 20 percent of the income of public colleges and 95 percent of the income of private colleges derive from tuition and fees (GUS 2007a: 306). It is also worth noting that Poland's public expenditures on education have increased during this period, but they have failed to keep up with the increasing number of students. In 2006, these expenditures amounted to 0.95 percent of GDP, which is 0.30 percent more than the amount spent ten years earlier; however, the number of students increased more dramatically. Comparable data from the OECD (which, for Poland relates only to students of public tertiary institutions) also indicate that the amount of money spent yearly on one student is one of the lowest in the OECD countries: US $3,893 in 2004 (converted using purchasing power parity), compared to an OECD average of almost US $8,000; again, this calculation refers only to public institutions.

The change in the nation's educational structure is a consequence of the rapid growth in the number of tertiary school students. The percentage of people with a tertiary education has more than doubled since the period just before the transformation (see figure 11.1). Similarly, growth took place in the percentage of people with a secondary education, the necessary credential to enter a college or university. Meanwhile, we saw a considerable decline in the number of people possessing only a primary education. These changes have obviously been caused by more than simply a broadening of the educational system; natural population trends have also played a role, as the older generation, less educated during the times of the Real Socialism, is dying out.

Research clearly suggests that the educational aspirations of Poles are growing, regardless of their achieved education level, age, and professional position. Public opinion surveys show that popular awareness of the importance of education has been growing on a yearly basis since the beginning of the last decade. Answers to the question, "Do you think that it is worthwhile to attain an education, to study in Poland nowadays, or that it isn't worthwhile?" were as follows: 42 percent responded "definitely yes" in 1993, 66 percent in 2002, 76 percent in 2004, and 70 percent in 2007. Those who replied in the negative declined from 20 percent in 1993 to 5 percent in 2007. The rate of those who wanted their children to achieve an education also grew (CBOS 2007). It was twenty percentage points higher among parents with primary and vocational educations, and about ten points higher among those with secondary and tertiary education, when comparing 2007

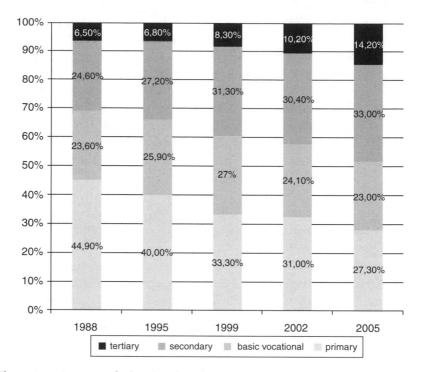

Figure 11.1 Structure of educational attainment, Poland 1988–2005.

Source: Glowny Urzad Statystyczny, 2007. *Maly rocznik statystyczny Polski.* Warsaw: GUS, table 6-66.

to 1993. Qualitative research indicates that even in poor families, who mainly live off various social security benefits, the education of children is a priority (Polawski 1999).

Now, nearly 80 percent of young people in Poland aged 12 through 15 expect to graduate from tertiary school, while during the early 1990s, fewer than 40 percentof young people did. Consequently, the percentage of those who plan to end their education at the primary or vocational school level has declined. The changes, described above, are not only the result of growing ambitions, but have also been produced by institutional changes in the educational system, which encourage people to attain knowledge at various levels. More discussion on this point will follow.

Meanwhile, public consciousness has also taken note of an important change in the realignment of education, earnings, and occupational prestige (see Rychard 2000). Apart from the shifts in attitudes toward education, there are important motivational changes as to why learning is worthwhile. High earnings are the most important motivation: more than 60 percent of respondents cited this. Other significant motivations are attaining an interesting profession, creating an easier life in the future, and avoiding unemployment. Interestingly, the percentage of those who cited higher earnings and the lower likelihood of unemployment as the most important motivations for learning changed, according to ongoing dynamics within the labor market. These factors were cited more often when unemployment was increasing and less frequently when the rate of unemployment was declining.

The problem is that higher education causes people to expect higher earnings and better conditions at work. Yet, there is a gap in Poland between expected earnings and actual earnings—a gap that is greatest for those with tertiary education. Evidence suggeststhat the most educated employees have the least accurate expectations about their earnings (Czapinski and Panek, 2007:166). Earlier, Czapinski and Panek (2005:127) also pointed out that the difference between prevailing and expected wages is much larger in the case of higher educated people; this means that they have a less realistic outlook about the financial benefits of their degrees than do those with a lower education.

More highly educated people expect higher incomes, but they rarely achieve their expected salaries. So what is the advantage of gaining an education in contemporary Poland? There are many signs of a modification in the rules of social stratification in Poland. Nowadays, it's not enough simply to attain education; that education needs to be appropriate in regard to specialization and achieved skills. Yet signs abound that that the public has not yet come to appreciate this second fact, at least not as readily as they understand the simple statistical relationship between educational levels and income and/or life opportunities.

PROFITS FROM EDUCATION

Education yields its profits in terms of both earnings and an impact on the general labor market. Available research suggests that throughout the period of transformation, salaries for employees with a tertiary education have been higher than for those with primary and vocational educations. In 2006, the average earnings of people with master's degrees or higher amounted to 147.3 percent of the average earnings in Poland; the earnings of people with a secondary education amounted to 89 percent of the average; for those with a basic vocational education, 73 percent; and for people with a primary education, 70 percent (GUS 2007b:64). Additionally, earnings growth has been greater for those with a tertiary education compared to others, with one exception: the earnings of people with a vocational education have also increased rapidly.

A similar pattern appears in regard to hourly rates of pay. An hour of work for a person with a tertiary school diploma is worth 170 percent of the average hourly rate of pay in Poland, while an hour of work for a person with a primary education is worth only 66 percent (GUS 2007b:69). It's also worth noting that educational differences in salaries are greater within the private sector than the public sector. In the private sector, the difference between the earnings of people with a tertiary education and those with a primary education amounts to 126 percent of the average earnings, whereas in the public sector, it is significantly lower, amounting to nearly 50 percent of average earnings in Poland. Thus, private employers value educational attainments much more than public employers do.

Salary level depends not only on the level of education but also on skills and expertise. Therefore, within the group of people commonly recognized as "experts" or "professionals," those who work at positions that almost always demand a tertiary education, the average monthly payment fluctuates from 220 percent of the average earnings in Poland (for lawyers) to 97 percent of that average (for teachers in primary schools) (GUS 2007b). Meanwhile, surveys indicate that profits from education are produced relatively quickly. The salaries of people who increased their qualifications during the two years prior to the survey (not only in educational institutions but also in various courses and training programs) currently amount to 154 percent of the salaries of those who didn't (Czapinski and Panek 2007:131).

The profitability of a private investment in education is confirmed as well by the results of analysis concerning the rate of return to education. Yet most research suggests a pattern: the bonus from education relates only to the university level. At other levels, the profitability of individual investments in education is lower, and again we see that it is connected not only to formal credentials but even more strongly to professional experience. According to Rutkowski (1996, 1997) the rate of return to education, as measured by additional earnings, significantly increased in the first period of the transformation: from 5 percent in 1987 to 8 percent in 1996. In 1992, 1995, and 1996, every year of learning by those employed in the private sector brought higher earnings than for those employed in the public sector, at a rate of 0.6, 0.9, and 0.8 percent, respectively. Similar results were obtained by Newell and Reilly (1997), who calculated the rate of return to education for people with a university diploma as 8 to 10 percent. Currently, this amount (disregarding some methodological differences in calculations) is stable. Strawinski (2007:17) calculated it at 10.2 percent of yearly earnings.

This favorable picture (for people who plan to educate themselves and those who promote the values of a common education) is somewhat altered, however, by an analysis presented by the authors of a panel survey (Czapinski and Panek 2003). The results of their calculations were quite surprising— first, because they did not confirm the profitability of investing in education at the college/bachelor level; and second, because they pointed out a distinct decline of profitability of investment in education at the master's degree level, when comparing the current situation to 1999. One of the authors commented on the study's findings as follows:

> A college/bachelor's degree, in comparison to a university/master's one, gives so little rate of return, especially for men, that the great popularity of such studies is very much surprising....The Poles have understood that tertiary education is a very good investment, but they don't recognize that the university/master's degree is something that really counts, or the offer of such education compared with college/bachelor's education is too modest. (2003:121)

The authors explain that the decline in the rate of return during the last four years is the result of less demand for graduates with popular majors, which are offered on a large scale by private schools at the college/bachelor's level. Most prominent among these majors are business studies (marketing, finance, bank management, etc.). Research indicates that 51 percent of graduates of tertiary schools in Poland—those who have achieved both bachelor's and master's degrees—have completed social science, business, and law studies; another 16 percent have completed education and training programs; and 8.5 percent, humanities and the arts. In the first category, Poland is the European leader in terms of the percentage of graduates. However, our country ranks last in the field of science and technology, with just 8 percent of all graduates in this area (European Commission 2005:318). As a result, the payoff of the educational miracle is actually not so apparent. In fact, educational benefits are significantly lower than might be expected because of the overproduction of graduates in those fields in which educational programs have proved to be inexpensive and simple to establish and maintain.

LABOR

In the prevailing situation in the Polish labor market, educated people are economically more active (this means they are either working or actively searching for work) than are people with relatively lower levels of education. We can also notice different dynamics of economic activity in both groups. Economic activity rates in 2006 were almost three times higher for people with tertiary school diplomas than for people with primary educations—86.7 and 31.2 percent, respectively (Grotkowska and Sztanderska 2007:130). The number of economically active people in each group has decreased in the last decade in Poland; this rate has also decreased for the population as a whole, from 65.9 percent in 1995 to 62.8 percent in 2005. It is worth noting that this is the worst employment decline in the EU. However, this decline has been uneven: the most dramatic decline has occurred in low-education categories, with a decrease of 28 percent among the group with only a primary education and a 10 percent decrease in economic activity among those with a vocational education. In the group of people with tertiary education, the decline has been the smallest, amounting to just 0.5 percent. Yet we notice that not only the quality of education but also specialization determine economic activity in the labor market. The decline of activity was less among people with a vocational education than for those with a general education (the decline of activity rates in the years 1995 to 2000 amounted to 7.6 percent for people with a vocational secondary education and 15.1 percent for those with a general secondary education).

Consequently, assuming that economic activity is the result of people's calculations regarding personal opportunities in the labor market and likely payoffs, it turns out that the balance of benefits and losses at work is really more profitable for people with a tertiary education. But the lack of economic activity among other groups also depends much more on skills than on formal credentials.

From 1990 to 1993, the unemployment rate in Poland increased, reaching the level of 16.4 percent; then, from 1994 to 1998, it declined and reached 10.4 percent. The next increase, which occurred from 1999 to 2003, produced unemployment near 20 percent, however, since 2004, the unemployment rate has declined by almost half, to a level of 11.5 percent. For people with a tertiary education, the level of unemployment was 3.6 percent in 1994, declining to 2 percent at the end of the decade; since then, along with the general tendency, it has increased, reaching 8 percent in 2006. In 2002, 3.8 percent of those unemployed had a tertiary education; in 2007, that figure reached 7 percent. At the same time, though, the percentage of the unemployed who had a basic vocational education decreased from 36 to 29.6 percent. In fact, when we analyze data regarding registered unemployment in Poland from the perspective of education, what worries us the most are the trends over time, and not the differing rates of unemployment between groups with varying education levels.

A general rule, as in the case of earnings, is simple: the lower the level of education, the bigger the risk of unemployment. The number of those unemployed who possess a relatively lower level of education is also considerably higher than of those with higher levels of education. Public opinion, as stated earlier, has accurately noted this relationship; surveys continually show that high earnings, as well as the hope for avoiding unemployment, are people's basic motivation for education. Yet we perceive a similar problem to that mentioned earlier: Some fields of study are less profitable than others, and it has not penetrated the social consciousness that the dynamics of unemployment are quire different among people with tertiary educations than for other educational groups.

The number of unemployed in particular areas of education has changed during the last ten years along with changes in the unemployment rate, yet long-term trends vary (see figure 11.2). Over a long period, the number of unemployed with relatively low education and, what is equally important, vocational training, has tended to decline. The opposite is the case when it comes to the unemployed with a tertiary education or a general secondary education (attained at schools that basically prepare people not to start working but to enter a college or a university): in both cases, we see an increasing trend over time. Similar patterns appear in the case of long-term unemployment, which lasts twelve months or longer.

The present trends could be interpreted in two ways: first, they demonstrate a strong resilience among people with tertiary education to changes in the economy, as well as greater vulnerability among those with relatively lower education; second, they reveal that, even during an economic boom, demand is lower for work that requires a tertiary education, and this trend becomes more pronounced each year. Forecasts for graduates in the labor market confirm these trends (Kabaj 2004).

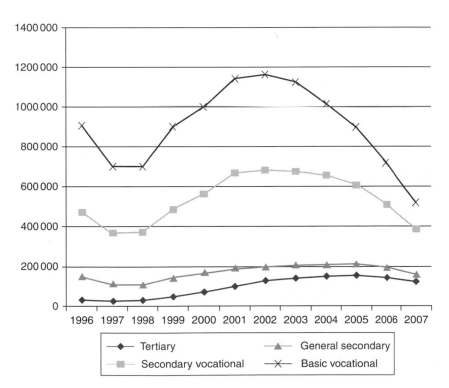

Figure 11.2 Unemployment by education level, Poland 1996–2007.

Source: Ministry of Labor and Social Affairs data on registered unemployment.

Some phenomena are more clearly seen when we consider unemployment among graduates. Unfortunately, the available statistics regarding
unemployment of graduates exist only up until 2003; since then, the category "graduate" has not been taken into consideration in statistics kept by
employment services and aggregated nationwide.

Figure 11.3 presents the number of registered unemployed graduates
from various types of schools. It shows clearly an increasing number of
unemployed graduates from tertiary schools at a time when the absolute
number of "educational boom" graduates was increasing as well. A consistent increase was also noticed among graduates of general secondary schools;
however, during this time of improving economic conditions, the number of
unemployed graduates from vocational schools decreased considerably. It
should be stressed that, although the trend of unemployed graduates from
tertiary schools was going up, the average time waiting for a new job was, in
their case, relatively short: only twelve months in 1968, while among the rest
of graduates the waiting time was sixteen months. The length of job searches
increased for all educational categories during the years that followed.

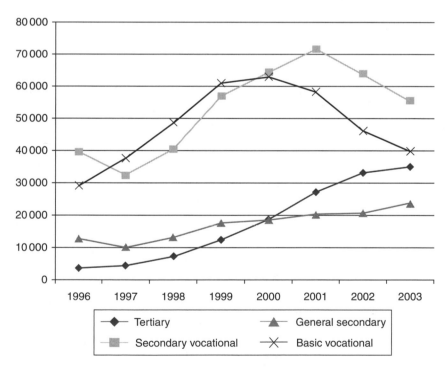

Figure 11.3 Unemployed graduates by education level, 1996–2003.

Source: Polish Ministry of Labor and Social Affairs data on registered unemployment.

Additionally, data from the labor market monitoring surveys that were carried out among employers show that the greatest number of vacancies were in jobs requiring a basic vocational education (49.6%). It is clear, therefore, that industry mostly requires employees with lower skills. Job vacancy rates in other categories were as follows: 34.3 percent for industrial workers and craftsmen; 15.3 percent for operators and fitters of machinery end equipment; and 17.1 percent for highly qualified experts. Most of the vacancies in the latter category were in institutions of public administration and national defense, social security services, and institutions of health and social welfare—that is, mainly in the public sector, which means that salaries were relatively lower.

In spite of the existence of unemployment, especially among graduates from tertiary schools, business executives in Poland complain about the lack of a qualified labor force (KPMG 2007). In 2007, 14 percent of companies surveyed mentioned the lack of qualified workers as the most important obstacle in the development of their companies (this compares to 3% in 2003). When companies seek highly qualified workers, they consider those who have a technical education, while seldom contemplating those who represent the most popular fields of study among graduates from Poland's tertiary institutions. Owing to underemployment problems and the lack of demand for their services, graduates from management, marketing, finance, and similar fields constitute a significant category of the Polish overeducated. But at this time, specific data are not available that would enable us to more precisely describe this category. Meanwhile, employers value not only formal qualifications but also experience. This may not be a particularly revealing conclusion, but it is a reasonable one worth noting, and it is confirmed both by surveys on registered unemployment (which find that there are greater numbers of unemployed among those who worked for shorter periods of time) and by qualitative research (Baba 2007).

THE CAUSES BEHIND THE SKILLS MISMATCH

Several factors are responsible for the above-described skills mismatch (that is, excess numbers of graduates from general studies in tertiary schools at the same time as there is a labor shortage among those with lower educational qualifications). These factors include migration, incomplete information, structure and characteristics of tertiary education after 1990, and the structure of secondary education after the reform of 1999.

In recent years, the media and public opinion have blamed Poland's lack of specialists on economic migration, especially to other EU countries. But there are not enough reliable data concerning even the size of this migration, let alone the structure of migrants as relates to their education or professional qualifications. Published estimates (INFOS 2006) have varied from 660,000 to 1.2 million; the media have even speculated that as many as 2 million people may have left Poland after its entry into the European Union.

Notwithstanding the difficulty in counting migrants, we do know that dynamics relating to departures, as well as the increasing number of Poles living abroad, have accelerated since 2002, when EU countries began to open their labor markets to workers from new member countries. We can also recognize the main directions of migration. From the moment of our entry to the European Union, Poles have chosen mainly to migrate to Great Britain, Ireland, and Germany, although the last of these countries has served primarily as a magnet for seasonal work (Bukowski 2007; Wisniewski 2006; CBOS 2006).

Information about the education levels of migrants is not consistent; OECD data suggest a relatively higher education level of migrants, as compared to the average education level of the populations of member countries; but the Polish Labor Force Survey reveals that, among Poles working abroad, a majority possess vocational educations (secondary vocational, 28.1%; and basic vocational, 30.9%; Grabowska-Lusinska and Okolski 2008). Meanwhile, better educated people and students tend to leave Poland for a short time and seldom combine their professional future with work abroad. That is a good example of Blau's paradox, mentioned at the beginning of this chapter: not returning to one's home country is associated with a high risk of not completing a tertiary education, which will lead to a decline in future earnings while wasting money already spent on education in one's country of origin.

Studies generally find that migrants fill gaps in the labor markets of those countries that accept them, rather than squeezing out local workers, who typically are not as willing to perform low-prestige, part-time, and/or lower paid jobs. Such data accord with findings relating to global trends: a basic mechanism accelerating migration is an increasing number of low-paid jobs in developed countries, as well as a lack of candidates willing to do this kind of work there (Sassen 1998).

If these assumptions are accurate, we are dealing with two different migration trends that influence the Polish labor market: first, the permanent flow of experts-craftsmen (in demand in Poland during a period of prosperity); and second, a short-term rotation of better educated graduates and students—that is, those who constitute the category of the overeducated in Poland.

Another factor causing a skills mismatch is incomplete information about the structure of labor-market demands. It is a case of imperfect information, as this is understood by welfare economists (e.g., Barr 2004). Personal investments in education, as is the case with all investments, are risky because it is hard to predict employment demand over a long period of time. There are, of course, some forecasts that predict the general trends—for example, an increasing demand for trained specialists and craftsmen (Kabaj 2004). The problem is that the implications of these forecasts are often ignored, or they may never have been publicized. The situation in Poland is unique, however, insofar as there were a variety of factors that encouraged the intensive development of a tertiary education, along with an increased supply of affordable educational options. Establishing new tertiary schools became possible owing to the fact that these would employ many academic workers quickly, and the profile of these schools was strongly influenced by the fact that social scientists constitute a majority among Poland's university personnel (GUS 2007a). Another factor producing incomplete information is the time sensitivity of the relationship between education and financial profits, as well as between supply and demand in the labor market. In one analsyis of the mismatch between labor supply and demand (Baba 2007:154), we can find a description of two surveys of classified advertisements. The first, from 1997, revealed that employers searching for workers generally didn't set or describe educational requirements, nor did they detail expected qualifications. In 2004, when similar research was conducted, it turned out that the majority of employers more precisely described those qualities they were looking for in an employee, including his or her education and qualifications. Within this period, therefore, employers were able to make their demands more precise, probably because of developments relating to the labor-market segmentation and dynamics.

From the start of educational reform in Poland, the notion has been promoted that, first and foremost, the modern economy requires flexibility in the workforce, yet that flexibility is encouraged by a general, nonvocational education. It may be that this notion has somewhat lost relevance along with changes in the labor market, only to be recognized by the labor force after some delay.

A mismatch between the demand for a specialized labor force and the supply of graduates with a tertiary education leads us to consider institutional factors—namely, the structure of the educational system in Poland. At the tertiary level of education, as mentioned earlier, the structure of the educational market, as well as secondary school graduates' preferences, has changed since the beginning of the 1990s. The numbers of teacher-training, technology, and humanities students have decreased, while there has been an increase in the areas of business, management, and social sciences (see table 11.2).

Table 11.2 Tertiary schools graduates by the field of education in 2006.

Field of Education	Students in '000	%	Graduates in '000	%
Education science and teacher training	250,6	12,8	59,9	15,2
Arts	22,2	1,1	3,7	0,9
Humanities	156,5	8,0	33,1	8,4
Social and behavioral science	264,7	13,5	56,7	14,4
Journalism and information	16,8	0,9	3,7	0,9
Business and administration	501,8	25,7	111,7	28,4
Law	54,6	2,8	8,2	2,1
Life science	13,7	0,7	3,1	0,8
Physical sciences	34,5	1,8	6,1	1,5
Mathematics and statistics	16	0,8	3,3	0,8
Computing	103,9	5,3	17,2	4,4
Engineering and engineering trades	153,5	7,9	22,7	5,8
Manufacturing and processing	28,1	1,4	3,9	1,0
Architecture and building	56,5	2,9	8,1	2,1
Agriculture, forestry and fishery	39,7	2,0	6,3	1,6
Veterinary	4,3	0,2	0,6	0,2
Health	92,1	4,7	19	4,8
Social services	1,9	0,1	0	0,0
personal services	64,2	3,3	13	3,3
Transport	16	0,8	2,3	0,6
Environmental protection	55,7	2,9	10,6	2,7
Security services	6,5	0,3	0,9	0,2

Source: GUS 2007, table. 16; own computations.

In the case of primary and secondary education, the reform of 1999 carried out structural changes with the goal of increasing opportunities and enhancing enrollment numbers, as well as educational choices. In the earlier system, a three-year vocational program or a five-year secondary technical school guaranteed vocational training along with a general education. Now, curricula in secondary schools do not guarantee labor-oriented skills, and specialized secondary schools include only some vocational courses. Curricula of secondary vocational schools more often cover courses that correspond to the most popular courses in tertiary education. In a sense, this strongly encourages students to continue their education in tertiary schools (at least through the college/bachelor level). Meanwhile, at the secondary education level, schools often institute graduation examination requirements: previously this wasn't necessary for students preparing for three-year vocational schools, although it was a requirement at the tertiary level.

Another problem for Poland is the country's dubious standards of teaching. Results of PISA cognitive competence surveys situate Polish students below average in OECD countries as relates to their mathematical preparedness to enter technical and science courses. (Changing dynamics suggest that this situation is improving, especially in general secondary schools—see MEN 2006). Additionally, The Adult Literacy Survey points out that almost half of the Polish population lacks functional literacy skills.

To summarize, the Polish educational system has been redesigned to provide easy access and a general education, rather than those skills that are genuinely valuable in the labor market. The fact that education must be related to labor-market demand has been overlooked. Skills mismatch has been an unintentional side effect of the reforms, producing a structural strain: available jobs do not meet the aspirations of young people who were encouraged by education. And these jobs are hardly comparable to those available elsewhere. It does not seem that Poland's educational system is prepared to meet these problems.

12

The Socioeconomic Integration of Immigrants in the EU

Effects of Origin and Destination Countries on the First and Second Generation

Fenella Fleischmann
Jaap Dronkers

Immigrant integration has received a great deal of attention in social scientific research, but this research has concentrated on the classic immigration countries and, most notably, the United States. There, starting with the work of the Chicago School in the 1920s and 1930s, a theory of assimilation was developed that predicted immigrants would, over time, become socio-economically, spatially, socio-culturally, and politically more like natives. However, after World War II waves of immigration from more diverse countries of origin led to a challenge to assimilation theory. Research among different ethnic groups in different urban settings in the United States has revealed that not all immigrant groups experience upward social mobility after arrival. While this still holds true for some immigrant groups, others were found to experience downward assimilation into a socioeconomic, but also racially or ethnically defined, underclass; meanwhile, still other groups were incorporated neither into the middle class nor into the underclass, but instead remained concentrated in ethnic niches or enclaves.

The debate is ongoing in the United States as to whether there is still a general trend toward assimilation for all groups or whether a process of segmented assimilation is at work instead (Alba and Nee 1997; Portes and Rumbaut 2001; Zhou 1997). In Europe, the debate about, and research into, the integration of immigrants is much newer, since most Western European countries have just started to acknowledge themselves as immigration societies. Moreover, policy approaches to immigrant integration vary greatly among European societies, which continue to define themselves as nation-states with heavy ethnic connotations. These different policies are often seen as an important explanation for the differential success of integration processes in the countries of the European Union. A cross-national comparison of the factors that hamper or promote immigrant integration is necessary to estimate the importance of these policy differences. Such a cross-national comparison is especially relevant because the European Union strives now for a common immigration and integration policy.

To avoid confusion, we want to make explicit what we mean by the "socioeconomic integration" of immigrants: we consider immigrants to be *integrated* if their work participation and unemployment rates, as well as their occupational status and their access to the most prestigious jobs, do not significantly differ from those of natives, after controlling for relevant predictors of these outcomes that apply to both immigrants and natives. In other words, successful integration is defined as the absence of significant effects of immigrant status.

Therefore, we want to find out which characteristics of both the countries of destination and the countries of origin promote or hamper the integration of immigrants, taking into account their individual characteristics. In this chapter, we focus on the position of immigrants in the labor market, thus limiting our scope to that socioeconomic dimension of integration. We do this in part for practical reasons: our data provide the most information about this dimension of integration; additionally, covering more than one dimension is hardly feasible within one chapter. But there are other reasons as well. We are in agreement with a number of scholars who have argued that the socioeconomic integration of immigrants is the first step—a precondition for subsequent spatial, socio-cultural, and political integration (Geddes et al. 2004; Waldenrauch 2001).

In addition to differences in the policies and other characteristics among countries of destination, it is expected that countries of origin affect the immigrants' socioeconomic integration. As Kao and Thompson (2003) have argued, immigrants' differences in religion and cultural values lead to different evaluations of achievement, which can partly explain differential outcomes of immigrants coming from different regions of the world. Furthermore, the levels of expected and experienced discrimination in the labor market differ among immigrant groups from different origins, which might partly be due to different levels of visibility for these immigrant groups.

While research on immigrant integration in Europe is still limited in comparison to studies conducted in the classic immigrant-receiving societies, there are already numerous studies comparing the processes and outcomes of integration in different European countries. However, many of them are limited either to a small number of destination countries or to a small number of immigrant groups (for example, see Koopmans and Statham 1999).

Others try to incorporate a larger number of destination countries, either by analyzing more countries separately (e.g., Heath and Cheung 2007) or by comparing national statistics (e.g., Werner 2003). There are several problems with this type of research. Obviously, separate analyses of destination countries do not allow for statistical testing across countries, so the comparison remains on an abstract, theoretical level. Moreover, the definition of who is an immigrant differs among destination countries (as does, to make things even more complicated, the terminology itself), leaving some doubt as to the usefulness of comparing national statistical data from various countries. A more serious problem, however, is that comparisons taking into account only one immigrant group in multiple destinations, or multiple immigrant groups in a single destination, do not allow for the separation of destination-country effects from origin-country effects. This is a serious drawback, since the composition of immigrant populations varies greatly among European countries. A single comparative approach, or a study including only a small number of destination countries, cannot establish whether the differential outcomes of immigration are due to individual factors or to macro-characteristics of either the destination country or the country of origin.

Only a few studies have been published, but these have suffered from a number of shortcomings, such as using such a double comparative multi-level approach (mostly owing to problems in data availability). Tubergen's work (2004; Tubergen, Maas, and Flap 2004) on immigrant integration in numerous countries does examine the effects of macro-characteristics of both destination countries and countries of origin, but his data include only first-generation immigrants. Although this research greatly improves on earlier work, the fact that it does not include the second generation is a serious drawback, since the fate of second-generation immigrants is a much stronger indicator of the degree to which integration is successful. Furthermore, these studies do not focus exclusively on Europe, and therefore they do not allow for detailed measures of intra-European differences in immigrant integration.

Similar approaches have revealed significant effects of both destination and origin countries on the school achievement of immigrant pupils (Dronkers and Levels 2007; Levels and Dronkers 2008; Levels, Dronkers, and Kraaykamp, 2008). These studies made it clear that both the sending and the receiving contexts affect the educational achievement of immigrants' children (next to the usual effects of both micro and meso characteristics, like parental background and school composition), and they report significant macro characteristics of both destination and origin, such as GDP per capita and religious composition.

Kogan (2007) uses an exclusively European focus in her comparison of immigrants' labor-market outcomes. For the EU-15 countries, she examines the effects of a number of macro characteristics, especially welfare regimes and labor-market structure on immigrants' positions. However, her data do not contain information about the immigrants' exact country of origin, which implies that she cannot take into account characteristics of these countries nor can she measure their effects on integration. In addition, her data excludes second-generation immigrants.

The second wave of the European Social Survey allows us to overcome these problems because it provides information on the place of birth for both the respondent and his or her parents, thus distinguishing the country of origin for both first- and second-generation immigrants. Furthermore, since we rely exclusively on one data source, our definition of immigrant status is consistent across countries, which is not always the case in cross-national comparisons. Following, we elaborate on the micro characteristics of individual immigrants and the macro characteristics of their countries of origin and countries of destination as we analyze labor-market outcomes for first- and second- generation immigrants in thirteen EU countries.

DATA AND METHODS

We use the second wave of the European Social Survey (Jowell et al. 2005), which contains data gathered in 2004 and 2005 on more than 45,000 respondents in twenty-three countries. The main aim of this chapter is to assess the impact on immigrants of social and labor-market policies in the destination countries. We measure the inclusiveness of social policies using the European Civic Citizenship and Inclusion Index (Geddes et al. 2004); unfortunately, at the time of this writing, the index was available only for the EU-15 countries. Since data from Italy were not yet available, we could include only fourteen destination countries. This number was further decreased to thirteen because we excluded data from Finland, given the low number of immigrant respondents in that country. Furthermore, we selected only respondents between the ages of 25 and 60, since this is the age span in which most respondents will have completed their education and in which their economic activity is concentrated. Our final sample of 15,602 respondents contains 2,541 immigrants (1,209 males and 1,332 females) from 132 different countries. In the remainder of this chapter we analyze the male immigrants; the results for female immigrants are published elsewhere (Fleischmann and Dronkers 2007).

We classified respondents as *immigrants* if one or both parents were born outside the country of survey. Respondents who were born abroad but to two native parents are not classified as immigrants because we assumed that these children of expats would be more like the native population than are children of mixed marriages and of first-generation immigrants. We used the following rules to establish the country of origin: if the respondent and both of his or her parents were born in the same country, this country was classified as the *country of origin*. If two out of three (parents plus child) were born in the same country, this was used as the country of origin, except if two out of three were natives in the country of survey. If all three were born in different countries, we looked at the language spoken at home. If this corresponded to one of the three countries, this country was used as the country of origin. If none of these conditions applied, we used the country of birth of the mother, arguing that parental culture is more influential in socialization (rather than using the country of birth of the respondent, which can be a temporary situation, especially when family backgrounds are diverse) and that "motherhood is a fact, whereas fatherhood is an opinion." With this procedure, we could distinguish 132 countries of origin, but many of them pertained to only few cases. We therefore aggregated the countries into *regions of origin* when there were fewer than twenty immigrants from a certain country, using a slightly adapted version of the United Nations classification of geographical regions (UN Statistical Office).[1] In the end, we had twenty-seven countries of origin and an additional twenty-one regions of origin, varying in number of immigrants from 2 (French-speaking Caribbean) to 209 (Germany).

On the one hand, our measurement of immigrant status as described above is much more accurate than taking into account only nationality (which is problematic, owing to differences in naturalization rates across countries and the colonial histories of many immigrants) or the respondent's country of birth (which excludes the second generation) (Kogan 2007). On the other hand, this method gives rise to problems, which cannot be solved with the data sets used here or with other available cross-national data.

A definitional problem concerns changing national boundaries, which is particularly relevant to Europe. Owing to changes in the political frontiers after 1945 (the annexation by Poland of some former German territory; the extension of Russia at the expense of Polish territory), and subsequent displacement of large populations, an unknown number of "indigenous" persons are measured as born outside their country (e.g., a German respondent or his or her parents born in Königsberg, East Prussia, now living in Germany; or a Polish respondent or his or her parents born in Lvov, Ukraine, and now living in Poland). Because we did not make a distinction between genuine migrants and border changes, we probably overestimated the number of better integrated immigrants. This failure highlights a conceptual problem in defining an immigrant: for how many generations must a Polish family live in Germany before they are no longer considered Polish? This issue extends to the large number of third-country immigrants originating in former European colonies and whose grandparents immigrated to Europe. Their grandchildren, born in these immigrant-receiving countries, are classified as natives; however, typically in these countries this third generation is still considered "immigrant," especially if they are a visible minority. Therefore, they might have lower levels of education and labor-market outcomes than natives (Portes and Rumbaut 2001).

Moreover, given the sampling procedures applied in constructing the data set used here, our data are unlikely to include illegal immigrants and immigrants with lower skills levels in the language of the destination country.

Dependent Variables

We concentrate our analysis of the socioeconomic integration of immigrants on their integration into the labor market. Four indicators are used to assess different dimensions of this integration. First, we analyze whether immigrants' labor-market participation differs from that of natives. The dichotomous variable economic activity contrasts respondents who either have paid employment or are unemployed but actively searching for a job with those who don't look actively for work. Second, among the economically active respondents, we distinguish between those who are unemployed and those who are currently employed. Third, for those respondents who have paid employment, we examine the occupational status of their current job, using the ISEI scale (Ganzeboom et al. 1992).[2] The occupational-status variable had 307 missing values, 51 of which were among immigrants. In order to avoid loss of information, we imputed missing values for the ISEI scale using a regression procedure in which we took into account the immigrant generation, the country of origin, the highest educational level achieved, and the respondent's gender. Given the disputed continuous character of this occupational status scale, and the lower chances that second-generation immigrants will enter the highest occupational class than will natives (Tesser and Dronkers 2007), we also need to analyze more specific barriers within the labor market. We therefore examine whether respondents succeed in entering the upper middle class, which we define as those occupations classified as higher and lower controllers in the EGP class-categories scheme (Erikson, Goldthorpe, and Portocarero 1979).

Independent Variables: The Macro Level

The main focus here is the question of whether, and if so how, indicators on the macro level, of both the destination and origin countries, affect immigrants' socioeconomic integration in the thirteen EU countries under study. As a measure of immigrant integration policies, we use the European Civic Citizenship and Inclusion Index (Geddes et al. 2004), which was developed for the EU-15 member states. This index contains five dimensions: labor-market inclusion, long-term residence rights, family reunion, naturalization, and anti-discrimination measures. We recoded index scores so that values between -1 and 0 represent less favorable policies on these dimensions, while values between 0 and 1 stand for more favorable policies—that is, policies that are more inclusive of immigrants. The assessment of each country's policies in these areas is based on an ideal, not real, legal framework, which means that the creators of the index made a judgment as to how close certain national policies came to what they consider to be ideal for the integration of immigrants. Next to the five separate dimensions, we include the mean score across these dimensions.

We test the hypothesis that immigrants in countries with a higher score on (one of the dimensions of) the European Inclusion Index are better integrated socioeconomically those in countries that score low on this index. Furthermore, we test the effects of different types of welfare regimes in the countries of destination. Based on the classic typology of Esping-Andersen (1990) and the work of other authors (Kogan 2007), we distinguish among four types of welfare regimes. The *liberal welfare regime*, represented by the United Kingdom and Ireland in our data, is characterized by market-based social insurance and a lack of active employment measures. In this type of welfare regime, universal transfers are very modest and typically only those occupying the lowest strata make use of them, which results in a considerable stigma of welfare dependence. Therefore, there is a strong incentive for success in the labor market and avoidance of welfare dependence. Combined with a deregulated labor market, this type of welfare regime should promote immigrants' access to the labor market and lower their risk of unemployment, although it is questionable whether it brings high-status jobs into close reach for immigrants.

The second type, the *social-democratic regime*, represented by Sweden and Denmark in our analysis, is, on the contrary, characterized by a high standard of universal social insurance for citizens. The objective of such a type of welfare regime is equalization of class differences. Owing to the rather generous transfers in this universalistic welfare regime, the incentive to take on low-skilled, modestly paid labor is strongly reduced for all who have access to the welfare state, including immigrants. This might lower the rates of labor-market participation, especially among immigrants with little human capital, but on the other hand, immigrants should be less likely to occupy mainly low-status jobs than they are with the liberal welfare regime.

In the third type, the *conservative or corporatist regime*, social insurance is state-based instead of market-based; however, in contrast to the social-democratic welfare regime, there is no aim at equalization of status and class differentials. Rather, transfers aim to maintain status differentials, making it difficult for newcomers to the labor market, especially those with few qualifications, to be upwardly mobile. We classify Belgium, France, Germany, Luxembourg, and the Netherlands as countries with conservative welfare regimes. We separately distinguish a fourth type, the *southern or Mediterranean regime*, which is found in Greece, Portugal, and Spain, since this region shares some elements with the conservative welfare regime, but additionally includes a high level of labor-market rigidity and rather low levels of welfare benefits.

Following Kogan (2007), who found a positive effect of the liberal welfare state on immigrants' socioeconomic integration, we argue that the type of welfare regime should be taken into account when analyzing between-country differences in immigrant integration into the labor market. We expect that the liberal welfare regime has a less closed labor market and social welfare system for outsiders than do other welfare regimes and, as a consequence, increases immigrants' opportunities for a successful socioeconomic integration.

Labor-market rigidity might even be more relevant for employment opportunities and ensuing occupational status of immigrants, since more stringent employment protection legislation (EPL) is likely to increase the effects of statistical discrimination and the penalty that immigrants are likely to experience of having outsider status in the labor market (Kogan 2007). EPL data are taken from the OECD's labor market statistics (OECD 2006). We averaged the available scores from 1990, 1998, and 2003 to reach a maximally reliable measure of labor-market rigidity. In our data, EPL ranges between 0.65 in the United Kingdom and 3.33 in Greece. We expect immigrants to be better integrated socioeconomically in countries with a more flexible labor market—that is, countries with lower legal employment protection.

We additionally control for the presence of left-wing parties in governments during the past thirty years. This measure has been used in previous cross-country research on immigrant integration (Tubergen 2004; Tubergen et al. 2004; Levels et al. 2008), but the problem with this indicator is that it is merely a proxy for concrete policies. In the presence of the policy indicators described above, we expect to learn little more from the presence of left-wing parties in the government. Based on the data provided by Beck et al. (2000), we compute a total score for every country, assigning 1 for every year in which the government is exclusively made up of left-wing parties and 0.5 for every year in which a left-wing party is part of a coalition with one or more center or right-wing parties. We expect that the presence of left-wing parties in the government promotes the socioeconomic integration of immigrants.

Furthermore, we control for GDP per capita (expressed in purchasing-power parity) and the Gini coefficient of both destination and origin countries. These measures are perceived to be internationally comparable indicators of the economic situation of a country and the degree of equality in the distribution of wealth within countries. Both indicators were taken from the Central Intelligence Agency *World Factbook* (2007), which provides the most recent information per country.[3] From the same source, we also obtained information about the net migration rate of both countries of destination and origin. We hypothesize that immigrants who come from countries in which these indicators differ only slightly from their destination countries will be better integrated socioeconomically.

For countries of origin, we also include Kaufmann, Kraay, and Mastruzzi's (2005) indicator of political stability, which assesses the probability that the current government will be overthrown in the near future. This internationally comparable measure is available for all countries of destination and origin, with the exception of the Faeroe Islands, Greenland, and Yugoslavia. Furthermore, we include an index of political freedom and civil rights developed and published for the last thirty years by Freedom House (2006). We recode this seven-point index so that higher values represent higher rates of political freedom.

By including these indicators of the political structure of the countries of origin, we introduce a control for potential political motives for migration. Although it is often difficult to strictly distinguish political migrants from economic migrants, we think that the motive for migration is a potential explanatory factor in immigrant integration. Because of the political background of their migration, political refugees might have a stronger bond with their country of origin since they might hope to return to this country after a regime change; furthermore, they might be less positively selected than labor migrants. We expect immigrants from politically less stable and less free countries to be less well integrated socioeconomically.

As a more comprehensive measure of the economic and social development of the countries of origin, we use the scale of the Human Development Index (2006). This index combines information on GDP per capita, education, life expectancy, and gender inequality, and it ranks countries according to these indicators. Owing to the larger economic and cultural differences among the countries of origin and destination, immigrants coming from countries that rank low on this index have less opportunity to become integrated in the EU countries of destination. We expect immigrants from less developed countries to have lower levels of socio-economic integration.

Lastly, we include a dummy variable for the prevalent religion in the country of origin. A religion was classified as prevailing in one country if at least 50 percent of the population belonged to this religious group (data from the CIA *World Factbook* 2007). If less than 50 percent of the population belonged to a single religious group, the country was classified as having no prevalent religion. The prevalent religion in the country of origin is an indicator of the cultural distance between the country of origin and the country of destination, a consideration that has been used in comparable research (Tubergen 2004, Tubergen et al. 2004; Levels et al. 2008). In this analysis, we can make a distinction between the individual religion of the immigrant and the dominant religion in his or her country of origin, which was not possible in earlier studies. We expect immigrants from non-Christian countries to have less favorable labor-market outcomes in the EU countries.

Independent Variables: The Individual Level

Since the process of socioeconomic assimilation of immigrants is expected to differ with different generations of immigrants, we distinguish two such generations. First-generation immigrants are those who were born outside the country of destination. This group makes up 58.3 percent of all immigrants in our sample. Second-generation immigrants are those who are born in the country of destination, but who have at least one parent who was born outside the country of destination. This group comprises 41.7 percent of our immigrant sample.[4] Our generation hypothesis is that the second generation should have more favorable labor-market outcomes than the first generation of immigrants.

Access to, and success in, the labor market depends to a large extent on educational qualifications. We therefore control for the highest level of education achieved by the respondents, using the seven-point ISCED-97 (UNESCO 1997) scale, which ranges from 0 (not completed primary education) to 6 (second stage of tertiary education). However, we had to collapse the "upper secondary" and "postsecondary, nontertiary" categories and the "first stage of tertiary" and "second stage of tertiary" categories owing to a different measurement in the U.K. The highest educational level achieved by a respondent's parents is computed by taking the maximum of the educational-level variable of both parents. These are measured with the same ISCED scale, and since there are no country-specific deviations, we keep the original scale, but we remind the reader that the measures of educational level differ between respondents and their parents. We imputed missing values for the highest level of education of the respondent (10 missing values, 3 of which are among immigrants) and his or her parents (219 missing values, 55 of which are among immigrants), using the mean of groups sorted according to gender, immigrant status, immigrant generation, and country of origin in the case of respondent's education and immigrant status, country of origin and respondent's education in the case of parents' education. In order to control for the effect of imputation, we add (stepwise) dichotomous variables that indicate whether these variables are imputed whenever we use the education variables.. Our education hypothesis is that the higher the respondents' education, and the higher the education of their parents, the better integrated they are socioeconomically.

Furthermore, we include respondents' religion in this step of the analysis. We add dummies for Muslims and those who adhere to no religion.[5] In addition, we assess religiosity with a self-classification measure for which respondents indicated their degree of religiosity on a ten-point scale ranging from "not religious at all" to "very religious." Lastly, we control for the intensity of religious practice, which we assess with a composite measure of prayer and service attendance, measured on a seven-point scale, with higher values indicating a higher intensity of religious practice.

Including individual religion is not common in the analysis of the socioeconomic integration of immigrants, but we have two reasons to expect effects in this respect. First, the cultural habitus of a religious group might affect labor-market outcomes—for example, through the differential evaluation of achievement (Kao and Thompson 2003). Second, European societies react differently to different religious groups, the primary example being the attitude toward Muslims after 9/11. Our religion hypothesis is that religious affiliation and the extent to which individuals follow the practices of their religious community will affect their socioeconomic integration, but we do not have clear expectations with regard to the signs of these effects for different religious groups.

In addition, we take into account whether respondents speak a minority language at home, whether they hold the citizenship of the country of destination, and whether they are born to one native and one immigrant parent. Based on earlier findings (Levels and Dronkers 2008), we hypothesize that immigrants who speak a minority language at home will have less favorable labor-market outcomes. Furthermore, we expect immigrants who are citizens of their destination country, or who are born to one native and one immigrant parent, to have higher levels of socioeconomic integration.

We argue that immigrants from certain countries of origin are likely to be better integrated socioeconomically than immigrants from other countries or regions of origin. Therefore, we coded the information according to whether the country of origin is a neighboring country to the country of destination,[6] whether the country of origin is one of the EU-15 member states (plus the largely comparable countries and silent EU member states, Switzerland and Norway), and whether the country of origin is a former colony or territory of the country of destination.[7] We expect immigrants from countries that fall into any of these categories will be better integrated socioeconomically than immigrants who come from countries that are less historically and culturally connected to the countries of destination in our analysis.

MACRO EFFECTS ON SOCIOECONOMIC INTEGRATION OF IMMIGRANTS

In this part, we present the results of our analyses of labor-market participation, unemployment, occupational status, and upper-middle-class position. Figures 12.1 and 12.2 show clear differences among the thirteen EU member states in both direction and strength of difference between natives and

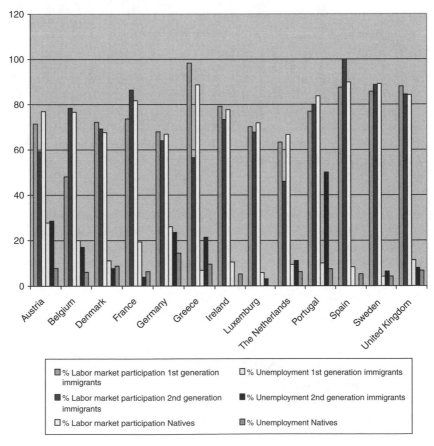

Figure 12.1. Labor market participation and unemployment rates of male first- and second-generation immigrants and natives in 13 EU countries.

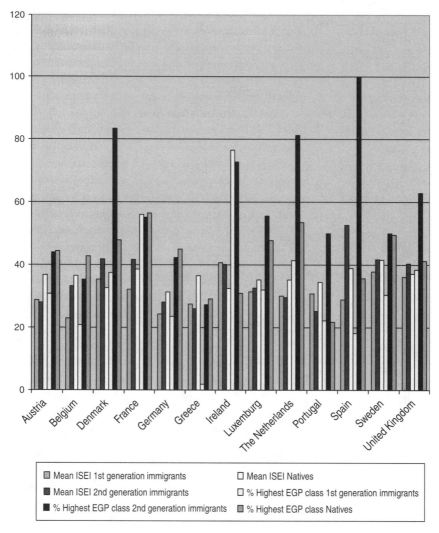

Figure 12.2. Occupational status of male first- and second-generation immigrants and natives in 13 EU countries.

immigrants in relation to these four aspects of labor-market participation. Figure 12.3 shows the differences on the four dimensions of socioeconomic integration for the largest immigrant groups. The differences in these figures are not controlled for individual characteristics.

To estimate the effects of the macro indicators, a cross-classified multilevel model is necessary, since the individual immigrants in our data are nested both within countries of origin and within countries of destination,

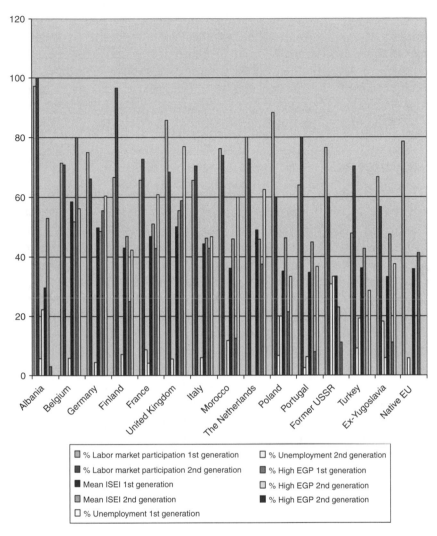

Figure 12.3. Labor market outcomes of male first- and second-generation immigrants from largest origin countries and EU 13 natives.

and these two levels crosscut each other instead of being nested within each other. We use only immigrants in this multilevel analysis because natives do not have a country of origin and destination. Because we include the average score of the native population on the dependent variable in every model as an independent variable, we can interpret the constant of the equations as the differences between the first-generation immigrants and the natives.

To promote the readability of this contribution, we present the final results in a summary table (table 12.1). Readers interested in the statistical specifications of these analyses and the differences in the coefficients of the various models are referred to Fleischmann and Dronkers (2007). We limit ourselves here to the description of the macro characteristics with significant effects. Those nonsignificant macro characteristics of table 12.1 that are significant in more economical models will be discussed in the text.

Labor-Market Participation

The first column of table 12.1 shows the results of the multilevel logistic regression of labor-market participation of immigrants. Macro characteristics of destination countries have significant effects. In countries with a more favorable naturalization policy, the labor-market participation of immigrants is higher. At the same time, immigrants in conservative welfare regimes are much less likely to be active in the labor market, while this likelihood increases in more unequal societies (i.e., those which have a higher Gini coefficient). Also, a higher labor-market participation of the natives in a destination country has a positive effect on the labor-market participation of immigrants.

In addition, we find a number of significant macro characteristics of the countries of origin. Immigrants from countries with more emigrants are less active, which means at the same time that immigrants from countries with high rates of emigration—that is, typical labor migrants—participate more. Immigrants from countries with higher rates of political freedom have somewhat lower participation rates. Immigrants from the EU countries and the postsocialist countries of Eastern Europe participate at higher rates than do natives.

Our model succeeds in explaining practically all of the variance at the level of both country of origin and country of destination.[8] The inclusion of the mean labor-market participation of natives accounts for the large decline in variance between countries of destination. In general, this variance is smaller than that between countries of origin. The explanation is that the thirteen EU countries resemble each other more than does the much larger and more diverse group of 132 countries of origin. Differences in immigrant labor-market participation among countries of destination appear to result mainly from the differential composition of the individual characteristics of immigrants in these countries.

Unemployment

In column 2 of table 12.1, we analyze the unemployment risks of immigrants. We find that the difference between first- and second-generation

Table 12.1 Individual and macro effects on labor-market participation, unemployment, occupational status (ISEI), and social class of male immigrants.

	Labor market participation	Unemploymert	Occupational status (ISEI)	Highest occupational class (EGP)
Individual level				
Second generation	0,122	0,029	**2,924**	**0,801**
One native, one immigrant parent	-0,132	**2,370**	-2,375	1,133
Speaking minority language at home	0,340	-0,466	4,841	0,622
Citizenship of the destination country	0,108	0,142	0,160	0,260
Age	**0,423**	-0,223	0,425	0,026
Age²	**-0,005**	0,002	-0,003	0,000
Highest level of education achieved	0,162	0,030	**7,086**	**1,384**
Missing value on highest level of education	-0,025	0,274	**-7,063**	-1,312
Maximum parental education	**-0,142**	-0,021	**0,992**	**0,181**
Missing value parental education	0,300	**1,222**	**-7,274**	-0,746
Number of children	0,091	0,192	**-0,978**	-0,056
No religion	-0,129	-0,090	0,314	-0,163
Islam	-0,086	**1,904**	2,844	0,106
Religiosity	0,022	0,002	-0,057	-0,025
Intensity of religious practice	-0,026	0,101	0,680	0,081
Education * 1 native, 1 immigrant parent	-0,027	**-0,638**	0,249	-0,466
Education * Minority language	-0,044	0,196	-1,873	-0,282
Education * Islam	-0,005	-0,689	-2,102	-0,202

(continued)

Table 12.1 Continued

	Labor market participation	Unemployment	Occupational status (ISEI)	Highest occupational class (EGP)
Macro level: countries of destination				
Mean native score on dependent variable	2,032	**12,954**	0,135	1,942
EII: Naturalization policy	0,567	n.s.	n.s.	1,265
Employment Protection Legislation	n.s.	n.s.	**-3,325**	**-0,685**
Social democratic welfare regime	n.s.	-0,056	n.s.	n.s.
Conservative welfare regime	**-0,693**	0,134	n.s.	n.s.
Presence of left-wing parties in the government	n.s.	n.s.	n.s.	-0,027
GDP per capita	n.s.	0,010	n.s.	n.s.
Gini coefficient	0,043	n.s.	n.s.	n.s.
Macro level: countries of origin				
Gini coefficient	n.s.	-0,013	n.s.	n.s.
Net migration rate	**-0,085**	n.s.	n.s.	n.s.
Human development Index	n.s.	0,008	-0,008	n.s.
Political stability	n.s.	-0,153	n.s.	-0,009
Political freedom	**-0,016**	n.s.	0,077	n.s.
Origin country prevalently Eastern Orthodox	n.s.	n.s.	-0,587	-0,281
Origin: EU15+	**0,605**	0,328	0,362	0,076
Origin: Neighboring countries	0,248	-0,573	1,716	-0,032
Origin: Former colony/territory	0,085	-0,055	1,648	-0,121
Origin: Post-socialist countries	**0,672**	0,698	**-7,161**	-0,625
Constant	**-9,781**	0,118	11,155	**-5,028**
N	**1188**	799	799	799

Note: Bold effects are significant at least at the .05 level.

immigrants and natives becomes nonsignificant, after controlling for individual human-capital characteristics—meaning that there is no general immigrant penalty in unemployment rates. If the unemployment rates of natives in a destination country are high, the unemployment of immigrants is also high in that country.

With respect to the countries of origin, we find only a few and mostly nonsignificant effects at the macro level. Immigrants coming from neighboring countries are unemployed less often than other immigrants. This can be caused by a selection effect (they migrate because they already have a job in a neighboring country) or by their larger knowledge of certain job opportunities in neighboring countries, which makes a successful immigration more probable. In addition, they might be commuting between countries owing to discrepancies in the labor and housing market between the neighboring countries.

Occupational Status

Column 3 of table 12.1 shows that, after controlling for individual human-capital characteristics, the occupational status of the first generation does not differ significantly from that of natives. The second generation, however, has jobs of a significantly higher status than the first generation, once we control for individual characteristics.[9] Although most (80.4%) of the total variation in this multilevel regression model lies at the individual level, and we succeed in accounting for 22.5 percent of this variance, the null-model (see Fleischmann and Dronkers 2007) shows that the occupational status of immigrants also varies among countries of destination (5.6% of the total variance is located at this level) and among countries of origin (which accounts for 14.0% of the total variance). The macro characteristics of these countries succeed in explaining practically all of this variance at both of the higher levels. We find that immigrants in countries with a more rigid labor market (i.e., higher levels of employment-protection legislation) are more often found in low-status jobs. The same holds for immigrants from less developed countries (thus higher scores on the Human Development Index) and for those coming from postsocialist societies.

Upper-Middle-Class Entrance

In column 4 of table 12.1, we present the results of the multilevel logistic regression of immigrants' chances of reaching the upper middle class. Throughout all models, we find that first-generation immigrants have significantly lower chances of reaching the highest occupational classes than do natives; for second-generation immigrants, the chances are somewhat better, but they are still less likely than natives to enter the upper middle class.

With respect to the countries of destination, we find that more favorable naturalization policies increase the likelihood of immigrants' entering the upper middle class, while stricter employment-protection legislation reduces immigrants' chances across all models. Including these explanatory factors accounts for a considerable part of the variance at this level. As in many other analyses, the variance is larger at the level of the country of origin, and we succeed in explaining practically all of this variance with our macro indicators. We find that immigrants from postsocialist societies have lower chances of entering the upper middle classes.

DISCUSSION

Our results provide some important insights into the socioeconomic integration of immigrants from various countries of origin for the thirteen European Union countries that we studied. First, we find quite marked differences in the effects on labor-market participation, unemployment, occupational status, and chances of reaching the highest segment of the labor market. These four indicators should, therefore, be regarded as separate, although interrelated dimensions of socioeconomic integration. Any study that is limited to only one of these factors will necessarily give only a partial, and therefore biased, account of the integration of immigrants into the labor markets of their destination countries. For the same reasons, certain dimensions of immigrants' integration, other than the labor market, might be related to different processes and mechanisms.

Effects of the Macro Level: The Importance of Origin and Destination

The prevalent religion in the country of origin was not found to play a role. This provides little support for the argument that cultural distance, expressed in religious differences between the country of destination and the country of origin, is an important predictor of immigrants' integration, at least in socioeconomic terms. Our data show that there is no evidence of a direct "clash of civilizations" (Huntington 1996) that would govern the relations between societies with different religions, especially the Islamic and the non-Islamic worlds. However, one can interpret the significant effects of individual Muslim affiliation as evidence of an indirect clash, either as a consequence of a religious habitus of Islam or, more likely in the absence of similar negative "Islam effects" in the classical immigration countries like the United States, of discrimination against Muslims in European labor markets.

Origin Inside or Outside the European Union. In general, immigrants originating in the EU-15 countries, Switzerland, or Norway have more favorable outcomes than do immigrants from neighboring countries. While immigrants from the postsocialist countries of Eastern Europe and Central Asia have considerably worse outcomes, there are no effects of coming from a former colony or territory of the destination country. In the case of immigrants from the EU and from neighboring countries, a possible explanation might be the smaller cultural distances between their countries of origin and their countries of destination. The higher integration rates of immigrants from the EU can be interpreted as evidence of the effective functioning of the European Union and the realization of its goals of free movement of capital, goods, and persons. The growing integration of national labor markets into a European economic system, the ongoing equalization of the European systems of vocational and higher education, and the dismantling of administrative barriers to intra-EU migration are likely to be among the reasons individuals moving within the European Union have fewer problems than others do in integrating into labor markets. The flip side of this success of the European Union is that immigrants from outside the union have more problems in the labor markets of EU societies.

Integration Policies of Destination Countries. The five dimensions of the European Civic Citizenship and Inclusion Index (Geddes et al. 2004) have no strong explanatory power. We find that more favorable naturalization policies are associated with higher labor-market participation, a finding that supports the argument behind the index. However, none of the other dimensions of the index has a significant impact on any of the four aspects of labor-market integration.

The meager results of the European Civic Citizenship and Inclusion Index and its five dimensions suggest that differences in policy approaches regarding immigrants among the thirteen destination countries do not have a large impact on the socioeconomic integration of these immigrants.

Labor-Market Protection in Destination Countries. One of the most important factors accounting for the differential labor-market outcomes of immigrants in the thirteen EU countries is the level of employment-protection legislation (EPL). In countries with a more rigid labor market, immigrants have significantly lower occupational status and are less likely to enter the upper middle class. This means that natives who hold high-status jobs profit most from high levels of job protection, since they do not have to compete with immigrants as much as natives do for jobs at the lower end of the occupational ladder.

The finding that EPL especially prevents immigrants from finding higher status jobs suggests that a consequence of higher EPL might be higher levels of statistical discrimination, since in a more rigid labor market the employers take more risks when hiring outsiders (immigrants), owing to the increased costs of getting rid of an unproductive employee. Statistical discrimination is hard to prove and difficult for policymakers to address. Therefore, it would be more efficient to loosen the employment-protection legislation in order to promote equal opportunities for immigrants in European labor markets. Although it is understandable that the employed population will not be pleased with lower levels of employment security, the perverse side effects of a high level of employment protection might pose larger problems for a society than would a less secure labor-market position. A lower level of socioeconomic integration of immigrants (irrespective of their generation) could lead in the long run to the emergence of an ethnic underclass. There seems to be the dilemma of choosing between a high level of job protection, on the one hand, and a lower socioeconomic integration of immigrants, on the other. This problem will become increasingly more urgent, if one believes immigration to Europe can no longer be prevented.

Welfare States and Immigrants.   In addition to the characteristics of the labor market, we find that welfare regimes play a role in explaining the integration of immigrants into the labor market. In contrast to Kogan (2007), we do not find liberal welfare regimes to have specifically beneficial effects, but our analysis suggests slightly better socioeconomic integration of immigrants in countries with a social-democratic welfare regime, and lower levels of integration in countries with a conservative or southern welfare regime. To be more precise, immigrants have lower unemployment rates in the social-democratic welfare regime, while they also tend to participate more in these countries. On the contrary, participation rates are lower among immigrants in the conservative welfare regime, highlighting the objective of this type of welfare state to maintain socioeconomic boundaries (in this case between insiders and outsiders in the labor market).

Political Freedom and Migration Rate in Origin Countries.   Political freedom in the countries of origin was found to lower the labor-market participation rates of immigrants. As we argued in the introduction, political stability and freedom in the country of origin might partly reflect the migration motives of immigrants, as well as their continuing hope to return to their origin country after a successful regime change. We do not find indications of a negative selection process of these immigrants. Immigrants who come from countries with high levels of emigration (such as many postsocialist societies or Morocco) are more likely to participate in the labor market, but they have lower chances of having high-status jobs. This makes clear that these are typical labor migrants, since being active in the labor market of the destination countries is their primary motive for immigration; they often choose occupations that generate financial resources in the short term but have lower returns in the long run.

Effects on the Individual Level

Religious Affiliation

Although individual religion is not conventionally taken into account in comparable analyses of immigrant integration, our results show that it is certainly worthwhile to include this factor. We found disadvantages specifically for Muslims, even after controlling for human capital, in all of the destination countries that we examined: Muslim immigrants have significantly higher unemployment rates than non-Muslim immigrants, and they tend to have lower returns to education on all of the four different labor-market outcomes. Our findings can be explained by three processes. First, it is possible that Muslims have a different religious habitus from non-Muslims that makes them less likely to succeed in the labor market—for instance, if one of their religious values (honor) partly contradicts one of the conditions of success in modern capitalism (productivity). This religious explanation deserves more detailed investigation—for example, with an examination of the large variations within the Muslim community (e.g., between Sunni and Shiite).[10]

A second explanation of our result might be discrimination against Muslims, be it direct or indirect, in the labor markets of the EU countries. The persistence of the negative effect of being a Muslim, after controlling for human capital and especially the lower returns to education that Muslims experience, makes this second explanation relevant. A third explanation is the deviant selectivity of the "guest workers" who were mainly imported from three Islamic countries (Morocco, Algeria, Turkey). The selection of these guest workers deviated from other immigrants from most other regions: they came from the poorest and most underdeveloped regions of these countries, and they were transported on a temporary basis to European countries (Belgium, France, Germany, the Netherlands); meanwhile, the European or Chinese immigrants came from the lower middle classes, rather than from the poorest or the most underdeveloped regions. Owing to negative selection, they and their children have more problems in the labor market than do other immigrants to Europe; this is also because they maintain family and marriage links to their regions of origin.

Citizenship

We found that the citizenship policy of the destination country does not play any role of significance in the labor-market success of its immigrants. The absence of an effect of citizenship is an important finding, since it has been argued many times that more generous naturalization policies are beneficial to immigrants' integration into their host societies. The creators of the European Civic Citizenship and Inclusion Index (Geddes et al. 2004) take a similar position when they rate naturalization policies as one of the five policy dimensions that are perceived to be crucial for immigrant integration. Although it is possible that differences in the naturalization rates of destination countries affect the socio-cultural integration, our analyses have shown that citizenship is not so crucial for socioeconomic integration. While this finding might be controversial, we are quite confident about its robustness, since we found no cross-country differences in the effects of citizenship, despite large variations in naturalization rates among the studied EU countries.

Speaking the Language of the Destination Country at Home

Not speaking the language of the destination country at home does not affect immigrants' labor-market participation, their unemployment, or their chances of reaching the higher classes, after controlling for other individual characteristics (especially educational level). Contrary to common expectations in the heated debates across Europe about language and immigrants, speaking the language of the destination country does not have much effect on immigrants' socioeconomic integration.

The Combination of Native and Immigrant Parents

Having both a native and an immigrant parent does not affect three of the four dimensions of socioeconomic integration for immigrants. The children of these mixed marriages do have higher unemployment rates, however, at the same time as they have higher rates of return to their education in terms of their ability to avoid unemployment. Mixed marriages of natives and immigrants thus hardly affect the socioeconomic or educational integration of their children. We must add one caveat to our unexpected finding: using the country of birth of both parents as an indicator of mixed marriage might be an unreliable measurement of having mixed married parents because the country of birth might simply be too incidental. However, better indicators are difficult to develop and are not yet available.

Education

The highest level of education is not significantly correlated with immigrants' labor-market participation and unemployment, but for those immigrants who have one native and one immigrant parent, more education has a beneficial effect on avoiding unemployment. Higher educational levels increase the occupational status of immigrants' jobs, as well as the chances of their reaching one of the higher classes.

Parental Education

Parental educational level does not always have the same effect as does educational attainment of their children on the four dimensions of socioeconomic integration. Higher parental education is associated with lower labor-market participation, while it increases the occupational status of their children and their chances of reaching the higher classes.

The nonsignificant interaction between parental education and immigrant generation shows that having highly educated parents is as important for natives as it is for immigrants. Compared with the smaller effects of mixed parental marriage, or of speaking the language of destination country at home, or of the nationality of the destination country, parental educational background is far more important for the integration of immigrants. This finding is particularly important with regard to the assimilation debate: given the low educational level of first-generation immigrants and the strong influence of parental education on children's labor-market outcomes, intergenerational social mobility appears hard to achieve.

CONCLUSION: PROGRESS IN THE SECOND GENERATION?

Our earlier overview of the effects of indicators at the macro level of the countries of both origin and destination has shown that these higher level effects have to be taken into account when analyzing the socioeconomic integration of immigrants across countries. While it is clear that the characteristics of the destination countries will affect both first-generation immigrants and their children (in fact, the second and later generations are likely to be even more influenced by the receiving context), it is less obvious that the characteristics of the origin country will continue to have effects on the integration of the second generation. However, we found that these macro processes affect the second generation in the same way as the first, since belonging to the second rather than the first generation of immigrants does not interact with the country of origin. An explanation of this might be the socialization processes within immigrant families or the emergence of transnational networks in the form of available mass media and affordable travel opportunities to the countries of origin. How exactly the influence of origin countries is transmitted from the first to later generations of immigrants (and after how many generations it will vanish) is certainly an interesting and challenging topic for future research.

The finding of the importance of the origin-country characteristics for later generations of immigrants is important for yet another reason. It makes clear that there is no uniform process of integration taking place among the immigrant generations in Europe. The degree to which immigrants integrate socioeconomically depends on their origin and is therefore not universal. Although the second generation has better labor-market outcomes than the first generation, it is still at a disadvantage compared to natives, even after controlling for human capital. Thus, a certain degree of upward social mobility between immigrant generations is possible, although there is a ceiling effect that prevents immigrants from reaching the most desirable positions in the labor markets of European countries.

Notes

1. The adaptations that we made all refer to the Caribbean and the Americas. Here, we did not stick with the strictly geographic distinction, but included information about national languages. We constructed the new category "Caribbean and South America," with the subcategories "Spanish Speaking," "English Speaking," "French Speaking" and "Dutch Speaking." This deviation from the general classification scheme of the UN is justified by the different migration patterns that go along with the different colonial histories that materialize in the languages spoken in these regions today.

2. The European Social Survey gives the occupational titles as four-digit ISCO-88, and we used these to recode the original variable into the more comprehensive and more widely used ISEI scale.

3. Information about the Gini coefficient was not available for all countries in the *World Factbook* (CAI 2007); however, it could instead be derived from the databases of the World Bank. For a detailed description of the sources used and our handling of missing values on macro variables, see Fleischmann Dronkers (2007).

4. We also tried to include the so-called 1.5 generation, which consists of individuals who were born outside the country of destination, but who migrated at such a young age that they received most or all of their education in the destination country. A problem in the construction of this category is that the European Social Survey (Jowell et al. 2005), does not provide exact information about the time since migration, since this is measured categorically. Using the maximum of these categories, we found small shares of the 1.5 generation. Therefore, we refrained from analyzing this group of immigrants separately.

5. Owing to the small numbers of adherents of other religions, this reference category consists mainly of Christians.

6. We use a liberal definition of "neighboring countries" that also includes countries that share sea borders with the country of destination. A list of the matches of neighboring countries can be found in Fleischmann Dronkers (2007).

7. These are, in the first place, countries that have been or still are colonies (for instance, India for the U.K., the Spanish-speaking countries of Latin America for Spain, and Brazil for Portugal). But in the case of Austria, Germany, the U.K., and Sweden, also included are those countries that were part of their former territories (for example, Hungary, Czechoslovakia, and the former Yugoslavia for Austria; Norway for Sweden).

8. The variance components of the various models can be found in Fleischmann and Dronkers (2007).

9. The positive main effect for the second generation means that they have higher status jobs than natives with comparable human capital. However, if human capital is not kept constant, the occupational status of the second generation does not differ significantly from those of natives. Hence, it appears that the composition of the second generation in terms of human capital is less favorable than that of the native population.

10. Unfortunately, this religious variation within the Muslim world is not measured in the European Social Survey.

13

Gender, Perceptions of Opportunity, and Investment in Schooling

Angel L. Harris

Beginning with the work of Emile Durkheim, understanding the link between societal conditions and individuals' behaviors has been a primary focus of sociology. Within the sociology of education, scholars have assessed the implication that the prevailing system of social mobility has on students' schooling behaviors via students' beliefs (e.g., Ogbu 1978; Mickelson 1990; Harris 2008). Ogbu (1978) argues that motivation for maximizing school achievement results from beliefs that more education leads to better jobs, higher wages, and greater social status. However, he cautions that not everyone shares the premise that education leads to success. Groups who experience or perceive persistent barriers to success with regard to future employment and earnings owing to structural inequalities become disillusioned about the future and doubt the value of schooling. Given women's lower educational returns (Joy 2003), it seems plausible that girls would lower their educational and occupational expectations to be more consistent with the realities they encounter. However, research shows that girls invest more in schooling than boys (Buchmann and DiPrete 2006; Jacobs 1996; Livingston and Wirt 2004).

This seemingly paradoxical pattern—girls' greater investment in school despite women's lower educational returns—has been referred to as "the anomaly of women's achievement" (Mickelson 1989). Despite receiving some recent attention (Mickelson 2003), there is a dearth of research on girls' perceptions of the opportunity structure and the implication of these perceptions on their investment in schooling. Most research on the link between perceptions of the opportunity structure and academic investment has focused on race. O'Connor (1999) did examine gendered narratives of opportunity among youths. However, her sample consisted of only black adolescents, which was appropriate given that her aim was to highlight the variations in how adolescents who share the same social positioning and social spaces account for structural constraints on upward mobility.

Given the lack of attention to girls' perceptions of the opportunity structure, it is unclear whether or not girls invest in schooling more than boys because of differences in their perceptions of rewards in the labor market. This chapter attempts to remedy this situation by including gender in the discourse on perceptions of the opportunity structure. The purpose here is to examine whether gender differences exist in perceptions of the opportunity structure among American adolescents and whether these differences explain girls' greater investment in schooling relative to boys. My aim is to determine whether girls are more academically invested *because* they perceive fewer barriers than boys or *despite* perceiving more barriers than boys. Whereas the former would suggest that girls lack motivation for achievement if they anticipate encountering barriers, the latter would suggest that girls are determined to overcome those barriers in the opportunity structure. Investigating the anomaly of girls' greater academic investment despite women's lower educational returns is important for understanding how groups perceiving or experiencing barriers maintain an achievement orientation.

This study accounts for the intersection of race and gender. Several scholars emphasize the importance of considering this intersection in sociological research on systems of stratification (for a review, see Browne and Misra 2003; Chafetz 1997). Browne and Misra write, "race is 'gendered' and gender is 'racialized,' so that race and gender fuse to create unique experiences and opportunities for all groups" (2003: 488). For example, focusing on women's disadvantage in economic relations overlooks more complex interactions: in many cities, white women earn more than black men (McCall 2000). Also, since black women represent two social subordinate groups, they are vulnerable to a race penalty in addition to the gender penalty experienced by white women. O'Connor's (1999) study provides another example of this intersection. She finds that black boys perceive the stigma of their having a greater potential for violence and incarceration, which affects their educational experiences in ways distinct from that of the "white kid" or "black girl." Thus, research on perceptions about future opportunities should consider *both* race and gender. Below, I briefly discuss the lower rewards experienced by women in the labor market and girls' greater investment in schooling than boys.

THE BASIS FOR THE ANOMALY OF GIRLS' GREATER INVESTMENT IN EDUCATION

The inequality experienced by women in the labor market is persistent and pervasive. For example, following rapid declines in the gap in gender earnings during the 1980s, any convergence in earnings has stalled since 1990. Today, women earn about 77 cents on every dollar that men earn (Cotter, Hermsen, and Vanneman 2004). The chosen college major accounts for only about one-tenth of the gender wage gap (Joy 2003; Marini and Fan 1997), perhaps owing to declines in gender segregation across majors during the past twenty years (NCES 1996). Even within similar fields of study, women earn less than men (Peter and Horn 2005). Joy (2003) finds that if women enter the workforce with similar educational credentials and labor-market preferences as men, the labor market still values them less. She notes that if women received similar returns to their qualifications as do men, their salaries would be 25 percent higher.

The labor market's differential reward system based on gender places school-aged girls in a group whose educational credentials are not rewarded to the same extent as are boys' credentials. According to oppositional culture theory, which posits that groups who experience or perceive discrimination in the opportunity structure disinvest from schooling, girls should hold an antagonistic view of the system of social mobility. However, research shows that girls invest more in schooling than do boys. Compared to boys, girls on average have higher grade point averages in high school (Marini and Fan 1997) and college (Buchmann and DiPrete 2006), repeat grade levels less, have higher graduation rates (Jacobs 1996), and outpace boys in the number of college preparatory courses and advanced placement examinations taken in high school (Bae et al. 2000). Furthermore, trend statistics reveal that over the past half-century, women have made significant gains in educational attainment relative to men; whereas 65 percent of all bachelor's degrees in 1960 were awarded to men, by 2004, 58 percent of all such degrees were awarded to women (Buchmann and DiPrete 2006). The greater increases in four-year degrees awarded to women relative to men are occurring across a wide range of majors (Livingston and Wirt 2004).

LIMITATIONS OF PREVIOUS RESEARCH ONR UNDERSTANDING GENDERED VIEWS OF OPPORTUNITIES

The literature on gender differences in perceptions of opportunities among adolescents is limited, for several reasons. First, scholars have focused primarily on race. This is in part owing to the extensive attention given to the oppositional culture theory (Ogbu 1978), which is perhaps the preeminent framework that links the prevailing system of social mobility with student schooling behaviors. The framework posits that those facing an unfair system of social mobility will disinvest from schooling. Although being the dominant theory linking societal conditions in the labor market to student behaviors, it is intended for understanding racial differences in school achievement. Therefore, studies assessing this aspect of the framework have focused on race (Ainsworth-Darnell and Downey 1998; Akom 2003; Carter 2005; Cook and Ludwig 1997; Harris 2006; O'Connor 1997; Tyson, Darity, and Castellino 2005; Mickelson 1990).

Second, few studies deal with the effect of these perceived barriers in the opportunity structure on adolescents' investment in schooling. Previous research has shown societal conditions affecting individuals' achievement via perceptions of the opportunity structure (Ford and Harris 1996; Mickelson 1990). The typical finding in this line of research is that students who believe in the achievement ideology (i.e., education leads to status attainment) experience academic success while those who challenge this belief do not. Thus, group differences in perceived barriers are typically assessed as differences in perceptions of educational returns. However, the focus on perceptions of rewards presents only a partial assessment of how societal conditions in the labor market influence schooling behavior. To fully assess the labor market—schooling behavior link, perceptions of *barriers* in the opportunity structure need to be examined, rather than estimated based on perceptions of educational returns. Thus, this chapter examines whether girls perceive fewer, similar, or more barriers to upward mobility than do boys, and whether these differences in perception explain the gender differences in academic investment.

GENDERED BELIEFS ABOUT THE OPPORTUNITY STRUCTURE: THE POLLYANNA HYPOTHESIS

Given the results of previous studies (e.g., Ford and Harris 1996; Mickelson 1990), it seems reasonable to expect that if girls were aware of their diminished opportunities relative to boys, or believed gender stratification would affect them in the opportunity structure, they would disinvest from schooling. Therefore, an assumption underlying girls' achievement advantage is that young women are either not aware of the gender stratification or consider it to be a thing of the past. This view has been referred to as the *Pollyanna hypothesis*, which suggests that "young women believe they have 'come a long way'—that barriers to successful careers in both the marketplace and the home have fallen by the wayside" (Mickelson 1989:55).

Mickelson's (1989) review of research on the Pollyanna hypothesis suggests that young women view having a family and a career as important and they do not believe these are incompatible goals. She reviews trend analyses based on data from Monitoring the Future—a nationally representative study of approximately 18,000 high school seniors—that suggest girls do not anticipate facing the sexist barriers experienced by their mothers (see Johnston, Bachman, and O'Malley 1975, 1985). However, she cautions that findings based on youths' attitudes toward marriage, family life, work, and gender roles provide an indirect test of the Pollyanna hypothesis. Thus, it is unclear whether gender differences exist among adolescents on their perceptions of barriers in the opportunity structure. In this chapter I provide a direct test of the Pollyanna hypothesis; and specifically, since girls are more academically invested than boys, I test whether they perceive fewer barriers to upward mobility than do boys. Because previous research suggests that belief in barriers leads to disinvestment from schooling, girls must not believe in such barriers or, at the very least, do not believe in them any more than boys do. I also assess the implications for gender differences in academic investment of beliefs about barriers based on sex and race.

It is important to remember that there is a racialized component to perceiving the opportunity structure. Given that blacks have experienced long-standing discrimination in the United States, black children are raised in households where parents have developed adaptive strategies particular to their position within the larger society (Taylor et al. 1990) The adaptive-strategies perspective closely parallels socialization theory, which describes the processes leading individuals to become functioning members of the society in which they live (Elkin and Handel 1984). Thus, children's socialization centers on their parents' perceptions of the opportunities, dangers, and barriers those children will likely face in society. Taylor et al. (1990:994) note that racial socialization is a main feature of children's socialization for black parents, as they attempt to "prepare their children for the realities of being black in America." Therefore, it is unclear whether perceptions of barriers to upward mobility will be similar for white and black females.

METHODS

Data

This study employs data from the Maryland Adolescence Development in Context Study (MADICS), which was drawn from a county on the Eastern seaboard of the United States and contains a unique collection of measures on 1,480 adolescents (51 percent male and 49 percent female). The study is used primarily by psychologists for understanding psychological determinants of behavior and developmental trajectories during adolescence; its richness allows for analyses not possible using most national data sets. The sample was selected from approximately 5,000 adolescents in the county who entered middle school during 1991, and it uses a stratified sampling procedure designed to obtain proportional representations of families from each of the county's twenty-three middle schools. Students' socioeconomic (SES) backgrounds were varied, as the sample included families from neighborhoods in low-income urban areas, middle-class suburban areas, and rural farm-based regions. Although the mean family income in the sample was normally $45,000–$49,000 (range $5,000–$75,000), white families reported significantly higher incomes ($50,000–$54,999) than black families ($40,000–$44,999).

Data were collected from the time the target youths entered middle school until they were three years removed from high school. The current study uses white and black students from the first three waves and the final wave of the MADICS, which were collected when they were in grades 7 ($n = 1407$), 8 ($n = 1004$), and 11 ($n = 951$), and three years post-high school ($n = 853$). In supplemental analyses not shown, blacks were *not* more likely to attrit than whites; also, the proportion of whites and blacks in the sample remained the same for each wave (66% black and 34% white). It is important to note most attrition occurs between grades 7 and 8; only 3 percent of the sample was lost between grades 8 and 11, suggesting that it is unlikely sample attrition resulted from students' dropping out of high school.

Analytic Plan

The analyses begin by assessing whether girls perceive barriers to upward mobility differently from boys. Thus, I begin with a series of gender comparisons by race regarding the extent to which adolescents (measured in grades 7 and 8) believe discrimination based on gender will prevent them from attaining their preferred job and level of education, and whether their gender is a barrier toward "getting ahead" in life. I also conduct this analysis with regard to race to determine whether girls perceive barriers along two dimensions of the social structure. These outcomes are regressed on three groups: black females, white females, and black males (white males omitted). Analyses control for socioeconomic (SES) factors associated with race, such as family income, parental education, and family structure.

The next set of analyses examine whether views about the opportunity structure have implications for student investment in schooling and for academic outcomes (measured in grade 11). Two types of investment are assessed: psychological and behavioral. *Psychological investment* is measured by students' educational aspirations, educational expectations, and the importance they attribute to school for later success in the labor market. *Behavioral investment* is measured by the frequency with which students seek help to improve academically and the amount of time they spend on school activities and in clubs (e.g., student government), homework, and

Table 13.1 Unadjusted means, standard deviations, and descriptions for variables used in the analysis.

Variable Name	Description	Metric	Whites		Blacks	
			Males	Female	Male	Female
Psychological Investment (High School)						
Educational Aspirations	If you could do exactly what you wanted, how far would you like to go in school?	1 = Less than H.S. 8 = J.D., Ph.D., M.D.	6.25 (1.60)	6.76 (1.39)	6.45 (1.54)	7.04 (1.35)
Educational Expectations	We can't always do what we most want to do. How far do you think you actually will go in school?	1 = Less than H.S. 8 = J.D., Ph.D., M.D.	5.54 (1.64)	6.15 (1.46)	5.56 (1.61)	6.28 (1.58)
Educ. Import	Achievement and effort in school lead to job success later on.	1 = Strongly Disagree 5 = Strongly Agree	3.78 (.95)	4.23 (.80)	4.00 (.88)	4.27 (.79)
Behavioral Investment (High School)						
Seek Help (Alpha = .61)	When you're having trouble on schoolwork, how often do you go to (a) your teachers for help? (b) other adults in the school, like a tutor, for help? (c) other students for help? (d) your parent(s) for help? (e) your friends for help?	1 = Almost Never 5 = Almost Always	2.57 (.72)	2.79 (.78)	2.71 (.72)	2.93 (.74)
School Activities/Clubs	During the last year how often did you spend time on any other school activities (such as clubs or student government)?	1 = Never 7 = Usually Every Day	2.76 (2.06)	3.75 (2.07)	2.60 (2.14)	3.42 (2.25)
Homework	Think about the last two weeks, about how often did you do homework?	1 = Never 6 = Daily, > An Hour	3.99 (1.74)	4.70 (1.54)	3.99 (1.56)	4.45 (1.59)

Variable	Description	Scale				
Educational Activities (Alpha = .62)	Think about the last two weeks, about how often did you (a) watch news, educational or cultural shows on TV? (b) read books or magazines for pleasure? (c) read newspapers?	1 = Never, 6 = Daily, More than 1 Hour	3.40 (1.15)	3.21 (1.09)	3.28 (1.18)	3.28 (1.25)
Academic Outcomes						
Grades in Grade 11	Self-reported GPA.	0 – 4.0	2.89 (.82)	3.16 (.74)	2.63 (.72)	2.99 (.68)
College Enrollment	Enrolled in college three years post-high school.	0 = No, 1 = Yes	.65 (.48)	.79 (.41)	.59 (.49)	.74 (.44)
Anticipated Discrimination Based on Gender & Race (Middle School)						
Gender/Job	How much do you think discrimination because of your sex might keep you from getting the job you want?	0 = Not at all, 1 = little to a lot	.08 (.28)	.48 (.50)	.34 (.48)	.60 (.49)
Gender/Educ.	How much do you think discrimination because of your sex might keep you from getting the amount of education you want?	0 = Not at all, 1 = little to a lot	.08 (.27)	.28 (.45)	.31 (.46)	.48 (.50)
Gender Barrier	Do you think it will be harder or easier for you to get ahead in life because you are a (boy/girl)?	1 = A lot easier, 5 = A lot harder	2.66 (.55)	3.24 (.64)	2.74 (.81)	3.22 (.84)
Race/Job	How much do you think discrimination because of your race might keep you from getting the job you want?	0 = Not at all, 1 = little to a lot	.18 (.38)	.30 (.46)	.62 (.49)	.69 (.46)

(continued)

Table 13.1 Continued

Variable Name	Description	Metric	Whites		Blacks	
			Males	Female	Male	Female
Race/Educ.	How much do you think discrimination because of your race might keep you from getting the amount of education you want?	0 = Not at all 1 = little to a lot	.08 (.27)	.25 (.43)	.57 (.50)	.55 (.50)
Race Barriers (Alpha = .84)	(a) Because of your race, no matter how hard you work, you will always have to work harder than others to prove yourself; (b) because of your race, it is important that you do better than other kids at school in order to get ahead.	1 = Strongly disagree 4 = Strongly agree	1.63 (.62)	1.50 (.64)	2.52 (.89)	2.48 (.97)

Notes: Numbers in parentheses are standard deviations. Valid cases range from 777 to 948 in the MADICS (82% or greater of the total sample).

educational activities outside of school. Finally, analyses are conducted for two academic outcomes: achievement (i.e., grades) and college enrollment. These outcomes are first regressed on gender and race interactions to determine the extent to which group differences exist on school investment. Students' perceptions of barriers in the opportunity structure are then included to the models to examine whether they lead to a decline in school investment.

Table 13.1 contains detailed information on all outcomes. Constructs comprising multiple items are weighted sums; responses were added and the sums divided by the number of items. Although group differences in means appear in table 13.1, models discussed above allow for systematic gender/race comparisons to be made after adjusting for SES. To account for missing data, each predictor was entered into the models with a "missing information" measure—coded 0 if not missing and 1 if missing. This yields estimates identical to those attained via "listwise deletion" for the variable with the substituted values and allows all cases with values on the outcome to remain in the analysis. Finally, since analyses are restricted to students present in grade 11, an assessment of exclusion bias is conducted in the Appendix.[1]

RESULTS

Differences in Perceptions of Barriers

The findings shown in table 13.2 provide a direct test of the Pollyanna hypothesis. The top panel of table 13.2 shows that girls are much more likely to believe they will experience discrimination based on gender in the job market (logit = 2.918 for black females and 2.312 for white females) and in education (logit = 2.418 for black females and 1.536 for white females). Interestingly, black males are more than five times more likely to believe this than white males. Girls also view their gender as a barrier in general more than boys (b = .594 for black females and .576 for whites females). The bottom panel of table 13.2 repeats these analyses with regard to race and shows that blacks view race as an obstacle in the labor market, in education, and in life in general more than do whites. However, relative to white males, white females are more likely to believe discrimination based on race will make it harder for them to get the job and education they want. In sum, table 13.2 provides no support for the hypothesis that girls perceive fewer barriers than boys. Instead, the findings show that white males are least likely to consider their gender and race as barriers in the opportunity structure.

Table 13.2 Unstandardized coefficients from regressions of anticipated discrimination based on gender and race (Pollyanna hypothesis).

| | Gender Discrimination | | | | |
| | Gender/Job | | Gender/Educ. | | Barrier |
Ind. Variables	(Logit)	Odds Ratio	(Logit)	Odds Ratio	(OLS)
Black Females	2.918***	18.511	2.418***	11.218	.594***
	(.347)		(.357)		(.083)
White Females	2.312***	10.099	1.536***	4.647	.576***
	(.358)		(.379)		(.091)
Black Males	1.909***	6.748	1.691***	5.424	.126
	(.349)		(.362)		(.084)
Constant	−3.800***		−2.677***		2.344***
	(.684)		(.686)		(.211)
χ^2, df / R^2	123***, 9		76***, 9		.112

| | Race Discrimination | | | | |
| | Race/Job | | Race/Educ. | | Barrier |
Ind. Variables	(Logit)	Odds Ratio	(Logit)	Odds Ratio	(OLS)
Black Females	2.536***	12.631	2.749***	15.634	.906***
	(.277)		(.358)		(.092)
White Females	.746*	2.108	1.400***	4.054	−.106
	(.294)		(.382)		(.101)
Black Males	2.215***	9.165	2.889***	17.977	.939***
	(.275)		(.360)		(.093)
Constant	−2.730***		−3.538***		1.316***
	(.643)		(.688)		(.236)
χ^2, df / R^2	148***, 9		144***, 9		.241

Notes: Numbers in parentheses are standard errors. White males are the omitted category for race. All analyses control for family structure, household income and parental education, and student achievement. Number of observations range from 777 to 794.

Subsequently, given the negative impact that perceptions of barriers are posited to have on academic investment, and the common finding that girls are more invested in schooling, the prediction made by the second hypothesis—that girls are more invested because they perceive fewer barriers—cannot be supported. Essentially, this suggests that girls have greater academic investment *despite* their substantially greater perceptions of barriers in the opportunity structure. This result calls into question the proposed negative link between perceptions of barriers and educational outcomes, which is a key component of the oppositional culture model discussed earlier. This is further examined in the next portion of the analyses.

Perceptions of Barriers on Psychological Investment

Table 13.3 examines three outcomes—educational aspirations, educational expectations, and educational importance—using OLS regression models. The first model in table 13.3 for each outcome yields no surprises. Similar to the findings in previous research, we see that girls are psychologically more invested in schooling than boys. Specifically, black girls have the highest educational aspirations ($b = .983$), followed by white girls ($b = .586$) and black males ($b = .348$); white males have the lowest educational aspirations net of socioeconomic factors. This is also the case with regard to educational expectations ($b = 1.058$ and $.708$ for black girls and white girls, respectively)—black boys do not differ from white boys. Similarly, all three groups have a

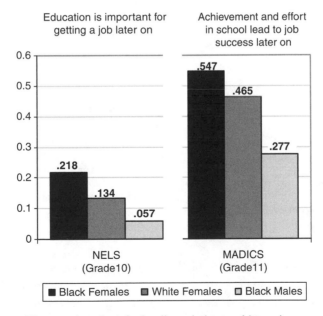

Figure 13.1. Differences in value of schooling relative to white males among adolescents in two datasets net of SES: NELS and MADICS.

Note: Findings are net of family income, parents' education, and family structure. Range is 1–4 for the NELS measure (constant = 3.285, $n = 7690$) and 1–5 for the MADICS measure (constant = 3.433, $n = 870$). All values are significant at the $p < .05$ level.

Source:

Table 13.3 Unstandardized coefficients for psychological investment on anticipated discrimination.

Ind. Variables	Educational Aspirations		Educational Expectations		Effort in School = Job Success	
	(1)	(2)	(1)	(2)	(1)	(2)
Group						
Black Females	.983***	.946***	1.058***	.997***	.547***	.587***
	(.148)	(.165)	(.156)	(.174)	(.088)	(.098)
White Females	.586***	.515***	.708***	.622***	.465***	.494***
	(.161)	(.169)	(.169)	(.179)	(.096)	(.101)
Black Males	.348*	.324*	.288	.265	.277**	.302**
	(.148)	(.165)	(.156)	(.174)	(.088)	(.098)
Gender Discrimination						
Gender/Job	—	.263	—	.237	—	−.032
		(.149)		(.157)		(.089)
Gender/Educ.	—	−.420**	—	−.231	—	−.103
		(.159)		(.168)		(.096)
Gender Barrier	—	.067	—	.070	—	−.019
		(.073)		(.077)		(.044)
Race Discrimination						
Race/Job	—	−.107	—	−.115	—	.082
		(.151)		(.160)		(.091)
Race/Educ.	—	.284	—	.188	—	.070
		(.158)		(.167)		(.095)
Race Barrier	—	−.046	—	−.035	—	−.056
		(.067)		(.071)		(.040)
Constant	3.733***	3.621***	2.164***	2.127***	3.433***	.203
	(.312)	(.230)	(.328)	(.401)	(.184)	(.238)
R^2	.124	.138	.169	.179	.053	.069

Notes: Numbers in parentheses are standard errors. White males are the omitted category for race. Analyses control for family structure, household income, and parental education. Number of observations range from 844 to 870.
* $p < .05$ ** $p < .01$ *** $p < .001$ (two-tailed tests)

stronger belief that effort in school will lead to future success in the labor market than do white boys, though this belief is stronger among girls ($b =$ .547 and .465 for black girls and white girls, respectively, and .277 for black boys). This pattern is similar to that observed in the National Educational Longitudinal Study (NELS), which is perhaps the most frequently used national data set among education researchers over the past ten to fifteen years (see figure 13.1). However, the second model for each outcome yields surprising results. With the exception of the negative effect of students' views about the extent to which gender will inhibit their educational

Table 13.4 Unstandardized coefficients for behavioral investment on anticipated discrimiration.

Ind. Variables	Seek Help (1)	(2)	Time on School Activities/Clubs (1)	(2)	Time on Homework (1)	(2)	Time on Educational Activities (1)	(2)
Group								
Black Females	.368***	.323***	.875***	.796***	.632***	.693***	-.094	-.188
	(.078)	(.087)	(.213)	(.237)	(.161)	(.178)	(.121)	(.133)
White Females	.228**	.221*	1.092***	1.045***	.757***	.752***	-.185	-.242
	(.085)	(.090)	(.234)	(.247)	(.178)	(.186)	(.133)	(.139)
Black Males	.171*	.143	.054	.044	.181	.186	-.087	-.177
	(.078)	(.087)	(.213)	(.234)	(.160)	(.175)	(.121)	(.132)
Gender Discrimination								
Gender/Job	—	.023	—	.237	—	-.030	—	.190
		(.078)		(.157)		(.161)		(.121)
Gender/Educ.	—	-.031	—	-.231	—	-.237	—	-.220
		(.084)		(.168)		(.171)		(.130)
Gender Barrier	—	.030	—	.070	—	-.067	—	-.012
		(.039)		(.077)		(.079)		(.059)
Race Discrimination								
Race/Job	—	.011	—	-.115	—	.052	—	-.206
		(.080)		(.160)		(.164)		(.122)
Race/Educ.	—	-.012	—	.188	—	.305	—	.365**

(continued)

Table 13.4 Continued

Ind. Variables	Seek Help		Time on School Activities/Clubs		Time on Homework		Time on Educational Activities	
	(1)	(2)	(1)	(2)	(1)	(2)	(1)	(2)
		(.083)		(.167)		(.172)		(.129)
Race Barrier	—	.031	—	-.035	—	-.138	—	.011
		(.036)		(.071)		(.071)		(.053)
Constant	2.450***	2.260***	.012	-.274	2.103***	2.619***	2.884***	2.987***
	(.166)	(.201)	(.437)	(.534)	(.331)	(.400)	(.247)	(.299)
R^2	.039	.052	.093	.097	.080	.097	.009	.031

Notes: Numbers in parentheses are standard errors. White males are the omitted category for race. Analyses control for family structure, household income, and parental education. Number of observations are 830 for *Seek Help*, 948 for *Time on School Activities/Clubs*, 924 for *Time on Homework*, and 934 for *Time on Educational Activities*.

* $p < .05$ ** $p < .01$ *** $p < .001$ (two-tailed tests)

opportunities on educational aspirations (b = -.420), perceptions of barriers with regard to gender and race have no effect on students' psychological investment in schooling.[2]

Perceptions of Barriers on Behavioral Investment

Table 13.4 repeats the previous analyses for measures of behavioral investment. Similar to the findings for psychological investment, the first model for each outcome in table 13.4 shows that girls are more invested in schooling than boys. Specifically, while all three groups seek help with schoolwork more than white boys, girls are more involved with school activities/clubs (b = .875 and 1.092 for black girls and white girls, respectively) and spend more time on homework than do boys (b = .632 and .757 for black girls and white girls, respectively). There are no group differences in time spent on educational activities outside school. However, as in the previous analyses, the second model for each outcome shows that perceptions of barriers with regard to gender and race in the opportunity structure have no effect on students' behavioral investment in schooling save one exception—perception of racial barriers in the domain of education lead to an increase in time spent on educational activities outside of school.

Perceptions of Barriers on Academic Outcomes

Given girls' concerns about gender discrimination in the opportunity structure, one might expect them to have lower school achievement. However, as previously mentioned, the finding that girls invest more in schooling is robust. Girls' greater school achievement is opposite to what the resistance model would predict and suggest that students' views of the system of social mobility have minimal impact on their school achievement.

Table 13.5 examines whether youths' views about an unfair opportunity structure affect their academic outcomes. Model 1 shows group differences in achievement (i.e., grades) before and after controlling for prior achievement (all prime models control for prior school achievement). As mentioned previously, this gendered pattern—girls' higher grades than boys—is also found among national data (see figure 13.2). Whereas prior achievement explains the black male disadvantage (b = -.174 in Model 1 and nonsignificant in Model 1□), it does not account for girls' higher achievement. Model 2 shows that anticipated discrimination based on gender does not compromise achievement. Instead, students who view their gender as an obstacle in the job market have higher school achievement than those who do not.

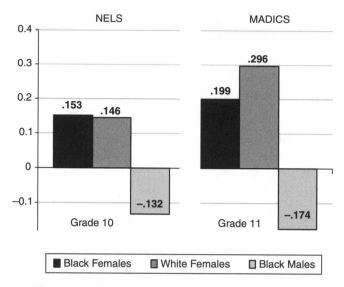

Figure 13.2. Differences in grades relative to white males among adolescents in two datasets net of SES: NELS and MADICS.

Note: Findings are net of family income, parents' education, and family structure. Range is 0–4 with constants of 1.996 and 1.903 for grades in the NELS (n = 6328) and MADICS (n = 789), respectively. All values are significant at the *p* < .05 level.

Model 2 also suggests that the reason black females outperform white males is that they anticipate discrimination in the labor force. Model 2 □ shows that the white female achievement advantage becomes nonsignificant when both prior achievement and anticipated gender discrimination are controlled. Finally, Model 3 shows that although anticipated barriers based on race adversely affect achievement, beliefs about racial discrimination in the system of social mobility have minimal effect on group differences in achievement.

The next set of models in table 13.5 examine whether youths' views about an unfair opportunity structure affect their likelihood of enrolling in college. The first model shows that net of SES, girls are more likely to be enrolled in college than boys. Black boys do not differ from white boys. However, prior to controlling for SES, black boys were less likely to be enrolled in college than white boys (not shown). Model 2 yields provocative findings about perceived barriers and college enrollment: perceived barriers *do not* adversely affect college enrollment; instead, students who perceive race as a barrier for education are almost twice as likely to be enrolled in college as those who do not see race as an obstacle (odds ratio = 1.908).

Table 13.5 Unstandardized coefficients for academic outcomes on anticipated discrimination.

| | Achievement (Grade 11)[a] | | | | | | College Enrollment | | | | |
Ind. Variables	(1)	(1')	(2)	(2')	(3)	(3')	Ratio Odds	(1)	Ratio Odds	(2)	Ratio Odds
Group											
Black Females	.199**	.186**	.136	.146	.195*	.174*	2.986	1.094***		.874**	2.396
	(.078)	(.073)	(.083)	(.078)	(.084)	(.079)		(.279)		(.313)	
White Females	.296***	.182*	.237**	.145	.279***	.173*	2.829	1.040***		.934**	2.546
	(.085)	(.080)	(.088)	(.083)	(.085)	(.080)		(.309)		(.328)	
Black Males	-.174*	-.023	-.198*	-.033	-.168*	-.032		.303		.054	
	(.078)	(.074)	(.080)	(.076)	(.085)	(.081)		(.279)		(.312)	
Gender Discrimination											
Gender/Job	—	—	.162*	.088	—	—		—		.488	
			(.067)	(.063)						(.301)	
Gender/Educ.	—	—	-.096	-.068	—	—		—		-.395	
			(.069)	(.064)						(.329)	
Gender Barrier	—	—	.044	.045	—	—		—		.009	
			(.038)	(.035)						(.156)	
Race Discrimination											
Race/Job	—	—	—	—	.126	.112		—		.019	
					(.068)	(.064)				(.298)	
Race/Educ.	—	—	—	—	.047	.026		—		.646*	1.908
					(.069)	(.064)				(.320)	

(continued)

Table 13.5 Continued

Ind. Variables	Achievement (Grade 11)[a]						College Enrollment			
	(1)	(1')	(2)	(2')	(3)	(3')	Ratio Odds (1)		Ratio Odds (2)	
Race Barrier	—	—	—	—	-.084*	-.053	—		-.051	
					(.035)	(.033)			(.129)	
Constant	1.903***	.121	1.763***	.022	1.975***	.203	-4.026***		-4.156***	
	(.164)	(.230)	(.193)	(.251)	(.174)	(.238)	(.632)		(.796)	
R^2	.120	.242	.131	.249	.136	.254	χ^2, df	99, 7	124, 19	

Notes: Numbers in parentheses are standard errors. White males are the omitted category for race. Analyses control for family structure, household income, and parental education. Number of observations are 789 and 668 for *achievement* and *college enrollment*, respectively.

[a] Prime models control for prior school achievement (measured during grade 7).

* $p < .05$ ** $p < .01$ *** $p < .001$ (two-tailed tests)

DISCUSSION

The purpose of this study was to include gender in the discourse on adolescents' perceptions of the opportunity structure. This study examined whether gender differences exist in perceptions of the opportunity structure and whether these perceptions affect students' investment in schooling. A data set containing a unique collection of measures on perceptions of the opportunity structure was used to assess students' views of barriers based on gender and race in the labor market. The analyses accounted for the intersection of race and gender, which allowed for the racialized aspects of gender to be considered. The findings reveal interesting patterns of how youths perceive their gender and race as barriers to upward mobility. Also, findings emerged that are important for understanding why females, a group that experiences and perceives persistent barriers to social mobility, do not disinvest from schooling. Each set of findings is discussed below.

The Pollyanna hypothesis was not supported. Girls are aware that they will encounter barriers in the opportunity structure. Interestingly, black boys perceive more barriers based on gender than do white boys. This may be the case for several reasons. Given that rates of black girls' and women's educational achievement and occupational attainment continue to increase, while those of black boys' and men's decrease (Cohen and Nee 2000; Cross and Slater 2000), black males may perceive that they have less educational/ occupational potential than black women. In addition, their higher rates of incarceration and contact with the criminal justice system (Brown et al. 2003) may contribute to negative stereotypes that black males are incapable of being upwardly mobile. O'Connor's (1999:153) work shows that students recognize the unique status of black men who are instantly stereotyped as convicts, gangbangers, and perpetrators, which they believe constrain their educational opportunity and employment prospects. Some students reported that "such a stigma (or stereotype) means that African American boys are less likely than white youths or African American girls to receive needed academic assistance and are more likely to receive severe sanctions for transgressing school norms" (O'Connor 1999:152). Ferguson (2000) finds school personnel view the dress and behavior of black males as recalcitrant and oppositional, and exert strict control over them. She notes that culturally based assumptions about black males lead them to face constant regulation of their dress, behavior, and speech. When viewed in this context, it makes sense that black boys would perceive their gender as an additional barrier to upward mobility.

Another interesting finding to emerge in this study is that white girls perceive their race as a barrier to upward mobility more than white boys.

However, this finding seems to be more indicative of white boys' feeling more protecte' or having a greater sense of privilege than of white girls' perceiving barriers based on race. White boys seem to have an awareness of their position of privilege that comes from being both male and white. Therefore, relative to white males, any perception of vulnerability with regard to race might result in group differences.

A surprising finding is that girls' awareness of gender stratification in the opportunity structure has little relevance for their investment in schooling—psychological and behavioral—and academic outcomes. Findings show that students' anticipation of an unfair system of social mobility—with regard to the labor market, school, and life in general—does not compromise their belief in education as a mechanism for upward mobility. It seems that girls do not dwell on the negative aspects of the system of social mobility. In contrast, rather than being discouraged by future barriers, the findings in table 13.5 suggest that they use this as motivation for school achievement. O'Connor (1999) also finds that high achievers are highly attuned to structural barriers to opportunity. Given these findings, I revisit whether the female achievement advantage is an anomaly, and why a group that receives lower educational returns and anticipates barriers in the labor market invests more in the system of social mobility than its better rewarded advantaged counterparts.

Is the Female Achievement Advantage an Anomaly?

The introduction to this study suggested that, when viewed within the context of the oppositional culture theory, girls' achievement advantage presents an anomaly. Given women's lower educational returns, when focusing on their greater investment in schooling, one is almost obligated to situate the issue within the context of oppositional culture theory. It has been *the* dominant theory linking academic investment to experiences or perceptions of inequality in the opportunity structure. Also, it has received enormous attention across numerous disciplines. Doing so leads one to derive girls' achievement advantage as an anomaly. However, Mickelson (1989) notes that girls' achievement advantage is not an anomaly if considered within the more fluid boundaries that separate women's public and private lives, which exist along a continuum rather than are a dichotomy. Drawing on feminist theory, she notes that women weave public and private roles into a single tapestry, and they are more likely to seek educational returns suitable for both spheres. Differently from men, women do not perform comparative cost-benefit analyses of educational returns when investing in school. Considering girls' achievement advantage, an anomaly assumes there is only one measure for educational returns.

2. Why Do Girls Invest in School More than Boys?

Women may actually be prone to investing more in education if they view things in relative terms. Mickelson (1989) raises this possibility (i.e., reference-group theory) and suggests that the notion that women do not care about the greater educational returns received by men requires a leap of faith. However, rather than comparing themselves to men—or even to other women—girls might be comparing themselves to the counterfactual: what their lives would be like without further investment in schooling. They know (or believe as the current findings suggest) that their chances for success in the job market will be better if they invest in schooling than if they do not.

Another possible reason for girls' greater investment in school is that they might realize things have actually been improving for women, both in education (i.e., currently higher graduation rates in college and a higher presence in graduate school than men) and in the workplace. While there remains a glass ceiling in the world of work, which the current study shows they not only perceive but also are motivated to shatter, girls may still feel their chances of attaining high positions are at an all-time best, since the outlook is much rosier than it was ten to twenty years ago. Research suggests that, in recent decades, the value of completing college—in terms of its combined impact on future earnings, marriage, standard of living, and insurance against income deprivation—has risen faster for women than for men (DiPrete and Buchman 2006). Also, Buchmann and DiPrete (2006) find that girls' advantage in completing college is partly due to the gender-distinctive effects of family background; there is a growing vulnerability of boys in families with fathers who have only a high school education or are absent, which is linked to declines in educational attainment.

CONCLUSION

It seems that the reason girls are able to remain academically invested, despite perceiving future barriers in the labor market, is that these perceptions have no implications for their investment in schooling. Future research should consider whether conditions might exist in which perceptions of barriers in the opportunity structure do become consequential. For example, it is possible that women and minorities are adversely affected by stereotype vulnerability (Steele 1988)—the need to consistently disavow group-based negative feedback. Steele (1997) notes that increased reminders of barriers and stereotypes in particular domains can compromise performance. He refers to this phenomenon as "stereotype threat," which occurs when individuals fear that their behavior(s) may confirm stereotypes (often negative) about a group to which they belong. Steele and Aronson (1995) found that black college students whose race was not made salient outperformed those whose race was made salient on academic tasks. Thus, the performance of women who aspire to be engineers might be affected by perceptions of barriers in that domain (e.g., engineering).

The lack of effect that perceptions of structural barriers to upward mobility have on academic outcomes show how groups that experience lower educational returns are able to maintain both psychological and behavioral investment in schooling. Also, the current findings are informative about the link between societal conditions and students' academic investment. This study shows that beliefs in barriers do not depress academic investment. Instead, when it comes to academic outcome, beliefs in barriers can serve as a motivating factor for girls.

APPENDIX

See table 13.6.

Table 13.6 Means and Mean Differences between the full sample, study sample, and excluded sample by race and gender on seventh-grade measures analogous to the outcomes in this study.

	Whites Males					Whites Females					Black Males					Black Females				
	Full	Study	Excluded	Differences		Full	Study	Excluded	Differences		Full	Study	Excluded	Differences		Full	Study	Excluded	Differences	
	(1)	(2)	(3)	(2–1)	(3–2)	(1)	(2)	(3)	(2–1)	(3–2)	(1)	(2)	(3)	(2–1)	(3–2)	(1)	(2)	(3)	(2–1)	(3–2)
Psychological Investment																				
Aspiration Educ.	7.45	7.55	7.23	.10	-.32	8.01	8.25	7.46	.24	-.79	7.53	7.67	7.30	.14	-.37*	8.23	8.11	8.53	-.12	.42
Expectation Educ.	7.56	7.44	7.83	-.12	.39	7.02	7.17	6.66	.15	-.51	6.84	7.09	6.40	.25	-.69	7.95	8.19	7.37	.24	-.82
Important Educ.	4.34	4.34	4.32	.00	-.02	4.40	4.48	4.22	.08	-.26*	4.42	4.50	4.27	.08	-.23*	4.60	4.60	4.61	.00	.01
Behavioral Investment																				
Seek Help	2.88	2.88	2.88	.00	.00	3.24	3.24	3.23	.00	-.01	3.10	3.12	3.06	.02	-.06	3.20	3.22	3.14	.02	-.08
School Act./ Clubs	1.40	1.64	0.90	.24	-.74*	1.48	1.48	1.48	.00	.00	1.19	1.18	1.21	-.01	.03	1.68	1.57	1.94	-.11	.37
Homework	4.85	4.86	4.83	.01	-.03	4.99	4.97	5.04	-.02	.07	4.85	4.88	4.79	.03	-.09	4.99	5.05	4.85	.06	-.20
Educ. Activities	2.92	3.00	2.74	.08	-.26	2.77	2.82	2.64	.05	-.18	2.87	2.89	2.84	.02	-.05	2.90	2.94	2.83	.04	-.11
Academic Outcome																				
Achievement	3.19	3.30	2.97	.11	-.33*	3.42	3.44	3.39	.02	-.05	2.96	3.00	2.90	.04	-.10	3.21	3.23	3.16	.02	-.07
N =	224	154	70			245	171	74			493	312	181			445	314	131		

Note: * Denotes differences are significant at the *p* < .05 level (two-tailed).

Notes

I am greatly indebted to Shannon Cavanaugh, Robert Hummer, Chandra Muller, Catherine Riegle-Crumb, Keith Robinson, Mary Rose, and Christine Williams for helpful comments. This research is supported in part by NICHD Grant #R01 HD33437 to Jacquelynne S. Eccles and Arnold J. Sameroff, and by the MacArthur Network on Successful Adolescent Development in High Risk Settings (Chair: R. Jessor).

1. The Appendix (table 13.6) serves as a further check for attrition bias. The first three columns for each group show the grade 7 (wave 1) means on measures analogous to the outcomes in this study (educational importance is measured as "I have to do well in school if I want to be a success in life") for the full sample, the study sample (i.e., students present in grade 11), and the excluded sample (i.e., students not present in grade 11). Column 2–1 shows that there are no significant differences on any of the outcomes between the study and full samples for all groups. Column 3–2—which is informative in determining who is excluded—shows that there are some differences between the study and the excluded sample. White males excluded from this study were less involved with school activities or clubs and had lower grades than white males in the study. Relative to the white females in this study, those excluded had lower educational expectations and rated education as less important. Relative to black males in this study, those excluded had lower aspirations and rated education as less important. Finally, there are no differences between the retained and excluded black female samples. Although the excluded sample differs from the study sample on 6 of the 32 comparisons, it is reasonable to expect that the implication of these differences for the discrimination/barriers effects is negligible.

2. In supplemental analyses, interaction terms were entered into a third model for each outcome to determine whether the effects of the discrimination measures vary across groups (e.g., black females x sex barriers). However, the interaction terms were not significant (results available upon request).

References

Ackerlof, George. 1976. "The Economics of Caste, and of the Rat Race and Other Woeful Tales." *Quarterly Journal of Economics* 90 (4): 599–617.

Ainsworth-Darnell, James W., and Douglas B. Downey. 1998. "Assessing the Oppositional Culture Explanation for Racial/Ethnic Differences in School Performance." *American Sociological Review* 63: 536–553.

Akom, A. A. 2003. "Reexamining Resistance as Oppositional Behavior: The Nation of Islam and the Creation of a Black Achievement Ideology." *Sociology of Education* 76: 305–325.

Alba, R., and V. Nee. 1997. "Rethinking assimilation in a new era of immigration." *International Migration Review* 31 (4): 826–874.

Altbach, Philip, and Jane Knight. 2006. *The Internationalization of Higher Education: Motivations and Realities. NEA Almanac of Higher Education.* Washington, DC: National Educational Association.

American Association of Community Colleges 2010. Accessed May 30, 2010; http://www.aacc.nche.edu/AboutCC/Pages/default.aspx.

Arneson, R. 1989. "Equality and Equality of Opportunity for Welfare." *Philosophical Studies* 56: 74–94.

Arrow, K. 1973. "The Theory of Discrimination." In *Discrimination in Labor Markets*, O. Ashenfelter and A. Rees, eds. (pp. 3–33). Princeton, NJ: Princeton University Press.

Arrow, K., S. Bowles, and S. Durlauf. 2000. *Meritocracy and Economic Inequality.* Princeton, NJ: Princeton University Press.

Arum, Richard, Adam Gamoran, and Yossi Shavit. 2007. "More Inclusion than Diversion: Expansion, Differentiation, and Market Structure in Higher Education." In *Stratification in Higher Education: A Comparative Study*, Yossi Shavit, Richard Arum, and Adam Gamoran, eds. (chap. 1). Stanford, CA: Stanford University Press.

Ashenfelter, O., and C. Rouse. 1998. "Income, Schooling, and Ability: Evidence from a New Sample of Identical Twins." *Quarterly Journal of Economics* 113 (1): 353–384.

Attias-Donfut, C. 2000. Rapports de générations: transferts intrafamiliaux et dynamique macrosociale, *Revue française de sociologie* 41 (4): 643–684.

Auerbach A. J., J. Gokhale, and L. J. Kotlikoff. 1994. "Generational Accounting: A Meaningful Way to Evaluate Fiscal Policy (in Symposia: Generational Accounting)." *Journal of Economic Perspectives* 8 (1): 73–94.

Aviezer, O., and M. Rosental. 1997. "A Comparison of Pre-School & Toddlers in City and Kibbutz." In *Kibbutz Education in Its Environment*, Y. Dror, ed. (pp. 37–58).

Tel Aviv: Tel Aviv University School of Education and Ramot Publishing. (Hebrew)

Avrahami, A. 1997. *Learning on the Way to the Future: Why Do Kibbutz Children Study?* Ramat Efal, Israel: Yad Tabenkin. (Hebrew with English abstract)

Baba, M. 2007. "Niezaspokojony pop ytna prace." In *Edukacja dla pracy. Raport o rozwoju spolecznym Polska 2007*, Ursula Sztanderska, ed. Warsaw: United Nations Development Program.

Bae, Yupin, Susan Choy, Claire Geddes, Jennifer Sable, and Thomas Snyder. 2000. *Trends in Educational Equity of Girls and Women*. U.S. Department of Education, National Center for Education Statistics. Washington, DC: U.S. Government Printing Office.

Ball, S. 2003. *Class Strategies and the Educational Market: The Middle Classes and Social Advantage*. London: RoutledgeFalmer.

Ball, S., M. Maguire, and S. Macrae. 2000. *Choice, Pathways and Transitions Post-16: New Youth, New Economies in the Global City*. London: RoutledgeFalmer.

Bambra, C. 2007. "Going Beyond the Three Worlds of Welfare Capitalism: Regime Theory and Public Health Research." *Journal of Epidemiology and Community Health* 61: 1098–1102.

Barbier J. C., and J. Gautié (dir.). 1998. *Les politiques de l'emploi en Europe et aux Etats Unis, Cahiers du CEE*. Paris: PUF.

Barr, Nicholas. 2004. *The Economics of the Welfare State*. New York: Oxford University Press.

Bashir, Sajitha. 2007. *Trends in International Trade in Higher Education: Implications and Options for Developing Countries*. Working paper series, no. 6. Washington, DC: World Bank.

Baudelot, R. Establet. 2000. *Avoir trente ans, en 1968 et 1998*. Paris: Éd. du Seuil.

Beck, T., et al. 2000. *New Tools and New Tests in Comparative Political Economy: The Database of Political Institutions*. Working paper series, no. 2283. Washington, DC: World Bank.

Becker, Gary S. 1967. *Human Capital and the Personal Distribution of Income*. Ann Arbor: University of Michigan Press.

———. 1971. *The Economics of Discrimination*. Chicago: Chicago University Press.

———. 1975. *Human Capital. A Theoretical and Empirical Analysis with Special Reference to Education*. New York: National Bureau of Economic Research.

Becker, H. A. 2000. "Discontinuous Change and Generational Contracts." In *The Myth of Generational Conflict. The Family and State in Ageing Societies*, S. Arber and C. Attias-Donfut, eds. (pp. 114–132). London /New York: Routledge.

Behrman, J. R., and P. Taubman. 1989. "Is Schooling 'Mostly in the Genes'? Nature-Nurture Decomposition Using Data on Relatives." *Journal of Political Economy* 97 (6): 1425–1446.

Behrman, J. R., M. R. Rosenzweig, and P. Taubman. 1994. "Endowments and the Allocation of Schooling in the Family and in the Marriage Market: The Twins Experiment." *Journal of Political Economy* 102 (6): 1131–1173.

Belfield, Clive R. 2000. *Economic Principles for Education: Theory and Evidence*. Cheltenham: Edward Elgar.

Bell, D. 1973. *Coming of Post-Industrial Society: A Venture in Social Forecasting*. New York: Basic Books.

Bell L., G. Burtless, T. Smeeding, and J. Gornick. 2007. "Failure to Launch: Cross-National Trends in the Transition to Economic Independence." In *The Price of Independence*, S. Danziger and C. E. Rouse, eds. (chap. 2). New York: Russell Sage Foundation.

Beller, M. 1994. "Psychometric and Social Issues in Admissions to Israeli Universities." *Educational Measurement: Issues and Practice* 13 (2): 12–20.

Belzil, C., and J. Hansen. 2002. "Unobserved Ability and the Return to Schooling." *Econometrica* 70 (5): 2075–2091.

Benabou, R. 2000. "Meritocracy, Redistribution, and the Size of the Pie." In *Meritocracy and Economic Inequality*, K. Arrow, S. Bowles, and S. Durlauf, eds. (chap. 12). Princeton, NJ: Princeton University Press.

Benavot, Aaron, Yun-Kyung Cha, David Kamens, John Meyer, and Suh-Ying Wong. 1991. "Knowledge for the Masses: World Models and National Curricula, 1920–1986. *American Sociological Review* 56 (1): 86–92.

Bennett, M. J. 2000. *When Dreams Came True: The GI Bill and the Making of Modern America*. Washington, DC: Brassey's.

Berman, Eli, John Bound, and Stephen Machin. 1998. "Implications of Skill-Biased Technological Change: International Evidence." *Quarterly Journal of Economics* 113 (4): 1245–1279.

Bernstein, Basil. 1971. *Class, Code and Control*. London: Routledge & Kegan Paul.

Betts, J. R., and J. E. Roemer. 2005. "Equalizing Opportunity for Racial and Socio-Economic Groups in the United States through Education Finance Reform." In *Schools and the Equal Opportunity Problem*, P. Peterson, ed. (pp. 209–238). Cambridge, MA: MIT Press.

Blanden, J., P. Gregg, and S. Machin. 2005. "Intergenerational Mobility in Europe and North America." Working Paper for London School of Economics' Center for Economic Performance. London, UK; http://cep.lse.ac.uk/about/news/IntergenerationalMobility.pdf.

Blanden, J., and S. Machin. 2004. "Educational Inequality and the Expansion of UK Higher Education." *Scottish Journal of Political Economy* 51 (2): 230–249.

Blau, Peter. M. 1994. *Structural Context of Opportunities*. Chicago: University of Chicago Press.

Blau, Peter, and O. D. Duncan. 1967. *Occupations in America*. New York: Basic Books.

Blinder, Alan. 1973. "Wage Discrimination: Reduced Form and Structural Estimates." *Journal of Human Resources* 8 (4): 436–455.

Boarini, R., and H. Strauss. 2007. *The Private Internal Rates of Return to Tertiary Education: New Estimates for 21 OECD Countries*. Economics Department working papers series, no. 591. Paris: Organization for Economic Cooperation and Development.

Boudon, R. 1974. *Education, Opportunity and Social Inequality*. New York: John Wiley.

Bourdieu, Pierre. 1977. "Cultural Reproduction and Social Reproduction." In *Power and Ideology in Education*, Jerome Karabel and A. H. Halsey, eds. (pp. 487–510). New York: Oxford University Press.

———. 1984. *Distinction*. Cambridge, MA.: Harvard University Press.

———. 1986. "The Forms of Capital." In *Handbook of Theory and Research for the Sociology of Education*, J. G. Richardson, ed. (pp. 241–258). New York: Guilford Press.

―――. 2003. *Distinction: A Social Critique of the Judgement of Taste*. London: Routledge.

Bourdieu, Pierre, and Jean Claude Passeron. 1977. *Reproduction in Education, Culture and Society*, Richard Nice, trans. Los Angeles: Sage.

Bourguignon, F., F. Ferreira, and M. Menendez. 2002. *Inequality of Outcomes, Inequality of Opportunities and Intergenerational Education Mobility in Brazil*. Working paper. Washington, DC: World Bank.

Bowles, S. 1973. "Understanding Unequal Opportunity." *American Economic Review* 63 (2): 346–356.

Bowles, Samuel, and Herbert Gintis. 1976. *Schooling in Capitalist America*. New York: Basic Books.

―――. 2002. "Schooling in Capitalist America Revisited." *Sociology of Education* 75: 1–18.

Bowles, Samuel, Herbert Gintis, and Melissa Osborn Groves. 2001. "The Determinants of Earnings: Skills, Preferences, and Schooling." *Journal of Economic Literature* 39 (4): 1137–1176.

―――. 2005. *Unequal Chances: Family Background and Economic Success*. Princeton, NJ: Princeton University Press.

Braudel, Fernand. 2002. *El Mediterráneo y el Mundo mediterráneo en la época de Felipe II*. México: Fondo de Cultura Económica.

Brantlinger, E. 2007. "(Re)Turning to Marx to Understand the Unexpected Anger Among 'Winners' in Schooling: A Critical Social Psychology Perspective." In *Late to Class: Social Class and Schooling in the New Economy*, J. A. Van Galen and G. W. Noblit, eds. (pp. 235–268). Albany: State University of New York Press.

Braslavsky, Cecilia. 2001. "Los procesos contemporáneos de cambios de la educación secundaria en América Larina: Análisis de casos en América del Sur." In *La Educación Secundaria, ¿Cambio o inmutabilidad?*, Cecilia Braslavsky, org. (pp. 165–192). Buenos Aires: Santillana.

Breen, R. 1996. *Regression Models: Censored, Sample Selected or Truncated Data*. Thousand Oaks, CA: Sage.

Breen, Richard, and Jan O. Jonsson. 2005. "Inequality of Opportunity in a Comparative Perspective: Recent Research on Inequality and Social Mobility." *Annual Review of Sociology* 31: 223–243.

Brown, Michael, Martin Carnoy, Elliot Currie, Troy Duster, David Oppenheimer, Marjorie Shultz, and David Wellman. 2003. *Whitewashing Race: The Myth of a Color-Blind Society*. Berkeley: University of California Press.

Brown, Tamara L. 2000. "Gender Differences in African American Students' Satisfaction with College." *Journal of College Student Development* 41: 479–487.

Browne, Irene, and Joya Misra. 2003. "The Intersection of Gender and Race in the Labor Market." *Annual Review of Sociology* 29: 487–513.

Brzinsky-Fay, C. 2007. "Lost in Transition? Labour Market Entry Sequences of School Leavers in Europe." *European Sociological Review* 23: 409–422.

Buchel, Felix, Andries de Grip, and Antje Mertens (Eds). 2003. *Overeducation in Europe: Current Issues in Theory and Policy*. Cheltenham, UK: E. Elgar.

Buchmann, Claudia, and Thomas A. DiPrete. 2006. "The Growing Female Advantage in College Completion: The Role of Family Background and Academic Achievement." *American Sociological Review* 71: 515–541.

Bukowski, M. (ed.). 2007. *Zatrudnienie w Polsce 2006–produktywnosc dla pracy*. Warsaw: Ministerstwo Pracy i Polityki Spoleczny (Ministry of Labor and Social Policy).

Bynner, John. 2005. "Rethinking the Youth Phase of the Life-course: The Case for Emerging Adulthood?" *Journal of Youth Studies* 8 (4): 367–384.

Bynner, John, Heather Joshi, and M. Tstatsas. 2000. *Obstacles and Opportunities on the Route to Adulthood: Evidence from Rural and Urban Britain*. London: Smith Institute.

Bynner, John, and Samantha Parsons. 2002. "Social Exclusion and the Transition from School to Work: The Case of Young People Not in Education, Employment, or Training (NEET)." *Journal of Vocational Behavior* 60 (2): 289–309.

Calsamiglia, C. 2004. *Decentralizing Equality of Opportunity*. Working paper, Department of Economics. Barcelona: Univeritat Autonoma de Barcelona.

Caplan, T., O. Furman, D. Romanov, and N. Zussman. 2006. "The Quality of Israeli Academic Institutions: What the Wages of Graduates Tell about It?" Samuel Neaman Institution for Advanced Studies in Science and Technology. Haifa, Israel: Technion-Israel Institute of Technology.

Card, David. 2001. "Estimating the Return to Schooling: Progress on Some Persistent Econometric Problems." *Econometrica* 69 (5): 1127–1160.

Card, David, and John E. DiNardo. 2002. "Skill-Based Technological Change and Rising Wage Inequality: Some Problems and Puzzles." *Journal of Labor Economics* 20 (4): 733–783.

Card, David, and T. Lemieux. 2000. *Can Falling Supply Explain the Rising Return to College for Younger Men?: A Cohort-Based Analysis*. Working paper series, no. 7655. Cambridge, MA: National Bureau of Economic Research.

Carnoy, Martín. 2007. "Improving Quality and Equity in Latin American Education: A Realistic Assessment." In *Pensamiento Educativo*, no. 40. Santiago: Facultad de Educación Universidad Católica de Chile.

Carnoy, Martín, Gustavo Cosse, Cristián Cox, and Enrique Martínez Larrechea. 2004. *Las reformas educativas en la década de 1990. Un estudio comparado de la Argentina, Chile y Uruguay*. Buenos Aires: Ministerios de Educación de Argentina, Chile y Uruguay, Grupo Asesor de la Universidad de Stanford.

Carter, M. R., and J. May. 2001. "One Kind of Freedom: Poverty Dynamics in Post Apartheid South Africa." *World Development* 29 (12): 1967–2148.

Carter, Prudence. 2005. *Keepin' it Real*. New York: Oxford University Press.

Case, A., and A. Deaton. 1998. "Large Cash Transfers to the Elderly in South Africa." *Economic Journal* 108 (450): 1330–1361.

Castel, R. 2003. *From Manual Workers to Wage Laborers: Transformation of the Social Question*. New Brunswick, NJ: Transaction.

Centeno, Miguel, and Katherine S. Newman (Eds.). 2010. *Discrimination in an Unequal World*. New York: Oxford University Press.

Central Bureau of Statistics (CBS). 1997. "Statistical 5." Jerusalem. Accessed June 1, 2010; http://www.cbs.gov.il/www/statistical/qibu-heb.pdf. (Hebrew)

———. 2007. "Statistical Abstract of Israel." Jerusalem. Accessed June 1, 2010; http://www.cbs.gov.il/reader/shnaton/shnatone_new.htm?CYear=2007&Vol=58 &CSubject=2.

Central Intelligence Agency (CIA). 2007. *World Factbook*. Accessed February 2007; https://www.cia.gov/cia/publications/factbook/index.html.

Centrum Badania Opinii Spolecznej (CBOS). 2004. *Opinie i Diagnozy nr 2: Mlodziez 2003. Raport z badan.* Warsaw: author.

———. 2006. *Praca Polakow w krajach UE Komunikat z badan.* Warsaw: author.

———. 2007. *Czy warto się uczyc? Komunikat z badan.* Warsaw: author.

Chan, T. W., and J. T. Goldthorpe. 2007. "Class and Status: The Conceptual Distinction and Its Empirical Relevance." *American Sociological Review* 72 (4): 512–532.

Chafetz, Janet Saltzman. 1997. "Feminist Theory and Sociology: Underutilized Contributions for Mainstream Theory." *Annual Review of Sociology* 23: 97–120.

Chauvel L. 1997. "L'uniformisation du taux de suicide masculin selon l'âge: effet de génération ou recomposition du cycle de vie?" *Revue française de sociologie* 38 (4): 681–734.

———. 1998. *Le destin des générations: structure sociale et cohortes en France au XXe siècle.* Paris: Presses Universitaires de France.

———. 2000. "Valorisation et dévalorisation sociale des titres: une comparaison France—Etats-Unis." In *L'état de l'école*, A. van Zanten, dir. (pp. 341–352). Paris: La Découverte.

———. 2002. *Le destin des générations, structure sociale et cohortes en France au XXe siècle* [2e éd. mise à jour, avec nouvel avant-propos pp. xiii–xxxiii]. Paris: PUF.

———. 2003. *Génération sociale et socialisation transitionnelle: Fluctuations cohortales et stratification sociale en France et aux Etats-Unis au XXe siècle.* Paris: Mémoire d'Habilitation à Diriger des recherches, Sciences-Po.

———. 2006. "Social Generations, Life Chances and Welfare Regime Sustainability." In *Changing France: The Politics that Markets Make*, Pepper D. Culpepper, Peter A. Hall, and Bruno Palier, eds. (pp. 341–352). Basingstoke, UK: Palgrave Macmillan.

———. 2007. "Generazioni sociali, prospettive di vita e sostenibilità del welfare." *La Rivista delle Politiche Sociali* 4 (3): 43–72.

Checchi, D. 1997. "Education and Intergenerational Mobility in Occupations: A Comparative Study." *American Journal of Economics and Sociology* 56 (3): 331–351.

Checchi, D., A. Ichino, and Rustichini, A. 1999. "More Equal but Less Mobile? Education Financing and Intergenerational Mobility in Italy and in the U.S." *Journal of Public Economics* 74: 351–393.

Chicello, P, M. Leibbrandt, and G. Fields. 2001. "Are African Workers Getting Ahead in the New South Africa? Evidence from KwaZulu Natal, 1993–1998." *Social Dynamics* 27: 1.

Christensen, Ronald. 1990. *Log-linear Models.* New York: Springer-Verlag.

Clogg, Clifford C., and E. S. Shihadeh. 1994. *Statistical Models for Ordinal Variables.* Thousand Oaks, CA: Sage.

Cohen, Cathy J., and Claire E. Nee. 2000. "Sex Differentials in African American Communities." *American Behavioral Scientist* 43: 1159–1206.

Cohen, G. A. 1989. "On the Currency of Egalitarian Justice." *Ethics* 99: 906–944.

Coleman, J. S. 1988. "Social Capital in the Creation of Human Capital." *American Journal of Sociology* 94: 95–120.

Colley, H., and P. Hodkinson, 2001. "Problems with *Bridging the Gap*: The Reversal of Structure and Agency in Addressing Social Exclusion." *Critical Social Policy* 21: 335–359.

Collins, Randall. 1971. "Functional and Conflict Theories of Educational Stratification." *American Sociological Review* 36: 1002–1019.

———. 1979. *The Credential Society: An Historical Sociology of Education and Stratification*. New York: Academic.

———. 1988. *Theoretical Sociology*. New York: Harcourt.

Comisión Económica para América Latina y Caribe (CEPAL). 2007. *Panorama Social de América Latina, 2006*. Santiago, Chile: División de Desarrollo Social y División de Estadística y Proyecciones Económicas.

Conley, D. 2001. "Capital for College: Parental Assets and Postsecondary Schooling." *Sociology of Education* 74: 59–72.

Cook, Philip J., and Jens Ludwig. 1997. "Weighing the 'Burden of Acting White': Are There Race Differences in Attitudes toward Education?" *Journal of Policy Analysis and Management* 16: 256–278.

Côté, J. E. 1996. "Sociological Perspective on Identity Formation: The Culture-Identity Link." *Journal of Adolescence* 19: 417–428.

Cotter, David A., Joan M. Hermsen, and Reeve Vanneman. 2004. *Gender Inequality at Work*. New York: Russell Sage.

Cox, Cristián. 2007. "Educación en el Bicentenario: dos agendas y calidad de la política." *Pensamiento Educativo* 40: 175–204.

———. 2008. "Las Reformas Educativas y su impacto sobre la cohesión social en Latinoamérica." In *Redes, estado y mercados. Soportes de la cohesión social latino-americana*. Eugenio Tironi, ed. Santiago, Chile: Uqbar, Colección Cieplan.

Crompton, R. 1998. *Class and Stratification: An Introduction to Current Debates*, 2nd ed. Cambridge, UK: Polity Press.

Cross, Theodore, and Robert Bruce Slater. 2000. "The Alarming Decline in the Academic Performance of African-American Men." *Journal of Blacks in Higher Education* 27: 82–87.

Crouch, L. A. 1996. "Public Education Equity and Efficiency in South Africa: Lessons for Other Countries." *Economics of Education Review* 15 (2): 125–137.

Crouch, Luis, Amber Gove, y Martin Gustafsson. 2007. *Educación y Cohesión Social*. Documento de Trabajo Proyecto Nacsal. Santiago, Chile: Cieplan-iFHC.

Czapinski, Janusz, and Panek Tomasz (Eds.). 2003. *Diagnoza spoleczna 2003. Warunki i jakosc zycia Polakow*, Warszawa: Wyzsza Szkola Finansow Zarazadzania (WSPiZ) (College of Management, Finance, and Public Administration).

———. 2005. *Diagnoza spoleczna 2003. Warunki i jakosc zycia Polakow*. Warsaw: Wyzsza Szkola Finansow Zarazadzania (WSPiZ) (College of Management, Finance, and Public Administration).

———. 2007. *Diagnoza spoleczna 2003. Warunki i jakosc zycia Polakow*. Warsaw: Rada Monitoringu Spolecznego.

Dahan, M., N. Mironichev, E. Dvir, and S. Shye. 2003. "Have the Gaps in Education Narrowed? On Factor Eligibility for the Israel Matriculation Certificate" *Israel Economic Review* 1 (2): 37–69.

Dar, Y. 1994. "Academic Achievement in Kibbutz and Urban Schools: Does Progressiveness Educe Achievement?" *Megamot Behavioral Science Quarterly* 35 (4): 344–58. (Hebrew)

De Ferranti, David, et al. 2004. *Inequality in Latin America. Breaking with History?* Washington, DC: World Bank.

Deaton, A. 1997. *The Analysis of Household Surveys: A Microeconometric Approach to Development Policy.* Baltimore: Johns Hopkins University Press.

Deng, Zhong, and Donald J. Treiman. 1997. "The Impact of Cultural Revolution on Trends in Educational Attainment in the People's Republic of China." *American Journal of Sociology* 103: 391.

Department for Children, Schools and Families (DCSF). Undated. *Statistical Bulletin: Youth Cohort Study: Education, Training, and Employment of 16–18 Year Olds in England and the Factors Associated with Non-Participation.* London: author.

Department for Education and Skills (DFES). 2005. *Participation in Education, Training and Employment by 16–18 Year Olds in England.* London: author.

Devine, F. 2004. *Class Practices: How Parents Help Their Children Get Good Jobs.* Cambridge, UK: Cambridge University Press.

Dinkelman, T., and F. Pirouz. 2002. "Individual, Household and Regional Determinants of Labour Force Attachment in South Africa: Evidence from the 1997 October Household Survey." *South African Journal of Economics* 70 (5): 865–891.

Di Gropello, Emmanuela. 2004. *Education Decentralization and Accountability Relationships in Latin America.* Policy Research working paper, no. 3453. Washington, DC: World Bank.

DiPrete, Thomas A., and Claudia Buchmann. 2006. "Gender-Specific Trends in the Value of Education and the Emerging Gender Gap in College Completion." *Demography* 43: 1–24.

Domanski, H. 1997. "Mobilnosc i hierarchie stratyfikacyjne." In *Elementy nowego ladu,* H. Domański and A. Rychard, eds. Warsaw: Instytut Filozofii i Socjologii Polskiej Akademii Nauk.

Dronkers, J., and M. Levels. 2007. "Do School Segregation and School Resources Explain Region-of-Origin Differences in the Mathematics Achievement of Immigrant Students?" *Educational Research and Evaluation* 13: 435–462.

Dryzek, John S. 1990. *Discursive Democracy: Politics, Policy and Political Science.* Cambridge, UK: Cambridge University Press.

Duncan, G. J., and S. D. Hoffman. 1981. "The Incidence and Wage Effects of Overeducation." *Economics of Education Review* 1 (1): 75–86.

Duru-Bellat, M. 2006. *L'inflation scolaire: les désillusions de la méritocratie.* Paris: Le Seuil.

Dworkin, R. 1981. "What Is Equality? Part 2: Equality of Resources." *Philosophy and Public Affairs* 10: 283–345.

Easterlin R. A. 1961. "The American Baby Boom in Historical Perspective." *American Economic Review* 51 (5): 869–911.

Easterlin, R. A. 1966. "On the Relation of Economic Factors to Recent and Projected Fertility Changes." *Demography* 3 (1): 131–153.

Easterlin R. A., C. M. Schaeffer, and D. J. Maucunovich. 1993. "Will the Baby Boomers Be Less Well off than Their Parents? Income, Wealth, and Family Circumstances over the Life Cycle in the United States." *Population and Development Review* 19 (3): 497–522.

Economic Commission for Latin America (ECLAC-UNESCO). 1992. *Education and Knowledge: Basic Pillars of Changing Production Patterns with Social Equity.* Santiago, Chile: author.

Education Bureau, Hong Kong. 2010. Accessed May 30, 2010; http://www.edb.gov. hk/index.aspx?nodeID=2&langno=1.

Education Commission Report. 2000. *Learning for Life, Learning through Life, Reform Proposals for the Education System in Hong Kong*. Hong Kong: Government printer.

Education For All (EFA—UNESCO). 2006. *Literacy for Life*. Global Monitoring Report. Paris: author.

Elkin, Frederick, and Gerald Handel. 1984. *The Child and Society: The Process of Socialization*. New York: Random House.

Elliot, James. 2001. "Referral Hiring and Ethnically Homogeneous Jobs." *Social Science Research* 30: 401–425.

Erichsen, G., and J. Wakeford. 2001. *Racial Discrimination in South Africa Before and After the First Democratic Election.*, Working paper, no. 01:49. Cape Town: Development Policy Research Unit.

Erikson, R., and J. H. Goldthorpe. 1992. *The Constant Flux: A Study of Class Mobility in Industrial Societies*. Oxford: Clarendon Press.

Erikson, R., J. H. Goldthorpe, and L. Portocarero. 1979. "Intergenerational Class Mobility in Three Western Societies: England, France and Sweden." *British Journal of Sociology* 30 (40): 415–441.

Esping-Andersen, Gøsta. 1990. *The Three Worlds of Welfare Capitalism*. Cambridge, UK: Polity Press.

———. 1999. *Social Foundations of Postindustrial Economies*. Oxford: Oxford University Press.

Esping-Andersen G., D. Gallie, A. Hemerijck and J. Myles. 2002. *Why We Need a New Welfare State*. Oxford: Oxford University Press.

Estevez-Abe, M., T. Iversen, and D. Soskice. 2001. "Social Protection and the Formation of Skills: A Reinterpretation of the Welfare State." In *Varieties of Capitalism*, Peter A. Hall and David Soskice, eds. (pp. 145–183), New York: Oxford University Press.

European Commission, 2005. *Key Data on Higher Education in Europe—2005 Edition*. Luxembourg: Office for Official Publications of the European Communities.

European Group for Integrated Social Research (EGISR). 2001. "Misleading Trajectories: Transition Dilemmas of Young Adults in Europe." *Journal of Youth Studies* 4 (1): 101–118.

Eurostat. 2004. *European Commission Population and Social Conditions Statistics*. Luxembourg: author.

Farkas, George. 1996. *Human Capital or Cultural Capital? Ethnicity and Poverty Groups in an Urban School District*. New York: De Gruyter.

Ferguson, Ann Arnett. 2000. *Bad Boys: Public Schools in the Making of Black Masculinity*. Ann Arbor: University of Michigan Press.

Feres Jr., João. 2005. "Ação afirmativa no Brasil: a política pública entre os movimentos sociais e a opinião douta." Trabalho apresentado no Seminário Internacional Ações afirmativas nas políticas educacionais: o contexto pós-Durban, September 20–22, Brasília.

Ferrer, Guillermo. 2004. *Las reformas curriculares de Perú, Colombia, Chile y Argentina. ¿Quién responde por los resultados?* Working paper, no. 45. Lima: Grade.

————. 2006. *Estado de situación de los sistemas de evaluación de logros de aprendizaje en América Latina.* Santiago, Chile: Partnership for Educational Revitalization in the Americas (PREAL).

Ferrera, M. 1996. "The 'Southern Model' of Welfare in Social Europe." *Journal of European Social Policy* 6 (1): 17–37.

Filgueira, Fernando, Juan Bogliaccini, and Carlos Gerardo Molina. 2006. "Centralismo y Descentralización como Ejercicio Iterativo." In *Descentralización de la Educación Pública en América Latina*, M. F. F. Filgueira, ed. Río de Janeiro: K. Adenauer Stiftung.

Fiske, Susan. 1998. "Stereotyping, Prejudice, and Discrimination." In *The Handbook of Social Psychology*, Daniel Gilbert, Susan Fiske, and Gardner Lindzay, eds. (pp. 357–411). New York: Oxford University Press.

Fleischmann, F., and J. Dronkers. 2007. *The Effects of Social and Labor Market Policies of EU Countries on the Socio-economic Integration of First and Second Generation Immigrants from Different Countries of Origin.* Working paper, RSCAS 2007/19. San Dominico di Fiesole, Fl, Italy: European University Institute.

Flynn, James R. 2007. *What Is Intelligence?* Cambridge, UK: Cambridge University Press.

Ford, Donna Y., and J. John Harris, III. 1996. "Perceptions and Attitudes of Black Students toward School, Achievement, and Other Educational Variables." *Child Development* 67: 1141–1152.

Fourastié, J. 1979. *Les Trente Glorieuses ou la révolution invisible.* Paris: Fayard.

Franzen, Eva M., and Anders Kassman. 2005. "Longer-term Labour-market Consequences of Economic Activity during Young Adulthood: A Swedish National Cohort Study." *Journal of Youth Studies* 8 (4): 403–424.

Freedom House. 2006. "Freedom in the World Country Ratings 1972–2006." Accessed March 2007; http://www.freedomhouse.org/template.cfm?page=15.

Freeman, R. B. 1976. *The Overeducated American.* New York: Academic Press.

Fry, Peter, et al. 2007. *Divisões Perigosas.* Rio de Janeiro: Record.

Furlong, Andy. 2006. "Not a Very NEET Solution: Representing Problematic Labour Market Transitions among Early School-Leavers." *Work, Employment and Society* 20 (3): 553–569.

Gajardo, Marcela. 1999. *Reformas Educativas en América Latina. Balance de una década.* Documentos PREAL no.15. Santiago, Chile: PREAL.

Gallie, Duncan, and Serge Paugam (Eds). 2000. *Welfare Regimes and the Experience of Unemployment in Europe.* Oxford: Oxford University Press.

Gamoran, Adam. 1986. "Instructional and Institutional Effects of Ability Grouping." *Sociology of Education* 59: 185–198.

Ganzeboom. H. B. G., P. de Graaf, D. J. Treiman, and J. De Leeuw. 1992. "A Standard International Socio-Economic Index of Occupational Status." *Social Science Research* 21: 1–56.

García-Huidobro, Juan Eduardo. 2005. "A modo de síntesis: Políticas Educativas y Equidad en Chile." In *Políticas Educativas y Equidad*. Santiago, Chile: Universidad Alberto Hurtado.

Geddes, A., et al. 2004. *European Civic Citizenship and Inclusion Index 2004.* British Council. Brussels. Accessed February 2007; http://www.britishcouncil.org/brussels-europe-inclusion-index.htm.

Gellner, Ernest. 1991. *Narody i nacjonalizm* [Nations and Nationalism]. Warsaw: Panstwowy Instytut Wydawniczy (PIW, National Institute for Publication).

Gilboa, Y. 2004. "Kibbutz Education: Implications for Nurturing Children from Low- Income Families." *Israel Economic Review* 2 (2): 107–123.

Glewwe, P. 1996. "The Relevance of Standard Estimates of Rates of Return to Schooling for Education Policy: A Critical Assessment." *Journal of Development Economics* 51: 267–290.

Goldin, Claudia, and Lawrence Katz. 2008. *The Race between Education and Technology*. Cambridge, MA: Harvard University Press.

Goldthorpe, J. H. 1997. "Class Analysis and the Reorientation of Class Theory: The Case of Persisting Differentials in Educational Attainment." *British Journal of Sociology* 47: 481–505.

———. 2000. *On Sociology: Numbers, Narratives, and the Integration of Research and Theory*. Oxford: Oxford University Press.

Gomes, Joaquim Barbosa. 2001. *Ação Afirmativa e Principio Constitucional da Igualdade*. Rio de Janeiro: Renovar.

Gordon, Robert J., and Ian Dew-Becker. 2008. *Controversies about the Rise of American Inequality: A Survey*, Working paper, no. 13982. Cambridge, MA: National Bureau of Economic Research (NBER).

Grabowska-Lusinska I., and M. Okolski. 2008. *Migracja z Polski po 1 maja 2004 r.: jej intensywnosc i kierunki geograficzne oraz alokacja migrantow na rynkach pracy krajow Unii Europejskiej*. Working paper, no. 33/91. Warsaw: Centre of Migration Research, University of Warsaw.

Granovetter, Mark. 1974. *Getting a Job: A Study of Contacts and Careers*. Cambridge, MA: Harvard University Press.

Greene, W. H. 2003. *Econometric Analysis*, 5th ed. Upper Saddle River, NJ. Prentice-Hall.

Greene, W. 1999. "Marginal Effects in the Censored Regression Model." *Economics Letters* 64 (1): 43–50.

Griliches, Z. 1969. "Capital-Skill Complementarity." *Review of Economics and Statistics* 5: 465–468.

Grindle, Merilee. 2004. *Despite the Odds. The Contentious Politics of Education Reform*. Princeton, NJ: Princeton University Press.

Groot, W., and M. van den Brink. 2000. "Overeducation in the Labor Market: A Meta-Analysis." *Economics of Education Review* 19: 149–158.

Grotkowska, G, and U. Sztanderska. 2007. "Czas trwania edukacji a aktywnosc zawodowa." In *Edukacja dla pracy. Raport o rozwoju spolecznym Polska 2007*, John Szczycinski, ed. Warsaw: United Nations Development Program.

Guimarães, Antonio S. A. 2003. "The Race Issue in Brazilian Politics (the Last Fifteen Years)." In *Brazil since 1985; Economy, Polity and Society*, Maria D'Alva Kinzo and James Dunkerley, eds. (pp. 251–268). London: Institute of Latin American Studies.

Glowny Urzad Statystyczny (GUS) (Central Statistical Office). 2007a. *Szkoly wyzsze i ich finanse w 2006 roku*. Warsaw: Central Statistical Office.

———. 2007b. *Struktura wynagrodzen wedlug zawodow w październiku 2006*. Warsaw: Central Statistical Office.

——— 2007c. *Popyt na pracę w 2006 roku*. Warsaw: Central Statistical Office.

Hall, P. A., and C. R. Taylor. 1996. "Political Science and the Three New Institutionalisms." *Political Studies* 44: 936–957.

Halsey, A. H., A. F. Heath, and J. M. Ridge. 1980. *Origins and Destinations: Family, Class and Education in Modern Britain.* Oxford: Clarendon Press.

Hanley, Eric, and Matthew McKeever. 1997. "The Persistence of Educational Inequalities in State Socialist Hungary: Trajectory Maintenance versus Counterselection." *Sociology of Education* 70: 1–18.

Hannum, Emily, and Yu Xie. 1994. "Trends in Educational Gender Inequality in China 1949–1985." *Research in Social Stratification and Mobility* 13: 73–98.

Hansen, M. N. 1997. "Social and Economic inequality in the Educational Career: Do the Effect of Social Background Characteristics Decline?" *European Sociological Review* 13 (3): 305–321.

Hart, B., and T. R. Risley. 1995. *Meaningful Differences in the Everyday Experiences of Young American Children.* Baltimore: Brookes.

Harris, Angel L. 2006. "I (Don't) Hate School: Revisiting 'Oppositional Culture) Theory of Blacks' Resistance to Schooling." *Social Forces* 85: 797–834.

Hastings D. W., and L. G. Berry. 1979. *Cohort Analysis: a Collection of Interdisciplinary Readings.* Oxford, OH: Scripps Foundation for Research in Population Problems.

Haveman, R., and K. Wilson. 2007. "Economic Inequality in College Access, Matriculation, and Graduation." In *Higher Education and Inequality*, Stacey Dickert-Conlin and Ross Rubinstein, eds. New York: Russell Sage Press.

Heath, A., and S. Cheung (Eds.). 2007. *Unequal Chances. Ethnic Minorities in Western Labor Markets.* Oxford: Oxford University Press.

Heckman, James, Alan Kreuger, and Benjamin Friedman. 2004. *Inequality in America: What Role for Human Capital Policies?* Cambridge, MA: MIT Press.

Heckman, James, Jora Stixrud, and Sergio Urzula. 2006. "The Effects of Cognitive and Noncognitive Abilities on Labor Market Outcomes and Social Behavior." *Journal of Labor Economics* 24 (3): 411–481.

Hega, G. M., and K. G. Hokenmaier. 2002. "The Welfare State and Education: A Comparison of Social and Educational Policy in Advanced Industrial Societies." *German Policy Studies* 2 (1): 1–29.

Heller, D. E. (Ed.). 2002. *Conditions of Access: Higher Education for Lower Income Students.* Westport, CT: Praeger.

Hertz, T. 2003. "Upward Bias in the Mincerian Returns to Education: Evidence for South Africa." *American Economic Review* 93 (4): 1354–1368.

Heston A., R. Summers, and B. Aten. 2006. *Penn World Table Version 6.2.* Center for International Comparisons of Production, Income and Prices, University of Pennsylvania.

Hirst, Paul Q. 1994. *Associative Democracy: New Forms of Economic and Social Governance.* Cambridge, UK: Polity Press.

Hong Kong Census and Statistics Department. *Summary Results for the Years of 1971, 1981, 1991, 2001, and 2006.* Hong Kong: Government Press.

Hong Kong Education Bureau. 2010. Accessed May 30, 2010; http://www.edb.gov. hk/index.aspx?nodeID=2&langno=.

Horn, Daniel. 2007. "Conservative States, Stratified Education, Unequal Opportunity: A Hypothesis on How Educational Regimes Differ." Paper presented to the ASPAnet Conference, Vienna, Austria.

Hout, Michael. 2004. *Maximally Maintained Inequality Revisited: Irish Educational Mobility in Comparative Perspective*. Working paper. Berkeley, CA: Survey Research Center, University of California.

————. 2006. "Maximally Maintained Inequality and Essentially Maintained Inequality: Crossnational Comparisons." *Sociological Theory and Methods* 21: 237–52.

Human Development Index. 2006. Accessed February 2007; http://hdr.undp.org/hdr2006/statistics.

Huntington, S. 1996. *The Clash of Civilizations and the Remaking of World Order*. New York: Simon & Schuster.

Iaies, Gustavo, and Andrés Delich. 2007. *Sistemas educativos y cohesión social: La reconstrucción de "lo común" en los estados nacionales del siglo XXI*. Documento de Trabajo Proyecto Nacsal. Santiago, Chile: Cieplan-iFHC.

Instituto Internacional de Planeamiento Educativo, Organización de Estados Iberoamericanos-UNESCO (IIPE-OEI). 2006. *Informe sobre Tendencias Sociales y Educativas en América Latina*. Buenos Aires: IIPE-UNESCO Buenos Aires and OEI.

INFOS. 2006. "Migracje zarobkowe Polakow do krajow UE. " Mimeo. Warsaw: Biuro Analiz Sejmowych.

Inui, A. 2005. "Why Freeter and NEET are Misunderstood: Recognizing the New Precarious Conditions of Japanese Youth." *Social Work and Society* 3: 244–251.

International Organization for Migration (IOM). 2008. *World Migration Report 2008: Managing Labour Mobility in the Evolving World Economy*. Geneva: author.

Jackson, B., and D. Marsden. 1962. *Education and the Working Class*. London: Routledge and Kegan Paul.

Jacobs, Jerry. 1996. "Gender Inequality and Higher Education." *Annual Review of Sociology* 22: 153–185.

Jencks, C. 1988. "Whom Must We Treat Equally for Educational Opportunity to Be Equal?" *Ethics* 98: 518–533.

Jin, Shen. 2000. "Elitist Educational System and Focus Schools." *Modern Education Study* 1: 3–9.

Johnston, Jack, and John Dinardo. 1997. *Econometric Methods*. New York: McGraw Hill.

Johnston, Lloyd D., Jerald G. Bachman, and Patrick M. O'Malley. 1975. *Monitoring the Future*. Ann Arbor, MI: Survey Research Center, Institutes for Social Research.

————. 1985. *Monitoring the Future*. Ann Arbor, MI: Survey Research Center, Institutes for Social Research.

Jowell, R., et al. 2005. *European Social Survey 2004/2005: Technical Report*. London: Centre for Comparative Social Surveys, City University.

Joy, Lois. 2003. "Salaries of Recent Male and Female College Graduates: Educational and Labor Market Effects." *Industrial and Labor Relations Review* 56: 606–621.

Kabaj, M. 2004."Prognoza podaży i popytu absolwentów wedóug poziomów wykształcenia." Mimeo. Warsaw: Instytut Pracy i Spraw Socjalnych (Institute for Labor and Social Affairs).

Kao, G., and J. S. Thompson. 2003. "Racial and Ethnic Stratification in Educational Achievement and Attainment." *Annual Review of Education* 29: 417–442.

Kaufmann, D., A. Kraay, and M. Mastruzzi. 2005. *Governance Matters IV: Governance Indicators for 1996–2004*. Policy Research working paper, no. 3630. Washington, DC: World Bank.

Kaufman, Robert R., and Joan M. Nelson. 2005. *Políticas de Reforma Educativa. Comparación entre Países*. Documentos PREAL no. 33. Santiago, Chile: PREAL.

Kerckhoff, Alan C. 1995. "Institutional Arrangements and Stratification Processes in Industrial Societies." *Annual Review of Sociology* 21: 323–347.

Kingdon, J. W. 2003. *Agendas, Alternatives and Public Policies*. New York. Longman.

Kingdon, G., and J. Knight. 1999. "Unemployment and Wages in South Africa: A Spatial Approach." Oxford: Centre for the Study of African Economies, Institute of Economics and Statistics, University of Oxford.

———. 2003. "Unemployment in South Africa: the Nature of the Beast." *World Development* 32 (3): 391–408.

Kogan, I. 2007. *Working Through Barriers: Host Country Institutions and Immigrant Labor Market Performance in Europe*. Dordrecht: Springer.

Kohn, M. L. 1977. *Class and Conformity: A Study in Values*, 2nd. ed. Chicago: University of Chicago Press.

Kooiman, J. 1993. "Governance and Governability: Using Complexity, Dynamics and Diversity." In *Modern Governance*, J. Kooiman, ed. (pp. 35–50). London: Sage.

Koopmans, R., and P. Statham. 1999. "Challenging the Liberal Nation-State? Postnationalism, Multiculturalism, and the Collective Claims Making of Migrants and Ethnic Minorities in Britain and Germany." *American Journal of Sociology* 105 (3): 652–696.

Korea Educational Development Institute (KRDI). 1994. *A Study of Consciousness of Education of Koreans*, RR 94–8. Seoul: author.

Korea National Statistical Office (KNSO). 2006. *Social Indicators of Korea 2006*. Seoul: author.

———. 2008. *Reports on the Private After School Education*. Seoul: author.

Koubi, M. 2003. "Les trajectoires professionnelles: une analyse par cohorte," *Économie et Statistique* 369–370: 119–147.

Kozol, Jonathan. 1991. *Savage Inequalities: Children in America's Schools*. New York: Crown.

KPMG. 2007. "Migracje pracownikow—szansa czy zagrozenie? Raport z badan." Mimeo. Warsaw: author.

Krugman, P. R. 1992. *The Age of Diminished Expectations: US Economic Policy in the 1990s*. Cambridge, MA: MIT Press.

Lam, D. 2001. "The Impact of Race on Earnings and Human Capital in Brazil, South Africa, and the United States." Paper presented at DPRU/FES Conference on Labour Markets and Poverty, Johannesburg, South Africa.

Lareau, A. 2000. *Home Advantages: Social Class and Parental Intervention in Elementary Education*. Lanham, MD: Rowman and Littlefield.

———. 2002. "Invisible Inequality: Social Class and Childrearing in Black Families and White Families." *American Sociological Review* 67 (October): 747–776.

———. 2003. *Unequal Childhoods: Class, Race and Family Life*. Berkeley, CA: University of California Press.

Levels, M., and J. Dronkers. 2008. "Differences in Educational Performance between First and Second-Generation Migrant-Pupils from Various Regions and Native Pupils in Europe and the Pacific Rim." *Ethnic and Racial Studies* 31 (8): 1404–1425.

Levels, M., J. Dronkers, and G. Kraaykamp. 2008. "Educational Achievement of Immigrants in Western Countries: Origin, Destination, and Community Effects on Mathematical Performance. *American Sociological Review* 73 (5): 835–853.

Lewis, O. 1959. *Five Families: Mexican Case Studies in the Culture of Poverty*. New York: Basic Books.

Livingston, Andrea, and John Wirt. 2004. *The Condition of Education 2004 in Brief.* NCES no. 2004–076, National Center for Education Statistics, Institute of Education Services. Washington, DC: U.S. Department of Education.

Lucas, Samuel R. 1999. *Tracking Inequality: Stratification and Mobility in American High Schools*. New York: Teachers College Press.

————. 2001. "Effectively Maintained Inequality: Educational Transitions and Social Background." *American Journal of Sociology* 106: 1642–1690.

Lundberg, S., and R. Startz. 1998. "On the Persistence of Racial Inequality." *Journal of Labour Economics* 16 (2): 292–323.

Luxembourg Income Study (LIS). 2010. Accessed May 31, 2010; http://www.lisproject.org.

Lynch, K., and Moran, M. 2006. "Markets, Schools and the Convertibility of Economic Capital: The Complex Dynamics of Class Choice." *British Journal of Sociology of Education* 27 (2): 221–235.

MacLeod, J. 2004. *Ain't No Makin' It: Aspirations and Attainment in a Low-Income Neighbourhood*. Boulder, CO: Westview.

Maddala, G. 1983. *Limited Dependent and Qualitative Variables in Econometrics*. New York: Cambridge University Press.

Maddison A. 1982. *Phases of Capitalist Development*. Oxford: Oxford University Press.

Mannheim K. 1928/1990. *Le problème des générations*. Paris: Nathan.

Marini, Margaret Mooney, and Pi-Ling Fan. 1997. "The Gender Gap in Earnings at Career Entry." *American Sociological Review* 62: 588–604.

Marshall, G., A. Swift, and S. Roberts. 1997. *Against the Odds*. Oxford: Clarendon Press.

Martin, J. P., and D. Grubb. 2001. "What Works and for Whom: A Review of OECD Countries' Experiences with Active Labour Market Policies." *Swedish Economic Policy Review* 8: 956.

Mason K. O., W. M. Mason, H. H. Winsborough, and W. H. Poole. 1973. "Some Methodological Issues in Cohort Analysis of Archival Data." *American Sociological Review* 38: 242–258.

Mayer, K. U. 2005. "Life Courses and Life Chances in a Comparative Perspective." In *Analyzing Inequality: Life Chances and Social Mobility in Comparative Perspective*, S. Svallfors, ed. (pp. 17–55). Palo Alto, CA: Stanford University Press.

Mayer, S. E. 1997. *What Money Can't Buy: Family Income and Children's Life Chances*. Cambridge, MA: Harvard University Press.

McCall, Leslie. 2000. "Explaining Levels of Within-group Wage Inequality in U.S. Labor Markets." *Demography* 37: 415–430.

McDonald, J., and R. A. Moffitt. 1980. "The Uses of Tobit Analysis." *Review of Economics and Statistics* 62: 318–321.

Mead, M. 1970. *Culture and Commitment; A Study of the Generation Gap*. New York: Doubleday (Published for the Natural History Press).

Mendras, H. 1988. *La seconde révolution française: 1965–1984*. Paris: Gallimard.

Mentré, F. 1920. *Les générations sociales*. Paris: Éd. Bossard.

Mickelson, Roslyn Arlin. 1989. "Why Does Jane Read and Write so Well?: The Anomaly of Women's Achievement." *Sociology of Education* 62: 47–63.

———. 1990. "The Attitude-Achievement Paradox among Black Adolescents." *Sociology of Education* 63: 44–61.

———. 2003. "Gender, Bourdieu, and the Anomaly of Women's Achievement Redux." *Sociology of Education* 76: 373–375.

Mincer, J. 1974. *Schooling, Experience and Earnings*. New York: Columbia University Press.

Mingpao. 2006. Accessed December 8; http://www.mingpaonews.com/20061208/gfd1.htm.

———. 2007a. Accessed January 16; http://www.mingpaonews.com/20070116/faa1.htm.

———. 2007b. Accessed July 5; http://www.mingpaonews.com/20070705/gxg1.htm.

———. 2007c. Accessed November 1; http://www/mingpaonews.com/20071101/gaa1.htm.

Ministerio de Educación. 2005. *Objetivos Fundamentales y Contenidos Mínimos Obligatorios de la Educación Media -Actualización 2005*. Santiago, Chile: author.

Ministerstwo Edukacji Narodowej (MEN). 2006. *Program Miedzynarodowej Oceny Umiejętnosci Uczniow PISA. Wyniki badania 2006 w Polsce*. Warsaw: author.

Ministerstwo Gospodarki i Pracy (MgiP). 2005. *Informacja o bezrobotnych wedlug grup zawodow i specjalności w II polroczu 2005 roku*. Warsaw: author. Available at http://www.praca.gov.pl/index.php?page=publications.

Ministerstwo Pracy i Spraw Socjalnych (MPiPS). 2006a. *Zarejestrowani bezrobotni oraz oferty pracy wedlug zawodow i specjalnosci w II polroczu 2007 roku*. Warsaw: author. Available at http://www.praca.gov.pl/index.php?page=publications.

———. 2006b. "Bezrobotni pozostajacy bez pracy powyzej 12 miesięcy. Analiza od 1993 roku." Mimeo. Warsaw: author.

———. 2008. *Ministerstwo Pracy i Spraw Socjalnych, 'Informacja o bezrobociu w grudniu 2007 roku do konca czerwca 2006 roku*. Warsaw: author.

Ministry of Education and Human Resource Department. 2006. *Statistical Yearbook of Education*. Seoul, Korea: author.

Ministry of Regional Development (MRD). 2007. *Human Capital Operational Programme. National Strategic Reference Framework 2007–2013*. Warsaw: author.

Mitchell, Michael. 1985. "Blacks and the Abertura Democrática." In *Race, Class and Power in Brazil*, Pierre-Michel Fontaine, ed. (pp. 95–119). Los Angeles: Center for Afro-American Studies, University of California.

Mokrzycki, E. 1997. "Od protokapitalizmu do prosocjalizmu: makrostrukturalny wymiar dwukrotnej zmiany ustroju." In *Elementy nowego ladu*, H. Domanski and A. Rychard, eds. Warsaw: IFiS PAN (Institute for Philosophy and Sociology of the Polish Academy of Sciences).

Moll, P. 1996. "The Collapse of Primary Schooling Returns in South Africa, 1960–1990." *Oxford Bulletin of Economics and Statistics* 58: 185–209.

Moore, R. 2004. *Education and Society: Issues and Explanations in the Sociology of Education*. Cambridge, UK: Polity Press.

Moura, Clóvis. "Organizações Negras." 1981. In *São Paulo: O povo em movimento*, Paul Singer, and Vinicius Caldeira Brant, eds. Petrópolis: Vozes.

Mulligan, C. 1997. *Parental Priorities and Economic Inequality*. Chicago: University of Chicago Press.

Murnane, Richard, Frank Levy, and John Willett. 1995. "The Growing Importance of Cognitive Skills in Wage Determination." *Review of Economics and Statistics 72* (2): 251–266.

Nash, R. 2006. "Controlling for 'Ability': A Conceptual and Empirical Study of Primary and Secondary Effects." *British Journal of Sociology of Education 27* (2): 157–172.

Nash, R. 2002. "The Educated Habitus, Progress at School, and Real Knowledge." *Interchange 33* (1): 27–48.

National Center for Education Statistics (NCES). 1996. *Integrated Postsecondary Education Data System (IPEDS) "Completions" Survey*. Washington, DC: U.S. Department of Education.

———. 2008. *Projections of Educational Statistics to 2017*. NCES study, no. 2008–078. Institute for Education Sciences. Washington, DC: U.S. Department of Education.

Nattrass, N. 2000. "The Debate about Unemployment in the 1990s." *Studies in Economics and Econometrics 24* (3): 129–142.

Navarro, Juan Carlos. 2006. *Dos clases de políticas educativas. La política de las políticas públicas*. Study no. 36. Santiago, Chile: PREAL.

Neumark, D. 1988. "Employer's Discriminatory Behavior and the Estimation of Wage Discrimination." *Journal of Human Resources 23* (3): 279–295.

———. 2000. *On the Job: Is Long Term Employment a Thing of the Past?* New York: Russell Sage.

Newell, A., and B. Reilly. 2007. *Rates of Return to Educational Qualifications in the Transitional Economies*. Discussion Papers in Economics, University of Sussex, Paper no. 03/97; available at http://citeseer.ist.psu.edu/newell97rates.html.

Newman, Katherine S. 1999. *Falling from Grace: Downward Mobility in Age of Affluence*. Berkeley, CA: University of California Press.

——— (Ed.). 2008. *Laid Off, Laid Low: The Social and Political Consequences of Job Instability*. New York: Columbia University Press.

Ng, J., and K. Y. Cheng. 2002. "Transfer of Associate Degree Students in Hong Kong: What Can We Learn from the US Model?" Mimeo. Conference on Continuing Education and Lifelong Learning, Hong Kong.

Oakes, Jeannie. 1985. *Keeping Track: How Schools Structure Inequality*. New Haven: Yale University Press.

Oaxaca, R. 1973. "Male-Female Wage Differentials in Urban Labor Markets." *International Economic Review 14*: 693–709.

Oaxaca, R., and M. Ransom. 1994. "On Discrimination and the Decomposition of Wage Differentials." *Journal of Econometrics 61*: 5–21.

O'Connor, Carla. 1997. "Dispositions toward (Collective) Struggle and Educational Resilience in the Inner City." *American Educational Research Journal 34*: 593–629.

———. 1999. "Race, Class, and Gender in America: Narratives of Opportunity among Low-Income African American Youths." *Sociology of Education 72*: 137–147.

Office of Prime Minister, 1994. *Annual Opinion Survey*. Tokyo, Japan: author.

Ogbu, John U. 1978. *Minority Education and Caste: The American System in Cross-Cultural Perspective.* New York: Academic Press.

Organization for Economic Cooperation and Development (OECD). 1998. *Human Capital Investment: An International Comparison.* Centre for Educational Research and Innovation. Paris: author.

————. 2004. *Reviews of National Policies of Education: Chile.* Paris: author.

————. 2007a. *Education at a Glance 2007:.* OECD *Indicators.* Paris: author.

————. 2007b. *No More Failures: Ten Steps to Equity in Education.* Paris: author.

————. 2007c. *Science Competencies for Tomorrow's World: PISA 2006. Vol. 1: Analysis. Vol. 2: Data.* Paris: author.

————. 2008. *Education at a Glance: OECD Indicators.* Centre for Educational Research and Innovation. Paris: author. Available at http://www.oecdbookshop.org/oecd/display.asp?CID=&LANG=EN&SF1=DI&ST1=5KZN0WRKCDTG.

Park, HyunJoon. 2007. "South Korea: Educational Expansion and Inequality of Opportunity for Higher Education." In *Stratification in Higher Education: A Comparative Study,* Yossi Shavit, Richard Arum, and Adam Gamoran, eds. (chap. 5). Stanford, CA: Stanford University Press.

Park, Hyunjoon, and Jeroen Smits. 2005. "Educational Assortative Mating in Korea: 1930–1988." *Research in Social Stratification and Mobility* 23: 103–127.

Parkin, Frank. 1971. *Class Inequality and Political Order: Social Stratification in Capitalist and Socialist Societies.* New York: Praeger.

Parish, William L. 1984. "Destratification in China." in *Class and Social Stratification in Post-Revolution China,* J. L. Watson, ed. (pp. 84–120). Cambridge, UK: Cambridge University Press.

Pavin, A. 2006. "The Kibbutz Movement—Facts and Figures 2006." Yad Tabenkin Research and Documentation Center of the Kibbutz Movement, Ramat Efal, Israel.

Pemberton, Simon. 2007. "Tackling the NEET Generation and the Ability of Policy to Generate a 'NEET' Solution—Evidence from the UK." *Environment and Planning C: Government and Policy* 26 (1): 243–259. Accessed June 2, 2010; http://www.envplan.com/abstract.cgi?id=c0654.

Peugny, C. 2009. *Le déclassement.* Paris: Grasset.

Peter, Katharin, and Laura Horn. 2005. *Gender Differences in Participation and Completion of Undergraduate Education and How They Have Changed Over Time.* NCES no. 2005–169, National Center for Education Statistics, Institute of Education Services. Washington, DC: U.S. Department of Education.

Pinto, Regina Pahim. 1993. *O movimento negro em São Paulo: luta e identidade.* São Paulo: FFLCH/USP.

Plug, E. 2004. "Estimating the Effect of Mother's Schooling on Children's Schooling Using a Sample of Adoptees." *American Economic Review* 94 (1): 358–368.

Pohl, Axel, and Andreas Walther. 2007. "Activating the Disadvantaged. Variations in Addressing Youth Transitions Across Europe." *International Journal of Lifelong Education* 26 (5): 533–553.

Pohoski, M. 1995. "Nierownosci społeczne w Polsce—kontynuacje i zmiany w okresie transformacji ustrojowej. " In *Ludzie i instytucje. Stawanie się ladu społecznego. Pamietnik IX Ogolnopolskiego Zjazdu Socjologicznego.* Lublin: Uniwersytet Marii Curie-Sklodowska [People and Institutions, Proceedings of the IX National Congress of Sociology, vol. I, Lublin].

Polawski, P. 1999. "Dzieci i mlodziez w sferze ubostwa. Dziedziczenie biedy i spolecznego nieprzystosowania." In *Marginalnos i procesy marginalizacji*, Kazimierz Frieske, ed. Warsaw: Instytut Pracy i Spraw Socjalnych (IPiSS) (Institute for Labor and Social Studies).

Popham, I. 2003. *Tackling NEETs: Research on Action and Other Factors that Can Contribute to a Reduction in the Numbers of Young People Not in Education, Employment or Training (NEET)*. Nottingham: Department for Education and Skills Publications.

Portes, A., and R. G. Rumbaut. 2001. *Legacies: The Story of the Immigrant Second Generation*. Berkeley: University of California Press.

Post, D. 1993. "Focus on Educational Attainment: Educational Attainment and the Role of the State in Hong Kong." *Comparative Education Review* 37 (3): 240–262.

Powell, Arthur G. 1996. *Lessons from Privilege: The American Prep School Tradition*. Cambridge, MA: Harvard University Press.

Power, S., T. Edwards, G. Whitty, and V. Wigfall. 2003. *Education and the Middle Class*. Buckingham, UK: Open University Press.

Powers, Daniel A., and Yu Xie. 2000. *Statistical Methods for Categorical Data Analysis*. New York: Academic Press.

Prince's Trust. 2007. *The Cost of Exclusion. Counting the Cost of Youth Disadvantage in the UK*. London, UK: The Prince's Trust. Accessed June 2, 2010; http://www.princes-trust.org.uk/PDF/Princes%20Trust%20Research%20Cost%20of%20Exclusion%20apr07.pdf.

Programa de Provisión de la Reforma Educativa (PREAL). 1999. *Descentralización educacional: aprendizaje de tres décadas de experiencia*. Series de Resúmenes de Políticas, no. 3. Santiago, Chile: author.

———. 2006. *Cantidad sin Calidad. Informe de Progreso Educativo en América Latina*. Santiago, Chile: author.

Psachararopoulos, G. 1994. "Returns to Investment in Education." *World Development* 22 (9): 1325–1343.

Psachararopoulos, G., and H. Patrinos. 2002. *Returns to Investment in Education: A Further Update*. Policy Research working paper, no. 2881. Washington, DC: World Bank.

Putnam, Robert. 2000. *Bowling Alone the Collapse and Revival of American Community*. New York: Simon & Schuster.

Queiroz, D. M. 2004. *Universidade e Desigualdade: brancos e negros no ensino superior*. Brasília: Liber Livros.

Quintini, Glenda, John P. Martin, and Sébastien Martin. 2007. *The Changing Nature of the School-to-Work Transition Process in OECD Countries*. Bonn: Institute for the Study of Labor.

Rabe-Hesketh, S., and B. Everitt. 2004. "Random Effects Models: Thought Disorder and Schizophrenia." In *A Handbook of Statistical Analyses Using Stata*, S. Rabe-Hesketh and B. Everitt, eds. (pp. 151–178). Boca Raton, FL: Chapman & Hall/CRC.

Raffo, Carol, and Michelle Reeves. 2000. "Youth Transitions and Social Exclusion: Developments in Social Capital Theory." *Journal of Youth Studies* 3 (2): 147–166.

Raftery, A. E. 1986. "Choosing Models for Cross-Classifications." *American Sociological Review* 51: 145–146.

Raftery, Adrian E., and Michael Hout. 1993. "Maximally Maintained Inequality: Expansion, Reform, and Opportunity in Irish Education." *Sociology of Education* 66: 41–62.

Reimers, Fernando. 2000. "Educational Opportunity and Policy in Latin America." In *Unequal Schools, Unequal Chances*, F. Reimers, ed. (chap. 1). Cambridge, MA: Harvard University Press.

Richiardi, Matteo. 2002. "What Does the ECHP Tell Us about Labour Status Misperception?" Working Paper Series #10. Moncalieri, Italy: LABORatorio R. Revelli (Center for Employment Studies), Collegio Carlo Alberto.

Roemer, J. E. 1996. *Theories of Distributive Justice*. Cambridge, MA: Harvard University Press.

———. 1998. *Equality of Opportunity*. Cambridge, MA: Harvard University Press.

———. 2000. "Equality of Opportunity." In *Meritocracy and Economic Inequality*, K. Arrow, S. Bowles, and S. Durlauf, eds. (chap. 2). Princeton, NJ: Princeton University Press.

Roemer, J. E., et al. 2003. "To What Extent Do Fiscal Regimes Equalize Income Acquisition among Citizens?" *Journal of Public Economics* 87 (3–4): 539–565.

Royster, Deidre. 2003. *Race and the Invisible Hand*. Berkeley: University of California Press.

Rutkowski, J. 1996. "High Skills Pay Off: The Changing Wage Structure During Economic Transition in Poland." *Economics of Transition* 4 (1): 89–111.

———. 1997. "Low Wages Employment in Transitional Economies of Central and Eastern Europe." *MOCT-MOST: Economic Policy in Transitional Economies* 7 (1): 105–130.

Rychard, A. 2000. "Przestrzen instytucjonalna." In *Strategie i system. Polacy w obliczu zmiany systemowej*, A. Giza-Poleszczuk, M. Marodyand, and A. Rychard, eds. Warsaw: Instute for Philosophy and Sociology of the Polish Academy of Sciences (IFiS PAN).

Ryder, N. B. 1965. "The Cohort as a Concept in the Study of Social Change." *American Sociological Review* 30: 843–861.

Sassen, Saskia. 1998. *Globalization and its Discontents. Essay on the New Mobility of People and Money*. New York: New Press.

Saunders, P. 2002. "Reflections on the Meritocracy Debate in Britain: A Response to Richard Breen and John Goldthorpe." *British Journal of Sociology* 53 (4): 559–574.

Savage, M. 2000. *Class Analysis and Social Transformation*. Buckingham, UK: Open University Press.

Savage, M., and M. Egerton. 1997. "Social Mobility, Individual Ability and the Inheritance of Class Inequality." *Sociology* 31 (4): 645–672.

Sayer, A. 2005. *The Moral Significance of Class*. Cambridge, UK: Cambridge University Press.

Scarr, S., and D. Yee. 1980. "Heritability and Educational Policy: Genetic and Environmental Effects on IQ, Aptitude and Achievement." *Educational Psychologist* 15 (1): 1–22.

Schnitzer, K., W. Isserstedt, J. Schreiber, and M. Schrödr. 1996. "Students in Germany: The 1994 Socio-Economic Picture." Bonn, Germany: Federal Ministry of Education, Science, Research and Technology.

Schofer E., and J. W. Meyer. 2005. "The World-wide Expansion of Higher Education in the Twentieth Century." *American Sociological Review* 70: 898–920.

Schriewer, Jurgen. 2004. *Multiple Internationalities: The Emergence of World-Level Ideology and the Persistence of Idiosyncratic World-Views.* Comparative Education Centre, Research paper, no. 14. Berlin: Humboldt University.

Schultz, G. 1961. "Investment in Human Capital." *American Economic Review* 51 (1): 1–17.

Schütz, G., H. W. Ursprung, and L. Woessmann. 2005. "Education Policy and Equality of Opportunity." Discussion paper, no. 1906. Bonn: Institut zur Zukunft der Arbeit (IZA) (Institute for the Study of Labor).

Sen, A. K. 1980. "Equality of What?" In *Tanner Lectures on Human Values: Volume 1,* S. McMurrin, ed. Cambridge, UK: Cambridge University Press.

Sennett, R. and J. Cobb. 1972. *The Hidden Injuries of Class.* New York and London: Norton and Company.

Shavit, Yossi, Richard Arum, and Adam Gamoran. 2007. *Stratification in Higher Education: A Comparative Study.* Stanford, CA: Stanford University Press.

Shavit, Yossi, and Hans Peter Blossfeld (Eds.). 1993. *Persistent Inequality: Changing. Educational Attainment in Thirteen Countries.* Boulder, CO: Westview Press.

Shavit, Yossi, S. Bolotin-Chavhashvili, H. Ayalon, and G. Menahem. 2003. "Diversification, Expansion and Inequality in Israeli Higher Education." Pinhas Sapir Center for Development, discussion paper, no. 1. Tel Aviv: University of Tel Aviv.

Sherer, G. 2000. "Intergroup Economic Inequality in South Africa: The Post Apartheid Era." *American Economic Review* 90 (2): 317–321.

Shorrocks, A. 1978. "The Measurement of Mobility." *Econometrica* 46: 1013–1024.

Sicherman, N. 1991. "Mismatch in the Labor Market." *Journal of Labor Economics* 9 (2): 101–122.

Simkus, Albert, and Rudolf Andorka. 1982. "Educational Attainment in Hungary." *American Sociological Review* 47: 740–751.

Slomczynski, K., and W. Wesolowski. 1974. "Uklady zgodności i niezgodnosci pozycji społecznych." In *Zroznicowanie spoleczne.* Wroclaw: Ossolineum.

Smith, Sandra. 2003. "Exploring the Efficacy of African Americans' Job Referral Networks." *Ethnic and Racial Studies* 26 (6): 1029–1045.

Smits, J., W. Ultee, and J. Lammers. 1998. "Educational Homogamy in 65 Countries: An Explanation of Differences in Openness Using Country-Level Explanatory Variables." *American Sociological Review* 63: 264–285.

Social Exclusion Unit. 1999. "Bridging the Gap: New Opportunities for 16–18 Year-olds not in Education, Employment or Training." Cm 4405, Social Exclusion Unit. London: Stationery Office.

Solon, G. 2002. "Cross-Country Differences in Intergenerational Earnings Mobility." *Journal of Economic Perspectives* 16 (3): 59–66.

Sorokin, P. A. 1927. *Social Mobility.* New York: Harper.

Spence, M. 1974. *Market Signaling: Informational Transfer in Hiring and Related Screening Devices.* Cambridge, MA: Harvard University Press.

StataCorp. 2005. *Survival Analysis and Epidemiological Tables.* College Station, TX: Stata Press.

Steele, Claude. 1988. "The Psychology of Self-Affirmation." *Advances in Experimental Social Psychology* 21: 261–302.

————. 1997. "A Threat in the Air: How Stereotypes Shape Intellectual Identity and Performance." *American Psychologist* 52: 613–629.

Steele, Claude M., and Joshua Aronson. 1995. "Stereotype Threat and the Intellectual Test Performance of African Americans. *Journal of Personality and Social Psychology* 69: 797–811.

Strawinski, P. 2007. "Changes in Return to Higher Education in Poland, 1998–2004." MPRA paper, no. 5185. Accessed June 2, 2010; http://mpra.ub.uni-muenchen.de/5185/.

Suter, Brigit, and M. Jandl. 2006. *Comparative Study on Policies towards Foreign Graduates. Study on Admission and Retention Policies towards Foreign Students in Industrialised Countries.* Vienna: International Centre for Migration Policy Development (ICMPD).

Sweeting, A. 2004. *Education in Hong Kong, 1941 to 2001: Visions and Revisions.* Hong Kong: Hong Kong University Press.

Szreter, S. R. S. 1993. "The Official Representation of Social Classes in Britain, the United States, and France: The Professional Model and "Les Cadres." *Comparative Studies in Society and History* 35 (2): 285–317.

Taylor, Robert, Linda M. Chatters, M. Belinda Tucker, and Edith Lewis. 1990. "Developments in Research on Black Families: A Decade Review." *Journal of Marriage and the Family* 52: 993–1014.

Teichler, Ulrich. 2007. *Higher Education Systems: Conceptual Frameworks, Comparative Perspectives, Empirical Findings.* Rotterdam: Sense Publishers.

————. 2009. *Higher Education and the World of Work: Conceptual Frameworks, Comparative Perspectives, Empirical Findings.* Rotterdam: Sense Publishers.

Tesser, P., and J. Dronkers. 2007. Equal Opportunities or Social Closure in the Netherlands? In *Unequal Chances. Ethnic Minorities in Western Labor Markets,* A. Heath and S. Cheung, eds. (pp. 359–402). Oxford: Oxford University Press.

Thernstrom, S. 1973. *The Other Bostonians: Poverty and Progress in the American Metropolis, 1880–1970.* Cambridge, MA: Harvard University Press.

Thomas, D. 1996. "Education across Generations in South Africa." *AEA Papers and Proceedings* 86 (2): 330–339.

Thorat, S., and K. Newman. 2009. *Blocked by Caste.* Oxford: Oxford University Press.

Thurow, L. C. 1969. "Poverty and Human Capital." In *Problems in Political Economy: An Urban Perspective,* David M. Gordon, ed. (pp. 85–90). Lexington MA: D.C. Heath.

Tilly, C. 1998. *Durable Inequality.* Berkeley: University of California Press.

Torres, C. A., and A. Antikainen (Eds). 2003. *International Handbook on the Sociology of Education: An International Assessment of New Research and Theory.* Lanham, MD: Rowman and Littlefield.

Treiman, Donald J., and Kam-Bor Yip. 1989. "Educational and Occupational Attainment in 21 Countries." In *Cross-National Research in Sociology,* Melvin L. Kohn, ed. (pp. 373–394). Newbury Park, CA: Sage.

Tubergen, F. van. 2004. *The Integration of Immigrants in Cross-National Perspective: Origin, Destination and Community Effects.* PhD dissertation, Utrecht University.

Tubergen, F. van, I. Maas, and H. Flap. 2004. "The Economic Incorporation of Immigrants in 18 Western Societies: Origin, Destination, and Community Effects." *American Sociological Review* 69: 704–727.

Tyson, Karolyn, William Darity, Jr., and Domini Castellino. 2005. "Black Adolescents and the Dilemmas of High Achievement." *American Sociological Review* 70: 582–605.

UNESCO. 1997. *International Standard Classification of Education* (ISCED). Paris: author.

———. 2005. *Education Trends in Perspective: Analysis of the World Education Indicators, 2005 Edition*. Montreal, Canada: UNESCO Institute for Statistics.

Ultee, W. C., and R. Luijkx, 1990. "Educational Hegerogamy and Father-to-Son Occupational Mobility in 23 Industrial Nations: General Societal Openness or Compensatory Strategies of Reproduction?" *European Sociological Review* 6: 125–149.

United Nations Statistical Office. 2007. "Composition of Macro Geographical (Continental) Regions, Geographical Sub-regions, and Selected Economic and Other Groupings." Accessed January–February 2007; http://unstats.un.org/unsd/methods/m49/m49regin.htm.

Van De Velde, C. 2008. *Devenir adulte, Sociologie comparée de la jeunesse en Europe*. Paris: Presses Universitaires de France.

Van Galen, J. A., and G. W. Noblit (Eds). 2007. *Late to Class: Social Class and Schooling in the New Economy*. Albany: State University of New York Press.

Veall, M., and K. Zimmerman. 1992. "Psuedo-R^2 in the Ordinal Probit Model." *Journal of Mathematical Sociology* 16: 333–342.

Vegas, Emiliana, and Jenny Petrow. 2007. *Raising Student Learning in Latin America: The Challenge for the 21st Century*. Washington, DC. World Bank.

Wacquant, Loic. 1998. "Negative Social Capital: State Breakdown and Social Destitution in America's Core." *Journal of Housing and the Built Environment* 13 (1): 25–40.

Waldrauch, H. 2001. *Die Integration von Einwanderern. Ein Index der rechtlichen Diskriminierung*. Wien: Campus.

Walther, Andreas. 2006. "Regimes of Youth Transitions. Choice, Flexibility and Security in Young People's Experiences across Different European Contexts." *Young: Nordic Journal of Youth Research* 14 (2): 119–139.

Walther, Andreas, and Axel Polh. 2005. *Thematic Study on Policy Measures Concerning Disadvantaged Youth: Study Commissioned by the European Commission: Final Report*. Tubingen: Institute for Regional Innovation and Social Research (IRIS).

Walther, Andrea, Barbara Stauber, Andy Biggart, Manuela du Bois-Reymond, Andy Furlong, Andreu Lopez Blasco, Sven Morch, and Jose Machado Pais (Eds.). 2002. *Misleading Trajectories—Integration Policies for Young Adults in Europe?* Opladen, Germany: Leske+Budrich.

Waters, J. L. 2006. "Emergent Geographies of International Education and Social Exclusion." *Antipode* 38 (5):1046–1068.

Weir, M. 2002. "The American Middle Class and the Politics of Education." In *Social Contracts Under Stress: The Middle Classes of America, Europe, and Japan at the Turn of the Century*, O. Zunz, ed. (pp. 178–203). New York: Russell Sage.

Werner, H. 2003. *"The Integration of Immigrants into the Labor Markets of the EU."* IAB topics, no. 52. Nuremberg, Germany: Institute for the Study of Labor (IAB).

Wesolowski, Wlodzimierz. 1980. *Klasy, warstwy i wladza*. Warsaw: Wydawnictwo Nalikowe PWN (Polish Scientific Publishers).

Wesolowski, Wlodzimierz, and Bogdan Mach. 1986. *Systemowe funkcje ruchliwosci spolecznej w Polsce.* Warsaw: Instytut Filozofii i Socjologic PAN (Insitute for Philospohy and Sociology of the Polish Academy of Sciences).

Whyte, Martin. 1975. "Inequality and Stratification in China." *China Quarterly* 64: 684–711.

———. 1981. "Destratification and Restratification in China." In *Social Inequality,* G. Berreman, ed. (pp. 309–336). New York: Academic Press.

Willis, P. 1977. *Learning to Labour.* Farnborough, UK: Saxon House.

Willis, Robert J. 1986. "Human Capital and the Rise and Fall of Families: Comment." *Journal of Labor Economics* 4 (3): S40–47.

Winkler, Don, and Alec I. Gershberg. 2000. *Los efectos de la descentralización del sistema educacional sobre la calidad de la educación en América Latina.* Documento de Trabajo, no. 17. Santiago, Chile: PREAL.

Wisniewski, Jakub. 2006. *Migracje zarobkowe Polaków po 1 maja 2004.* Warsaw: Instytut Spraw Publicznych.

Wittenberg, M. 2003. "Job Search in South Africa: A Nonparametric Analysis." *South African Journal of Economics* 70 (8): 1163–1197.

Wong, Y. L. 2004. "A Unified Middle Class or Two Middle Classes? A Comparison of Career Strategies and Intergenerational Mobility Strategies between Teachers and Managers in contemporary Hong Kong." *British Journal of Sociology* 55 (2): 167–186.

———. 2007. "How Middle-Class Parents Help Their Children Obtain an Advantaged Qualification: A Study of Strategies of Teachers and Managers for Their Children's Education in Hong Kong Before the 1997 Handover." *Sociological Research Online* 12 (6); http://www.socresonline.org.uk/12/6/5.html.

Wooldridge, Jeffrey M. 2002. *Econometric Analysis of Cross Section and Panel Data.* Cambridge, MA/London: MIT Press.

World Bank. 2004. *Making Services Work for Poor People.* World development report, 2005. Washington, DC: author.

———. 2005. *Equity and Development.* World development report, 2006. Washington, DC: author.

Wright, Erik Olin. 1985. *Classes.* London: Verso.

———. 1997. *Class Counts.* Cambridge, UK: Cambridge University Press.

Yang Dongping. 2003. "China Education Development Report 2002." In *China in 2003–2004: Analysis and Forecast of Social Situation,* Lu Xin, Lu Xiuyi, and Li Peilin, eds. (pp. 55–59). Beijing: Social Science Press.

Yates, Scott, and Malcolm Payne. 2006. "Not so NEET? A Critique of the Use of 'NEET' in Setting Targets for Interventions with Young People." *Journal of Youth Studies* 9 (3): 329–344.

Yuji, G. 2005. "The NEET Problem in Japan." *Social Science Japan* 32: 3–4.

Zhou, M. 1997. "Segmented Assimilation: Issues, Controversies and Recent Research on the New Second Generation." *International Migration Review* 31 (4): 975–1008.

Zhou, Xueguang, Phyllis Moen, and Nancy Brandon Tuma. 1998. "Educational Stratification in Urban China: 1949–94." *Sociology of Education* 71: 199–222.

Index

Note: Page numbers followed by "*f*" and "*t*" denote figures and tables, respectively.